Profession
Visual Studio® 2008

G000065857

Professional
Visual Studio® 2008 Extensibility

Keyvan Nayyeri

WILEY

Wiley Publishing, Inc.

Professional Visual Studio® 2008 Extensibility

Published by
Wiley Publishing, Inc.
10475 Crosspoint Boulevard
Indianapolis, IN 46256

Copyright © 2008 by Wiley Publishing, Inc., Indianapolis, Indiana

Published simultaneously in Canada

ISBN: 978-0-470-23084-8

Manufactured in the United States of America

10 9 8 7 6 5 4 3 2 1

Library of Congress Cataloging-in-Publication Data is available from the publisher

For my mother and my father, who are not only my parents, but also support me in the technical world even though they aren't software gurus! We've passed hard days of war and life. They really believe in me.

About the Author

Keyvan Nayyeri is a software architect and developer who has a bachelor of science degree in applied mathematics. He was born in Kermanshah, Kurdistan, in 1984.

Keyvan's main focus is on Microsoft development technologies and their related technologies, such as markup languages. He also has a serious passion for community activities and open-source software. As a result, he has authored many well-known .NET communities and has published various articles and tutorials on them. He is also a team leader and developer for several .NET open-source projects, where he increases his knowledge in many areas, including writing code for special purposes. As an old ASP.NET developer, Keyvan is also a big fan and follower of Telligent products and holds an MVP award for Community Server as well. Before this book, Keyvan recently co-authored *Wrox Professional Community Server* (Wrox, 2007).

When he's not writing code, he enjoys blogging, reading technical books, listening to music, and playing video games. You can check out his blog, which contains his thoughts about matters both technical and personal, at www.nayyeri.net.

About the Technical Editor

Cody Reichenau is a professional software developer with Catapult Systems in beautiful Austin, Texas. He has a wonderful wife, two terrific daughters, a neurotic yellow dog, and an unproductive obsession with console gaming.

Credits

Acquisitions Editor
Katie Mohr

Development Editor
William Bridges

Technical Editor
Cody Reichenau

Production Editor
William A. Barton

Copy Editor
Luann Rouff

Editorial Manager
Mary Beth Wakefield

Production Manager
Tim Tate

Vice President and Executive Group Publisher
Richard Swadley

Vice President and Executive Publisher
Joseph B. Wikert

Proofreader
Jennifer Larsen, Word One

Indexer
Robert Swanson

Project Coordinator, Cover
Lynsey Osborn

Acknowledgments

First of all, thanks to God for my existence and for everything! While I was writing this book, I was also doing my required military service and frequently had to be away from home, so I had a very limited time to work. God helped me get this book about such a special topic, Visual Studio Extensibility, done, and ahead of schedule. Moreover, thanks to God for making me such a lucky guy to get the help of a great editorial team. I was writing this book on one side of the world while the editorial team was editing it on the other side.

Thanks to Bill Bridges and Cody Reichenau, the development and technical editors of this book, who closely collaborated with me in order to deliver the best possible content to readers. If it's good, it's their great work, and if it's bad, it's my bad work!

Bill spent a lot of time editing and applying the changes I made to the content. Working with a kid and a non-English author wasn't easy for him. I made some major changes to the manuscript as the writing proceeded and even renamed it. The current simplicity of the text reflects the excellent job he did with the original. Thanks, Bill, for your patience and the great effort you put into the book. (I'm sure you'll edit this page to be much better than the original acknowledgments!)

As technical editor, Cody helped me to fill many gaps in technical details and improve the content. Editing a title about Visual Studio Extensibility isn't so easy, believe me. He caught my technical mistakes and helped me solve them. Like Bill, Cody has had an important effect on the quality of the content. Thank you, Cody!

I also have to give credit to the acquisitions editor of the book, Katie Mohr. The original idea of this book was hers — she suggested that I write a book about Visual Studio add-ins and extensions based on the C# language. She was also, in effect, the book's director, helping match different people on the team to various tasks and answering questions about the book's publishing progress. It was a pleasure to work with her and many others at Wiley.

My special thanks also go to Tom Dinse, senior editor, who connected me and the editorial team with other teams and solved problems during the writing process.

I thank anyone else who helped to complete this book, both inside Wiley and Wrox and outside, including Ken Levy, the product manager of the Visual Studio Ecosystem team at Microsoft, and Simone Chiaretta, my dear friend in Italy, who helped me with some translations.

Finally, I want to thank my best friend, Mehrdad Ebrahimi. He has been a great friend and support for me in life and helped me with his thoughtful comments during the writing process.

Contents

Contents

Contents

Contents

Contents

Contents

Introduction

Visual Studio is a development IDE created by Microsoft to enable easier development for Microsoft programming languages and development technologies. Visual Studio has been the most popular IDE for working with Microsoft development products for a decade.

Visual Studio, itself, is extensible. This extensibility has many aspects and includes several options. Extensibility is a key feature of Visual Studio — important enough to dedicate a book (or even several books) to the subject. A growing number of community requests for more resources on Visual Studio Extensibility encouraged Wrox to think about publishing such a book. Unlike other Microsoft technologies, this part of Visual Studio doesn't have rich resources. Only a few books have been written, back in the days of .NET 1.0 and 1.1, and they didn't cover the topic thoroughly (they just focused on add-ins and macros). Moreover, some new features have been added to VS Extensibility over the years that definitely warrant coverage in a book.

Wrapping Up

When Katie Mohr, the acquisitions editor of this book, suggested that I work on a title about Visual Studio add-ins and extensions with C#, I had no idea how broad and deep this topic could be! During the writing process, I learned many new things, which made me change a lot in the book, even its title! To ensure that readers understand the subject correctly, this introduction is somewhat different from most other Wrox books. I'm assuming that readers have at least a minimum level of knowledge about topics related to Visual Studio Extensibility before reading the book. I won't be leaving the main topic to teach general .NET concepts, because I want to keep chapters as short and simple as possible.

Technology evolves quickly, so developers need to quickly learn new techniques and concepts. Of course, books can't reflect everything about a topic, so I thought it would be a good idea to share some ideas, tricks, and new material about Visual Studio Extensibility on an online resource. With that in mind, I've joined with the authors of *Professional Visual Studio 2008* (Wrox, 2008) to set up a dedicated website about Visual Studio, in order to write about related topics and provide readers with additional help. This site is online at www.professionalvisualstudio.com. A work in progress, the authors of *Professional Visual Studio 2008* and I are continuously improving and adding to this site, and developing it further to be another resource about Visual Studio.

You can also check out my blog at www.nayyeri.net where I share technical material with my subscribers. I use both sites as complementary resources for the content provided in this book.

About Visual Studio Extensibility

Working on a book about Visual Studio Extensibility (VSX) and spending a lot of time on aspects of this topic in depth (or at least more depth than what most developers are accustomed to), I found that many developers consider Visual Studio Extensibility a hard topic to learn, and its APIs very complex.

Microsoft has made several attempts to address this in recent months (before the release of Visual Studio 2008 and in parallel with it), and one of its main strategies was generating a good solid community for Visual Studio Extensibility.

Despite this support, however, anyone who is working with VSX needs a good understanding of the current position of the topic and its community. Note that I'm writing this introduction in December 2007, just a few weeks after Visual Studio 2008 was released and while Microsoft was trying hard to fill the holes that I outline in a moment.

I agree that Visual Studio Extensibility is hard to learn, especially in comparison with most .NET-related topics, but this isn't because of its inherent nature, which I'll say more about in a moment. I also agree that Visual Studio APIs, especially those related to extensibility features, aren't written well. Some call these APIs "dirty" because there is no good structure, naming convention, or consistency between these APIs.

This Old COM-Based Product

One reason for the difficulty is that Visual Studio is now 10 years old. This product was created in COM days for COM programming, but migrated to .NET. Now that .NET is the common way to develop software for Microsoft products, developers learn .NET codes easier and faster because it has more references from which to learn, and because .NET has a great design, with simplicity at its core.

Visual Studio is built on COM components, and most of traditional extensibility relies heavily on COM programming. Moving forward from COM to .NET, Visual Studio has revamped itself in order to look more familiar to .NET users, while retaining its COM nature. It has used .NET and COM interoperability at advanced levels to do this. However, many .NET developers may not know about .NET and COM interoperability at this level, making it hard for them to work with Visual Studio Extensibility.

Some new features of Visual Studio Extensibility are based on newer technologies, and thus are easier to learn — or at least Microsoft has tried to provide these extensibility points in a way that developers can work with easily, without worrying about the underlying layers. An example of this is code snippets, which are easy to develop and deploy even when you don't know what's going on under the hood. In any case, the main extensibility options, such as add-ins, VSPackages, and the Visual Studio Shell, rely on COM components and interfaces.

Variety of Extensibility Options

Another reason for its difficulty is the sheer variety of Visual Studio Extensibility options. During the past 10 years, Visual Studio has continued to grow and new extensibility features have been added to it. Learning all these options with their different purposes, natures, and implementations isn't so easy. Many extensibility features are broad topics themselves, such as add-ins, macros, the Visual Studio Shell, or the new domain-specific language tools in Visual Studio. Conversely, extensibility options can be grouped at different levels based on their priority. Learning all these topics can present quite a challenge, especially because these options aren't closely related to general .NET programming topics — they're completely new and specific to Visual Studio.

Design Considerations

Going back and forth in Visual Studio Extensibility and looking at its APIs, code, and structure, as well as the architecture of the automation model, you may or may not share my personal opinion that they aren't designed very well. Being an old product built on two technologies (.NET and COM) has produced inconsistency in code. Moreover, different teams and developers have worked on Visual Studio at different times, a factor that has added to the inconsistency.

Because Visual Studio is built on COM components, interfaces couldn't be avoided. Having a ton of interfaces and their implementations in a complex inheritance hierarchy makes the API hard to explore and learn, especially when you can't find a consistent structure among all the APIs. The large number of interfaces and their implementations is another negative point that can frustrate developers when they first enter this world.

The most important drawback of interfaces are apparent here, and Visual Studio APIs are probably the best way to demonstrate the extensibility of interfaces in APIs. As you know, extending interfaces requires extra effort in any framework, and in Visual Studio you face many class and interface names that have a number index at the end to specify their version — such as Solution, Solution2, and the new Solution3 in Visual Studio 2008. This naming convention isn't recommended, but it seems the best way to handle the variety of interfaces and classes in Visual Studio and its automation model.

Naming Convention Inconsistency

Another annoying aspect about Visual Studio Extensibility is the poor naming conventions for many interfaces, classes, properties, and methods. In some places you see unrelated names that don't make sense at all. This, in conjunction with poor documentation for these programming elements, makes it difficult (if not impossible) to learn about them! I faced two such instances while writing this book, and I couldn't find any resource that knew anything about them. It's never a good sign when the only way to understand something is to ask the Microsoft developers!

You already know the importance of a good naming convention and choosing related and meaningful names in code, but Visual Studio lacks this programming principle. A possible reason for this may be that these parts of VS code weren't originally supposed to be used publicly; therefore, Microsoft's developers may not have worried about them much.

Documentation

The last point I want to mention is about documentation. Even though some parts of Visual Studio Extensibility have excellent documentation, that can't be said in general. Fortunately, the Visual Studio Ecosystem team is working hard to improve documentation, so this may not be a problem for developers in the near future.

Conclusion

These problems aside, I think we'll see a better future for Visual Studio Extensibility. Microsoft changed its strategy and has gathered all the teams that were working on the extensibility of Visual Studio under the single umbrella mentioned above — the Visual Studio Ecosystem team. It would be difficult to change the current structure of the Visual Studio API completely, but I think this team can solve many of its current problems and make VS simpler and easier to learn and use.

Still, by its nature, Visual Studio Extensibility isn't an easy topic to learn. As I've noted, the variety of extensibility options, their different purposes and implementations, and of course the depth of each option, make it harder to learn than many other .NET programming topics.

Ultimately, I hope that this book, which I have written to help the community, enables you to get a grasp of the subject, and that it assists you in learning about Visual Studio Extensibility in a straightforward way. Of course, despite my best efforts to keep it simple and useful, I know that no book is perfect, and I welcome feedback on any aspect of it.

Why Extend Visual Studio?

For experienced developers, this question has an obvious answer. The development process involves a lot of repetitive tasks, so doing things easier and quicker is a main goal for developers. Here, the development environment plays a key role in simplifying things. Fortunately, Visual Studio has some really great features for simplifying development tasks, and many features have been added to this tool over the years. Some of these features were the direct result of requests from the developer community.

Although Visual Studio is a full-featured product that is both simple and fast, developers often need other features for their daily work, features that are not a part of the product. These features may reflect common requests by a number of developers or special cases for an individual developer.

Like other development tools, the extensibility of Visual Studio is important. Recognizing this need, Microsoft has devoted a lot of effort to making Visual Studio as extensible as possible. As a result, developers can enjoy numerous extensibility features in Visual Studio for different requirements.

Being aware of the extensibility options in Visual Studio is essential for every developer who works with this IDE professionally. Today, many helpful extensions are available for Visual Studio, some of them commercial, and others open source and free.

Why C#?

The primary programming language for this book is C#, one of the .NET programming languages and one that has become highly popular in recent years. C# has a similar syntax to C and C++. Following are a few reasons why C# was chosen for this book:

❑ Writing a book with multiple programming languages wouldn't be a good idea, especially a book like this, which covers a topic for more experienced developers. I've noticed over the years that .NET developers are able to read and understand code in Visual Basic or C#, so writing in two languages would waste time and paper.

❑ C# is becoming increasingly popular. The .NET community is going to accept it as the first programming language for .NET, and most code samples are provided in C#, making it a good choice for this book.

❑ You won't find any other title about Visual Studio Extensibility with C#. The few recent books about VSE used Visual Basic as the main language. Having a book with the C# language will be helpful for the community.

Even though I chose C# as the main language, Visual Basic is the language used in Chapter 22 to discuss Visual Studio macros, because technically it's not possible to write macros with any other language. In addition, Visual C++ is used for Chapter 15 to discuss Visual Studio Shell, for the same reason as in Chapter 22.

If you're a developer in one of the .NET languages with a good background in .NET and some familiarity with C programming languages, don't worry about this and just go ahead and read the book. I'm pretty sure that you'll understand all the code. I know both C# and Visual Basic very well and Visual C++ to some extent, and I've written all the examples in a way that enables .NET developers to learn them.

Whom This Book Is For

This book is for .NET developers who are interested in extending Visual Studio as their development tool. In addition to this essential interest, you need to know the following material well:

- ❑ Object-oriented programming (OOP)
- ❑ The .NET Framework and .NET programming
- ❑ C# or Visual Basic languages (for VB developers, having a familiarity with C programming languages is mandatory). You also need some familiarity with Visual C++, which is used for a chapter in this book.
- ❑ XML and its related topics. You should have a general understanding of XML for some chapters.
- ❑ Visual Studio structure and usage

In addition to these main prerequisites, a familiarity with COM programming and different .NET technologies is advantageous.

Note that this book isn't a complete reference about Visual Studio Extensibility. Readers who are familiar with the style of the Wrox Professional series know that the series is different from the Programmer's Reference series. Therefore, you shouldn't expect this book to provide a comprehensive description about each topic in Visual Studio Extensibility. Instead, it teaches you how to use it, including common topics and techniques. It is geared toward experienced .NET developers (as described above) and explains how to develop Visual Studio extensions up to a professional level (but not an expert level). Obviously, the general topic of Visual Studio Extensibility can be divided into many specific topics, each warranting its own book — something I hope we'll see in the near future.

Aims of This Book

This book is written with some main considerations in mind. I tried to gather all the ideas and requests of the community in order to write something helpful, both for community members and developers. The following are the aims of this book:

- ❑ Provide an overview of all aspects of Visual Studio Extensibility
- ❑ Enable readers to know where and when to use extensibility options

- ❏ Familiarize readers with VS Extensibility in detail (which isn't the same as discussing everything, though)

- ❏ Show readers the first steps and let them follow through with their own experiences

- ❏ Use examples, sample code, and real-world case studies to demonstrate things in a way that helps readers understand the concepts

- ❏ Avoid bothering readers with long discussions and useless code samples

With these aims in mind, I also tried to provide some tips and tricks, because these are things that can't be learned easily.

What You Need to Use This Book

There are some technical requirements for getting the most out of this book. You need to have the following two packages installed on your machine to be able to read and understand the chapters and test code samples:

- ❏ Visual Studio 2008 Team System Edition (or other commercial editions)

- ❏ Visual Studio 2008 SDK 1.0 (or its newer versions)

Because Visual Studio 2008 is a commercial product, you need to buy it to register for an evaluation version. Free Express editions of Visual Studio don't support extensibility options, so you can't use them. The Visual Studio SDK is mandatory in order to read some chapters in this book and can be downloaded as a free package.

The operating system doesn't matter for the content of this book, but I wrote all code with Visual Studio 2008 Team System Edition in Windows Vista x86.

What This Book Covers

The following list provides a brief description of the main topics of each chapter in this book:

- ❏ **Chapter 1** provides an introduction to Visual Studio and walks you through a short history of its evolution.

- ❏ **Chapter 2** talks about the .NET Framework, its different versions, .NET programming languages, .NET technologies, and the correlation between .NET and Visual Studio.

- ❏ **Chapter 3** is a quick tour of the main extensibility options in Visual Studio, including a few simple examples.

- ❏ **Chapter 4** offers an introduction to the automation model and its relationship to extending Visual Studio.

- ❏ **Chapter 5** walks through the Add-in Wizard and describes each of its steps.

❑ **Chapter 6** shows you the anatomy of add-ins and explains how to create add-ins and how they work.

❑ **Chapter 7** discusses how to manipulate solutions, projects, and project items via your code to build add-ins.

❑ **Chapter 8** shows you how to deal with documents and code editors in your add-ins.

❑ **Chapter 9** explains how to work with programming codes and manipulate their elements, as well as working with the build process.

❑ **Chapter 10** describes some ways to work with user interface elements, Windows Forms, and controls via code in your add-ins. It also talks about manipulating some common windows in the Visual Studio IDE.

❑ **Chapter 11** discusses the Tools Options page and uses add-ins as the case study to show you how to create your own Tools Options pages.

❑ **Chapter 12** teaches you how to debug and test your add-ins.

❑ **Chapter 13** shows you how to deploy your add-ins.

❑ **Chapter 14** completes the discussion about add-ins by talking about resources and localization of add-ins.

❑ **Chapter 15** discusses a new feature in Visual Studio 2008: the Visual Studio Shell. You'll learn some general topics about this feature.

❑ **Chapter 16** talks about domain-specific language tools, which are a part of Visual Studio Extensibility. You'll also work with domain-specific languages in Visual Studio and build them, and see a quick overview of DSL tools in this chapter.

❑ **Chapter 17** discusses an important part of Visual Studio: debugging and how to extend debugging features.

❑ **Chapter 18** talks about VSPackages as a way to extend Visual Studio functionality and add something new to its existing packages.

❑ **Chapter 19** teaches you what a code snippet is and how to write and manage code snippets in Visual Studio to make your coding process easier.

❑ **Chapter 20** talks about Visual Studio project templates and starter kits and how to write your own project templates.

❑ **Chapter 21** focuses on MSBuild and writing custom builds for Visual Studio and .NET applications.

❑ **Chapter 22** discusses Visual Studio macros in detail and explains how to build a Visual Studio macro.

❑ **Appendix A** contains a list of helpful third-party add-ins and extensions to give you some ideas about real-world scenarios.

❑ **Appendix B** contains a list of useful resources for further reading, including communities, blogs, and other books.

How to Use This Book

You can read this book chapter by chapter in a linear fashion and then read the appendices, but if you're interested in a specific topic, then this short guide to reading the book may be useful. Chapters 1, 2 and 3 give you an introduction to the basic concepts you need to use in the rest of the book. Chapter 4 discusses the automation model, which is an important prerequisite for many chapters in this book about add-ins, macros, and VSPackages.

In Chapters 5 to 14, we'll use add-ins as a case study to learn about main aspects of the automation model and some common techniques in Visual Studio Extensibility development. If you need to learn about add-in development, you can read each of these chapters one by one, but if you're interested in learning about a specific topic, then you can just jump right to it. I wrote these chapters so that each one can be understood independently of the others.

Each of the rest of the chapters is dedicated to a specific extensibility option. They're independent of each other and you can read them in any order. However, you may need to know some basic information about the automation model, which you can get from Chapters 4 to 14.

The appendices provide information about some third-party add-ins and extensions that you can check out to get some ideas from the real world. They also list some online resources and books for further reading.

I recommend that you read Chapter 3, "Quick Tour," and Chapter 4, "The Automation Model," to get a basic idea about Visual Studio Extensibility and the automation model, and then follow your own path to the other chapters.

What Is Visual Studio?

Having a good background in Visual Studio and knowing its history and features can help you understand all the chapters in this book better. Of course, such an understanding is a prerequisite for reading this book, but it is likely that readers have acquired their knowledge from different resources and from their daily experience with this IDE, and therefore may be unfamiliar with some aspects of it. This chapter describes a few things that may be helpful as you read the book.

First, I'll provide a short history of Visual Studio and the main features and enhancements in each of its versions. After that I'll cover Visual Studio 2008 (code-named Orcas) and its new features and requirements, and the installation process. Then, after an overview of the Visual Studio IDE, you will learn about extensibility in Visual Studio and the Visual Studio SDK.

Introduction to Visual Studio

Visual Studio is one of the most famous Microsoft products and is specifically designed for development goals. It's the most popular tool for all developers who use Microsoft development technologies and is widely used by developers around the world. It is built on an Integrated Development Environment (IDE) and enables users to build different types of applications using Microsoft programming languages.

Visual Studio, which is abbreviated as VS by community members (and is used frequently throughout this book), supports several platforms and programming languages "out of the box," that is, without requiring additional installations, plug-ins, expansion packs, or products.

Because a good background in the history of VS and how its features have improved in each version can help you get a good picture of what Visual Studio is and how it has reached this point in its development, this chapter provides a short history of Visual Studio and its features over the past 11 years and offers a brief introduction to Visual Studio 2008 and its installation process. Chapter 2 discusses the .NET Framework and its correlation with Visual Studio and different pieces of this development framework. Other chapters discuss all aspects of Visual Studio extensibility, with a primary focus on the latest version, Visual Studio 2008.

History

Visual Studio is an old and famous Microsoft product that was created for development purposes. In 1997 and later, Microsoft built some visual development languages for its Windows operating system. It also built an IDE to support these languages in a visual manner and named it Visual Studio. Visual Studio has changed a lot during the past 11 years. Not only has it become richer, it has enhanced the way it integrates with Microsoft programming languages and technologies. Over the years, Microsoft also added several new features to support database technologies, markup languages, web development tools, unit-testing features, and team work management.

In the following sections, we'll take a look at the history of six versions of Visual Studio released during these years, including all their major improvements, changes, and new features.

Visual Studio 97

1997 was the first year in which Microsoft tried to build a single environment for developing in multiple languages. In that year, it introduced Visual Studio as an IDE for development, and it included the following elements and languages:

❑ Visual Basic 5.0

❑ Visual C++ 5.0

❑ Visual FoxPro 5.0 (for xBase programming)

❑ Visual J++ 1.1 (for Java programming for Windows)

❑ Visual InterDev (for creating dynamic web pages with ASP)

❑ MSDN (Microsoft Developer Network)

Visual C++, Visual J++, Visual InterDev, and MSDN used the same environment, named Developer Studio, while Visual Basic and Visual FoxPro had their own environments.

Visual Studio 97 was a first attempt and a first version, but even then it was a great development environment. Back then, every developer could enjoy working in this IDE. Current versions of Visual Studio are very different, in terms of both the user interface and the features that are included.

The internal version of Visual Studio 97 was 5.0.

Visual Studio 6.0 (98)

In 1998, Microsoft tried to integrate its development tools more consistently than in the past and took the first steps toward what we now have as the .NET Framework.

In that year, Microsoft released Visual Studio 6.0 with the same components as Visual Studio 97, but updated their version numbers to 6.0. Even Visual J++ and Visual InterDev version numbers were updated to 6.0 from 1.1 and 1.0, respectively.

Visual Studio 6.0 included the last version of Visual Basic as we knew it, because current Visual Basic (known as Visual Basic .NET) is different from that earlier Visual Basic in some fundamental ways. Visual Studio 6.0 was also the last version of Microsoft development tools for the Windows 9x platform.

At this point, Visual J++ died, and Microsoft no longer supported any programming language for the Java Virtual Machine (JVM).

Other changes were reflected in the number of environments. Visual Studio 98 had one more environment than Visual Studio 97. Visual J++ and Visual InterDev left the environment they had and got their own environments.

Visual Studio 6.0 (98) was the last link of a chain that ended at this point. After Visual Studio 6.0, Microsoft focused mainly on building a single compiler and environment by introducing the .NET Framework.

Visual Studio .NET 2002

2002 saw a revolution in Microsoft development tools and programming languages. After some years of hard work and planning, Microsoft released the .NET Framework, Visual Studio .NET, and the .NET programming languages. This marked the first point of complete integration and consistency between Microsoft development products. The beta version of Visual Studio 2002 was available to MSDN subscribers in 2001, but the final version appeared on the market in 2002.

The .NET Framework 1.0 was the most important release that year. It introduced managed code to Microsoft developers. In the .NET Framework, programs compile to *Microsoft Intermediate Language (MSIL)* or *Common Intermediate Language (MIL)*, rather than compile to machine language. You'll read more about the .NET Framework in Chapter 2, "The .NET Framework."

Visual Studio .NET 2002 (with 7.0 as the internal version) was the first version of Visual Studio that required NT-based operating systems for installation. It could support four languages out of the box:

- ❑ **Visual Basic .NET:** This was the first member of the Basic family languages that could support object-oriented programming 100 percent. It differed in some fundamental ways with Visual Basic 6.0, which had been one of most popular programming languages for years. Visual Basic .NET was (and still is) the most popular programming language around the world.

- ❑ **C#:** This was a completely new language in the .NET Framework 1.0. Later, it would catch the interest of many developers. It still has a growing number of fans, and it's likely to be the most popular Microsoft programming language for the near future. C# uses C syntax but is simpler than other Visual languages with C-family syntax, such as Visual C++.

- ❑ **Visual J#:** Like C#, J# was a new language introduced in the .NET Framework. It can be considered a replacement for Visual J++, which died after Visual Studio 6.0. It has a Java syntax, but unlike Visual J++ it can build applications only for the .NET Framework, not the Java Virtual Machine (JVM).

- ❑ **Visual C++:** Like its preceding versions, Visual C++ is a programming language with a C-family syntax. It is still available as part of the .NET Framework with enhancements.

Using these programming languages and a single compiler, the .NET Framework provides a rich set of tools to build various kinds of desktop, web, and embedded-device applications. It includes several technologies, such as ASP.NET, ADO.NET, and web services. The .NET Framework and its related technologies are covered in Chapter 2, "The NET Framework," in more detail.

Visual Studio .NET 2003

A year after Visual Studio .NET 2002 was released, Microsoft shipped Visual Studio .NET 2003 (with 7.1 as the internal version), which could support the .NET Framework 1.1, the new version of the .NET Framework.

The .NET Framework 1.1 had built-in support for building mobile applications and included some other new features, as well as bug fixes. It was the first stable version of the .NET Framework and it has been widely used. Visual Studio .NET 2003 was even more stable and popular than the 2002 release.

There were four editions for this 2003 version:

❑ Professional

❑ Enterprise Developer

❑ Enterprise Architect

❑ Academic

The Enterprise Architect version offered built-in support for Microsoft Visio, which enables *Unified Modeling Language (UML)* for application architecture.

Microsoft released Service Pack 1 for Visual Studio .NET 2003 in September 2006.

Visual Studio 2005

In October 2005, Microsoft released the new version of the .NET Framework, the .NET Framework 2.0, and a new version of Visual Studio that was code-named Whidbey and later used 2005 as its version number. The internal version of Visual Studio 2005 is 8.0. At this point, Microsoft removed the ".NET" suffix from the name of its products such as Visual Studio and Visual Basic, bit it still supports the .NET Framework.

Visual Studio 2005 was enhanced to support the .NET Framework 2.0. It had the following features and changes:

❑ ASP.NET 2.0

❑ ADO.NET 2.0

❑ Generics in .NET 2.0

❑ Enhanced IntelliSense

❑ Addition of new project types

❑ A local web server to test ASP.NET applications without Internet Information Services (IIS)

❑ Support for 64-bit applications

The other major change in VS 8.0, in comparison to its predecessors, was that its editions were introduced in a different way. It had the following editions:

❑   Express

❑   Standard

❑   Professional

❑   Tools for Office

❑   Team System

There were two new editions for VS 2005: Express and Team System. Express editions are free and suitable for small business and individuals who just want to build small applications. Four express editions are available for all available languages in the .NET Framework, as well as a Visual Web Developer to create ASP.NET applications. Express editions don't offer all the professional features of Visual Studio, however.

There are five Team System editions. Four of them have a major role in building software: Developers, Architects, Testers, and Database Designers. The other one, Visual Studio Team Suite edition, has all these four capabilities in a single edition.

After the initial release of Visual Studio, some other products were shipped along with it for special purposes:

❑   **Visual Studio Team System (VSTS):** This is suitable for team work. It uses the Visual Studio 2005 IDE, but it adds some applications such as Visual Studio Team Foundation Server, a powerful source control, which includes a free client as an add-in for Visual Studio and great integration with VS.

❑   **Visual Studio Tools for Office (VSTO):** This enables the use of Microsoft Office document data in other applications and Microsoft Office APIs. It also enables developers to use Microsoft Office controls in other applications.

❑   **Visual Studio Tools for Applications (VSTA):** This is the enhanced version of Visual Basic for Applications (VBA). VSTA has a customized version of the VS 2005 IDE that includes a runtime that can be used in other applications via the .NET object model.

Service Pack 1 for Visual Studio 2005 was released in December 2006. This service pack replaced the ASP.NET websites with ASP.NET web applications as the default project type for ASP.NET applications. This was the default option in Visual Studio 2002 and 2003 as well, and was a change requested by many community members.

Microsoft launched the .NET Framework 3.0 in 2006, when Visual Studio 2005 was the latest version of Visual Studio. Thus, there are add-ins for Visual Studio 2005 that enable development for *Windows Presentation Foundation*, *Windows Communication Foundation*, and *Windows Workflow Foundation* as main new technologies in the .NET Framework 3.0. You'll read more about these technologies in Chapter 2.

You can find more information about Visual Studio 2005 from Wrox's *Professional Visual Studio 2005*, by Andrew Parsons and Nick Randolph (ISBN: 9780764598463).

Visual Studio 2008

The latest available version of Visual Studio (sixth version) is code-named Orcas and should be launched by Microsoft by the time you read this book, with 9.0 as the internal version. It was released earlier (at the end of 2007) to MSDN subscribers. The next version of Visual Studio (code-named Hawaii) is under development.

Visual Studio 2008 is the first version that supports three different versions of the .NET Framework out of the box: 2.0, 3.0, and 3.5. The .NET Framework versions 2.0 and 3.0 were available before Visual Studio 2008, but the .NET Framework 3.5 shipped with Visual Studio Orcas. The default framework for VS 2008 assemblies is 3.5, but you can choose which version of the .NET Framework you prefer to compile your assemblies with.

Orcas focuses primarily on Windows Vista and Office 2007, as well as new features in the .NET Framework 3.0 and 3.5, while keeping all the goodies from Visual Studio 2005.

Here's a list of new features and changes in Visual Studio 2008:

❑   Built-in support for *Windows Presentation Foundation* and an excellent designer, originally called Cider, for XAML layouts

❑   Built-in support for *Windows Communication Foundation*

❑   Built-in support for *Windows Workflow Foundation,* and a powerful workflow designer

❑   A new language feature in .NET 3.5, LINQ, which is available in new versions of Visual Basic and C# and a LINQ to SQL designer (to define type mappings for SQL data)

❑   Addition of Microsoft Silverlight projects, a new type of web project that brings the great features of Windows Presentation Foundation and XAML to web applications

❑   JavaScript IntelliSense and debugger

❑   A powerful XHTML/CSS editor

❑   J# is no longer included

Visual Studio 2008 ships with the same editions as Visual Studio 2005. Visual Studio Team System 2008 was originally named Rosario and was released with Visual Studio 2008.

You can read more about Visual Studio 2008 in Wrox's *Professional Visual Studio 2008,* by Nick Randolph and David Gardner (ISBN: 9780470229880).

Extensibility

Visual Studio is a tool for development and for extending other things, but it's extensible itself. Obviously, the built-in features of Visual Studio won't be enough for some developers, who need something more or something special. Many current VS features are community requests from developers, and some of them have been implemented by third-party components and open-source projects before they were incorporated into Visual Studio.

I won't bother reviewing the necessity of extensibility features in a tool like Visual Studio, because you already know many of the reasons from your own experience. Instead, this section provides a brief introduction to the extensibility features in this tool.

Fortunately, Microsoft has put some extensibility features into Visual Studio to help developers extend VS easily. Add-ins, macros, and packages are three common ways of extending Visual Studio and they have been a part of VS extensibility features for a long time.

Add-ins enable users to gain access to VS's underlying APIs for IDE, in order to automate tasks such as coding and deployment. Macros are a way to automate frequently repeated tasks in Visual Studio. Developers can create macros by recording them or writing them programmatically. Packages, created using the Visual Studio SDK, enable a deeper integration between the IDE and programming languages.

In addition, compared to the 2005 version, a few new extensibility options have been added to Visual Studio, such as visualizers and Visual Studio Shell. This book will cover all these extensibility options in enough detail to make readers familiar with extensibility in Visual Studio. Initially, documentation and community activities related to Visual Studio extensibility were weak before the release of Visual Studio 2008. However, after a Microsoft TechEd 2007 conference (when Visual Studio 2008 was in beta 1 stage), the Visual Studio Extensibility team at Microsoft tried to improve this situation. One such improvement was new documentation about VS extensibility. This book enhances that documentation and should be a good resource for the Visual Studio community, whose members are asking for more information.

Extensibility features for Visual Studio aren't available in Express free editions. You must have a commercial edition (Professional or above) to get all the benefits of extensibility features. You'll read more about extensibility later in this book, but I wanted to introduce the various options here.

Visual Studio SDK

The Visual Studio SDK (Software Development Kit) is a free downloadable package for Visual Studio that contains a set of documentation, code samples, and other materials to help you develop applications that integrate with Visual Studio.

The Visual Studio SDK contains all three extensibility options mentioned in the previous section (add-ins, macros, and packages) as well as other options that are new or not as well known.

This Visual Studio 2008 SDK offers a new extensibility option: *Visual Studio Shell*. This new tool enables you to build your applications based on a core foundation of VS and with a similar look to its IDE. This is helpful, as developing such applications gets easier, and the user interface more familiar, for many users.

Visual Studio Shell works in two modes: integrated mode and isolated mode. Integrated mode is good for programming languages, whereas isolated mode is helpful for special tools. You'll read more about the Visual Studio SDK later in the book.

Installation

Although all of the code samples and discussions in this book are about Visual Studio 2008, the latest available version, most of the material is applicable to previous versions with few or no changes.

Here, I'm referring to installation of the Visual Studio 2008 Team System edition. I chose this edition because it's becoming more widely used than other editions. In addition, all its features and capabilities are also available in other commercial editions. You can download a free 90-day trial of this edition from the Microsoft downloads site in order to work through this book and test its sample code. For the purposes of this book, there is no difference between the Professional or later editions of Visual Studio, and you can even use the Standard edition for many of the chapters.

In the following sections, I talk about system requirements and the installation process of Visual Studio 2008 Team Suite edition, but other editions have very similar requirements and the same installation process.

System Requirements

According to Microsoft's documentation, the supported operating systems for Visual Studio 2008 are various editions of Windows Vista, Windows 2003, and Windows XP.

Minimum installation requirements for Visual Studio 2008 Professional edition are as follows:

- ❑ Processor: 1.6 + GHz
- ❑ RAM: 384 + MB of available physical RAM
- ❑ Display: 1024 × 768

Recommended settings, however, are as follows:

- ❑ Processor: 2.2 + GHz
- ❑ RAM: 1024 + MB of available physical RAM
- ❑ Display: 1280 × 1024

For Windows Vista, you need a 2.4 GHz CPU and 768 MB of RAM.

For this book, I used Visual Studio 2008 Team System edition on Microsoft Windows Vista Ultimate x86, but nothing is different from other operating systems.

Installation Process

After running the Visual Studio setup file, you will see a window like the one shown in Figure 1-1.

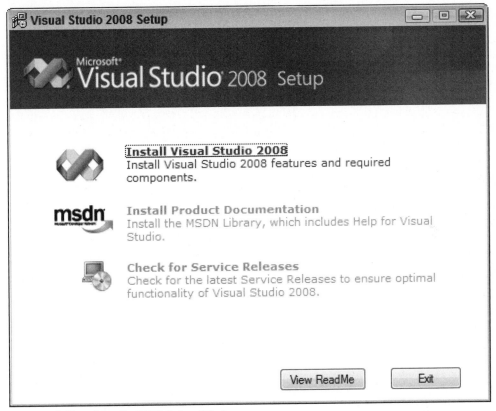

Figure 1-1: Visual Studio 2008 Setup Window

By clicking the first option, Install Visual Studio 2008, you can begin the installation process. The second option installs the MSDN library, and the third option installs service releases, which keep your Visual Studio installation up to date.

The installation process for Visual Studio 2008 is similar to that for Visual Studio 2005. After opening the installer, you need to accept the terms and license agreement and choose the appropriate type of installation (Default, Full, or Custom) to install Visual Studio at the specified path.

After finishing the installation, you can launch your Visual Studio IDE. On its first run, Visual Studio asks you to choose your preferred environment settings based on the programming language and the type of development that you frequently use (see Figure 1-2).

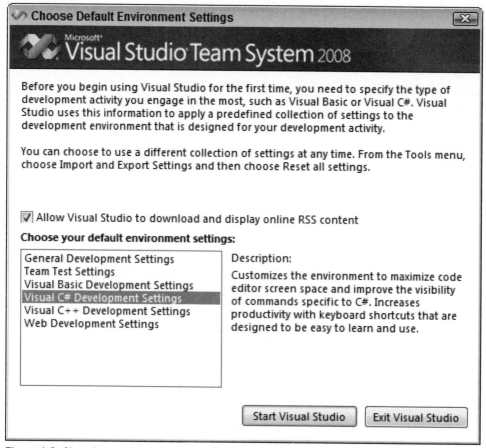

Figure 1-2: Choosing your preferred settings at first startup

Installing the SDK

You can download the Visual Studio 2008 SDK 1.0 from http://tinyurl.com/3brqyy. This installer contains everything you need to set up the Visual Studio SDK. This is the only available version at the time of writing, but Microsoft releases new versions of the Visual Studio SDK on a regular basis, so you may be able to get a newer version by the time you read this.

An Overview of the IDE

This section provides you with an overview of the IDE. I know that most readers are already familiar with these principles, but it is important that every reader has seen them before stepping into the content. After a short introduction to the structure of the IDE, I'll introduce the main elements of the Visual Studio environment.

General Structure of the IDE

The first time you load Visual Studio, you will see an environment like the one shown in Figure 1-3.

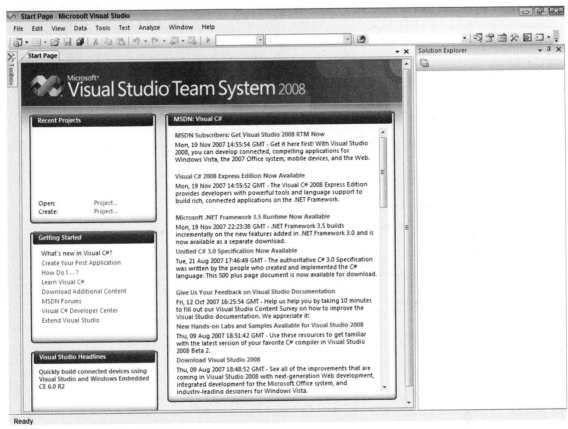

Figure 1-3: Visual Studio 2008 IDE

The VS IDE has a tabular structure, which means that it opens the main content in several tabs in the center of the IDE. It also contains several windows that can be docked to one of corners, as well as a collection of different toolbars for development purposes. The Visual Studio IDE is completely customizable — you can change the layout and look of most of its elements. Using the Solution Explorer, you navigate through your solutions and projects, choose your code files, and open them in new tabs. Other windows enable you to easily accomplish necessary tasks.

Windows and toolbars play the main role in using Visual Studio for development, and you'll use them to achieve the benefits of different features of Visual Studio.

Main Elements of the IDE

This book describes how to extend Visual Studio. Any extension of Visual Studio has its own goals, but regardless of the goals of an extension, it extends one of the main parts of this environment. Because most of the time you are dealing with some of the main elements of the VS IDE for extensibility, it's worthwhile to review all these elements in one place and learn what they do. Therefore, in the next few sections, you'll learn about all these windows and how they help you do your work.

Solution Explorer

The Solution Explorer, shown in Figure 1-4, is an important window in Visual Studio. It enables you to navigate between your solutions, projects, and project files in an hierarchical manner, using a tree control.

Figure 1-4: Solution Explorer

By clicking on each item, a new tab opens in the middle of the IDE and you can see the content of that item. You can also gain access to the properties of each item by right-clicking on it. Some common tasks are available for each item in the right-click menu.

Properties Window

The Properties window, shown in Figure 1-5, is another common window in Visual Studio.

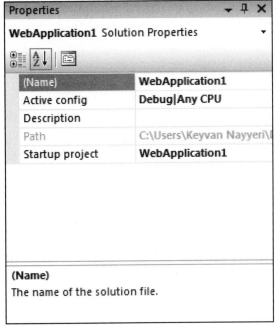

Figure 1-5: Properties window

This window shows all available properties of an item and can sort them alphabetically or by group. Using this window, you can set the properties of a solution, project, file, control, or any other item easily.

Toolbox

The Toolbox, shown in Figure 1-6, is a window that contains a list of controls that you can drag and drop into your Windows Forms, web pages, XAML windows, or workflow designer.

In the toolbox, controls are grouped and are displayed based on the type of application that you're developing. You can also add new groups and custom controls manually.

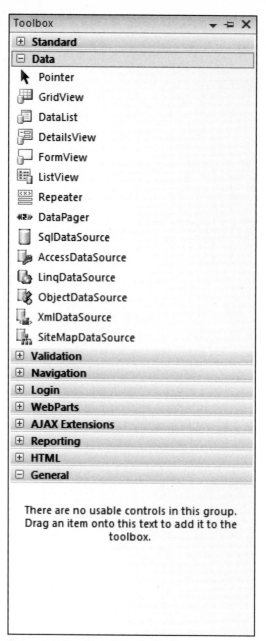

Figure 1-6: The Visual Studio Toolbox

Server Explorer

The Server Explorer window, shown in Figure 1-7, is another window that enables you to navigate through local and remote servers in order to gain access to databases as well as resources and services of servers.

Figure 1-7: Visual Studio's Server Explorer window

Class View

This window, shown in Figure 1-8, displays all the available classes in a solution (in addition to built-in classes in the .NET Framework) and groups them according to their namespaces.

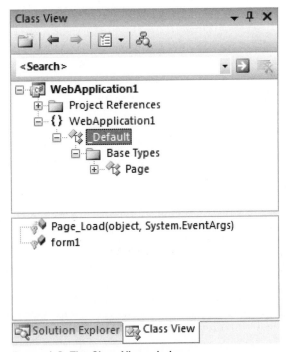

Figure 1-8: The Class View window

Error List

All errors in your code, either at the time of writing the code or upon compilation, are shown in the Error List window, shown in Figure 1-9.

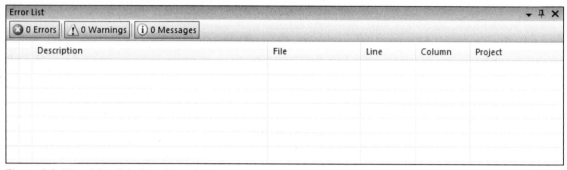

Figure 1-9: Visual Studio's Error List window

This window lists all warnings and errors. By clicking on an item in the list, you can access the original code that caused the warning or error.

Output

The last important Visual Studio window is the Output window, shown in Figure 1-10. This window provides a list of messages about all the processes that are occurring in Visual Studio.

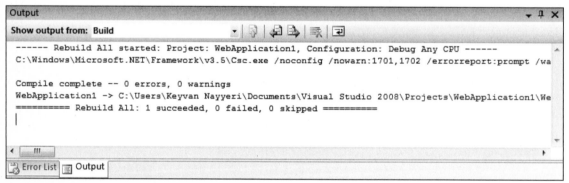

Figure 1-10: The Output window

Most of the actions and tasks in Visual Studio have a corresponding command, and these commands generate output. The output of actions is helpful for debugging and finding the status of a task. You can also write your own texts into the Output window for debugging purposes.

Summary

In this first chapter of the book, you took a brief walk through the history of Visual Studio over the past 11 years, including the features and changes of the six versions of this product that have been released during this period. After that, you learned about the extensibility options in Visual Studio and were introduced to the Visual Studio SDK. In addition, you learned the installation requirements and procedures for Visual Studio. Finally, you took a quick tour of the Visual Studio IDE and its main elements.

The .NET Framework

After reviewing the history of Visual Studio, its features, and its main elements in Chapter 1, it's time to look at another basic topic — the Microsoft .NET Framework. Visual Studio targets the .NET Framework and supports its programming languages and technologies, so it seems reasonable to dedicate a chapter to this framework. Here you will find a brief introduction to its architecture, programming languages, and technologies, and examine its correlation with Visual Studio.

The .NET Framework is important in this book for two reasons:

❑ Developers want to extend Visual Studio to simplify their daily development tasks with it, in order to develop something with .NET programming languages and technologies. For example, you may want to write an add-in to automate some coding tasks with C#, or perhaps you need to write a visualizer to debug an ASP.NET cache. Yet another reason may be to write a macro to create a fixed layout for a Windows Presentation Foundation application. In order to extend Visual Studio for any of these scenarios, you have to know the .NET Framework very well.

❑ You use .NET to extend Visual Studio! In every chapter of this book, I apply .NET programming languages, programming techniques, and various concepts of .NET technologies to illustrate the topics; readers definitely should have a good background in the .NET Framework.

Therefore, this chapter covers the following main topics:

❑ The .NET Framework, including its available versions and their features

❑ The architecture of the .NET Framework

❑ Available programming languages in .NET

❑ Technologies included in the .NET platform

❑ Integration between the .NET Framework and Visual Studio 2008

Let's begin with an introduction to Microsoft .NET.

What Is Microsoft .NET?

.NET is Microsoft's answer to the necessity for an integrated multi-purpose software development platform, which had been requested by developers for a decade or so. In the late 1990s, Microsoft finally began the work to build a single platform in software development for desktop, web, and embedded-device applications, under the name the .NET Framework. A framework has its own meaning and .NET is truly a framework, and probably the best software development framework ever created. For more information about software frameworks, the .NET Framework, and designing a good software framework with .NET, check out *Framework Design Guidelines* by Krysztof Cwalina and Brad Abrams (Addison-Wesley, 2005).

The .NET Framework was designed with the following goals in mind:

❑ **Language independence:** This means building applications that work independently of the programming language they've been written with, making it possible to build an application with multiple languages.

❑ **Platform independence:** One of main goals of the .NET Framework is to design applications that run on other platforms and computers, regardless of their resource limitations and other specifications. Until now, Microsoft, other companies, and open-source teams have tried to implement the .NET Framework on other platforms, but their results were not completely successful.

❑ **Security:** Writing more secure applications

❑ **Easier deployment:** Making the deployment easier both for desktop and web applications

❑ **Interoperability:** Being compatible with older technologies such as COM

The .NET Framework uses a single runtime for different languages to build different kinds of software, including local desktop applications, smart clients, web applications, and embedded-device applications. Programs written with .NET can run on all versions of the Microsoft Windows operating system (although some of them require service packs). Also in the works are some projects to port the .NET Framework to other operating systems such as Linux and Apple Macintosh.

The .NET Framework has a rich Base Class Library (BCL) of pre-coded frameworks for web applications, user interfaces, data access, and communications. You use this class library along your own code to build your applications.

The great thing about .NET is that it uses the Common Language Runtime (CLR) in the core. The CLR enables you to build your applications independently of the specification of the system that is running them. For example, you don't need to worry about CPU usage for your application's execution — the CLR does this for you.

The class library and the CLR make up the .NET Framework. In the following sections, you'll read more about the .NET architecture and how it works. For now, it's worthwhile to have a look at the five available versions of the .NET Framework.

The .NET Framework 1.0

Released in 2002 with Visual Studio .NET 2002, the .NET Framework 1.0 included the first versions of Visual Basic .NET, C#, and J#, as well as the new .NET version of Visual C++. It also had ASP.NET 1.0 and ADO.NET 1.0 at its core.

The .NET Framework 1.1

The second version, released in 2003 with Visual Studio .NET 2003, was an update to .NET 1.0, including bug fixes, minor feature improvements, and support for embedded-device development. It included new versions of all programming languages, ASP.NET 1.1, ADO.NET 1.1, and updates to the CLR classes.

The .NET Framework 2.0

In 2005 Microsoft released the .NET Framework 2.0 and Visual Studio 2005 together. New versions of the .NET programming languages, ASP.NET 2.0, ADO.NET 2.0, and some new features, such as generic types in .NET languages, were a part of .NET 2.0. .NET 2.0 marked a milestone in .NET's life and it is still an important version. Later, Microsoft added new features to the .NET Framework 2.0 and released the .NET Framework 3.0 and 3.5.

Since this version, the .NET moniker has been removed from the name of the .NET programming languages and Visual Studio.

The .NET Framework 3.0

The .NET Framework 3.0 was released in 2006 and didn't have a corresponding version of Visual Studio. It wasn't a completely new framework; in fact, it was an extension to the .NET Framework 2.0, which added four new technologies to .NET:

- ❑ Windows Presentation Foundation (WPF)
- ❑ Windows Communication Foundation (WCF)
- ❑ Windows Workflow Foundation (WWF or WF)
- ❑ Windows CardSpace (WCS)

Also included was a new markup language based on XML. Named XAML, it worked with Windows Presentation Foundation. The .NET Framework 3.0 was the first version of the .NET Framework to target Windows Vista and Windows Server 2008, even though it could run on Windows XP Service Pack 2 and Windows Server 2003.

The .NET Framework 3.0 didn't have its own CLR or any architecture changes and used the 2.0 version of the CLR.

The .NET Framework 3.5

.NET 3.5 released with Visual Studio 2008 in November 2007 and is the latest available stable version of the .NET Framework. It removes the J# language from the supported languages and adds some improvements to Windows Presentation Foundation, Windows Communication Foundation, Windows Workflow Foundation, and Windows CardSpace. It also has new versions of the .NET programming languages as well as a new language feature named LINQ.

Also included in .NET 3.5 is a new web technology named Silverlight. Silverlight is a compact version of Windows Presentation Foundation that can be executed in web browsers to display Silverlight animations and other things. Silverlight is a competitor of Adobe Flash and tries to accomplish similar goals in a better and easier way.

Common Language Runtime (CLR)

As mentioned previously, .NET applications run with the Common Language Runtime (CLR). The CLR is like a virtual machine for applications. In other words, the CLR helps developers write their applications without regard to the capabilities of the CPU. The CLR manages the runtime for an application and its runtime requirements. It also has some other main features, including memory management, error handling, and security mechanisms.

The CLR is Microsoft's implementation of the Common Language Infrastructure (CLI). Designed by Microsoft, the CLI is an international open specification defining an environment that enables multiple languages to be used on different platforms, avoiding the need to rewrite code for different architectures.

There are some other implementations for the CLI, such as the .NET Compact Framework (.NET CF) for portable devices and Mono, and the .NET implementation for Linux, sponsored by Novell.

In the next few paragraphs, I'll discuss different parts of the .NET Framework, their roles, and the process that is followed to compile and run an application written in .NET with the CLR. A schematic view of this process is shown in Figure 2-1.

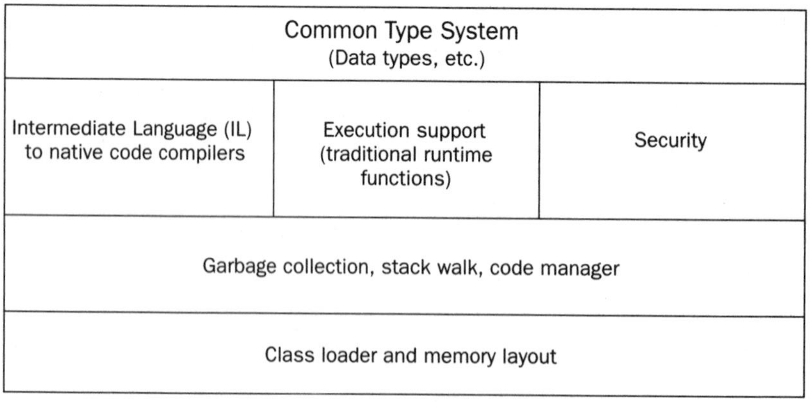

Common Type System (Data types, etc.)		
Intermediate Language (IL) to native code compilers	Execution support (traditional runtime functions)	Security
Garbage collection, stack walk, code manager		
Class loader and memory layout		

Figure 2-1: CLR structure

An application written with one of .NET's programming languages can be compiled using a specific compiler for that language. Visual Basic, C#, and Visual C++ have their own compilers. The source code of programs is compiled into an Intermediate Language (IL) or Microsoft Intermediate Language (MSIL). IL codes are similar for all .NET languages, so the final code for all languages is the same. This paves the way for the language independence goal of the .NET Framework, enabling you to develop an application with multiple languages.

IL codes with other resources such as images and files are added to managed assemblies. Managed assemblies have .exe or .dll extensions and contain a manifest to provide information regarding their type, version, number, and culture.

At runtime, the program's IL code is loaded to the CLR, and this may have some effect on the IL based on the manifest. If security conditions are met, then the CLR performs just-in-time (JIT) compilation to convert the IL to machine instructions.

Architecture of the .NET Framework

The .NET Framework has the efficient architecture shown in Figure 2-2.

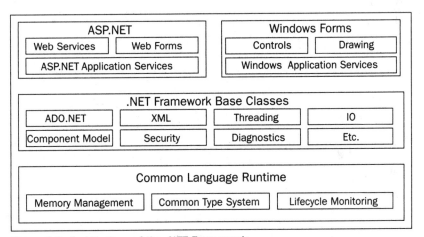

Figure 2-2: Architecture of the .NET Framework

This architecture consists of three layers:

❑ At the upper layer are ASP.NET and Windows Forms and their children, such as web services, controls, services, and interface components in general.

❑ The middle layer represents the Base Class Library (BCL), which includes ADO.NET, XML, IO, security, and threading.

❑ Finally, at the lower layer is the Common Language Runtime (CLR), which manages the runtime.

Programming Languages

There are three languages in the .NET Framework 3.5 — Visual Basic, C#, and Visual C++. J# is dead — Microsoft stopped developing it after the .NET Framework 2.0. In addition to Microsoft programming languages included in the .NET Framework, many other .NET languages, created by other companies and open-source projects, can design applications for .NET. Also included as a plug-in part of ASP.NET, and designed by Microsoft, is an IronPython language that enables Python programmers to write ASP.NET applications with Python syntax.

Let's examine in a little more detail the three programming languages available in .NET 3.5 and Visual Studio 2008. From a technical point of view, there's no difference between Visual Basic and C# as the most common .NET languages, because both provide the same features and represent the base class library and CLR classes. For users who are coming from the Basic world, however, VB is suitable; and for those who are coming from the C/C++ world, C# is better. Conversely, Visual Basic is easier to learn and use than C#. There is also a pre-compilation feature in Visual Basic that provides code with an additional level of IntelliSense and error checking.

Programming *into* Your Language, Not *in* It

The title of this sidebar and its topic are drawn from Steve McConnell's great book about software development, *Code Complete, 2nd ed.* (Microsoft Press, 2004). In this book, Steve discusses programming languages and why developers should program *into* a language, not *in* it. In other words, he says he doesn't limit himself by what a programming language provides as built-in features and capabilities. If he wants something that's not part of the language, then he develops it himself. In other words, he writes anything necessary for his applications to move them *into* the language and doesn't put any limitation on himself *in* a language.

This is what I want to illustrate here, too. The point isn't what programming language you're using or its capabilities. What's important is that you should be able to do whatever you want with it — which most likely depends on you, not on the programming language. If you don't know your platform very well, you may waste time writing something that's already there. If you don't know how to write a good program, you can't succeed, even if you write it with the most suitable language for your purpose. However, don't forget that a language with more features and libraries is absolutely better than a language without them. For example, C# is better than C++ or C, both for someone who needs its enhanced features and for someone who wants to develop for the Microsoft .NET platform.

The .NET Framework has removed the difference between the capabilities of its programming languages, because they're representing the same libraries with different syntaxes. Two languages from two popular language families — Visual Basic and C# — enable developers with older versions to migrate easily to .NET.

There have been many debates about Visual Basic and C# and which is the better language, but there's no definitive answer. Visual Basic is easier to use and learn, so it's popular. C# is harder to learn and use, but it's popular with professional developers because new language features usually appear in C# sooner than they do in VB, and because some famous Microsoft developers use it and provide more samples.

In my own opinion, there's no important difference between these two languages. Personally, I'm able to use both to develop my projects, and I can't find a good reason to recommend one over the other. In recent years, I've used C# more frequently than VB, but I still frequently use VB for daily development and small projects.

Using both languages for this book would have wasted time and resources. Everybody with a background in .NET and C languages can understand the C# codes used in this book, even if he or she is a VB developer. Similarly, a C# developer can easily understand VB codes because they're closer to human language. Moreover, you can find several commercial or free code converters to convert C# codes to VB and vice versa.

Visual Basic

Microsoft's own programming language, Visual Basic (VB), attains its latest version (9.0) in the .NET Framework 3.5. Visual Basic is a programming language with a syntax similar to traditional Basic languages such as GWBasic and QBasic. Before .NET, Visual Basic was a popular language but it didn't support object-oriented programming (OOP) 100 percent. Visual Basic .NET 7.0 (2002), the first .NET version of VB, made many fundamental changes to support object-oriented programming completely. Current versions of Visual Basic are still object-oriented. Visual Basic is the only case-insensitive language in .NET. VB can be used, among some other languages, for developing ASP.NET web applications.

Although Visual Basic is still widely used, its popularity has declined in recent years. Microsoft's new language, C#, and Java (from Sun) have replaced it to some extent. In this book, you'll use Visual Basic in Chapter 22 for developing Visual Studio macros, as Visual Basic is the only language supported for building macros.

C#

C# is Microsoft's implementation of C languages for .NET. C# has a syntax similar to C/C++ but it's simpler than Visual C++, and it was born at the same time as the .NET Framework. It's becoming increasingly popular, and many professional .NET developers use it for daily development. Like other C languages, it's case sensitive; and for some it has a more complicated learning curve than Visual Basic.

As in Visual Basic, you can use C# for developing ASP.NET applications.

C# is the language I used for all the chapters in this book, but VB developers shouldn't worry, because anyone who is basically familiar with the C family and has a good background in .NET can read this book and understand its code easily.

Visual C++

Visual C++ with .NET is the newer version of the Visual C++ languages that come from the COM days. Visual C++ uses the same syntax for developing .NET applications and can't be used for ASP.NET development. It's case sensitive, and it's harder to learn than other .NET programming languages. Visual C++ isn't widely used for developing common applications but it still has its own place in systems programming.

In this book, I used Visual C++ for Chapter 15, "Visual Studio Shell," because that is the language that Microsoft has used for developing Visual Studio Shell applications. This is related to the nature of Visual Studio itself, because it's created with Visual C++ as well.

Technologies

The .NET Framework provides several technologies out of the box. Some of these technologies were part of .NET from its early days, and some were added with newer versions. I reviewed a bit of their history in previous sections. Now I want to provide an introduction to these technologies, their goals, and their main features. This is helpful because you'll often want to extend Visual Studio in order to simplify tasks related to these technologies, especially the newer ones.

ASP.NET

The next generation of classic Active Server Pages (ASP) was designed specifically for building websites. ASP.NET is an enterprise technology for building web pages and web portals with .NET languages. Great integration between ASP.NET and other technologies is included in the .NET Framework and the base class libraries. It's also 100 percent integrated with Visual Studio 2008.

ASP.NET is probably the most popular technology in the .NET Framework, and developers around the world are using it. ASP.NET, in conjunction with Internet Information Services (IIS), has been the most trustworthy platform for building enterprise sites and portals.

ASP.NET with the addition of SharePoint makes a great choice for building web portals.

ASP.NET AJAX is an important technology that's included in ASP.NET. This technology enables rich client applications. AJAX stands for Asynchronous JavaScript and XML, and it has become a common web development technology in recent years. There are other implementations for AJAX in ASP.NET and other technologies such as PHP, but ASP.NET AJAX from Microsoft is the most popular choice for ASP.NET developers.

Web Services

Web services can be considered part of ASP.NET's features. The growing number of service-oriented applications and sites led Microsoft to create an efficient and easy-to-use built-in mechanism for working with web services.

Web services are completely based on XML and provide different types of flexibility and security mechanisms for developers, based on SOAP and WSDL specifications. Web services were part of .NET from its early versions, but later, in .NET 3.0, Microsoft added a new technology for service-oriented architecture (SOA), named Windows Communication Foundation (WCF).

ADO.NET

ADO.NET was part of the .NET Framework from its early days. ADO.NET is responsible for data access functionality and features, and for providing different data types for working in relational database systems such as SQL Server, Access, and Oracle. It can also work with nonrelational data storages. It's a part of the base class library and can be compared to ActiveX Data Objects (ADO) from COM days, but it has changed extensively and can be considered a completely new thing.

XML, XSD, XPath, and XSLT

Extensible Markup Language (XML) entered the software world in the late 1990s and opened many doors to software developers. XML was well supported in the .NET Framework from the start; built-in controls, classes, and services are provided to work easily with XML files and data.

In addition to XML itself, some XML-related technologies are supported in the .NET Framework:

❑ XML Schema Datatype (XSD) is the XML schema that enables you to define the structure of an XML file in order to validate XML files and ensure that they're suitable for your purposes. XSD is one of three approaches to validating an XML file. The other two are Document Type Definitions (DTD) and RELAX NG.

❑ XML Path Language (XPath) is another XML-related technology designed to address different pieces of an XML file and perform some computations on the content of XML files.

❑ Extensible Stylesheet Language Transformations (XSLT) provides a way to convert an XML file to other XML files or to other formats such as HTML or XHTML.

Windows Presentation Foundation and XAML

Windows Presentation Foundation (WPF), code-named Avalon, was introduced in the .NET Framework 3.0 as a new graphic engine for Windows Vista. It uses an XML-based markup language named Extensible Application Markup Language (XAML) to define the layout and appearance of applications.

On compilation, XAML codes are compiled to Binary Application Markup Language (BAML), and WPF displays the final interface to users. There is a one-to-one mapping between CLR classes and XAML elements, and they can be accessed via .NET code.

Windows Communication Foundation

Windows Communication Foundation (WCF), code-named Indigo, was another new technology introduced in .NET 3.0. It's the next generation of technologies for building distributed systems based on service-oriented architecture (SOA).

Along with some basic functionalities such as those in web services, WCF provides more enhanced mechanisms and tools to build services and clients for distributed applications that run on multiple machines located far from each other.

Windows Workflow Foundation

Windows Workflow Foundation (WWF or WF) was the third new technology in .NET 3.0 to accomplish workflow-based tasks and build applications based on workflows. Two general types of workflows are supported in Windows Workflow: sequential workflows and state machine workflows.

Windows CardSpace

Windows CardSpace (WCS), code-named InfoCard, was the last new technology in .NET 3.0. WCS is a component that enables the storage of a user's digital identity in a secure way. It also retrieves it later for specific tasks such as web-site authentication.

LINQ

Language Integrated Query (LINQ) is a new technology included in the .NET Framework 3.5. Its primary goal is to add native querying syntax similar to Transact SQL to .NET languages. LINQ is supported by C# 3.0 and Visual Basic 9.0.

It enables code written in .NET languages to create, filter, and enumerate different types of data collections with the same syntax. Those collections may come from .NET enumerable classes, arrays, XML files, or relational databases.

LINQ uses some new features in programming languages, such as extension methods, lambda expressions, and anonymous types.

Silverlight

Microsoft Silverlight, which was named WPF/e previously, is a light version of WPF that can be installed on web browsers in order to move the great features of WPF and XAML to web applications. Using Silverlight, you can build dynamic user interfaces for web applications with XAML codes.

Silverlight is similar to Adobe Flash, but its files are smaller and its development is easier.

The .NET Framework and Visual Studio 2008

Unlike the support for the .NET Framework 3.0 in Visual Studio, which wasn't possible without installing add-ins for Visual Studio 2005, the .NET Framework 3.5 offers excellent integration with Visual Studio 2008.

In addition to feature improvements and bug fixes for older versions of the .NET Framework, Visual Studio 2008 includes support for new versions of the .NET Framework, 3.0 and 3.5, and their related technologies.

Visual Studio 2008 is the first version of Visual Studio that targets three different versions of the .NET Framework (2.0, 3.0, and 3.5) and supports them out of the box. This means that you can choose among these three versions of the .NET Framework for building your projects. It's also possible to filter project templates based on the version of the .NET Framework.

Visual Studio has built-in support for .NET 3.0 and its technologies, including Windows Presentation Foundation, Windows Communication Foundation, Windows Workflow Foundation, and their project templates. There is also a fine XAML designer for XAML files, named Cider.

Finally, there is also excellent support for the .NET Framework 3.5. Silverlight project templates are provided, and you can develop Silverlight applications easily. Similarly, LINQ is completely integrated with VS and all its auto-generated code templates and project references.

.NET and COM

Before .NET came into play, the Component Object Model (COM) was common. As mentioned earlier, interoperability between .NET and older technologies such as COM was one of Microsoft's main considerations in building the .NET Framework. Thus, there is excellent support for COM components in .NET, and new .NET technologies have interoperability options for COM.

Interoperability between .NET and COM is introduced here because you need COM for developing add-ins. In fact, add-ins are COM components, and you need some familiarity with them to some extent. A complete discussion about .NET and COM interoperability are beyond the scope of this chapter, so I'll just present a common scenario involving interoperability — using a COM component in .NET applications.

Suppose you have a COM component such as a DLL file that is implementing an interface, and you need to use it in a .NET application. To do this, you should register the interface on the machine. If you build this DLL on the same machine, then it will be registered automatically, but if you're moving this DLL from another machine, then you can register it using the `regsvr32` command that can be found in `C:\Windows\system32`. Here is a command to do this (assuming that your DLL is named `MyComponent.DLL`):

```
regsvr32 MyComponent.dll
```

After this, your component is registered on the machine and you can use it in your .NET application. To add this interface to your .NET application, right-click on the project name and choose the Add Reference option, and then navigate to the COM tab and select your COM component to add to your project references. After this step, you can use this COM interface like a normal .NET reference in your application.

Additional Resources

This chapter covered .NET programming languages and technologies. Most readers will not know all these technologies in depth and may be interested in learning more about them. Having a profound understanding of these technologies isn't a prerequisite for reading this book, but if you want to consult additional resources for more information, Wrox has published many books about these topics. You can read them beginning with the lower levels and advancing to the more professional ones.

❑ *Professional VB 2008* (ISBN: 9780470191361)

❑ *Professional C# 2008* (ISBN: 9780470191378)

❑ *Professional ASP.NET 3.5: in C# and VB* (ISBN: 9780470187579)

❑ *Professional ADO.NET 3.5 with LINQ and the Entity Framework* (ISBN: 9780470182611)

❑ *Professional XML* (ISBN: 9780471777779)

❑ *Professional WPF Programming: .NET Development with the Windows Presentation Foundation* (ISBN: 9780470041802)

❑ *Professional WCF Programming: .NET Development with the Windows Communication Foundation* (ISBN: 9780470089842)

❑ *Professional Windows Workflow Foundation* (ISBN: 9780470053867)

❑ *Professional Silverlight 1.1* (ISBN: 9780470193938)

Summary

This chapter was dedicated to the .NET Framework to introduce some basic information about it and get you started with the essential knowledge you'll need in this book.

We began the chapter with an overview of the .NET Framework and its available versions. After that, you looked at the Common Language Runtime and the architecture of the .NET Framework. The next topics were .NET programming languages and .NET technologies, with short descriptions of them. Before finishing the chapter, you looked at the integration between the .NET Framework and Visual Studio 2008. The chapter finished with a discussion of .NET and COM interoperability, because for building add-ins you need a good knowledge of COM.

3

Quick Tour

It's time to wade in and get your feet wet with the main topic of this book: extending Visual Studio. In this chapter you'll look at three common options for extending Visual Studio: macros, add-ins, and visualizers.

Before getting into a detailed discussion about these extension options, it may be worthwhile to take a quick tour so you can see what they are. Some readers may not be aware of what these extensions really do or may not have a detailed understanding of them. This tour also provides a few simple examples; later you'll get a full discussion of all extension options, including real-world examples.

You may see some new material throughout this chapter and in the sample code, but don't worry. I'll describe the content on a need-to-know basis. If you have questions, keep in mind that you'll revisit this subject again in subsequent chapters and more detailed information will be provided.

Here's what you'll discover in this chapter:

❑ Different options to extend Visual Studio

❑ A short introduction to macros, including an example

❑ A short introduction to add-ins, including an example

❑ A short introduction to visualizers, including an example

❑ How to use the MSDN library and VS Help to learn more about extension options

After finishing this chapter, you'll move on to the main part of this book and go beyond the basic information presented in the first three chapters.

Different Ways to Extend Visual Studio

Visual Studio is extensible in different ways. The extensibility of Visual Studio was important enough for Microsoft to dedicate a development team specifically for it. The daily job of the Visual Studio Ecosystem team is to improve existing extensibility features, fix bugs, and add new features. Visual Studio extensibility is often abbreviated by Microsoft and community members as VSX, and you'll see that term in this book as well.

The current version of Visual Studio (2008) supports the following major extensibility options:

- Macros
- Add-ins
- Visualizers
- VSPackages
- Code snippets
- Project templates
- MSBuild
- Visual Studio Shell
- Domain-specific languages tools

Note that some of these options can be considered extensibility features directly, whereas others are features that open the doors for developers to automate or simplify their tasks. For example, macros and add-ins are two familiar aspects of VS extensibility, but project templates and MSBuild are also ways to automate some tasks, such as creating project files and custom builds.

What Is a Macro?

A macro is a way to simplify repetitive tasks by recording an instance and running it as many times as you want. For example, suppose that you need to generate an ASP.NET site-map file from all available web pages in an ASP.NET web application. You can do this manually by adding all nodes to the ASP.NET site-map XML file, but for large projects this method doesn't seem like a good idea, does it?

One handy solution would be to use a Visual Studio macro to automatically go through all available web pages and generate a site-map file based on their hierarchy. This is only one of many possible examples.

> *Microsoft MVP Scott Allen has written an ASP.NET 2.0 site-map macro to generate a site map automatically. You can find his macro on his blog, including a description, the source code, and installation instructions. See* http://odetocode.com/Blogs/scott/archive/2006/10/17/8168.aspx.

The concept of a macro isn't limited to Visual Studio. Many Microsoft products support macros to simplify repetitive tasks in their respective environments. You can find macros in Microsoft Office products such as Word or Excel as well.

Visual Studio macros can be created in two ways:

- ❑ Recording a repetitive tasks with a macro recorder
- ❑ Developing macros with programming codes

The first way is simple. You use a macro recorder to record all the steps that you would take to perform the action in your VS IDE. This recorder generates everything necessary to create a macro, and later you can just run the macro to repeat the same steps.

The second way requires a background in programming, but it provides more flexibility and features. With it, you use codes to develop a macro to carry out repetitive tasks.

Previously, Visual Basic for Applications (VBA) was the language for writing macros for products such as Word or Excel. For Visual Studio and new versions of Microsoft Office, however, you can use the Visual Basic language that's part of the .NET Framework (and Visual Studio Tools for Office for Office products).

Macros have an IDE similar to the Visual Studio IDE, in which you can develop your macros. The name of this IDE is Macros IDE, and it's accessible by selecting Tools ⇨ Macros ⇨ Macros IDE, or the Alt+F11 shortcut. This IDE provides the same features and the same look and feel as the main Visual Studio IDE, and it creates an environment in which you can code your macros with the Visual Basic language. Yes, you must develop your macros with Visual Basic because it's not technically possible to develop macros with any other language.

Macros IDE doesn't include some concepts, such as Solution; this is one of the differences between this IDE and the VS IDE. Macros IDE has an explorer similar to the VS Solution Explorer, named Project Explorer. The job of this feature is to explore between macro projects.

Macros are stored in files with a .vsmacros extension. These files keep Visual Basic codes for the macros, and a single macro file can hold as many macros as you like. Each macro can be defined as a separate Visual Basic subroutine.

The term macro *as used in this book actually refers to VSMacro, which is the original name of the Visual Studio macro defined by Microsoft. But "macro" is the common term for VS macros among all developers, so I also use this term unless it's necessary to refer specifically to VS macros.*

When authoring a macro, you have access to some APIs. The most important and common API is DTE (Development Tools Extensibility), and it's especially important for VS extensions. You'll read more about DTE in Chapter 4, "The Automation Model."

Macros are covered in detail in Chapter 22, and you might want to read that chapter right after finishing this one. As C# is the main language for this book and macros can't be written with Visual Basic, I made the chapter on macros the final chapter in the book. For now, you can become familiar with a very simple macro in the next section.

Sample Macro

Suppose you want to write a macro to resize the main IDE window to 600 × 480 from its original size (which is usually maximized). To do this, you have to follow some steps:

1. Open the Macro Explorer by choosing the Tools ⇨ Macros ⇨ Macro Explorer menu or pressing Alt+F8. This will put the Macro Explorer on the right-hand side of the Visual Studio IDE. Macro Explorer is shown in Figure 3-1.

Figure 3-1: Macro Explorer

2. After this, you can create a new macro project by right-clicking on Macros text at the root of the Macro Explorer tree and choosing the New Macro Project item.

3. In the opened window, choose a name for your project (Chapter 3) and create your macro project. This adds a new node named Chapter 3 to your Macro Explorer and a file named Module1 to it. By clicking on Module1, Visual Studio brings up the Macros IDE and shows the code for Module1, enabling you to implement your code.

The auto-generated code for Module1 looks like Listing 3-1.

Listing 3-1: Auto-generated Code for Module1

```
Imports System
Imports EnvDTE
Imports EnvDTE80
Imports EnvDTE90
Imports System.Diagnostics

Public Module Module1


End Module
```

As you can see, some references have been added to this module. EnvDTE, EnvDTE80, and EnvDTE90 refer to the general Visual Studio DTE API, the Visual Studio 2005 DTE API, and the Visual Studio 2008 DTE API, respectively. System.Diagnostics is there to enable you to get access to debugging information and system processes.

Now you can add a subroutine to this module and name it ResizeMainIDE to implement your macro logic there. After adding this simple logic, your module has code like what is shown in Listing 3-2.

Listing 3-2: Code Logic for the Macro

```
Imports System
Imports EnvDTE
Imports EnvDTE80
Imports EnvDTE90
Imports System.Diagnostics

Public Module Module1
    Sub ResizeMainIDE()
      Dim window As Window
      window = DTE.MainWindow
      window.Width = 640
      window.Height = 480
    End Sub
End Module
```

Let me describe how this code works. First, I created a Window object and set it to the DTE.MainWindow, which refers to the main window of the Visual Studio IDE. By changing the Width and Height properties of this window, I can resize the main IDE window.

In order to run this macro, I can either press F5 in the Macros IDE window (when implementing the macro) or I can right-click on the `ResizeMainIDE` subroutine in Macro Explorer and choose the Run item. This runs the macro to resize the IDE, as shown in Figures 3-2 and 3-3.

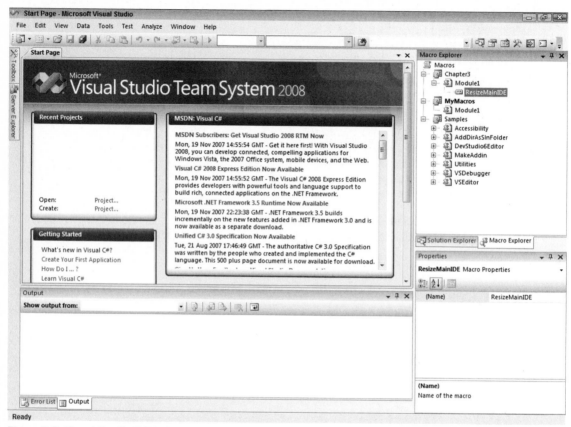

Figure 3-2: Visual Studio IDE before running the macro

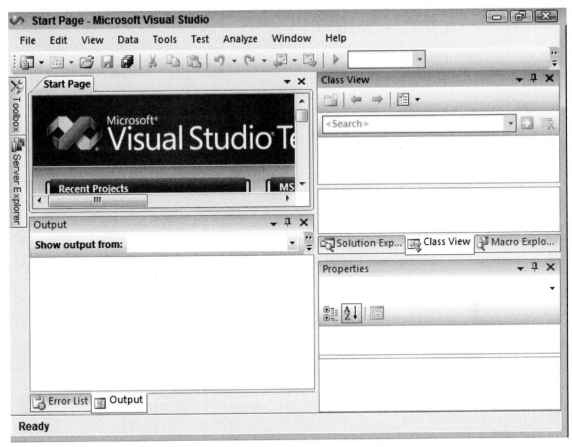

Figure 3-3: Visual Studio IDE after running the macro

What Is an Add-In?

An add-in is a kind of extension that completely integrates with the Visual Studio environment and adds new functionality to it. Add-ins have full access to IDE tools and APIs and can interact with them. In this way, add-ins and macros are similar, because add-ins can have access to the same APIs that macros have. The difference is in the way Visual Studio deals with add-ins and macros.

A macro is source code that can be run by Visual Studio but isn't an integrated part of the IDE. Because a macro isn't a compiled assembly, you need to distribute the source code in order to move and install a macro. An add-in, however, is a compiled DLL file that can be loaded by Visual Studio when the IDE starts up, and it can be integrated completely with the IDE. Therefore, you don't need to distribute the source code of an add-in in order to move or deploy it.

The other difference is that while you can write a macro only with Visual Basic, an add-in can be written with different programming languages. In fact, any .NET programming language that compiles its code to Intermediate Language (IL) can be used to write an add-in. Some common languages for writing add-ins are Visual Basic and C#.

An add-in is a compiled COM component that can be loaded and unloaded by Visual Studio. Add-ins can have (and should have) a look and feel similar to Visual Studio.

Add-ins can work with solutions, projects, code files, and other windows, and modify them. Therefore, add-ins are the most professional way to extend Visual Studio and add custom features to it. Developers use many commercial or free add-ins for Visual Studio in their daily development work. Some popular add-ins are listed in Appendix A, "Third-Party Add-Ins and Extensions."

The COM root of an add-in enables it to implement an interface. An interface has a list of pre-defined methods that enable it to be called by Visual Studio for some specific tasks defined for it. When dealing with add-ins, you need to work with some interfaces that are discussed later in this book, but the most common one is the IDTExtensibility2 interface. You must implement this interface in order to write an add-in. Your add-ins class has some code-logic implementations for methods defined in this interface. Visual Studio calls these methods at appropriate times to use your add-ins. In fact, these methods are related to five events for your add-ins that are described later in Chapter 6, "The Anatomy of an Add-In."

A Story about IDTExtensibility2 and IDTExtensibility

Seeing the "2" index in IDTExtensibility2 may have you wondering why Microsoft put that 2 at the end of the interface name. I want to describe the reason briefly here because throughout the book you may see similar indexing.

Because most add-ins come from COM days and have their roots in COM interfaces, there are many similarities between APIs in this part of the book and older APIs. There have been some additions to older technologies, but the basic concepts of older APIs are still correct and useful. Therefore, Microsoft has used this 2 index at the end of some class names to indicate a new version of an older class. IDTExtensibility2 is simply the new version of IDTExtensibility. There are some other examples of this as well.

The same indexing rule is applied to other classes. For example, as you've seen in the previous section for macros, EnvDTE80 and EnvDTE90 are new versions of EnvDTE for Visual Studio 2005 and 2008, respectively. We still use EnvDTE in the core, but EnvDTE80 and EnvDTE90 add some new features that can be helpful to us.

You'll read more about add-ins in subsequent chapters of this book, where add-ins are described in detail, from the basics to more enhanced topics. For now, take a moment to examine the very basic example provided in the next section.

Sample Add-In

This section contains a very basic Visual Studio add-in for showing a MessageBox with a text, which appears when Visual Studio starts up. This simple example offers just a quick tour of the basic concept of an add-in, it doesn't reflect a real-world situation.

To begin writing an add-in, you need to create a new project. When the New Project dialog appears, you should choose the Other Project Types and Extensibility category, and then choose the Visual Studio Add-in project template from the templates list. I chose the SampleAddin name for my project (see Figure 3-4).

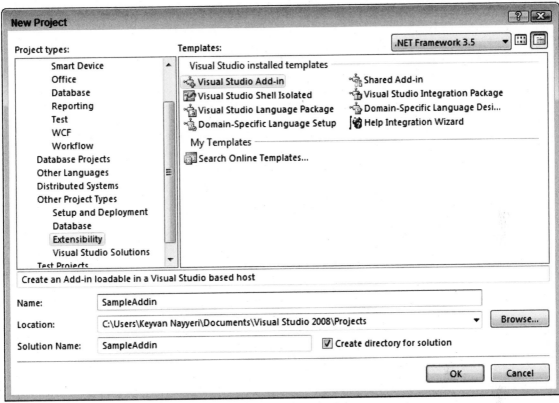

Figure 3-4: Choosing the Visual Studio SampleAddin project template

Clicking the OK button starts the Visual Studio Add-in Wizard. This wizard is covered in detail in Chapter 5, "Add-In Wizard," so we won't spend much time with it here, other than to demonstrate a short step-by-step guide to the process.

The first part of this wizard is just an introduction. To begin the wizard, click the Next button and follow the steps:

❑ Step 1: This page asks you to choose the development language for your add-in. There are several options, but I chose Create an Add-in using Visual C#.

❑ Step 2: Here you can choose the host for your application. You can choose the Visual Studio IDE and the Macros IDE as the host. For my example, I chose both.

❑ Step 3: Enter a name and description for your add-in. This information is used by Visual Studio to display the name and description of your add-in.

❑ Step 4: In this page, you can choose from three options for your add-in. I checked the second option for my add-in and left the first and last options unchecked.

❑ Step 5: You can also have an "About" dialog box for your add-in and enter a text for it.

❑ Step 6: The last page just shows a summary of your selections. By clicking the Finish button, you confirm these choices.

After finishing the wizard, Visual Studio registers the add-in and creates a new project for you with some files in it. These files contain some auto-generated code resulting from your selections in the wizard, among other code that is required to build an add-in. For now, you can ignore all files except the Connect.cs file, which is the main code file for add-ins.

Connect is the class that implements the IDTExtensibility2 interface and is the main class for implementing the add-in. It contains method definitions and some codes for five methods available in the IDTExtensibility2 interface. This auto-generated code is shown in Listing 3-3. Note that XML code comments are removed from the code to keep it simple and to save space.

Listing 3-3: Auto-generated Code for the Connect.cs Class

```csharp
using System;
using Extensibility;
using EnvDTE;
using EnvDTE80;
namespace SampleAddin
{
  public class Connect : IDTExtensibility2
  {
    public Connect()
    {
    }

    public void OnConnection(object application, ext_ConnectMode connectMode,
      object addInInst, ref Array custom)
    {
      _applicationObject = (DTE2)application;
      _addInInstance = (AddIn)addInInst;
    }

    public void OnDisconnection(ext_DisconnectMode disconnectMode, ref Array
custom)
    {
    }

    public void OnAddInsUpdate(ref Array custom)
    {
    }

    public void OnStartupComplete(ref Array custom)
    {
    }

    public void OnBeginShutdown(ref Array custom)
```

```
    {
    }

    private DTE2 _applicationObject;
    private AddIn _addInInstance;
  }
}
```

To implement my simple logic for the add-in, I can add a reference to `System.Windows.Forms` to my project and my class file, and put a line of code at the end of the `OnConnection` method to show a MessageBox. Listing 3-4 shows the new code for the `OnConnection` method.

Listing 3-4: OnConnection Method

```csharp
public void OnConnection(object application, ext_ConnectMode connectMode,
  object addInInst, ref Array custom)
{
  _applicationObject = (DTE2)application;
  _addInInstance = (AddIn)addInInst;

  MessageBox.Show("Sample add-in!");
}
```

The preceding snippet adds one line of code to show the MessageBox. The rest of the code is generated by Visual Studio and I'll describe it later in subsequent chapters.

Now I can build this project and restart my Visual Studio to see a MessageBox when it starts, as shown in Figure 3-5.

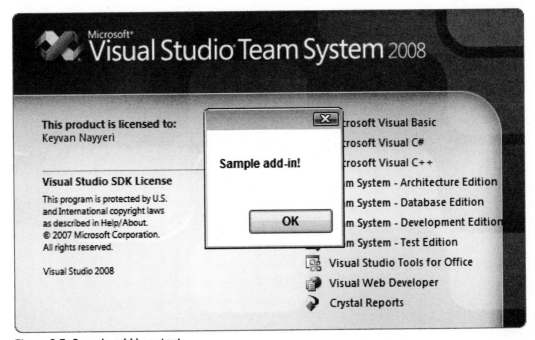

Figure 3-5: Sample add-in output

The source code for this sample add-in is available as part of the download package for this chapter on the book's Web site.

Working with Visualizers

Visualizers were added to Visual Studio after the 2005 version. A visualizer is a debugging feature, and it attracted the interest of .NET developers quickly. It's a very popular and handy tool for debugging .NET code in Visual Studio.

The main goal of a visualizer is to show different property values of an object in a visual way at each step of runtime. In other words, you can use visualizers to monitor the properties of an object while your code is running.

Listing 3-5 is a console application that adds some string values to a generic list of strings at runtime. You can insert a visualizer somewhere after the addition of items, to monitor the values and run your application.

Listing 3-5: Test Code for the List Visualizer

```
using System;
using System.Collections.Generic;
using System.Linq;
using System.Text;

namespace ListVisualizerSample
{
  class Program
  {
    static void Main(string[] args)
    {
      Console.Title = "Example of List Visualizer";

      List<string> names = new List<string>();

      names.Add("Katie Mohr");
      names.Add("Bill Bridges");
      names.Add("Cody Reichenau");

      foreach (string name in names)
        Console.WriteLine(name);

      Console.ReadLine();
    }
  }
}
```

Figure 3-6 shows this visualizer in action. This is a List visualizer; and as you can see, it displays the list of values in a list of strings.

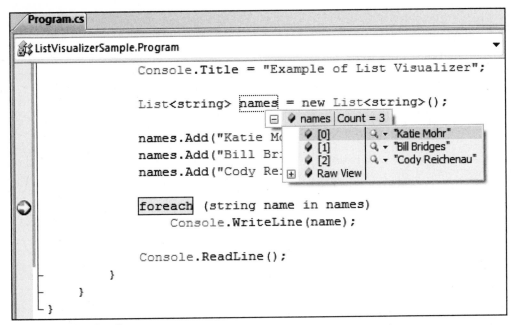

Figure 3-6: List visualizer

If you insert a breakpoint in your code, wait until it stops running, and then move your mouse over the name of a variable, you can use a visualizer to see its properties at that stage of runtime. This is very helpful because typically you're interested in monitoring variable values step by step to see what they contain. For example, suppose you have a null reference exception and don't have any idea where this exception is coming from. A good solution would be to use some breakpoints and check visualizer values to determine where your variable is going null, and thus solve the problem.

You may argue that you can use a watch window to monitor the property values, but keep in mind that some complex types can't represent their values in the watch window very well. Visualizers come into play at this point, by letting you monitor your values in any way you desire. For example, you can use an XML visualizer that shows XML objects in an XML editor.

Visualizers are mapped to their corresponding types. This means that each visualizer can be used for a specific type to display properties of its instances. There are two general types of visualizers:

❑ Built-in visualizers that are already a part of Visual Studio for some common types

❑ Custom visualizers that are implemented by community members and open-source projects and can be ported to Visual Studio to debug uncommon types and custom types

Talking about debugging techniques in Visual Studio is beyond the scope of this book, but you can check out other books for more information. Here, you'll see only how to extend debugging features to simplify your debugging process.

Visualizers are described in Chapter 17, "Extending the Debugger," among other ways to extend the debugging features in Visual Studio.

Sample Visualizer

Let's follow this brief tour of visualizers by looking at a simple example. This example creates a visualizer to monitor Stream objects by showing their content as plain text.

The first step in creating a visualizer is to start a Class Library project. Then, add a debugger visualizer item to your project. This is an item template that generates some necessary codes for your visualizer. The auto-generated code for my visualizer is presented in Listing 3-6.

Listing 3-6: Auto-generated Code for the Stream Visualizer

```
using Microsoft.VisualStudio.DebuggerVisualizers;
using System;
using System.Collections.Generic;
using System.Windows.Forms;

namespace SampleVisualizer
{
   // TODO: Add the following to SomeType's definition to see this visualizer when
debugging instances of SomeType:
   //
   // [DebuggerVisualizer(typeof(StreamVisualizer))]
   // [Serializable]
   // public class SomeType
   // {
   //  ...
   // }
   //
   /// <summary>
   /// A Visualizer for SomeType.
   /// </summary>
   public class StreamVisualizer : DialogDebuggerVisualizer
   {
     protected override void Show(IDialogVisualizerService windowService,
       IVisualizerObjectProvider objectProvider)
     {
       // TODO: Get the object to display a visualizer for.
```

```
//     Cast the result of objectProvider.GetObject()
//     to the type of the object being visualized.
object data = (object)objectProvider.GetObject();

// TODO: Display your view of the object.
//     Replace displayForm with your own custom Form or Control.
using (Form displayForm = new Form())
{
    displayForm.Text = data.ToString();
    windowService.ShowDialog(displayForm);
}
}

// TODO: Add the following to your testing code to test the visualizer:
//
//  StreamVisualizer.TestShowVisualizer(new SomeType());
//
/// <summary>
/// Tests the visualizer by hosting it outside of the debugger.
/// </summary>
/// <param name="objectToVisualize">The object to display in the visualizer
.</param>
public static void TestShowVisualizer(object objectToVisualize)
{
    VisualizerDevelopmentHost visualizerHost =
        new VisualizerDevelopmentHost(objectToVisualize, typeof(StreamVisualizer));
    visualizerHost.ShowVisualizer();
}
}
}
```

Auto-generated code for a visualizer is derived from `DialogDebuggerVisualizer` and contains definitions for two methods:

❑ **Show:** This method is the main way to show visualizers to end users. The main logic for a visualizer should be implemented here.

❑ **TestShowVisualizer:** This helper method is handy when you want to test your visualizer easily and quickly. Generally, you don't need to change the auto-generated code for this method because it does the job for you.

The code for the `Show` method has a `Form` object by default. This form is where you can show the values of an object, so what you need is implementing logic to show the values of a type in this form.

Listing 3-7 shows the code implementation for the preceding Show method. I don't need to change the auto-generated code for the TestShowVisualizer method.

Listing 3-7: Code Implementation for the Stream Visualizer

```
protected override void Show(IDialogVisualizerService windowService,
   IVisualizerObjectProvider objectProvider)
{
   Stream data = (Stream)objectProvider.GetObject();

   using (Form displayForm = new Form())
   {
      TextBox textbox = new TextBox();
      textbox.Width = 400;
      textbox.Height = 300;
      textbox.Multiline = true;
      textbox.ScrollBars = ScrollBars.Both;
      displayForm.Controls.Add(textbox);

      StreamReader reader = new StreamReader(data);
      textbox.Text = reader.ReadToEnd();

      displayForm.Width = 420;
      displayForm.Height = 340;
      displayForm.MaximizeBox = false;

      displayForm.Text = data.ToString() + " Visualizer";
      windowService.ShowDialog(displayForm);
   }
}
```

In this code, I first retrieved an object of type Stream from the objectProvider.GetObject method, and then built a textbox on-the-fly in which to show the text content of my object. Then, using a StreamReader, I loaded the content of my object to the textbox and finally added this textbox to my form.

Now it's time to test the visualizer. To do this, I add a Console Application to my solution and add references to Microsoft.VisualStudio.DebuggerVisualizers and my SampleVisualizer project. I also embed a text file resource to show its content in my visualizer.

After doing these things, I write the code in Listing 3-8 to call the TestShowVisualizer method to test my visualizer. Note that it's necessary to add references to your project and file for the System.IO namespace.

Listing 3-8: Code to Test the Visualizer

```
static void Main(string[] args)
{
   Stream stream = new MemoryStream(File.ReadAllBytes("SampleFile.txt"));

   SampleVisualizer.StreamVisualizer.TestShowVisualizer(stream);
}
```

Running this code results in the output shown in Figure 3-7.

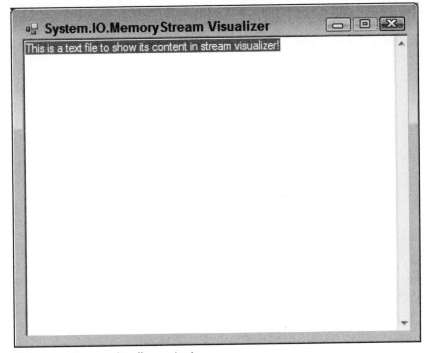

Figure 3-7: Stream visualizer output

The source code for this sample is provided in the code downloads for this chapter. You'll learn more about building visualizers and deploying them in Chapter 17, "Extending Debugger."

Using the Help Options

You'll read a lot in this book about Visual Studio Extensibility (VSX) in all its aspects, but it would be impossible to address every possible topic and question. However, you can find several helpful online and offline resources. Some of these community sites and blogs are listed in Appendix B. Current documentation and online and offline help for Visual Studio extensibility features isn't as full and rich as what you have likely found for other Microsoft products, but since the first beta version of Visual Studio 2008, Microsoft has tried to improve its documentation and provide better support to online communities. This book is another attempt to improve these resources.

One of the first references to check for answers to questions about Microsoft products is the Microsoft Developer Network (MSDN). Both offline and online versions of the MSDN are available. The offline version can be installed as a stand-alone package and it integrates with Visual Studio. The online version is accessible via http://msdn2.microsoft.com in some languages. You can search thousands of documentations and articles on the MSDN to find your answers. Contents are grouped according to criteria such as product categories, and you can browse these easily.

Two main menus in Visual Studio can help you check help and documentation easily: Community and Help. Visual Studio Help uses either the offline or the online version of the MSDN. If the offline version isn't available, then it searches the online version and displays the results for you.

The Community menu provides shortcuts to common help options. By choosing the Ask a Question item, you can search for answers. The Help menu has some other options for search, as well as index help options based on categories and products. Figure 3-8 shows the help window displayed when it returns search results for the "Visual Studio add-in" keywords in the C# language and the "Addins & Macros" content type.

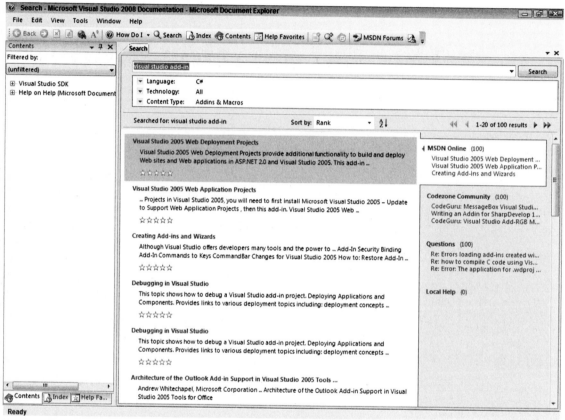

Figure 3-8: Visual Studio Help

Summary

This chapter completes the book's introductory material, provding you with a quick tour of Visual Studio's extensibility options. After a brief look at these options, you learned about macros, add-ins, and visualizers, three common examples of VS extensibility. Along with these three options, you explored three simple examples of each. Finally, you got a quick guide to using online and offline help on the MSDN to get additional information and answers to your questions.

The Automation Model

After the opening introductory chapters, I want to discuss add-ins and some topics related to them. In my experience, add-ins have been the most common way to extend Visual Studio during the last decade or so.

In addition to add-ins, this chapter discusses some general topics about Visual Studio Extensibility, and uses add-ins to apply them. These topics are something you'll need to know for other extensibility options. The topic of this chapter, the automation model, is important because you need to use it for macros and VSPackages — and because it's a general API for Visual Studio Extensibility.

Therefore, reading this chapter can be helpful for those who want to dive into the details of topics in subsequent chapters. For now, let's get to a major theme of this chapter, Development Tools Extensibility (DTE), which will remain an important topic for the rest of the book. What is DTE? I'll answer that completely in this chapter, but at this point I want to mention that DTE is an API that has been a part of Visual Studio for a long time and is actually the main representation of the automation model in code. Microsoft has improved it over the years in each new version.

Development Tools Extensibility enables you to get access to different properties, methods, and events of the Visual Studio IDE in order to manipulate it. Obviously, this is important for extending Visual Studio.

This chapter provides a general overview and discussion about the automation model based on Development Tools Extensibility (DTE). In subsequent chapters, you'll learn more about each major aspect of the automation model.

Here's what is covered in this chapter:

❑   General overview of the automation model and its concept

❑   The architecture of the automation model and Development Tools Extensibility (DTE)

❑   Main aspects of the automation model and a short description of each

❏   What can and can't be done with the automation model

❏   The automation model and the Macros IDE

In preparation for the longer discussion of Visual Studio Extensibility in later chapters, we'll start with an introduction to the automation model and Development Tools Extensibility, one of your most powerful tools throughout the book.

Note that this chapter is primarily a theoretical, general discussion about a broad topic and is designed just to get you started with it. A more detailed discussion about each aspect of the automation model and DTE APIs can be found in the rest of the book.

What Is the Automation Model?

The automation model and its code representation, Development Tools Extensibility (commonly known as DTE), are a set of APIs related to Visual Studio. It can be considered as a Visual Studio API because DTE is used by most of the extensibility options of Visual Studio to manipulate different objects in the development environment, including getting access to solutions, projects, project items, files, and codes.

DTE can be considered a class representation of the automation model in Visual Studio. This automation model is actually a set of different models for different aspects of Visual Studio. Each model is responsible for a major part, and each model includes some APIs for use with extending an aspect of Visual Studio functionality.

Seven models are part of the Visual Studio automation model:

❏   **Environment model:** This model is the core of the automation model and collaborates with other models. It's responsible for most parts of the IDE, such as windows, commands, and events.

❏   **Project model:** This model provides some tools to work with solutions, projects, and project items in Visual Studio and to manipulate them.

❏   **Code model:** Using this model, you can work with code and files. It can work with classes, interfaces, and other code types.

❏   **Editor model:** This model is responsible for providing tools to work with text editors in Visual Studio and for performing operations such as insert, delete, copy, and format.

❏   **Forms model:** This provides different objects to work with Windows Forms and their properties (but not web forms).

❏   **Debugger model:** The debugger model offers extensibility options for Visual Studio debugging features.

❏   **Build model:** This last model helps you work with build operation and configuration for solutions and projects, and enables you to set some configurations for them.

Most features for these models are constant between different .NET languages, but for some models the Visual Studio C++ language provides extra features to work with models; hence, Visual Studio C++ is suitable for advanced scenarios.

The collaboration of these models is shown in Figure 4-1.

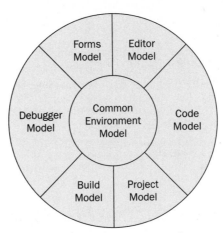

Figure 4-1: Visual Studio automation model diagram

As shown in the figure, the environment model is at the core, and other models collaborate with it to get the job done. From a development point of view, there are no clear boundaries for these models and it's not easy to distinguish among them in code and namespaces; however, some models have separate assemblies.

The main part of this book discusses these models in more detail and tries to apply them to the add-ins topic to demonstrate their concepts with real-world examples. The same concepts are applicable to other extensibility options such as macros and VSPackages, but these topics are not covered here. In general, there are three ways to use an automation model in Visual Studio: add-ins, macros, and VSPackages. Actually, I use add-ins as a case study to show concepts related to the automation model.

These extensibility points can be sorted into different levels (see Figure 4-2). From the perspective of ease of development, macros are easier to write than add-ins, and add-ins are easier to write than VSPackages. However, as far as capabilities and advanced scenarios are concerned, VSPackages are more powerful than add-ins, and add-ins are more powerful than macros.

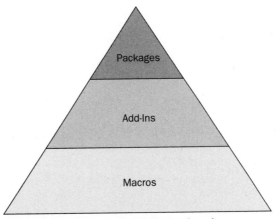

Figure 4-2: Levels of extensibility options in Visual Studio

The Architecture

The architecture of the automation model is strongly correlated with Visual Studio architecture because usually it represents Visual Studio IDE elements. DTE is the topmost object in the automation model, and most jobs in the Visual Studio IDE are done by DTE.

Consider first Figure 4-3, which shows how complicated the automation object model is.

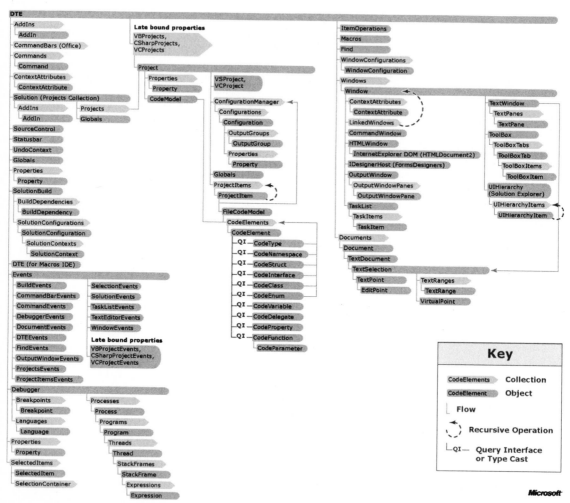

Figure 4-3: The automation object model

If you're saying, "Wow! The structure of namespaces and classes looks really complicated!" you are right! Working with DTE and an automation model requires some experience, and you need some training in order to understand the structure. That's why the main part of the book is devoted to chapters about this model, in order to show each aspect in some detail.

The architecture is complicated for the following reasons:

❑   Visual Studio itself is complicated, and as DTE is representing Visual Studio elements, it's complicated as well.

❑   The automation model and Development Tools Extensibility have their roots in COM. The interoperability between .NET and COM requires some extra work, and this extra work makes the architecture somewhat more complicated.

One general point you should be aware of is the correlation between DTE and COM objects. DTE (like the Visual Studio IDE) relies heavily on COM objects, so in your work with DTE you encounter various interfaces that have a corresponding class implementation, and these pairs build the infrastructure of DTE. Therefore, keep in mind that most of the classes that you use in DTE are an implementation of corresponding interfaces.

Development Tools Extensibility classes and interfaces are located in the EnvDTE namespace. EnvDTE is a .NET component that you can add to your projects.

The topmost class in this namespace hierarchy is DTE. DTE is the container for all other classes, interfaces, and enumerators, and it represents the automation model. DTE implements an interface called _DTE (see Figure 4-4).

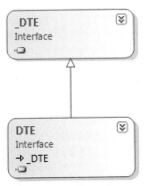

Figure 4-4: DTE implements the _DTE interface.

If you need to get a DTE object, you have to implement the IDTWizard interface in your class. This interface doesn't have anything more than an Execute method to implement (see Figure 4-5).

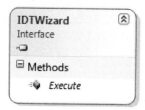

Figure 4-5: The IDTWizard interface

Returning to the automation model structure shown in Figure 4-3, you'll notice that DTE is the root class in this structure, and some other classes are direct or indirect children of this class. Direct children are major groups of Visual Studio or Macros IDE elements. For example, AddIns is a direct child for add-ins and Commands is another direct child for Visual Studio commands. Solution and Project are responsible for solutions and projects, and Events is responsible for various events that can occur in VS or the Macros IDE.

There are also items for Properties and Windows. Some common windows inside the VS IDE, such as OutputWindow, TaskList, TextWindow, and ToolBox, are children of the Windows item.

DTE hasn't been a constant across different versions of Visual Studio. In each version Microsoft solved some issues and added new features or improvements to the DTE.

In Visual Studio 2005, for example, Microsoft added several changes to DTE and used the EnvDTE80 namespace (8.0 is the internal version of Visual Studio 2005) to represent changes in this version and include all new classes, interfaces, events, and enumerators there. This namespace contains various classes with the same names as classes included in the original EnvDTE namespace but with a two-number index indicating that they're newer. For example, CodeFunction2 is the new version of CodeFunction in the Visual Studio 2005 DTE.

Conversely, in Visual Studio 2008, Microsoft made some updates as well, but not as many changes were made as in Visual Studio 2005. There were a few changes in DTE, and these are included in a new namespace named EnvDTE90 (9.0 is the internal version of Visual Studio 2008).

This new namespace has a few new classes and interfaces, and, like EnvDTE80, most of them have a number index at the end to specify the version. For example, 3 is the number that Microsoft has added to the names of classes and interfaces. Thus, Solution3 is the new version of Solution2 in Visual Studio 2005 DTE and of Solution in the original DTE.

Considering this history and the number of changes that attended each new version, we can consider Visual Studio 2005 DTE as a milestone in the DTE life cycle, whereas Visual Studio 2008 DTE is just an update with minor changes.

The other point to remember about DTE changes in these versions is that new versions of classes, interfaces, and the like usually are derived from the previous versions and just extend them. Therefore, they don't replace and outdate previous versions at all.

Let's take a look at this concept in an example. Debugger is one of main interfaces in DTE and it has undergone changes in both Visual Studio 2005 and 2008. Figure 4-6 shows the inheritance hierarchy for this interface in these versions.

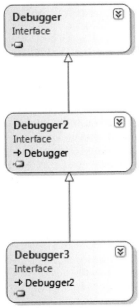

Figure 4-6: Debugger interface inheritance hierarchy through different versions

Debugger3 is the new version of the Debugger2 interface in Visual Studio 2005 DTE for Visual Studio 2008. Debugger2 itself is the new version of the original Debugger interface for Visual Studio 2005 DTE. As shown in the figure, Debugger3 is derived from Debugger2, and Debugger2 is derived from Debugger, so each new version just extends the previous version, it doesn't replace it.

The last important point is about the DTE class itself. This class has a new version in Visual Studio 2005 named DTE2, and in most cases you will use this for your projects. There isn't any updated class for Visual Studio 2008.

Main Parts of DTE

Development Tools Extensibility (DTE) consists of five main parts that act as a container for other elements. These five parts represent the main elements of the Visual Studio IDE. This section briefly introduces these elements, which you already know provide the main functionality of Visual Studio:

❑   Solutions and projects

❑   Commands

❑ Events

❑ Documents

❑ Debugger

Later in this book you'll learn about these in detail.

Solutions and Projects

Two main classes are responsible for solutions and projects in DTE. DTE.Solution is the code representation of the currently opened solution and is of type Solution.

This object contains a set of different properties and methods related to the solution and its projects to help you access this information and manipulate it. For example, Listing 4-1 shows some simple code for an OnConnection event of a sample add-in that uses this object in order to show the FullName property of the current solution in a MessageBox.

Listing 4-1: Using the Solution Object

```
public void OnConnection(object application, ext_ConnectMode connectMode, object
addInInst, ref Array custom)
{
    _applicationObject = (DTE2)application;
    _addInInstance = (AddIn)addInInst;

System.Windows.Forms.MessageBox.Show(this._applicationObject.Solution.FullName);
}
```

Figure 4-7 shows the result.

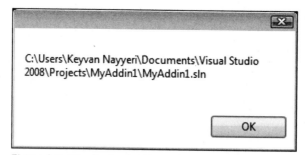

C:\Users\Keyvan Nayyeri\Documents\Visual Studio
2008\Projects\MyAddin1\MyAddin1.sln

OK

Figure 4-7: Result of using the Solution object

Conversely, the Solution class (which is a class that implements the Solution interface) includes some properties for accessing projects inside the solution, and you can find them in the Solution.Projects property.

Listing 4-2 is an example of using this property to show the number of projects inside the current solution.

Listing 4-2: Using the `Solution.Projects` property

```
public void OnConnection(object application, ext_ConnectMode connectMode, object
addInInst, ref Array custom)
{
    _applicationObject = (DTE2)application;
    _addInInstance = (AddIn)addInInst;

    System.Windows.Forms.MessageBox.Show
        (string.Format("Number of projects = {0}",
        this._applicationObject.Solution.Projects.Count.ToString()));
}
```

The output is shown in Figure 4-8.

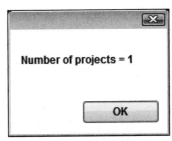

Figure 4-8: Result of using the `Solution.Projects` property

Commands

Commands are a fundamental concept in Visual Studio. In fact, most of the actions in Visual Studio are related to appropriate commands, and there are various built-in commands in Visual Studio. You can also define your own commands to implement various actions, and then add your commands to the list of commands in the IDE to make it available to Visual Studio.

`DTE.CommandBars`, `DTE.CommandLineArguments`, and `DTE.Commands` are three properties that help you manipulate Visual Studio commands (even though there are some other properties and methods that play a role in this). For example, `DTE.Commands` enables you to access all commands within the Visual Studio IDE. Listing 4-3 uses this property to show the number of commands. You can see its output in Figure 4-9.

Listing 4-3: Showing the Number of Commands in the VS IDE

```
public void OnConnection(object application, ext_ConnectMode connectMode, object
addInInst, ref Array custom)
{
    _applicationObject = (DTE2)application;
    _addInInstance = (AddIn)addInInst;

    System.Windows.Forms.MessageBox.Show
        (string.Format("Number of commands = {0}",
        this._applicationObject.Commands.Count.ToString()));
}
```

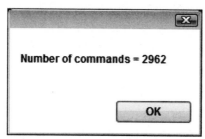

Figure 4-9: Result of using the **DTE**
.Commands property

Events

Events are another main aspect of the Visual Studio IDE. DTE.Events is the main property that plays a role for events in the DTE object. It includes some properties that work as containers for different groups of Visual Studio events, and you can add your own event handlers to these events.

Listing 4-4 shows an example of this property to add a new event handler for the OnStartupComplete event. I added this new handler in the OnStartupComplete event of a sample add-in.

Listing 4-4: Adding a New Handler to OnStartupComplete

```
public void OnStartupComplete(ref Array custom)
{
    this._applicationObject.Events.DTEEvents.OnStartupComplete
        += new
_dispDTEEvents_OnStartupCompleteEventHandler(DTEEvents_OnStartupComplete);
}

void DTEEvents_OnStartupComplete()
{
    System.Windows.Forms.MessageBox.Show("Startup Complete!");
}
```

Now if I restart the IDE, a MessageBox appears after the loading process is finished, as shown in Figure 4-10.

Startup Complete!

OK

Figure 4-10: A MessageBox appears after the loading process is finished.

Documents

You can also manipulate documents in the Visual Studio IDE with some properties of the DTE object. DTE.ActiveDocument helps you work with the currently active document in the IDE, and the DTE.Documents property helps you work with all available documents in the IDE.

Listing 4-5 illustrates a method that checks the active document to determine whether it's saved; if not, it saves all changes into the document.

Listing 4-5: Using the `ActiveDocument` object

```
void SaveCurrentDocument()
{
    if (!this._applicationObject.ActiveDocument.Saved)
        this._applicationObject.ActiveDocument.Save
            (this._applicationObject.ActiveDocument.Name);
}
```

Debugger

DTE.Debugger is the main type for working with debugging tools in the Visual Studio IDE, including such things as breakpoints and processes. As presented in Listing 4-6, the code indicates the number of breakpoints in the code by using the DTE.Debugger.Breakpoints.Count property.

Listing 4-6: Using `DTE.Debugger` **object**

```
public void OnConnection(object application, ext_ConnectMode connectMode, object
addInInst, ref Array custom)
{
    _applicationObject = (DTE2)application;
    _addInInstance = (AddIn)addInInst;

    System.Windows.Forms.MessageBox.Show
        (string.Format("Number of breakpoints = {0}",
        this._applicationObject.Debugger.Breakpoints.Count.ToString()));
}
```

If I put three breakpoints in my code and run the add-in, the MessageBox shown in Figure 4-11 appears.

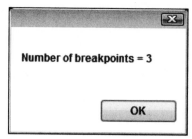

Figure 4-11: Using `DTE.Debugger`
to show the number of breakpoints
in the code

What You Can't Achieve with the DTE

DTE is a rich set of APIs, and Microsoft has added many new features to it in order to improve your capabilities when writing extensibility code for Visual Studio. In general, you can achieve a great many things with the properties and methods provided for a DTE object — but there still are things you can't do.

For example, there is a popular add-in for .NET bloggers in Visual Studio 2003, 2005, and 2008 named CopySourceAsHtml. This add-in enables you to copy your code in Visual Studio to the clipboard with HTML formatting and then paste it to other editors to use on sites and blogs. This add-in can work with a wide range of code documents such as classes, interfaces, enumerators, structures, XML documents, and text documents. However, it doesn't work with ASPX files in ASP.NET. This is a technical restriction of the DTE object that prevents you from getting access to information in the editor that's required in order to do this.

When using DTE for your add-ins, macros, or VSPackages, you may encounter similar cases. For that reason, you should have a good understanding of DTE and all its capabilities in order to decide whether it can be used to accomplish a task or not. If you can't use DTE, then there are some alternative methods that cost more. You can use underlying APIs in Visual Studio to accomplish some goals. One common example of these APIs is the integrated mode of Visual Studio Shell (described later in this book).

Nonetheless, you still may encounter situations in which you can't do anything! This rarely happens, but remember that you can't extend something without having enough extensibility options for it, especially when you don't have access to the source code of the original product (in our case, Visual Studio). In Visual Studio 2008, Microsoft is trying to provide source code for the .NET Framework and Visual Studio for easier debugging, but this doesn't help you very much.

Keeping this in mind, follow the rest of the book to see how many tools you have in hand to extend Visual Studio.

The Automation Model and Macros IDE

As mentioned in the previous sections, by using DTE you can access the Macros IDE elements as well. Even though there are some similarities between the main Visual Studio IDE and the Macros IDE, there are also some differences that prevent you from applying some extensibility options to the Macros IDE. For example, add-ins must be specifically designed to work with the Macros IDE in order to function there; otherwise, they're not available in the Macros IDE. This may be as easy as enabling the Visual Studio add-in in the Macros IDE or it may not. It depends on the APIs you have used in your add-in.

When writing macros, you commonly use the DTE object (this is described in Chapter 22). In the opposite direction, DTE also provides some properties and methods to work with the Macros IDE, such as DTE.Macros and DTE.MacrosIDE. This is an interesting aspect of DTE, because these two properties enable you to write add-ins and macros for the Macros IDE.

Summary

In this chapter, which is dedicated to add-ins, along with general extensibility topics, you got an overview of the automation model as one of main topics in Visual Studio extensibility.

You first learned about the automation model in general, including its code representation, Development Tools Extensibility, and saw what it is exactly. Then you explored their architecture in Visual Studio. In the next section, you learned important aspects of DTE, which included brief descriptions and simple examples. At the end, you read about what you can and can't achieve with DTE, and about the use of DTE in the Macros IDE.

We haven't finished our work with DTE; this chapter was just a starting point. In the upcoming chapters, you'll read more about different parts of DTE in more detail and will use add-ins to apply these concepts in real-world examples.

5

Add-In Wizard

In Chapter 3 you got a quick overview of building a very simple add-in for Visual Studio. As you discovered there, the first step to create an add-in is to choose the appropriate project template and then provide a name for your add-in. This simple process will invoke the Visual Studio Add-in Wizard.

The topic of this chapter is that wizard. At first glance, it may seem like this wizard doesn't play a very important role in building an add-in, and dedicating a chapter to it may seem like a waste of time. In fact, however, this wizard accomplishes more than meets the eye, and it's worthwhile to know more about it.

The Add-in Wizard collects your selections for building an add-in and then generates necessary code templates and configuration files, configuring the local machine to run your add-in. These steps would take a great deal of time if you, as a developer, had to do them manually, but thanks to the wizard you can create the best code for this purpose in a few seconds.

A developer who just wants to create a simple add-in doesn't care about the behind-the-scenes part of this wizard, but a professional developer who buys and reads this book should be interested to know what's going on there. This chapter is the first in a series that covers add-ins and discusses how to build an add-in. In this chapter you'll learn the first steps in the process.

Here are the major topics that you'll read about in this chapter:

❑ What you should do before building an add-in

❑ Different steps in the Add-in Wizard

❑ What happens behind the scenes for each step of the wizard

❑ A general overview of what the wizard does and the generated solution and code

❑ A short introduction to shared add-ins and the Shared Add-in Wizard, which can be used to create add-ins for Microsoft Office products

Even though you can write all the code that the Add-in Wizard generates for you, you'll probably agree that this would take too much of your time. Therefore, let's get started with the first topic: the pre-build requirements to create an add-in.

Before Building an Add-In

As with any other software, in order to build a Visual Studio add-in you need to know the requirements. Therefore, before beginning your work on the add-in, you should collect some information about the add-in you're going to create and identify some details about it.

This information includes the development language you want to use for your add-in, the environment you want to target (Visual Studio IDE or Macros IDE or both), the availability of your add-in via commands, and some other general information about your add-in. You will need this information when executing the Add-in Wizard and while writing your add-in.

After collecting this information, you can begin the development process. As in other applications, you must first create a new project in Visual Studio with an appropriate template. The project template for Visual Studio add-ins is located in the Other Project Types ⇨ Extensibility category in the New Project dialog. There you can find the Visual Studio Add-in and Shared Add-in templates (see Figure 5-1).

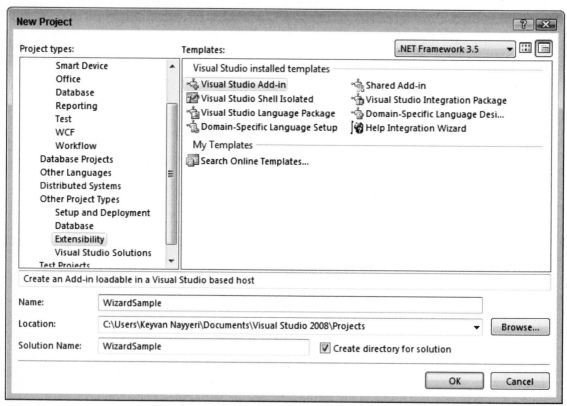

Figure 5-1: Choosing the Visual Studio Add-in template from the New Project dialog

Visual Studio Add-ins is the template for VS add-ins that we discuss in this book; Shared Add-in is a template for some other add-ins that you can write for Microsoft Office. There are many similarities between these two types that I'll describe in subsequent chapters, but for now just focus on the Visual Studio Add-in template.

Note that you may have some other project templates in the Other Project Types ⇨ Extensibility category (such as those shown in Figure 5-1). These project templates appear there after the installation of the Visual Studio SDK for VSPackages and Domain Specific Languages (described later in this book).

Add-in Wizard

After choosing the appropriate project type and setting its name and storage path, Visual Studio opens the Add-in Wizard. This wizard consists of a welcoming page and six main steps, which are described in the following subsections. Before talking about these steps, however, note a general structural feature of this wizard: its capability to go back and forth between all the steps, enabling you to change your selections at any time (before finishing the wizard).

Welcome

The welcome page, shown in Figure 5-2, is very simple — nothing more than a starting page for the wizard. It merely indicates that this wizard gathers information about the add-in and generates starter code for it.

Figure 5-2: Add-in Wizard welcome page

Page 1

The next page of the wizard (see Figure 5-3) is where you actually begin configuration and setup of your add-in.

In this step you choose the development language you want to use to create your add-in. Four languages are available:

❑   Visual C#

❑   Visual Basic

❑   Visual C++/CLR

❑   Visual C++/ATL

You can develop an add-in with any of these four languages, but as the focus of this book is on C#, C# is used here (refer to Figure 5-3).

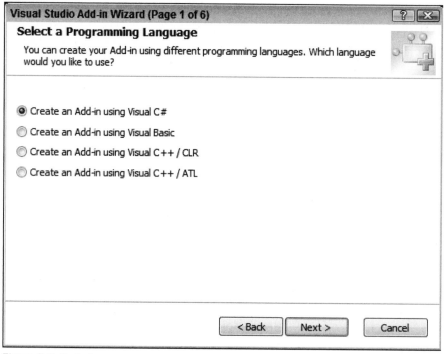

Figure 5-3: Page 1

Visual Studio generates a starting code template for your add-in based on your development language choice.

Page 2

In the second step of the wizard (see Figure 5-4) you can choose the application host for your add-in. This application host is where users can find your add-ins and use them. For your add-ins in Visual Studio, two application hosts are available:

❑ Visual Studio IDE

❑ Visual Studio Macros IDE

You can choose either of these applications hosts or both of them, to make your add-ins compatible with both.

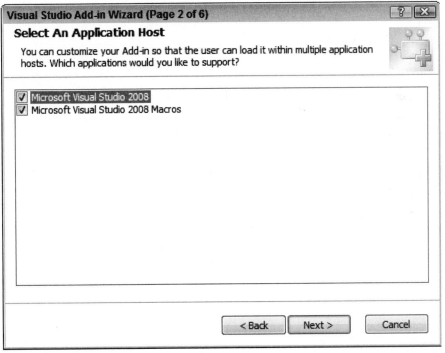

Figure 5-4: Page 2

Page 3

In the third step of the wizard (see Figure 5-5) you can set a name and description for your add-in. These two text values are what end users see for your add-ins in Visual Studio (Add-in Manager).

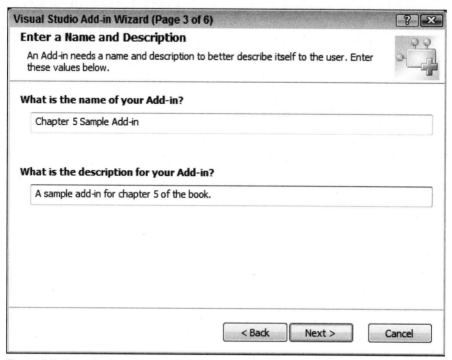

Figure 5-5: Page 3

Page 4

Step 4 of the wizard (see Figure 5-6) is where you can set some configuration options for your add-in. Three checkboxes are available.

The first option is to create a command bar UI for the add-in. If you choose this option, a Tools menu item will be created, which your add-in loads when the user clicks this option.

Two other options enable you to fine-tune when your add-in will load. The first option configures it to load when the host application (Visual Studio IDE or Macros IDE) starts. The second option specifies that the add-in doesn't have a modal UI and you can use it with command-line builds. You'll learn more about this option later in the book.

Page 5

The fifth page of the wizard (see Figure 5-7) provides information about setting an About page for your add-in. In this case, after checking an option, you can enter a text value for the About box.

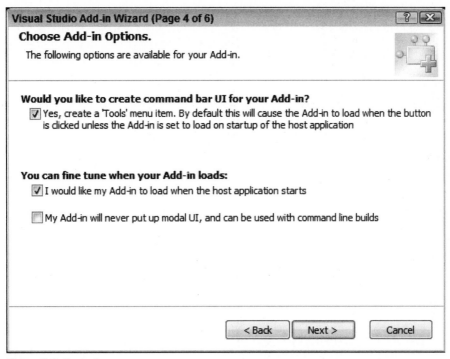

Figure 5-6: Page 4

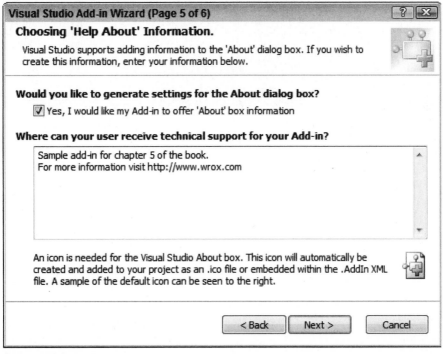

Figure 5-7: Page 5

This page also indicates that Visual Studio automatically creates a default icon for your add-in project and embeds it in your add-in project, although you can change this later. You'll learn more about this in subsequent chapters.

Page 6

The last page (see Figure 5-8) is where Visual Studio reports a summary of your options in the previous pages. At this point, you can go back and change your options, or you can accept them by clicking the Finish button. If you click Finish, then Visual Studio will begin the generation of code and items for you.

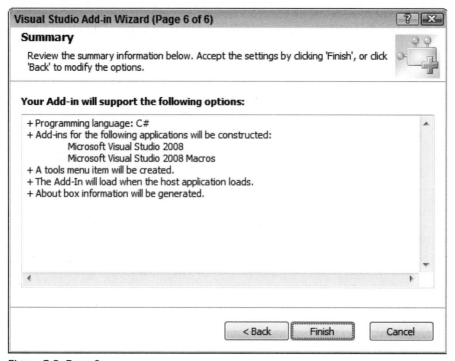

Figure 5-8: Page 6

What Is Generated for You

After accepting your options in the last step of the wizard, Visual Studio generates some code files, configuration files, and a few other files based your selections, enables your add-in in Visual Studio, and adds it to the Visual Studio IDE and/or Macros IDE on the local machine.

In general, Visual Studio generates three main files for your add-in:

❏ CommandBar.resx

❏ Connect.cs

❏ WizardSample.AddIn

The first file, CommandBar.resx, is a resource file that is generated to keep a list of values for command-bar text values. The second file, Connect.cs, is a C# class that keeps the main class for add-in logic implementation. The default code for this class is presented in Listing 5-1. You'll find more information about this file in Chapter 6.

Listing 5-1: Connect.cs Default Code

```csharp
using System;
using Extensibility;
using EnvDTE;
using EnvDTE80;
using Microsoft.VisualStudio.CommandBars;
using System.Resources;
using System.Reflection;
using System.Globalization;

namespace WizardSample
{
 /// <summary>The object for implementing an Add-in.</summary>
 /// <seealso class='IDTExtensibility2' />
 public class Connect : IDTExtensibility2, IDTCommandTarget
 {
        /// <summary>Implements the constructor for the Add-in object. Place your
initialization code within this method.</summary>
        public Connect()
        {
        }

        /// <summary>Implements the OnConnection method of the IDTExtensibility2
interface. Receives notification that the Add-in is being loaded.</summary>
        /// <param term='application'>Root object of the host application.</param>
        /// <param term='connectMode'>Describes how the Add-in is being
loaded.</param>
        /// <param term='addInInst'>Object representing this Add-in.</param>
        /// <seealso class='IDTExtensibility2' />
        public void OnConnection(object application, ext_ConnectMode connectMode,
object addInInst, ref Array custom)
        {
                _applicationObject = (DTE2)application;
                _addInInstance = (AddIn)addInInst;
                if(connectMode == ext_ConnectMode.ext_cm_UISetup)
                {
                        object []contextGUIDS = new object[] { };
                        Commands2 commands = (Commands2)_applicationObject.Commands;
                        string toolsMenuName;

                        try
                        {
                                //If you would like to move the command to a
different menu, change the word "Tools" to the
                                // English version of the menu. This code will take
the culture, append on the name of the menu
                                // then add the command to that menu. You can find a
list of all the top-level menus in the file
```

(continued)

Listing 5-1 *(continued)*

```
                        // CommandBar.resx.
                        string resourceName;
                        ResourceManager resourceManager = new
ResourceManager("WizardSample.CommandBar", Assembly.GetExecutingAssembly());
                        CultureInfo cultureInfo = new
CultureInfo(_applicationObject.LocaleID);

                            if(cultureInfo.TwoLetterISOLanguageName == "zh")
                            {
                                    resourceName =
String.Concat(cultureInfo.Name, "Tools");
                            }
                            else
                            {
                                    resourceName =
String.Concat(cultureInfo.TwoLetterISOLanguageName, "Tools");
                            }
                            toolsMenuName = resourceManager.
GetString(resourceName);
                    }
                    catch
                    {
                     //We tried to find a localized version of the word Tools,
but one was not found.
                            // Default to the en-US word, which may work for the
current culture.
                            toolsMenuName = "Tools";
                    }

                    //Place the command on the tools menu.
                    //Find the MenuBar command bar, which is the top-level
command bar holding all the main menu items:
                            Microsoft.VisualStudio.CommandBars.CommandBar
menuBarCommandBar =
((Microsoft.VisualStudio.CommandBars.CommandBars)_applicationObject.CommandBars)
["MenuBar"];

                    //Find the Tools command bar on the MenuBar command bar:
                    CommandBarControl toolsControl =
menuBarCommandBar.Controls[toolsMenuName];
                            CommandBarPopup toolsPopup = (CommandBarPopup)toolsControl;

                    //This try/catch block can be duplicated if you wish to add
multiple commands to be handled by your Add-in,
                            // just make sure you also update the QueryStatus/Exec
method to include the new command names.
                            try
                            {
                            //Add a command to the Commands collection:
```

```
                         Command command =
commands.AddNamedCommand2(_addInInstance, "WizardSample", "WizardSample", "Executes
the command for WizardSample", true, 59, ref contextGUIDS, (int)vsCommandStatus.vsC
ommandStatusSupported+(int)vsCommandStatus.vsCommandStatusEnabled,
(int)vsCommandStyle.vsCommandStylePictAndText, vsCommandControlType.
vsCommandControlTypeButton);

                                 //Add a control for the command to the tools menu:
                                 if((command != null) && (toolsPopup != null))
                                 {
                                         command.AddControl(toolsPopup.CommandBar, 1);
                                 }
                         }
                         catch(System.ArgumentException)
                         {
                                 //If we are here, then the exception is probably
because a command with that name
                                 // already exists. If so there is no need to
recreate the command and we can
         // safely ignore the exception.
                                 }
                     }
             }


         /// <summary>Implements the OnDisconnection method of the
IDTExtensibility2 interface. Receives notification that the Add-in is being
unloaded.</summary>
         /// <param term='disconnectMode'>Describes how the Add-in is being
unloaded.</param>
         /// <param term='custom'>Array of parameters that are host application
specific.</param>
         /// <seealso class='IDTExtensibility2' />
         public void OnDisconnection(ext_DisconnectMode disconnectMode, ref Array
custom)
         {
         }

         /// <summary>Implements the OnAddInsUpdate method of the IDTExtensibility2
interface. Receives notification when the collection of Add-ins has changed.
</summary>

         /// <param term='custom'>Array of parameters that are host application
specific.</param>
         /// <seealso class='IDTExtensibility2' />
         public void OnAddInsUpdate(ref Array custom)
         {
         }

         /// <summary>Implements the OnStartupComplete method of the
IDTExtensibility2 interface. Receives notification that the host application has
completed loading.</summary>
```

(continued)

Listing 5-1 *(continued)*

```csharp
        /// <param term='custom'>Array of parameters that are host application
specific.</param>
        /// <seealso class='IDTExtensibility2' />
        public void OnStartupComplete(ref Array custom)
        {
        }


        /// <summary>Implements the OnBeginShutdown method of the
IDTExtensibility2 interface. Receives notification that the host application is
being unloaded.</summary>
        /// <param term='custom'>Array of parameters that are host application
specific.</param>
        /// <seealso class='IDTExtensibility2' />
        public void OnBeginShutdown(ref Array custom)
        {
         }

        /// <summary>Implements the QueryStatus method of the IDTCommandTarget
interface. This is called when the command's availability is updated</summary>
        /// <param term='commandName'>The name of the command to determine state
for.</param>
        /// <param term='neededText'>Text that is needed for the command.</param>
        /// <param term='status'>The state of the command in the user
interface.</param>
        /// <param term='commandText'>Text requested by the neededText
parameter.</param>
        /// <seealso class='Exec' />
        public void QueryStatus(string commandName, vsCommandStatusTextWanted
neededText, ref vsCommandStatus status, ref object commandText)
        {
                if(neededText ==
vsCommandStatusTextWanted.vsCommandStatusTextWantedNone)
                {
                        if(commandName == "WizardSample.Connect.WizardSample")
                        {
                                status =
(vsCommandStatus)vsCommandStatus.vsCommandStatusSupported|vsCommandStatus.
vsCommandStatusEnabled;
                                return;
                        }
                }
        }

        /// <summary>Implements the Exec method of the IDTCommandTarget
interface. This is called when the command is invoked.</summary>
        /// <param term='commandName'>The name of the command to execute.</param>
        /// <param term='executeOption'>Describes how the command should be
run.</param>
        /// <param term='varIn'>Parameters passed from the caller to the command
handler.</param>
        /// <param term='varOut'>Parameters passed from the command handler to the
caller.</param>
```

```
        /// <param term='handled'>Informs the caller if the command was handled or
not.</param>
        /// <seealso class='Exec' />
        public void Exec(string commandName, vsCommandExecOption executeOption, ref
object varIn, ref object varOut, ref bool handled)
        {
            handled = false;
             if(executeOption ==
vsCommandExecOption.vsCommandExecOptionDoDefault)
            {
                    if(commandName == "WizardSample.Connect.WizardSample")
                    {
                            handled = true;
                            return;
                    }
            }
        }
        private DTE2 _applicationObject;
        private AddIn _addInInstance;
    }
}
```

The third file, WizardSample.AddIn, is an XML configuration file for your add-in. It contains default code that looks like what is shown in Listing 5-2. This file is also discussed in Chapter 6.

Listing 5-2: Add-in File

```xml
<?xml version="1.0" encoding="UTF-16" standalone="no"?>
<Extensibility xmlns="http://schemas.microsoft.com/AutomationExtensibility">
 <HostApplication>
 <Name>Microsoft Visual Studio Macros</Name>
 <Version>9.0</Version>
 </HostApplication>
 <HostApplication>
 <Name>Microsoft Visual Studio</Name>
 <Version>9.0</Version>
 </HostApplication>
 <Addin>
 <FriendlyName>Chapter 5 Sample Add-in</FriendlyName>
 <Description>A sample add-in for chapter 5 of the book.</Description>
 <AboutBoxDetails>Sample add-in for the chapter 5 of the book.\r\nFor more
information visit www.wrox.com</AboutBoxDetails>
 <AboutIconData>
  <!-- This section is removed to save the space -->
 </AboutIconData>
 <Assembly>WizardSample.dll</Assembly>
 <FullClassName>WizardSample.Connect</FullClassName>
 <LoadBehavior>1</LoadBehavior>
 <CommandPreload>1</CommandPreload>
 <CommandLineSafe>0</CommandLineSafe>
 </Addin>
</Extensibility>
```

In the following chapters, you'll learn more about these items and add-ins.

Shared Add-In Wizard

As mentioned previously, the Other Project Types ➪ Extensibility of New Project dialog offers you another option: shared add-ins. Shared add-ins are very similar to Visual Studio add-ins and have the same structure and code files, but they target Microsoft Office applications in order to extend them.

As shared add-ins are related to Microsoft Office products, we won't focus on them in this book, but it's still worth taking a look at the Shared Add-in Wizard to see how similar these add-ins are to Visual Studio add-ins. The Shared Add-in Wizard is the equivalent of the Add-in Wizard for Visual Studio add-ins and consists of five steps and a welcoming page. The latter is shown in Figure 5-9.

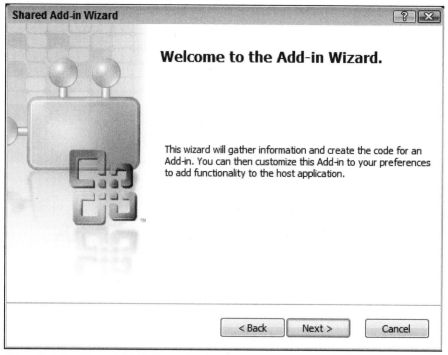

Figure 5-9: The Shared Add-in Wizard welcome page

In the first step of this wizard you can choose the development language for your add-in (see Figure 5-10). For Visual Studio add-ins, you have four options, but for shared add-ins you have only three; Visual C++/CLR isn't available.

In the second page (see Figure 5-11) you choose the host application for your shared add-in. Here you have many more options than with Visual Studio add-ins: You can choose from the list of all Microsoft Office products. Choosing each product makes the shared add-in available to that product.

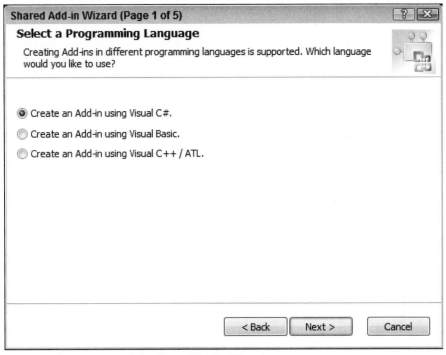

Figure 5-10: First page of the Shared Add-in Wizard

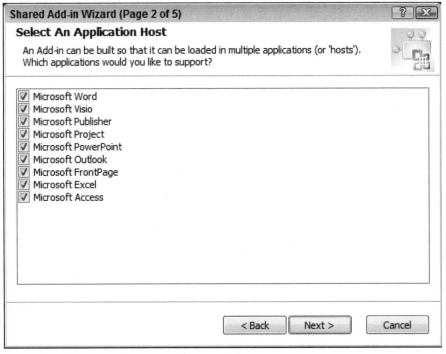

Figure 5-11: Page 2 of the Shared Add-in Wizard

On Page 3 (see Figure 5-12) you enter a name and description for your shared add-in.

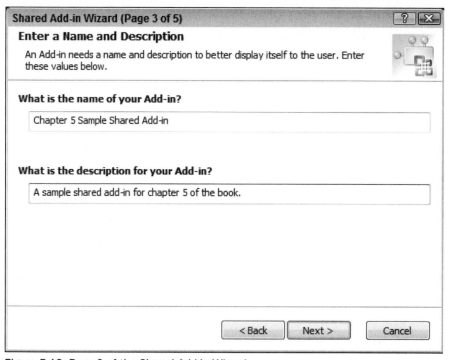

Figure 5-12: Page 3 of the Shared Add-in Wizard

Page 4 of the wizard, shown in Figure 5-13, provides two options for your add-in. One enables the add-in to be loaded when the host application loads. Selecting the second option makes it available to all users of the computer on which the add-in is installed, not just the installer. This option may be disabled, depending on your operating system configuration and the current user.

The last step, shown in Figure 5-14, displays the summary of your selections. You can either change them at this point or accept them to generate the shared add-in code.

After accepting your options, Visual Studio generates two projects in a solution for you. The first is a C# project that contains a main Connect.cs file whose structure is very similar to the Visual Studio add-in file. This project is the main one for your shared add-in and where you implement it. The second project is a setup one for your shared add-in to simplify the installation process.

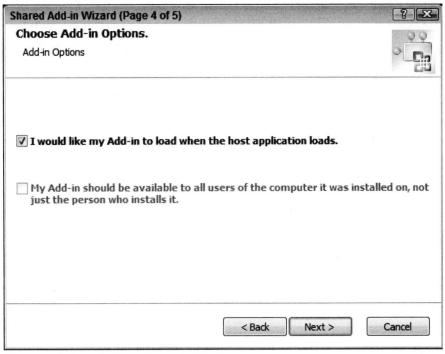

Figure 5-13: Page 4 of the Shared Add-in Wizard

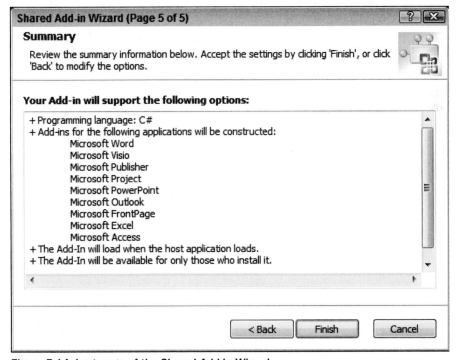

Figure 5-14: Last page of the Shared Add-in Wizard

Summary

This chapter provided an overview of the Add-in Wizard in Visual Studio, showing how it generates starting code for your Visual Studio add-ins. You learned the steps involved and how to use the wizard. You also read about what kinds of things are generated for you by this wizard. You also learned about shared add-ins and the Shared Add-in Wizard in Visual Studio, with which you can create add-ins for Microsoft Office products.

In the following chapters you'll read more about Visual Studio add-ins and the technical details of creating add-ins.

6

The Anatomy of an Add-In

After executing the Add-in Wizard to generate a starting code for your add-in, now you need to begin customizing this code and implementing your code logic for the add-in. Without your own code implementation, add-ins do not provide any capability and don't work at all.

The goal of this chapter, therefore, is to learn the anatomy of an add-in in order to be able to work with and develop them. Add-ins are just an implementation of a programming interface, and nothing more. Even though this implementation is sometimes simple, there are many complicated add-ins available that interact with the user interface and extend different aspects of Visual Studio.

Understanding the anatomy of an add-in is a key part of successfully developing add-ins because it's like providing the foundation of a building that may look simple but supports a very complicated structure. All add-ins (without exception) have the same structure. Some of them may be simple and others may be complicated. If you know the structure, then you can follow up the code for all add-ins easily.

The anatomy of an add-in consists of two main parts: an implementation of an interface and a configuration file.

This chapter covers both parts of the add-in, and includes the following topics:

- ❏ The structure of an add-in class
- ❏ A closer look at each event in add-in implementation
- ❏ The purpose of an add-in configuration file and its structure
- ❏ How to add a Toolbar menu item for an add-in
- ❏ How to run an add-in from the command line
- ❏ How to add an add-in to a toolbar
- ❏ A brief look at shared add-ins and their similarities to and differences from Visual Studio add-ins

After reading this chapter, you should be able to develop simple add-ins easily. In the following chapters, you'll learn about the main parts of the automation model so you can use them to write more enhanced add-ins.

The Structure of an Add-In

As a first step, let's take a look at the structure of add-in classes and the interface they implement. Add-ins are COM components by nature, and like any COM component they must implement an interface. Add-ins implement a single interface called IDTExtensibility2 located in the Extensibility assembly. Figure 6-1 shows the structure of this interface.

The class that implements an add-in (hence, the IDTExtensibility2 interface) is named `Connect` by default, but you can change this name. The IDTExtensibility2 interface has five methods, which must be implemented by classes you want to implement this interface:

- ❑   OnAddInsUpdate
- ❑   OnBeginShutdown
- ❑   OnConnection
- ❑   OnDisconnection
- ❑   OnStartUpComplete

Figure 6-1: Structure of the IDTExtensibility2 interface

I'll discuss each of these methods and their signatures later in the chapter.

> *As mentioned in Chapter 4, in the discussion about the automation model and Development Tools Extensibility (DTE), the "2" suffix in the name of the IDTExtensibility2 interface indicates that this interface is added to Visual Studio 2005 to improve the capability of add-ins.*

The class file for an add-in (after it's generated by the Add-in Wizard) is very simple and just has code definitions for the preceding methods, along with a public constructor and a few fields (see Figure 6-2).

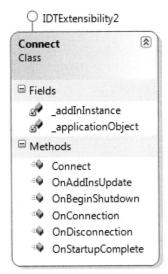

Figure 6-2: Structure of the add-in class

The add-in class has two fields:

❑   `applicationObject`: This is of the DTE2 type and keeps an instance of DTE for the add-in so you can access DTE properties and methods when writing your add-in. You read about Development Tools Extensibility (DTE) in Chapter 4.

❑   `addInInstance`: This is of the AddIn type and keeps an instance of the add-in so you can access some information about your add-in. You'll learn more details about the AddIn interface later in this chapter.

In addition to the class file for an add-in, there is a file with an .AddIn extension that functions as a configuration file for the add-in. It is actually an XML file with a specific structure. There is also another file with the same extension for test purposes that initially has a similar structure to the main .AddIn file. This file helps you when developing your add-in. The structure of these .AddIn files is described later in this chapter.

As add-ins are COM components, they have to be registered on a machine in order to work. However, you no longer need to do this manually because after the release of Visual Studio 2005, a new mechanism helps you deploy your add-ins more easily.

Now that you're familiar with some basic principles about add-ins, let's take a look at the five available methods in the IDTExtensibility2 interface as they are implemented in the default-generated code for the add-ins, and their parameters.

OnConnection

OnConnection is an event that occurs whenever an add-in is loaded into the Visual Studio environment. This method is probably the most common one in the add-in implementation. This method is called for all add-ins when they're being loaded, so you can use it for several purposes.

OnConnection has four parameters:

❑ application: This is of the Object type but it keeps a reference to an instance of the DTE that holds information about the environment where this add-in is loaded.

❑ connectMode: This is of the ext_ConnectMode enumeration value and specifies the way in which the add-in is loaded into the Visual Studio IDE.

❑ addInInst: This is of the Object type but it keeps an instance of the AddIn interface and holds some information about the add-in. The AddIn interface is discussed later in this chapter.

❑ custom: This is a reference to an array that you can use to pass some data to the caller code scope.

The ext_ConnectMode enumeration has six possible values, which are described in Table 6-1.

Table 6-1: The ext_ConnectMode Enumerator

Value	Description
ext_cm_AfterStartup	Add-in is loaded after Visual Studio startup
ext_cm_CommandLine	Add-in is loaded from command line
ext_cm_External	Add-in is loaded by an external code. This option is no longer supported in Visual Studio.
ext_cm_Solution	Add-in is loaded with a solution
ext_cm_Startup	Add-in is loaded with Visual Studio startup
ext_cm_UISetup	Add-in is loaded for user interface setup

The default code implementation for the OnConnection method is presented in Listing 6-1.

Listing 6-1: Default Implementation for the OnConnection Method

```
public void OnConnection(object application, ext_ConnectMode connectMode,
    object addInInst, ref Array custom)
{
    _applicationObject = (DTE2)application;
    _addInInstance = (AddIn)addInInst;

}
```

In this default implementation, Visual Studio has generated some very simple code that sets the two fields of the add-in class to appropriate values. These values are passed from the environment as parameters to the OnConnection method.

After converting the first application parameter to a DTE2 object, the value of the _applicationObject field is set to it to keep an instance of the appropriate DTE object.

The second line of the implementation for this method casts the addInInst parameter to an AddIn instance and sets the value of the addInInstance field to it in order to hold some information about the loaded add-in.

OnDisconnection

This event occurs when an add-in is disconnected from Visual Studio. In this case, the Visual Studio IDE doesn't shut down but is still running. This is the main distinction between the OnDisconnection and OnBeginShutdown methods that you'll see in a moment.

OnDisconnection has two parameters:

❑ RemoveMode: This is an ext_DisconnectMode enumeration value and specifies the reason why the add-in is disconnected.

❑ custom: This is a reference to an array that you can use to pass some data to the caller code scope.

Table 6-2 lists all possible values for the ext_DisconnectMode enumeration value.

Table 6-2: The ext_DisconnectMode Enumerator

Value	Description
ext_dm_HostShutdown	Add-in is disconnected because Visual Studio is shut down
ext_dm_SolutionClosed	Add-in is disconnected because the solution is closed
ext_dm_UISetupComplete	Add-in is disconnected because the user interface is set up
ext_dm_UserClosed	Add-in is disconnected by the user but Visual Studio is still running

The default code implementation for the OnDisconnection method is empty, as shown in Listing 6-2.

Listing 6-2: Default Implementation for the OnDisconnection Method

```
public void OnDisconnection(ext_DisconnectMode disconnectMode, ref Array custom)
{
}
```

OnAddInsUpdate

OnAddInsUpdate occurs whenever an add-in is loaded or unloaded in the Visual Studio IDE. This method is most suitable for checking dependencies between add-ins in Visual Studio.

This method has only one parameter, custom, which is actually a reference to an array that you can use to pass some data to the calling code.

The default implementation for this method is also empty, as shown in Listing 6-3.

Listing 6-3: Default Implementation for the OnAddInsUpdate Method

```
public void OnAddInsUpdate(ref Array custom)
{
}
```

OnStartupComplete

OnStartupComplete occurs whenever an add-in loads with Visual Studio when the IDE starts. In this case, the add-in must be configured to load when the IDE starts.

This method comes in handy in certain cases. Suppose you have an add-in that has a dependency with a component, and this component is not loaded while Visual Studio is being loaded. In this case, your add-in can't be loaded correctly with the OnConnection method. In such a situation, OnStartupComplete helps you control the loading process of your add-in.

The method signature for this method is similar to the OnAddInsUpdate method, and it has a custom parameter that is a reference to an array for passing your data to the caller code. This method also has an empty default implementation (see Listing 6-4).

Listing 6-4: Default Implementation for the OnStartupComplete Method

```
public void OnStartupComplete(ref Array custom)
{
}
```

OnBeginShutdown

The last method is OnBeginShutdown, which occurs whenever the Visual Studio IDE shuts down (and therefore stops the running add-in).

The shutdown process of the Visual Studio IDE can be cancelled, but OnBeginShutdown can't. Therefore, you have to assume that all shutdowns lead to closing all add-ins and write your code logic based on this.

OnBeginShutdown has an empty default implementation (see Listing 6-5) and a single custom parameter, just as the OnAddInsUpdate and OnStartupComplete methods do.

Listing 6-5: Default Implementation for the `OnBeginShutdown` Method

```
public void OnBeginShutdown(ref Array custom)
{
}
```

AddIn Interface

In the previous section you saw the frequent use of some parameters and fields of the AddIn type located in the EnvDTE assembly, so discussing this topic is mandatory here; you will deal with this type when writing your add-ins.

The AddIn interface represents an add-in available in Visual Studio through the Add-in Manager. Using this interface, you can access information about each add-in in Visual Studio.

Each add-in in the Visual Studio environment has a GUID to make it unique. Similarly, the AddIn interface also has a `GuidAttribute` to make it unique.

Let's take a look at properties and methods of the AddIn interface. This interface has nine properties and a single method. Table 6-3 lists all properties of this method, with a short description of each.

Table 6-3: AddIn Interface Properties

Value	Description
Collection	A read-only property, it returns a collection that contains the current instance of the AddIn object
Connected	A Boolean value to specify whether an add-in is loaded or not
Description	A text description for a current instance of an AddIn object
DTE	A read-only property that returns the DTE object for the add-in
Guid	A read-only property that returns the string value of the AddIn object's GUID
Name	A read-only string property for the name of the AddIn object
Object	An object that specifies the current AddIn object and represents this object
ProgID	A read-only string property for the add-in registry item
SatelliteDllPath	A read-only string property that specifies the path of a DLL file containing the localized resource items

This interface also has a `Remove` method that has no parameter and simply removes the add-in from the collection of available add-ins and actually unloads it.

Listing 6-6 applies some properties of the AddIn interface in the `OnConnection` method to show them in a MessageBox.

Listing 6-6: Sample Showing Use of the AddIn Interface Properties

```csharp
public void OnConnection(object application, ext_ConnectMode connectMode, object
addInInst, ref Array custom)
{
    _applicationObject = (DTE2)application;
    _addInInstance = (AddIn)addInInst;

    string stringToShow = string.Empty;
    stringToShow += string.Format("Parent collection count: {0}\n",
        this._addInInstance.Collection.Count.ToString());
    stringToShow += string.Format("Connected: {0}\n",
        this._addInInstance.Connected.ToString());
    stringToShow += string.Format("Description: {0}\n",
        this._addInInstance.Description);
    stringToShow += string.Format("GUID: {0}\n",
        this._addInInstance.Guid);
    stringToShow += string.Format("ProgID: {0}\n",
        this._addInInstance.ProgID);
    stringToShow += string.Format("SatelliteDllPath: {0}\n",
        this._addInInstance.SatelliteDllPath);

    MessageBox.Show(stringToShow);
}
```

This code creates a string variable, adds the value of some properties to the string, and finally shows it in a MessageBox.

Figure 6-3 shows the result of this code.

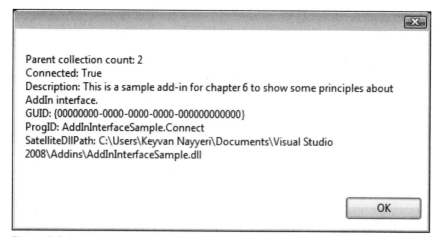

Figure 6-3: Result of using AddIn interface properties

The complete source code for this sample add-in is provided in the code download package for this chapter.

Other Options to Load an Add-in

Even though you can run an add-in from Visual Studio startup and load it into the IDE, for many real-life scenarios this doesn't tell the whole story. In fact, there are four ways to run an add-in, and so far you've only learned the first way:

❑   Run an add-in from different events in Visual Studio, such as startup.

❑   Run an add-in from a toolbar window.

❑   Run an add-in by clicking on a menu item in the Visual Studio IDE.

❑   Run an add-in from the command window.

Yes, everything that you learned in the previous chapter and this chapter up to this point was related to the simplest form of an add-in. Of course, this is also fundamental, and by understanding the simplest method you can learn more enhanced concepts faster.

In Chapter 5, where you were introduced to the Add-In Wizard, you learned two options for the add-in whereby you could create a Tools menu item for your add-in and make it available through the command line.

By checking these options, Visual Studio generates some additional code for you. Now it's time to learn how to load an option from the Tools menu item and command line.

If you check the item in Page 4 of the Add-In Wizard that specifies "Yes, create a 'Tools' menu item," by default this will result in more complicated code for your add-in generated at the end. This code is presented in Listing 6-7.

Listing 6-7: Auto-generated Add-in Code after Choosing the Tools Menu Item Option

```
using System;
using Extensibility;
using EnvDTE;
using EnvDTE80;
using Microsoft.VisualStudio.CommandBars;
using System.Resources;
using System.Reflection;
using System.Globalization;

namespace ToolsMenuSample
{
    /// <summary>The object for implementing an Add-in.</summary>
    /// <seealso class='IDTExtensibility2' />
    public class Connect : IDTExtensibility2, IDTCommandTarget
    {
        /// <summary>Implements the constructor for the Add-in object.
        /// Place your initialization code within this method.</summary>
```

(continued)

Listing 6-7 *(continued)*

```
public Connect()
{
}

/// <summary>Implements the OnConnection method of the IDTExtensibility2
/// interface. Receives notification that the Add-in is being loaded.</
summary>
/// <param term='application'>Root object of the host application.</param>
/// <param term='connectMode'>Describes how the Add-in is being loaded.</
param>
/// <param term='addInInst'>Object representing this Add-in.</param>
/// <seealso class='IDTExtensibility2' />
public void OnConnection(object application, ext_ConnectMode connectMode,
    object addInInst, ref Array custom)
{
    _applicationObject = (DTE2)application;
    _addInInstance = (AddIn)addInInst;
    if (connectMode == ext_ConnectMode.ext_cm_UISetup)
    {
        object[] contextGUIDS = new object[] { };
        Commands2 commands = (Commands2)_applicationObject.Commands;
        string toolsMenuName;

        try
        {

            //If you would like to move the command to a different menu,
change the word "Tools" to the
            //  English version of the menu. This code will take the
culture, append on the name of the menu
            //  then add the command to that menu. You can find a list of
all the top-level menus in the file
            //  CommandBar.resx.
            string resourceName;
            ResourceManager resourceManager = new
ResourceManager("ToolsMenuSample.CommandBar",
                Assembly.GetExecutingAssembly());
            CultureInfo cultureInfo = new
CultureInfo(_applicationObject.LocaleID);

            if (cultureInfo.TwoLetterISOLanguageName == "zh")
            {
                System.Globalization.CultureInfo parentCultureInfo =
cultureInfo.Parent;
                resourceName = String.Concat(parentCultureInfo.Name,
"Tools");
            }
            else
```

Listing 6-7 *(continued)*

```
                {
                        resourceName = String.Concat(cultureInfo
.TwoLetterISOLanguageName, "Tools");
                }
                toolsMenuName = resourceManager.GetString(resourceName);
        }
        catch
        {
                //We tried to find a localized version of the word Tools, but
one was not found.
                //  Default to the en-US word, which may work for the current
culture.
                toolsMenuName = "Tools";
        }

        //Place the command on the tools menu.
        //Find the MenuBar command bar, which is the top-level command bar
holding all the main menu items:
        Microsoft.VisualStudio.CommandBars.CommandBar menuBarCommandBar =

((Microsoft.VisualStudio.CommandBars.CommandBars)_applicationObject.
CommandBars)["MenuBar"];

        //Find the Tools command bar on the MenuBar command bar:
        CommandBarControl toolsControl = menuBarCommandBar
.Controls[toolsMenuName];
        CommandBarPopup toolsPopup = (CommandBarPopup)toolsControl;

        //This try/catch block can be duplicated if you wish to add
multiple commands to be handled by your Add-in,
        //  just make sure you also update the QueryStatus/Exec method to
include the new command names.
        try
        {
            //Add a command to the Commands collection:
            Command command = commands.AddNamedCommand2(_addInInstance,
                "ToolsMenuSample", "ToolsMenuSample", "Executes the command
for ToolsMenuSample",
                true, 59, ref contextGUIDS,
(int)vsCommandStatus.vsCommandStatusSupported +
                (int)vsCommandStatus.vsCommandStatusEnabled,
(int)vsCommandStyle.vsCommandStylePictAndText,
                vsCommandControlType.vsCommandControlTypeButton);

            //Add a control for the command to the tools menu:
            if ((command != null) && (toolsPopup != null))
            {
                command.AddControl(toolsPopup.CommandBar, 1);
            }
        }
```

(continued)

89

Listing 6-7 *(continued)*

```
                catch (System.ArgumentException)
                {
                    //If we are here, then the exception is probably because a
command with that name
                    //  already exists. If so there is no need to recreate the
command and we can
                    //  safely ignore the exception.
                }
            }
        }

        /// <summary>Implements the OnDisconnection method of the IDTExtensibility2
interface. Receives notification that the Add-in is being unloaded.</summary>
        /// <param term='disconnectMode'>Describes how the Add-in is being
unloaded.</param>
        /// <param term='custom'>Array of parameters that are host application
specific.</param>
        /// <seealso class='IDTExtensibility2' />
        public void OnDisconnection(ext_DisconnectMode disconnectMode, ref Array
custom)
        {
        }

        /// <summary>Implements the OnAddInsUpdate method of the IDTExtensibility2
interface. Receives notification when the collection of Add-ins has changed.
</summary>
        /// <param term='custom'>Array of parameters that are host application
specific.</param>
        /// <seealso class='IDTExtensibility2' />
        public void OnAddInsUpdate(ref Array custom)
        {
        }

        /// <summary>Implements the OnStartupComplete method of the
IDTExtensibility2 interface. Receives notification that the host application has
completed loading.</summary>
        /// <param term='custom'>Array of parameters that are host application
specific.</param>
        /// <seealso class='IDTExtensibility2' />
        public void OnStartupComplete(ref Array custom)
        {
        }

        /// <summary>Implements the OnBeginShutdown method of the IDTExtensibility2
interface. Receives notification that the host application is being unloaded.
</summary>
```

Listing 6-7 *(continued)*

```
        /// <param term='custom'>Array of parameters that are host application
specific.</param>
        /// <seealso class='IDTExtensibility2' />
        public void OnBeginShutdown(ref Array custom)
        {
        }

        /// <summary>Implements the QueryStatus method of the IDTCommandTarget
interface. This is called when the command's availability is updated</summary>
        /// <param term='commandName'>The name of the command to determine
state for.</param>
        /// <param term='neededText'>Text that is needed for the command.</param>
        /// <param term='status'>The state of the command in the user interface.
</param>
        /// <param term='commandText'>Text requested by the neededText parameter.
</param>
        /// <seealso class='Exec' />
        public void QueryStatus(string commandName, vsCommandStatusTextWanted
neededText,
            ref vsCommandStatus status, ref object commandText)
        {
            if (neededText == vsCommandStatusTextWanted.
vsCommandStatusTextWantedNone)
            {
                if (commandName == "ToolsMenuSample.Connect.ToolsMenuSample")
                {
                    status =
(vsCommandStatus)vsCommandStatus.vsCommandStatusSupported |
                        vsCommandStatus.vsCommandStatusEnabled;
                    return;
                }
            }
        }

        /// <summary>Implements the Exec method of the IDTCommandTarget
interface. This is called when the command is invoked.</summary>
        /// <param term='commandName'>The name of the command to execute.</param>
        /// <param term='executeOption'>Describes how the command should be run.
</param>
        /// <param term='varIn'>Parameters passed from the caller to the command
handler.</param>
        /// <param term='varOut'>Parameters passed from the command handler to the
caller.</param>
        /// <param term='handled'>Informs the caller if the command was
handled or not.</param>
        /// <seealso class='Exec' />
        public void Exec(string commandName, vsCommandExecOption executeOption,
            ref object varIn, ref object varOut, ref bool handled)
```

(continued)

Listing 6-7 *(continued)*

```
        {
            handled = false;
            if (executeOption == vsCommandExecOption.vsCommandExecOptionDoDefault)
            {
                if (commandName == "ToolsMenuSample.Connect.ToolsMenuSample")
                {
                    handled = true;
                    return;
                }
            }
        }
        private DTE2 _applicationObject;
        private AddIn _addInInstance;
    }
}
```

As you see, there are four main additions to the code:

❑ The IDTCommandTarget interface to the list of interfaces to implement

❑ Some code logic to the OnConnection method

❑ The QueryStatus method

❑ The Exec method

The following sections explore these additions in more detail.

Tools Menu Item

The code in Listing 6-8 highlights the new code added to the OnConnection method. The main job of this code is to handle the logic to create a Tools menu item for the add-in and show the appropriate text for it.

Listing 6-8: Changes in the OnConnection Method

```
public void OnConnection(object application, ext_ConnectMode connectMode, object
addInInst, ref Array custom)
{
    _applicationObject = (DTE2)application;
    _addInInstance = (AddIn)addInInst;
    if (connectMode == ext_ConnectMode.ext_cm_UISetup)
    {
        object[] contextGUIDS = new object[] { };
        Commands2 commands = (Commands2)_applicationObject.Commands;
        string toolsMenuName;

        try
```

```
        {
            //If you would like to move the command to a different menu, change the
word "Tools" to the
            //  English version of the menu. This code will take the culture,
append on the name of the menu
            //  then add the command to that menu. You can find a list of all
the top-level menus in the file
            //  CommandBar.resx.
            string resourceName;
            ResourceManager resourceManager = new ResourceManager
                ("ToolsMenuSample.CommandBar", Assembly.GetExecutingAssembly());
            CultureInfo cultureInfo = new CultureInfo(_applicationObject.LocaleID);

            if (cultureInfo.TwoLetterISOLanguageName == "zh")
            {
                resourceName = String.Concat(cultureInfo.Name, "Tools");
            }
            else
            {
                resourceName = String.Concat(cultureInfo.TwoLetterISOLanguageName,
"Tools");
            }
            toolsMenuName = resourceManager.GetString(resourceName);
        }
        catch
        {

            //We tried to find a localized version of the word Tools, but one was
not found.
            //  Default to the en-US word, which may work for the current culture.
            toolsMenuName = "Tools";
        }

        //Place the command on the tools menu.
        //Find the MenuBar command bar, which is the top-level command bar holding
all the main menu items:
        Microsoft.VisualStudio.CommandBars.CommandBar menuBarCommandBar =

((Microsoft.VisualStudio.CommandBars.CommandBars)_applicationObject
.CommandBars)["MenuBar"];

        //Find the Tools command bar on the MenuBar command bar:
        CommandBarControl toolsControl = menuBarCommandBar.Controls[toolsMenuName];
        CommandBarPopup toolsPopup = (CommandBarPopup)toolsControl;

        //This try/catch block can be duplicated if you wish to add multiple
commands to be handled by your Add-in,
        //  just make sure you also update the QueryStatus/Exec method to include
the new command names.
```

(continued)

Listing 6-8 (continued)

```
            try
            {
                //Add a command to the Commands collection:
                Command command = commands.AddNamedCommand2(_addInInstance,
    "ToolsMenuSample",
                    "ToolsMenuSample", "Executes the command for ToolsMenuSample",
    true, 59,
                    ref contextGUIDS, (int)vsCommandStatus.vsCommandStatusSupported +
    (int)vsCommandStatus.vsCommandStatusEnabled,
                    (int)vsCommandStyle.vsCommandStylePictAndText, vsCommandControlType
    .vsCommandControlTypeButton);

                //Add a control for the command to the tools menu:
                if ((command != null) && (toolsPopup != null))
                {
                    command.AddControl(toolsPopup.CommandBar, 1);
                }
            }
            catch (System.ArgumentException)
            {

                //If we are here, then the exception is probably because a command with
    that name
                //  already exists. If so there is no need to recreate the command and
    we can
                //  safely ignore the exception.
            }
        }
    }
```

Although the code may be self-explanatory to some readers, let's take a closer look to make sure you understand it before moving on.

This code runs when the add-in is loaded from a user interface setup (Tools window item). First it gets a list of available commands in the IDE and stores them in a variable named `commands`. Then, in a `try...catch` block of code, it tries to find the resource name for the Tools menu based on the current culture and stores this value in the `toolsMenuName` string variable.

After that, it creates an instance of the CommandBar object in order to create a CommandBarControl and a CommandBarPopup instance.

At the end, in another `try...catch` block, it adds a new command to the list of available commands for the menu item. This will map the `click` event of the Tools menu item to the appropriate command. In the next section, you'll see how this command is handled in the add-in.

Now, if you register this add-in and restart the Visual Studio IDE, then you'll notice the addition of a new item in the Tools menu, as shown in Figure 6-4.

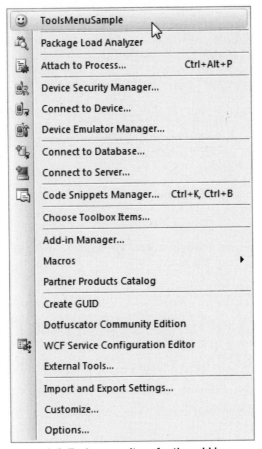

Figure 6-4: Tools menu item for the add-in

Localization resources for an add-in are stored in the CommandBar.resx file that is generated automatically by the Add-In Wizard.

Command Line

Another addition to the generated Connect class code was the IDTCommandTarget interface, which is responsible for providing two methods for handling the add-in commands. You'll see that the click event of the Tools menu item is also routed to a command.

Figure 6-5 shows the structure of this interface, which includes two method definitions for the Exec and QueryStatus methods.

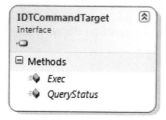

**Figure 6-5: IDTCommandTarget
interface structure**

Let's take a closer look at these two methods and their responsibilities.

Exec

This is an event that arises whenever a user enters an appropriate command to load your add-in. In this case, your `Exec` method receives the command.

The `Exec` method has four parameters:

❑   commandName: String value of the command name that is executed by the user

❑   executeOption: A vsCommandExecOption enumeration value that specifies the execution option

❑   varIn: An object that is passed to the command

❑   varOut: An object that can be returned to the caller after execution of the event

❑   handled: Specifies whether a command event is handled or not

You can see the default implementation for this event in Listing 6-9.

Listing 6-9: Default Implementation of the Exec Method

```
public void Exec(string commandName, vsCommandExecOption executeOption,
    ref object varIn, ref object varOut, ref bool handled)
{
    handled = false;
    if (executeOption == vsCommandExecOption.vsCommandExecOptionDoDefault)
    {
        if (commandName == "ToolsMenuSample.Connect.ToolsMenuSample")
        {
            handled = true;
            return;
        }
    }
}
```

This code first sets the `handled` variable to false to specify that the event is unhandled; then it checks to see whether the default execution option is passed to it. If true, then it checks for the appropriate command name and sets the event as handled.

Listing 6-10 modifies this code to show a MessageBox whenever the command is executed.

Listing 6-10: Modifying the Exec Event to Show a MessageBox

```
public void Exec(string commandName, vsCommandExecOption executeOption,
    ref object varIn, ref object varOut, ref bool handled)
{
    handled = false;
    MessageBox.Show("Command is executed!");
    if (executeOption == vsCommandExecOption.vsCommandExecOptionDoDefault)
    {
        if (commandName == "ToolsMenuSample.Connect.ToolsMenuSample")
        {
            handled = true;
            return;
        }
    }
}
```

Now if I type the `ToolsMenuSample.Connect.ToolsMenuSample` command in the command window (see Figure 6-6), I'll get a MessageBox like the one shown in Figure 6-7.

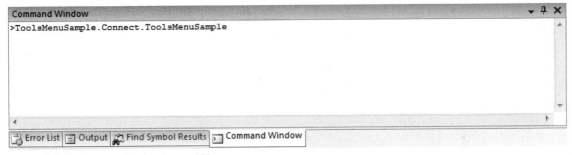

Figure 6-6: A command to load an add-in

Figure 6-7: Result of running
the command

QueryStatus

The other method of the IDTCommandTarget interface is QueryStatus. QueryStatus is a method that is called by the Visual Studio IDE in order to check whether a command is available for the add-in to execute. In other words, if this method doesn't set the appropriate value for the status of the command, then the Exec event can't be called.

This method has four parameters:

❑ commandName: String value of the command name

❑ neededText: A vsCommandStatusTextWanted enumeration value that specifies whether any information is returned from the check process and what kind of information is returned

❑ status: A vsCommandStatus enumeration value that is passed by reference and specifies the status of the command. This is the variable that you can use to control the availability of your command.

❑ commandText: A string value that is passed by reference and can be used to return text if the neededText variable is set

Here a short discussion about the vsCommandStatus enumeration value is necessary. This enumeration value takes six possible values, which are described in Table 6-4. Understanding the purpose of Latched and Ninched is one of reasons you're reading this book.

Table 6-4: The vsCommandStatus Enumerator

Value	Description
vsCommandStatusEnabled	The command is enabled.
vsCommandStatusInvisible	The command is invisible (hidden).
vsCommandStatusLatched	The command is latched. This means that the command is switching between two states, such as being enabled or disabled, but right now it's enabled. Latched isn't a common status.
vsCommandStatusNinched	The command is ninched. This means that the command consists of several commands and each command has its own status. Ninched isn't a common status.
vsCommandStatusSupported	The command is supported.
vsCommandStatusUnsupported	The command is not supported.

Listing 6-11 is the default implementation of the QueryStatus method.

Listing 6-11: Default Implementation of the QueryStatus Method

```
public void QueryStatus(string commandName, vsCommandStatusTextWanted neededText,
    ref vsCommandStatus status, ref object commandText)
{
    if (neededText == vsCommandStatusTextWanted.vsCommandStatusTextWantedNone)
```

```
        {
            if (commandName == "ToolsMenuSample.Connect.ToolsMenuSample")
            {
                status = (vsCommandStatus)vsCommandStatus.vsCommandStatusSupported |
                    vsCommandStatus.vsCommandStatusEnabled;
                return;
            }
        }
    }
```

This code first checks the neededText variable to see whether a text value is wanted, and then checks the commandName variable to ensure that it has the appropriate command name for the add-in. If true, then it returns a status value to let the IDE know that the add-in supports the commands.

Toolbar

The last option for loading an add-in is via a toolbar item. This option actually involves loading the command for the add-in via a toolbar item.

To create a toolbar item for an add-in, you first need to make sure that the add-in has a command available and that the add-in is loaded into the Visual Studio IDE. Then choose Tools ⇨ Customize from the menu, navigate to the Commands tab, and choose the Addins category from the left pane (see Figure 6-8).

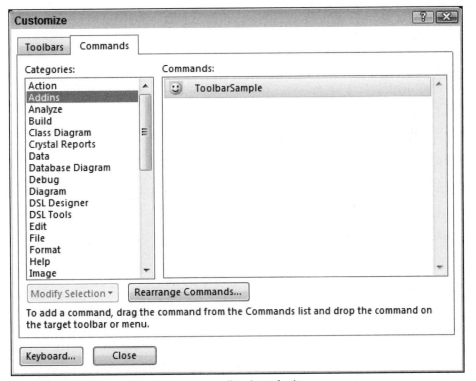

Figure 6-8: Select an add-in to create a toolbar item for it.

Now drag and drop the command item for your add-in from the right pane to the toolbar that you want (see Figure 6-9).

Figure 6-9: Create a toolbar item for the add-in.

.AddIn File

One of the things the Add-In Wizard generates for you is an XML file (with an .AddIn extension) for use as a configuration file for your add-in. The Visual Studio IDE uses this file to recognize your add-in and retrieve some information about it.

Actually, the Add-In Wizard creates two .AddIn files. One file is for testing purposes and the other one is the file that you can use to deploy your add-in. The test file is set to be copied to the Addins folder of your Visual Studio 2008 projects folder when you create the add-in. It helps you debug your add-ins easily and then disappears from your project files and from the Addins folder as soon as you close the IDE that contains your add-in project when opened for the first time.

For example, Listing 6-12 shows an .AddIn file with the structure you have after running the Add-in Wizard.

Listing 6-12: Sample .AddIn File

```xml
<?xml version="1.0" encoding="UTF-16" standalone="no"?>
<Extensibility xmlns="http://schemas.microsoft.com/AutomationExtensibility">
  <HostApplication>
    <Name>Microsoft Visual Studio Macros</Name>
    <Version>9.0</Version>
  </HostApplication>
  <HostApplication>
    <Name>Microsoft Visual Studio</Name>
    <Version>9.0</Version>
  </HostApplication>
  <Addin>
    <FriendlyName>AddIn File Sample</FriendlyName>
    <Description>This is a sample add-in for .AddIn file.</Description>
    <AboutBoxDetails>For more information about , see the  website at\r\nhttp://www
.wrox.com</AboutBoxDetails>
    <AboutIconData>
      <!-- This section is removed to save the space -->
    </AboutIconData>
    <Assembly>AddInFileSample.dll</Assembly>
    <FullClassName>AddInFileSample.Connect</FullClassName>
    <LoadBehavior>5</LoadBehavior>
    <CommandPreload>1</CommandPreload>
    <CommandLineSafe>1</CommandLineSafe>
  </Addin>
</Extensibility>
```

As you can see, this XML file contains an `<Extensibility>` root element that has an XML namespace set to `http://schemas.microsoft.com/AutomationExtensibility`. After inserting this XML namespace in your file, Visual Studio gives you the IntelliSense to edit this file more easily.

This `<Extensibility>` element doesn't have any attributes but it has three possible elements:

- `<HostApplication>`
- `<Addin>`
- `<ToolsOptionsPage>`

<HostApplication>

The `<HostApplication>` element represents a host application for an add-in. Each `<Extensibility>` element can have one or more `<HostApplication>` elements for all its host applications. For Visual Studio add-ins, you can have a maximum of two `<HostApplication>` elements (for the main Visual Studio IDE and the Macros IDE).

The `<HostApplication>` doesn't have any attributes but it has two child elements:

- `<Name>`: Specifies the name of the host application. For the main Visual Studio IDE it can be set to "Microsoft Visual Studio" and for the Macros IDE it can be set to "Microsoft Visual Studio Macros."
- `<Version>`: Determines the version of the host application (internal version). For Visual Studio 2008 it can be set to 9.0 and for Visual Studio 2005 it can be set to 8.0. Using this value, you may be able to upgrade Visual Studio 2005 add-ins for Visual Studio 2008.

Listing 6-13 shows a simple .AddIn file with definitions for the `<HostApplication>` elements.

Listing 6-13: Adding `<HostApplication>` Elements to an .AddIn File

```xml
<?xml version="1.0" encoding="UTF-16" standalone="no"?>
<Extensibility xmlns="http://schemas.microsoft.com/AutomationExtensibility">
  <HostApplication>
    <Name>Microsoft Visual Studio Macros</Name>
    <Version>9.0</Version>
  </HostApplication>
  <HostApplication>
    <Name>Microsoft Visual Studio</Name>
    <Version>9.0</Version>
  </HostApplication>
</Extensibility>
```

<Addin>

This element specifies some information about the add-in itself. Like the `<HostApplication>` element, this element doesn't have any attributes but it can contain the following elements:

- `<AboutBoxDetails>`: Set to the information that you entered in the Add-In Wizard. This information will be shown in the Help About dialog for Visual Studio.

❑ `<AboutIconData>`: Binary equivalent of add-in icon data

❑ `<AboutIconLocation>`: This element can be set to the fully qualified path of the icon or the fully qualified path of an assembly with the ID of a resource that contains the icon data or binary data for the icon in hex digit pairs.

❑ `<Assembly>`: The assembly name that contains the add-in

❑ `<CommandLineSafe>`: Specifies whether the add-in is command-line safe and displays the user interface or not. 0 indicates that it does show a user interface, and 1 indicates that it doesn't do this.

❑ `<CommandPreLoad>`: Specifies whether add-ins should be pre-loaded, which means that an add-in can be loaded the first time that Visual Studio IDE starts

❑ `<Description>`: The text description of the add-in that appears in the Add-in Manager dialog

❑ `<FriendlyName>`: The friendly name for the add-in that appears in Add-in Manager dialog

❑ `<FullClassName>`: The fully qualified class name for the add-in. If you rename the default `Connect` class to something else, you need to change this value as well.

❑ `<LoadBehavior>`: Determines when an add-in loads. 0 specifies that the add-in is not loaded when the IDE starts up and must be started manually; 1 specifies that the add-in is loaded when the IDE starts up, and 4 specifies that the add-in is loaded when the IDE is loaded from a command line with a build switch.

Listing 6-14 is an example of adding the `<Addin>` element to an .AddIn file.

Listing 6-14: Adding the `<Addin>` Element to an .AddIn File

```xml
<?xml version="1.0" encoding="UTF-16" standalone="no"?>
<Extensibility xmlns="http://schemas.microsoft.com/AutomationExtensibility">
  <HostApplication>
    <Name>Microsoft Visual Studio Macros</Name>
    <Version>9.0</Version>
  </HostApplication>
  <HostApplication>
    <Name>Microsoft Visual Studio</Name>
    <Version>9.0</Version>
  </HostApplication>
  <Addin>
    <FriendlyName>AddIn File Sample</FriendlyName>
    <Description>This is a sample add-in for .AddIn file.</Description>
    <AboutBoxDetails>For more information about , see the  website at\r\nhttp://www.
wrox.com</AboutBoxDetails>
    <AboutIconData>
      <!-- This section is removed to save the space -->
    </AboutIconData>
    <Assembly>AddInFileSample.dll</Assembly>
    <FullClassName>AddInFileSample.Connect</FullClassName>
    <LoadBehavior>5</LoadBehavior>
    <CommandPreload>1</CommandPreload>
    <CommandLineSafe>1</CommandLineSafe>
  </Addin>
</Extensibility>
```

<ToolsOptionsPage>

This element can be used to define an options page for the add-in, and it's not as common as the first two elements.

Using this element you can configure your add-in to display options in the Tools ➪ Options menu of Visual Studio under a specific category and subcategory.

`<ToolsOptionsPage>` doesn't have any attributes but it has a `<Category>` child element that has a `Name` attribute. `<Category>` itself has a `<SubCategory>` child element with the `Name` attribute.

`<SubCategory>` needs to have an `<Assembly>` and a `<FullClassName>` child element set for it. In Chapter 11 you'll learn how to create an options page for your add-ins.

Shared Add-ins

For the last time in this book, I'll talk here about shared add-ins and their minor differences from Visual Studio add-ins. After this, I'll focus just on Visual Studio add-ins.

In a comparison of the anatomy of Visual Studio add-ins and shared add-ins, you can notice many similarities and a few differences. Both kinds of add-ins implement the IDTExtensibility2 interface and have the same fields. They also have the same class name (`Connect`). Unlike Visual Studio add-ins, you don't have an .AddIn file for shared add-ins, which have only a class file for implementation. The other difference is in the references for a shared add-in, which are a little different from Visual Studio add-ins. Here you don't need to deal with EnvDTE anymore because appropriate references exist for Microsoft Office products.

Writing a shared add-in is easy if you know how to write a Visual Studio add-in. Only a few extra concepts about Microsoft Office APIs are necessary to write shared add-ins.

Summary

This chapter provided a detailed explanation of the anatomy of add-ins. You learned first about the structure of an add-in, and then the interface that add-ins implement, with a description of its methods.

After that, you learned about other ways to load an add-in in Visual Studio and saw sample codes for them. The chapter then covered the .AddIn file and its structure. At the end, you read a short discussion about shared add-ins and their similarities to and differences from Visual Studio add-ins in general.

7

Manipulating the Solutions, Projects, and Project Items

Solutions, projects, and project items are the fundamental parts of development in Visual Studio, and you always need to deal with them in order to develop an application.

Therefore, Document Tools Extensibility (DTE) has to provide a rich set of APIs to work with these main elements, and it does! This chapter covers solutions, projects, project items, and other related material.

The development model and structure in Visual Studio have changed over the last decade, but the structure has remained constant since the birth of .NET technology. We'll focus now on this structure, with its solutions, projects, and project items.

Most extensibility scenarios share the common purpose of using these elements in order to get something done. Using the automation model, you can do whatever you want with these elements in the Visual Studio IDE, including creating solutions and projects, adding project items, removing these elements, and much more.

In this chapter you'll learn about the following topics:

- ❑ An introduction to the structure of solutions, projects, and project items in Visual Studio development
- ❑ The Solution object, including a detailed discussion about its properties and methods
- ❑ The Project object, with details about its properties and methods
- ❑ The ProjectItem object, including a discussion about working with project items
- ❑ Visual Studio events related to solutions, projects, and project items

Each of these topics is covered in a practical way. That is, we will go over them one by one, looking at common scenarios and applications for each, including sample source codes.

We begin the chapter with a short background about the concepts you'll deal with frequently in the chapter.

Background

This short introduction to the structure of development elements in Visual Studio may be familiar to you already, but it never hurts to review the basic principles.

In Visual Studio, you can open only one solution at a time. Such a solution may contain one, two, or many projects, or none at all. Projects can be of different types and of different development languages.

Each project can contain several project items, including classes, modules, structures, enumerators, configuration files, resources, and files.

Figure 7-1 shows this hierarchy in a schematic view.

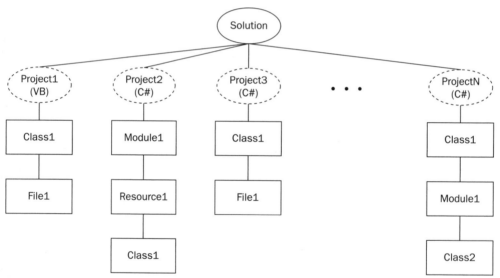

Figure 7-1: The structure of Visual Studio development elements

To extend Visual Studio in order to add something to the default behavior of solutions, projects, and project items, you need to deal with some main objects in the automation model and Development Tools Extensibility (DTE), which are covered in the following sections in detail.

Three classes play main roles in your development for these elements:

❑   Solution

❑   Project

❑   ProjectItem

As their names suggest, they represent the solution, project, and project item, respectively, in the automation model.

Solution

Solution is the parent of all other elements in programming for the development structure of Visual Studio. EnvDTE.Solution is a class that represents a solution in the automation model, and it provides several properties and methods for working with solutions. You can access instances of this object for the current Visual Studio IDE via the DTE2.Solution property. Solution inherits from the _Solution interface.

Conversely, you need to convert your solutions to the Solution3 object in the EnvDTE90 assembly, which is derived from the Solution2 object in the EnvDTE80 assembly and is derived from _Solution as well (see Figure 7-2).

In the upper level, _Solution is derived from the IEnumerable interface, which means it and all its derived classes are enumerable. In fact, they represent a collection of projects in a solution that you can iterate through.

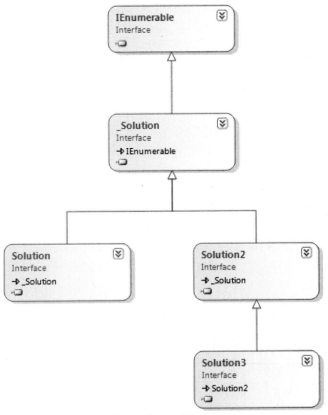

Figure 7-2: Solution inherits from _Solution

Table 7-1 lists the properties of this class and describes them briefly. Properties that come from the IEnumerable interface are omitted.

Table 7-1: The Solution Properties

Property	Description
AddIns	A read-only instance of the EnvDTE.AddIns object, and a collection of add-ins available in the IDE
DTE	A read-only DTE instance for the environment where the solution is located
ExtenderCATID	A read-only string value that returns the category ID for the extender object
ExtenderNames	Returns the list of EnvDTE.Extender object names for the solution
FileName	A read-only string value of the solution's filename
FullName	A read-only string value of the solution's full name
Globals	A read-only instance of the EnvDTE.Globals object that contains add-in values that may be saved in the solution or project file
IsDirty	A Boolean value that is reserved for internal use in Microsoft
IsOpen	Indicates whether a solution is open or not
Parent	Returns the parent DTE object for the solution
Projects	A read-only instance of EnvDTE.Projects that represents a collection of projects in the solution. You'll read more about this in the next section.
Properties	Returns an instance of the EnvDTE.Properties object related to the solution
Saved	Gets or sets a Boolean value and indicates whether the solution is saved from the last modification
SolutionBuild	Returns an instance of the EnvDTE.SolutionBuild object to manage the build process of the solution

Table 7-2 describes each of the methods of this class. Methods that come from the IEnumerable interface are omitted.

Table 7-2: The Solution Methods

Method	Description
AddFromFile	Adds an existing new project to the solution
AddFromTemplate	Adds a new project to the solution based on a project template
AddSolutionFolder	Adds a new solution folder to the solution with the specified name
Close	Closes the solution
Create	Creates a new empty solution with a specified name and path
FindProjectItem	Finds and returns an EnvDTE.ProjectItem object located in a project
GetProjectItemTemplate	Returns the path of a project-item template by getting the filename of the template and its language
GetProjectItemTemplates	Returns an instance of the EnvDTE90.Templates for the list of all the project item templates for a specified language
GetProjectTemplate	Returns the path of a project template by getting the filename of the template and its language
Item	Returns an EnvDTE.Project object located in the specified index in the list of projects
Open	Opens a specified solution
ProjectItemsTemplatePath	Gets the string value of a project item template type and returns the file path for that project item template
Remove	Removes a project from the solution
SaveAs	Saves the solution with the specified filename

After taking a quick look at the properties and methods of this class, let's look at some practical scenarios for the Solution object.

Creating a Solution

Obviously, the first scenario that comes to mind is how to create a solution. Thanks to the Create method of the Solution class, this is very simple!

This Create method gets two string parameters: the path where you want to store the solution and the name of the solution. The Create method merely creates the solution on-the-fly; it doesn't store it unless you call the SaveAs method to store the solution in the specified path.

Listing 7-1 is a simple example of this. It creates an empty solution. Note that the `CreateSolution` method is called from the `Exec` method of an add-in. You can find the full source sample of this example in the download package for this chapter.

Listing 7-1: Creating a Solution

```
private void CreateSolution()
{
  // Get the instance of the Solution
  Solution3 solution = this._applicationObject.Solution as Solution3;

  // Create a solution
  solution.Create(@"c:\solutions", "SampleSolution");
}
```

Running this add-in results in a new empty solution in the IDE (see Figures 7-3 and 7-4).

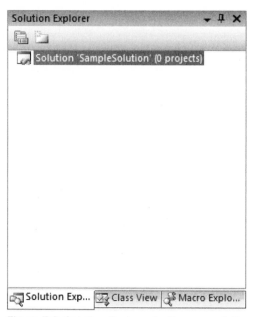

Figure 7-3: Solution Explorer for the new solution

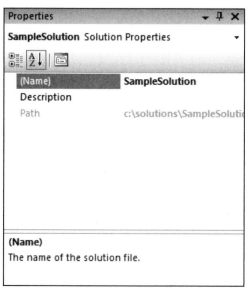

Figure 7-4: Properties window for the new solution

Opening and Closing a Solution

To open a solution, you need to use the `Open` method of the `Solution` class by passing the path of the solution file as a parameter.

In the reverse direction, if you want to close a solution, you need to call the `Close` method of the `Solution` class by passing a Boolean parameter specifying whether it should save the solution before closing it or not.

Listing 7-2 is an example of these actions. It presents two methods, OpenSolution and CloseSolution, that respectively open and close a solution.

Listing 7-2: Opening and Closing a Solution

```
private void OpenSolution()
{
  // Get the instance of the Solution
  Solution3 solution = this._applicationObject.Solution as Solution3;

  // Open the solution
  solution.Open(@"C:\Solutions\Solution1.sln");
}

private void CloseSolution()
{
  // Get the instance of the Solution
  Solution solution = this._applicationObject.Solution;

  // Close the solution
  solution.Close(true);
}
```

Adding a Project to the Solution

Another common scenario is adding a project to a solution. You have two options for creating a new project and adding it to the solution. You have these options in the Visual Studio IDE as well:

❑   Add an existing project from a file

❑   Add a completely new project based on a project template

Adding an Existing Project

To add an existing project to the solution, you need to use the AddNewFile method of the Solution class by establishing two parameters. The first one is the address of the project file; the second one is a Boolean value that indicates whether the project should be loaded in the current solution or its own solution.

Listing 7-3 provides an example showing how to use this method to add an existing C# project to the solution.

Listing 7-3: Adding an Existing Project to a Solution

```
private void AddProject()
{
  // Get the instance of the Solution
  Solution3 solution = this._applicationObject.Solution as Solution3;

  // Add an exisiting project to the solution
  solution.AddFromFile(@"C:\Projects\GenericList\GenericList.csproj", false);
}
```

Figure 7-5 shows the result of running this add-in. Note that here the code in Listing 7-1 is called before the code in Listing 7-3.

Figure 7-5: Adding an existing project to the solution

Adding a New Project

The second option is to add a completely new project to the solution based on a project template. Project templates for Visual Studio projects are located on the physical drives, and you need to pass their address to the AddFromTemplate method of the instance of the Solution object. This method also takes two other string parameters: the destination path of the project storage location and its name, as well as a Boolean parameter specifying whether it should be loaded in the current solution or its own solution.

To get the template path of a project, call the GetProjectTemplate method of the Solution instance. This method gets two parameters: the string value of the project template filename and the string value of the development language name.

Listing 7-4 shows you how to add a new C# project to the solution.

Listing 7-4: Adding a New Project to a Solution

```
private void AddNewProject()
{
  // Get the instance of the Solution
  Solution3 solution = this._applicationObject.Solution as Solution3;

  string templatePath = solution.GetProjectTemplate("ClassLibrary.zip", "CSharp");

  // Add a new project to the solution
```

```
    solution.AddFromTemplate(templatePath, @"c:\solutions\NewProject", "My New
Project", false);
}
```

The result is shown in Figure 7-6.

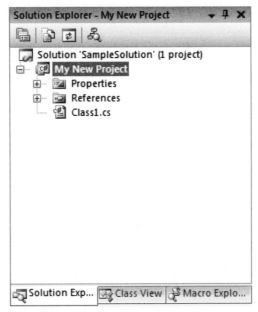

Figure 7-6: Adding a new project to the solution

Removing a Project from the Solution

You can also remove a project from the solution by calling the Remove method of the Solution instance. This method gets an instance of the Project object. Later in this chapter, you'll read more about Project.

Listing 7-5 is an example of removing a project from the solution.

Listing 7-5: Removing a Project from the Solution

```
private void RemoveProject()
{
   // Get the instance of the Solution
   Solution3 solution = this._applicationObject.Solution as Solution3;

   Project project = solution.Item(0);

   // Remove the project
   solution.Remove(project);
}
```

Saving the Solution

The last thing you need to make sure of is that you've saved your solution after applying changes. You may create or open a solution but none of your changes are stored unless you call the SaveAs method of the Solution instance by passing the path of the solution filename to it.

You can see this in action in Listing 7-6.

Listing 7-6: Saving the Solution

```
private void SaveSolution()
{
  // Get the instance of the Solution
  Solution3 solution = this._applicationObject.Solution as Solution3;

  // Save the solution
  solution.SaveAs(@"c:\solutions\SampleSolution.sln");
}
```

Project

The second element in Visual Studio development is the Project. The Project interface is the code presentation of a project in the automation model, located in the EnvDTE assembly.

Table 7-3 lists the properties of this interface and describes them briefly.

Table 7-3: The Project Properties

Property	Description
CodeModel	A read-only property that returns the EnvDTE.CodeModel object instance for the project
Collection	Returns an instance of the EnvDTE.Projects object that represents the collection of projects, including the current project
ConfigurationManager	Returns an instance of the EnvDTE.ConfigurationManager object for the project
DTE	Returns the DTE object for the project
Extender	Returns an instance of the Extender object for the project if it exists
ExtenderCATID	Returns the string value of the category ID for the Extender object
ExtenderNames	Returns a list of Extender names for the project
FileName	Returns the filename of the project
FullName	Returns the path and name of the project

Property	Description
Globals	Returns an instance of EnvDTE.Globals object
IsDirty	A Boolean value that is reserved for internal use by Microsoft
Kind	Returns the string value of a GUID that indicates what kind of project this is
Object	Gets an object for the solution that can be used for development
ParentProjectItem	Returns an instance of the EnvDTE.ProjectItem for nested projects, and contains the parent project item for the current project
ProjectItems	Returns an instance of the EnvDTE.ProjectItems that contains a list of project items for the project
Properties	Returns an instance of the EnvDTE.Properties that contains some properties related to the project
Saved	A Boolean value indicating whether the project has been saved since the last modification or not
UniqueName	Returns a unique name for the project that distinguishes the project from other projects with same name

Table 7-4 describes the methods for the Project interface.

Table 7-4: The Project Methods

Method	Description
Delete	Removes the project from the solution
Save	Saves the project
SaveAs	Saves the solution, project, and project item

Usually, a project is correlated with project items, so you'll see examples of the Project interface in the next section, which covers project items.

Project Items

Project items are what you use to develop your applications. Several project-item types are available in Visual Studio, depending on the different project-item templates, and you can even write your own project-item templates. This is covered in Chapter 20.

Two similarly named interfaces play the main roles regarding project items: ProjectItem and ProjectItems. ProjectItem is the representation of a project item, whereas ProjectItems is a collection of project items.

ProjectItem

This interface represents a project item. Properties of this interface are described in Table 7-5.

Table 7-5: The ProjectItem Properties

Property	Description
Collection	Returns an instance of the EnvDTE.ProjectItems object as a collection of project items, including the current item
ConfigurationManager	Returns an instance of the EnvDTE.ConfigurationManager object for the item
ContainingProject	Returns the project that contains the current item
Document	If there is any document for the current item, this returns the related EnvDTE.Document.
DTE	Returns the DTE for the item
Extender	Returns the EnvDTE.Extender object for the item
ExtenderCATID	Returns the category ID for the Extender object related to the item
ExtenderNames	Returns the list of all Extenders for the item
FileCodeModel	Returns an EnvDTE.FileCodeModel object instance for the item
FileCount	Returns the number of files associated with the item
FileNames	Returns the list of full paths for the files associated with the item
IsDirty	A Boolean value that is reserved for internal use by Microsoft
IsOpen	Indicates that a project item is open
Kind	Returns the string value of a GUID that indicates what kind of project it is
Name	The string value of the name of the item
Object	Gets an object for the item that can be used for development
ProjectItems	Returns an instance of the EnvDTE.ProjectItems object that contains a collection of items containing the current item
Properties	Returns an instance of the EnvDTE.Properties that contains some properties related to the item
Saved	A Boolean value that indicates whether the item has been saved since the last modification
SubProject	For nested projects, if the item is the root of a subproject, then this property returns an instance of the EnvDTE.Project object for that subproject.

Methods of the ProjectItem interface are listed in Table 7-6.

Table 7-6: The ProjectItem Methods

Method	Description
Delete	Deletes the item from the project
ExpandView	Expands the Solution Explorer to show the items
Open	Opens a ProjectItem object
Remove	Removes the item from the collection (not from the project)
Save	Saves the project item
SaveAs	Saves the project item with a specified name and path

ProjectItems

The ProjectItems interface represents a collection of project items. Table 7-7 describes its properties.

Table 7-7: The ProjectItems Properties

Property	Description
ContainingProject	Returns the project that contains the project items
Count	Returns the number of items in the collection
DTE	Returns the DTE object for the item collection
Kind	Returns the string value of a GUID that indicates what kind of project it is
Parent	Returns the parent object of the ProjectItems

Methods of the ProjectItems interface are listed in Table 7-8.

Table 7-8: The ProjectItems Methods

Method	Description
AddFolder	Add a new folder
AddFromDirectory	Adds project items from a directory to the ProjectItems collection
AddFromFile	Adds an item from a file to the collection
AddFromFileCopy	Copies a file and adds it to the collection
AddFromTemplate	Adds a new item from an item template to the project
Item	Returns a ProjectItem in the collection at the specified index

Let's explore some common examples.

Listing Project Items in a Project

One common scenario for project items is listing them to see what is there. To do this, you need to choose a project in the solution by referring to it via its index and the `Item` method of the Solution instance, and then iterate through the `ProjectItems` property of this project (see Listing 7-7).

Listing 7-7: Listing All Project Items

```
private void ListItems()
{
  // Get the instance of the Solution
  Solution3 solution = this._applicationObject.Solution as Solution3;

  solution.Open(@"C:\solutions\SampleSolution.sln");

  string output = string.Empty;

  // Iterate through items
  foreach (ProjectItem item in solution.Item(1).ProjectItems)
  {
    output += item.Name + "\n";
  }

  MessageBox.Show(output);
}
```

The result is shown in Figure 7-7.

Class1.cs
Properties

OK

Figure 7-7: Listing
project items

Adding a Project Item to the Project

To add a new item to a project, you need to have an open solution. Then you call one of the appropriate methods of the Project.ProjectItems instance to add a new item to it. There are four methods for this purpose: `AddFromDirectory`, `AddFromFile`, `AddFromFileCopy`, and `AddFromTemplate`:

- ❑ AddFromDirectory: Adds project items from a directory

- ❑ AddFromFile: Adds an existing file to the project

- ❑ AddFromFileCopy: Copies a file and adds it to the project

- ❑ AddFromTemplate: Adds a file based on an item template to the project

As an example, Listing 7-8 adds an interface file to the project. It uses the `GetProjectItemTemplate` method of the Solution instance to get the path of the interface item template, and then uses the `AddFromTemplate` method of the ProjectItems to add a new interface to the project.

Listing 7-8: Adding a New Item to the Project

```
private void AddItem()
{
    // Get the instance of the Solution
    Solution3 solution = this._applicationObject.Solution as Solution3;

    solution.Open(@"C:\solutions\SampleSolution.sln");

    Project project = solution.Item(1);

    // Get the template path
    string templatePath = solution.GetProjectItemTemplate("Interface.zip", "CSharp");

    // Add the new item to the project
    project.ProjectItems.AddFromTemplate(templatePath, "MyInterfaceFile.cs");
}
```

As shown in Figure 7-8, this add-in adds a new interface file to the solution.

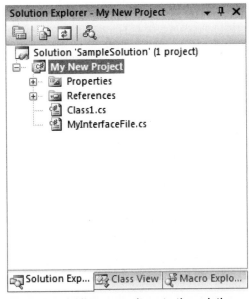

Figure 7-8: Adding a new item to the solution

ActiveSolutionProjects

DTE.ActiveSolutionProjects is an array of currently available projects in the solution and it provides a quick alternative way to access projects in the current solution. By default, it's of the general Object type, but you can convert it to an array, get access to its individual items, and then convert them to a project.

Listing 7-9 is an example of this, which uses this property to list the names of all projects in the IDE in a MessageBox.

Listing 7-9: Using ActiveSolutionProjects to List Available Projects

```
private void IterateProjects()
{
  Solution3 solution = this._applicationObject.Solution as Solution3;

  solution.Open(@"C:\solutions\SampleSolution.sln");

  Array projects = this._applicationObject.ActiveSolutionProjects as Array;

  string output = string.Empty;

  foreach (Object item in projects)
  {
    Project project = item as Project;
    output += project.Name + "\n";
  }

  MessageBox.Show(output);
}
```

It obtains the list of projects as an object from ActiveSolutionProjects, converts this object to an array, and iterates through its items and converts them to Project objects. You can check the output in Figure 7-9.

Figure 7-9: Using the ActiveSolutionProjects object

Events

Solutions, projects, and project items include some related events that you can use in order to execute some code on specific events.

Two groups of events located in the DTE.Events namespace provide what we need for this:

❑ SolutionEvents: For solution and project events

❑ SolutionItemEvents: For project item events

Table 7-9 lists the events in SolutionEvents.

Table 7-9: SolutionEvents Events

Event	Description
AfterClosing	Occurs when a solution is closed
BeforeClosing	Occurs before closing a solution
Opened	Occurs when a solution or project is opened
ProjectAdded	Occurs when a project is added to the solution
ProjectRemoved	Occurs when a project is removed from the solution
ProjectRenamed	Occurs when a project is renamed in the solution
QueryCloseSolution	Occurs right before the BeforeClosing event
Renamed	Occurs when a solution is renamed

Table 7-10 describes all the events in the SolutionItemEvents.

Table 7-10: SolutionItemEvents Events

Event	Description
ItemAdded	Occurs when a project is added to the solution or an item is added to the project
ItemRemoved	Occurs when a project is removed from the solution or an item is added to the project
ItemRenamed	Occurs when a project or item is renamed

Each of these events has its own parameters that provide some information related to the event, and you can use these parameters to handle events.

For example, a `ProjectAdded` event has a parameter of type Project that enables you to access information about the project that is added to the solution in order to customize it.

These events are very handy when writing add-ins and different extensions for Visual Studio, because you will typically need to handle one of the events in the IDE in order to get something done.

Summary

In this chapter you learned how to manipulate solutions, projects, and project items in Visual Studio using automation model objects.

First you read a short introduction to the main elements in Visual Studio development, including solutions, projects, and project items. Then you read a detailed discussion about Solution, Project, ProjectItem and ProjectItems objects in the DTE. After this, you learned about the DTE.ActiveSolutionProjects object as an alternative for iterating through projects in the solution quickly.

Finally, you read about events related to these elements in the Visual Studio automation model.

Manipulating Documents

The other common scenario for writing an add-in and extending the Visual Studio environment is to extend editor functionality and manipulate active documents and their content.

You often need to change something in your code automatically or update the text in your windows in order to perform a task. For example, you may want to add a method to the top of a class file.

In general, because the most common task in Visual Studio is coding, it's predictable that extending the editor and coding features, and providing better and easier ways to use them, is a main feature of Visual Studio extensibility.

The code model is one of several automation models that enable you to access appropriate APIs in order to work with coding features and manipulate code and text in documents. Besides the project model (described in Chapter 7), the code model is a helpful part of the automation model that's been enhanced in Visual Studio 2005 and 2008 to offer more features.

The main topic of this chapter (and Chapter 9) is the code model and how to manipulate text and code in windows. In this chapter you'll read about the following topics:

- ❑ An introduction to the code model
- ❑ The Documents collection
- ❑ The Document class
- ❑ The TextSelection, TextPoint, EditPoint, VirtualPoint, and TextDocument interfaces
- ❑ How to use DTE objects to manipulate texts

As in Chapter 7, these topics are covered in a practical way, including common real-world scenarios and related code samples.

Background

Visual Studio has a mechanism to present the main content of files and documents in a tabular structure in the center of the IDE using several tabs. In this chapter, these tabs are referred to as documents. Each document is a code or module file or any other type of file that can be viewed in Visual Studio.

At any one time, you can have many documents open in the IDE in different tabs. The Visual Studio automation model enables you to access all these documents easily. This is possible through the code model.

Development Tools Extensibility (DTE) provides some classes that enable you to manipulate the text in these documents and modify them at any time. The features of these APIs also allow many great third-party add-ins and extensions for Visual Studio, which enable you to further simplify your coding process. Some of these add-ins and extensions are listed in Appendix A and are handy tools for manipulating your code within the Visual Studio environment.

Two interfaces play the main roles in manipulating the text in documents: Documents and Document. *Documents* is a collection of `Document` objects and is actually the presentation of all available documents in the Visual Studio IDE as a collection. *Document* is the presentation of a single document in the IDE, and it provides methods and properties to work with documents and the text included in them.

> *The content of Document is not limited to programming codes, and you may have text or XML or other types of content in the documents. In this chapter we focus on the general text content in the documents and editor, and in Chapter 9 you will learn how to manipulate programming code.*

Documents

Documents is an interface that implements the IEnumerable interface itself. This collection contains a set of `Document` objects for all available documents in the IDE. It includes a few methods and properties that help you work with this collection and the documents it contains (see Figure 8-1).

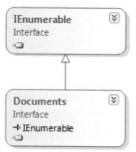

Figure 8-1: The Documents class structure

Table 8-1 describes the three properties of this interface.

Table 8-1: The Documents Properties

Property	Description
Count	Returns the number of documents included in the collection
DTE	Returns the DTE instance containing the Documents collection
Parent	Returns the direct parent object of the collection

Table 8-2 lists a few methods of the Documents interface.

Table 8-2: The Documents Methods

Method	Description
Add	Adds a new document to the collection
CloseAll	Closes all documents in the IDE. It takes a parameter of the EnvDTE.vsSaveChanges enumeration type to determine whether to save the changes or not: vsSaveChangesNo doesn't save the changes; vsSaveChangesPrompt prompts whether to save the changes or not, and vsSaveChangesYes saves all changes.
Item	Returns an instance of the Document object for the specified index from the collection
Open	Opens a document and returns an instance of the EnvDTE.Document object corresponding to the opened document
SaveAll	Saves all open documents in the Visual Studio IDE

The following common scenarios will help you get familiar with the applications of this interface.

Listing All Documents

To iterate through all open documents in the IDE you can write a for...each loop that counts each item in the Documents object instance and gets access to each Document instance.

Listing 8-1 illustrates this theory in action with a simple example that shows the names of all open documents in a MessageBox.

Listing 8-1: Listing All Documents in the IDE

```
private void ListAllDocuments()
{
    Documents documents = this._applicationObject.Documents;

    string output = string.Empty;

    foreach (Document document in documents)
    {
        output += document.Name + "\n";
    }

    MessageBox.Show(output);
}
```

The resulting MessageBox is shown in Figure 8-2.

Figure 8-2: The result of listing all documents in the IDE

The Documents collection doesn't contain the Visual Studio Start Page, so it's not included in the result. Other Visual Studio windows such as Object Browser or other built-in windows aren't listed either.

Closing All Documents

You have two options to close all documents in the Visual Studio environment:

❑   Iterate through all documents and close them one by one

❑   Use the `CloseAll` method of the Documents interface

The first option generally isn't very appropriate, so let's take a closer look at the second one.

The `CloseAll` method of the Documents interface takes an argument of the EnvDTE.vsSaveChanges enumeration type and has three possible values that specify how open documents should be saved before closing. `CloseAll` closes all open documents by saving them based on the passed parameter.

For example, the code in Listing 8-2 uses one line of code to close all documents in the IDE by prompting for each modified item. As shown in Figure 8-3, Visual Studio tries to close all documents and asks you to save or ignore the changes for each modified item before closing it.

Listing 8-2: Closing All Documents in the IDE.

```
private void CloseAllDocuments()
{
    this._applicationObject.Documents.CloseAll
        (vsSaveChanges.vsSaveChangesPrompt);
}
```

Figure 8-3: Closing all documents by prompting the user

Document

Document is the main interface in the code model. It represents an open document in the Visual Studio IDE. Obviously, there is a mapping between an open document and a corresponding project item in a project.

Unlike other common interfaces that you see in the DTE, Document doesn't implement another interface. It works as a stand-alone interface and provides 18 properties and 11 methods. These properties and methods are important because they give you a lot of power.

Table 8-3 describes all the properties of the Document interface.

Table 8-3: The Document Properties

Property	Description
ActiveWindow	Returns the active window in the environment. It may be null if no window is open.
Collection	Returns an instance of the EnvDTE.Documents interface containing the document
DTE	Returns the DTE instance containing the document
Extender	Returns an instance of the EnvDTE.Extender if one is available
ExtenderCATID	Returns the category ID for the Extender object
ExtenderNames	Returns a list of Extender names
FullName	Returns the full path and name of the document's file
IndentSize	Returns the indentation size of the document
Kind	Returns the string value of a GUID representing the type of the project
Language	Returns the string value of the language name for the document
Path	Returns the path of the document's file
ProjectItem	Returns an instance of the EnvDTE.ProjectItem object corresponding to the document
ReadOnly	Indicates whether the open document is read-only
Saved	Indicates whether the document is saved after the last modification
Selection	Returns an object that represents the selection part of the document
TabSize	Returns the tab size of the document
Type	Returns the string value of the document type name
Windows	Returns an instance of the EnvDTE.Windows object for the windows that are displayed for the document

Table 8-4 describes the Document interface's methods.

Table 8-4: The Document Interface Methods

Method	Description
Activate	Activates the document and moves the focus to it
ClearBookmarks	Clears all bookmarks in the document
Close	Closes the document and takes a parameter of the EnvDTE.vsSaveChanges enumeration type that specifies how changes should be saved: vsSaveChangesNo doesn't save the changes; vsSaveChangesPrompt prompts whether to save the changes, and vsSaveChangesYes saves all changes.
MarkText	Marks a part of the text in the document by getting a pattern and the number of flags
NewWindow	Creates an instance of the EnvDTE.Windows object to enable you to view the document in a new window
Object	Returns an object of a specified kind that you can use for your development
PrintOut	Prints the content of the document
Redo	Works like the Redo button in any editor
ReplaceText	Finds a specified text and replaces it with a new text based on a specified number of flags
Save	Saves the document with the specified filename
Undo	Works like the Undo button in any editor

Note that root DTE object has an ActiveDocument read-only property that enables you to quickly access the Document instance for the current document in the Visual Studio IDE.

The Document interface, in conjunction with five other interfaces, provides the capability to manipulate code and text in documents:

- ❑ TextSelection
- ❑ TextPoint
- ❑ EditPoint
- ❑ VirtualPoint
- ❑ TextDocument

In the next four sections you'll read more about these five interfaces and their properties and methods.

TextSelection

This interface provides several properties and methods for editing the selected text in documents.

TextSelection represents the editor commands in the Visual Studio IDE, and it may fail to perform an editing task if your document is opened in read-only mode.

Table 8-5 provides a short description of the TextSelection properties.

Table 8-5: The TextSelection Properties

Property	Description
ActivePoint	Returns an instance of the EnvDTE.VirtualPoint object that shows the current endpoint of the selected text
AnchorColumn	Returns the origin column index of the selected text
AnchorPoint	Returns an instance of the EnvDTE.VirtualPoint object that represents the origin point of the selected text
BottomLine	Returns the index of the bottom line of the selected text
BottomPoint	Returns an instance of the EnvDTE.VirtualPoint object that represents the bottom point of the selected text
CurrentColumn	Returns the index of the current column in the selected text
CurrentLine	Returns the index of the current line in the selected text
DTE	Returns the DTE object instance in which this object is located
IsActiveEndGreater	Indicates whether the active point is equal to the bottom point
IsEmpty	Indicates whether the anchor point is equal to the active point
Mode	A property of vsSelectedMode enumeration type that specifies whether dragging the mode selects the text in box or stream mode. The vsSelectionModeBox value is for box mode and the vsSelectionModeStream value is for stream mode.
Parent	Gets the direct parent of the current object
Text	A string property that gets or sets the selected text
TextPane	Returns an instance of the TextPane object that represents the text pane containing the selected text
TextRanges	Returns an instance of the TextRanges collection object. It contains several TextRange objects for each line in the selected text.
TopLine	Returns the index of the top line in the selected text in the document
TopPoint	Returns an instance of the VirtualPoint object that specifies the coordination of the top point in the selected text in the document

Table 8-6 describes all the methods for the TextSelection interface.

Table 8-6: The TextSelection Interface Methods

Method	Description
Backspace	Removes the specified number of characters to the left
Cancel	Cancels any applied change
ChangeCase	Changes the case option to the specified value. It gets a vsCaseOptions enumeration value as a parameter: vsCaseOptionsCapitalize capitalizes the text; vsCaseOptionsLowercase specifies lowercase, and vsCaseOptionsUppercase specifies uppercase.
CharLeft	Moves the object the specified number of characters to the left.
	For example, if you select a text with the mouse, then this moves the selection the specified number of characters to the left.
CharRight	Moves the object the specified number of characters to the right
ClearBookmark	Clears all bookmarks in the selected text
Collapse	Collapses the text to the active point
Copy	Copies the text to the clipboard
Cut	Copies the text to the clipboard and removes it from the buffer
Delete	Deletes the text
DeleteLeft	Deletes the specified number of characters from the left
DeleteWhitespace	Deletes all whitespace (empty) characters around the current location horizontally or vertically
DestructiveInsert	Adds the new text and overwrites the current text
EndOfDocument	Moves the object to the end of the document
EndOfLine	Moves the object to the end of the line
FindPattern	Searches for a specified pattern in the text from the current point to the end of the document
FindText	Searches for the specified text in the document from the active point to the end of the document
GotoLine	Moves the active point to the specified line
Indent	Indents all lines in the selected text by the specified number of indentations
Insert	Inserts the given string in the current location of the text
InsertFromFile	Inserts the content of the specified file in the active point of the text

(continued)

Method	Description
LineDown	Moves the object to the next line
LineUp	Moves the object to the previous line
MoveTo	Moves the active point to the specified point
MoveToAbsoluteOffset	Moves the active point to the specified one-based character offset
MoveToDisplayColumn	Moves the active point to the specified display column
MoveToLineAndOffset	Moves the active point to the specified location
MoveToPoint	Moves the active point to the specified location
NewLine	Adds the specified number of new-line breaks to the active point
NextBookmark	Moves the active point to the next bookmark
OutlineSection	Creates an outline section in the active point
PadToColumn	Adds whitespace characters to the text in the specified column
PageDown	Moves the active point to the next page
PageUp	Moves the active point to the previous page
Paste	Pastes the content of the clipboard to the active point
PreviousBookmark	Moves the active point to the previous bookmark
ReplacePattern	Replaces the pattern text with the new text in the selected text
ReplaceText	Replaces the text matching the pattern with the new text
SelectAll	Selects the entire text in the buffer
SelectLine	Selects the entire text in the current line
SetBookmark	Inserts a bookmark at the current line
SmartFormat	Formats the selected text
StartOfDocument	Moves the active point to the beginning of the document
StartOfLine	Moves the active point to the beginning of the current line
SwapAnchor	Replaces the position of the active and anchor points
Tabify	Converts all space characters to tabs in the selected text
Unindent	Removes all indents from the selected text
WordLeft	Moves the selected text to the left of the specified number of words
WordRight	Moves the selected text to the right of the specified number of words

Yes, there are indeed many properties and methods for this interface. Moreover, there are many methods with similar applications and different parameters. This large number of properties and methods gives you plenty of power to manipulate your code. Each method comes in handy for a given scenario and saves you from writing a lot of code.

TextPoint

This interface represents a location in the text within a document in general form. It provides base properties and methods to find the location of text in the document.

TextPoint is the root interface in an interface hierarchy, and the EditPoint and VirtualPoint interfaces (described later) are in the lower levels of this hierarchy (see Figure 8-4).

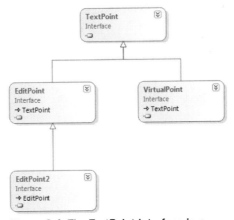

Figure 8-4: The TextPoint interface in a hierarchy

TextPoint has many similarities with EditPoint, but there is a main distinction between them: TextPoint acts on the text in the text editor, whereas EditPoint acts on the text in the text buffer.

However, the TextPoint interface has fewer properties and methods than EditPoint. Its properties are outlined in Table 8-7.

Table 8-7: The TextPoint Properties

Property	Description
AbsoluteCharOffset	Returns an offset (based on one) for the object from the beginning of the document
AtEndOfDocument	Indicates whether the object is at the end of the document
AtEndOfLine	Indicates whether the object is at the end of the line

(continued)

Property	Description
AtStartOfDocument	Indicates whether the object is at the start of the document
AtStartOfLine	Indicates whether the object is at the start of the line
CodeElement	Returns an instance of the `CodeElement` object for the object
DisplayColumn	Returns the display column index for the object
DTE	Returns an instance of the DTE object containing the `TextPoint` object
Line	Returns the line number of the object
LineCharOffset	Returns the character offset of the object
LineLength	Returns the length of the line, including the object
Parent	Returns the direct parent object of the `TextPoint` object

The methods of the TextPoint interface are described in Table 8-8.

Table 8-8: The TextPoint Methods

Method	Description
CreateEditPoint	Creates and returns an instance of the `EditPoint` object to edit the document
EqualTo	Compares a given `TextPoint` object with the current object and indicates whether the `AbsoluteCharOffset` property of the current object is equal to the same property of the given object
GreaterThan	Compares a given `TextPoint` object with the current object and indicates whether the `AbsoluteCharOffset` property of the current object is greater than the same property of the given object
LessThan	Compares a given `TextPoint` object with the current object and indicates whether the `AbsoluteCharOffset` property of the current object is less than the same property of the given object
TryToShow	Tries to display the `TextPoint` location

EditPoint

The EditPoint interface enables you to edit the text in your documents and represents a point in the document. As you saw in the previous section, this interface is derived from the TextPoint interface.

EditPoint is one of the interfaces that underwent some improvements in Visual Studio 2005, so a new EditPoint2 interface that derives from the original EditPoint was added to the automation model.

EditPoint provides more properties and methods than TextPoint, enabling you to apply many changes to your code and text. Properties of this interface are listed in Table 8-9. They're similar to properties of the TextPoint interface.

Table 8-9: The EditPoint Properties

Property	Description
AbsoluteCharOffset	Returns an offset (based on one) for the object from the beginning of the document
AtEndOfDocument	Indicates whether the object is at the end of the document
AtEndOfLine	Indicates whether the object is at the end of the line
AtStartOfDocument	Indicates whether the object is at the start of the document
AtStartOfLine	Indicates whether the object is at the start of the line
CodeElement	Returns an instance of the CodeElement object for the object
DisplayColumn	Returns the display column index for the object
DTE	Returns an instance of the DTE object containing the EditPoint object
Line	Returns the line number of the object
LineCharOffset	Returns the character offset of the object
LineLength	Returns the length of the line, including the object
Parent	Returns the direct parent object of the EditPoint object

The methods of the EditPoint interface are listed in Table 8-10.

Table 8-10: The EditPoint Methods

Method	Description
ChangeCase	Changes the case option to the specified value. It gets a vsCaseOptions enumeration value as a parameter: vsCaseOptionsCapitalize capitalizes the text; vsCaseOptionsLowercase specifies lowercase, and vsCaseOptionsUppercase specifies uppercase.
CharLeft	Moves the object a specified number of characters to the left
CharRight	Moves the object a specified number of characters to the right
ClearBookmark	Clears all bookmarks in the selected text
Copy	Copies the text to the clipboard

(continued)

Method	Description
CreateEditPoint	Creates and returns an instance of the `EditPoint` object at the active point
Cut	Copies the text to the clipboard and removes it from the buffer
Delete	Deletes the text
DeleteWhitespace	Deletes all whitespace (empty) characters around the current location horizontally or vertically
EndOfDocument	Moves the object to the end of the document
EndOfLine	Moves the object to the end of the line
EqualTo	Compares a given `EditPoint` object with the current object and indicates whether the `AbsoluteCharOffset` property of the current object is equal to the same property of the given object
FindPattern	Searches for a specified pattern in the text from the current point to the end of the document
GetLines	Returns a string of the text between two specified lines
GetText	Returns a string of the text between the current point and the specified point in the text buffer
GreaterThan	Compares a given `TextPoint` object with the current object and indicates whether the `AbsoluteCharOffset` property of the current object is greater than the same property of the given object
Indent	Indents all lines in the selected text by the specified number of indentations
Insert	Inserts the given string in the current location of the text
InsertFromFile	Inserts the content of the specified file in the active point of the text
LessThan	Compares a given `TextPoint` object with the current object and indicates whether the `AbsoluteCharOffset` property of the current object is less than the same property of the given object
LineDown	Moves the object to the next line
LineUp	Moves the object to the previous line
MoveToAbsoluteOffset	Moves the active point to the specified one-based character offset
MoveToLineAndOffset	Moves the active point to the specified location
MoveToPoint	Moves the active point to the specified location
NextBookmark	Moves the active point to the next bookmark
OutlineSection	Creates an outline section in the active point
PadToColumn	Adds whitespace characters to the text at the specified column
Paste	Pastes the content of the clipboard to the active point

Method	Description
PreviousBookmark	Moves the active point to the previous bookmark
ReadOnly	Indicates whether the specified range has a read-only text
ReplacePattern	Replaces the pattern text with the new text in the selected text
ReplaceText	Replaces the text matching the pattern with the new text
SetBookmark	Inserts a bookmark at the current line
SmartFormat	Formats the selected text
StartOfDocument	Moves the active point to the beginning of the document
StartOfLine	Moves the active point to the beginning of the current line
TryToShow	Tries to display the EditPoint location
Unindent	Removes all indents from the selected text
WordLeft	Moves the selected text to the left of the specified number of words
WordRight	Moves the selected text to the right of the specified number of words

VirtualPoint

This interface enables you to manipulate the text outside the margins of the text in a document. VirtualPoint is derived from TextPoint and is similar to it, but it can refer to a virtual space in the document and can cover spaces to the right or left of the text.

Table 8-11 describes the list of properties for the VirtualPoint interface.

Table 8-11: The VirtualPoint Properties

Property	Description
AbsoluteCharOffset	Returns an offset (based on one) for the object from the beginning of the document
AtEndOfDocument	Indicates whether the object is at the end of the document
AtEndOfLine	Indicates whether the object is at the end of the line
AtStartOfDocument	Indicates whether the object is at the start of the document
AtStartOfLine	Indicates whether the object is at the start of the line
CodeElement	Returns an instance of the CodeElement object for the object
DisplayColumn	Returns the display column index for the object

(continued)

Property	Description
DTE	Returns an instance of the DTE object containing the `VirtualPoint` object
Line	Returns the line number of the object
LineCharOffset	Returns the character offset of the object
LineLength	Returns the length of the line, including the object
Parent	Returns the direct parent object of the `VirtualPoint` object
VirtualCharOffset	Returns the column offset of a virtual point
VirtualDisplayColumn	Returns the display column index of the current virtual point

You can check the methods of this interface in Table 8-12.

Table 8-12: The VirtualPoint Methods

Method	Description
CreateEditPoint	Creates and returns an instance of the `EditPoint` object to edit the document
EqualTo	Compares a given `VirtualPoint` object with the current object and indicates whether the `AbsoluteCharOffset` property of the current object is equal to the same property of the given object
GreaterThan	Compares a given `VirtualPoint` object with the current object and indicates whether the `AbsoluteCharOffset` property of the current object is greater than the same property of the given object
LessThan	Compares a given `VirtualPoint` object with the current object and indicates whether the `AbsoluteCharOffset` property of the current object is less than the same property of the given object
TryToShow	Tries to display the `VirtualPoint` location

TextDocument

TextDocument is another interface related to the code editor in the Visual Studio IDE. This interface is based on the Visual C++ 6.0 version of the `Document` object and represents a text file that is open in the Visual Studio code editor.

I won't describe all the properties and methods of this interface because they're similar to what you've seen many times in this chapter; instead, I'll just provide a quick overview about the use of this interface.

Sometimes TextDocument is a good alternative for TextSelection, especially when you're working with a text editor and the code contained in it. In this case, it's better to use the TextDocument interface, rather than TextSelection, because it's simpler and provides appropriate properties and methods for working with a code editor. This interface is a good starting point before you to move to other interfaces, such as TextPoint, EditPoint, and VirtualPoint, to manipulate the code.

You can get an instance of this interface by setting your object instance to the `Object` method of the `ActiveDocument` of the DTE interface.

Document Manipulation Samples

Now that you've looked at the key interfaces used in document manipulation in the automation model, let's take a look at some examples that illustrate how they work together.

A wide range of examples could be used here, but I've limited the examples to only some common and simple ones in order to highlight the basic principles and get you started. Training is a key indicator for success in programming, so I strongly recommend that you take a look at the source code of open-source (or shared source) add-ins to learn more about the code model.

Commenting a Piece of Code

This first example is a common sample in all extensibility references and is very simple. Suppose that you want to select a piece of C# code and comment it out in the editor by running an add-in. This feature is supported by Visual Studio out of the box, but it is covered here to demonstrate how to use these interfaces.

Listing 8-3 shows the main method that does this job. (You can download the full source package for this chapter from the Web site.)

Listing 8-3: Commenting a Piece of Code

```
private void CommentCode()
{
    // Create an instance of the TextSelection for selected text
    TextSelection selectedText =
        this._applicationObject.ActiveDocument.Selection as TextSelection;
    // Create an instance of the EditPoint of the top point of the selected text
    EditPoint topPoint = selectedText.TopPoint.CreateEditPoint();
    // Create an instance of the TextPoint of the bottom point of the selected text
    TextPoint bottomPoint = selectedText.BottomPoint;

    while (topPoint.LessThan(bottomPoint))
    {
        // Insert the comment characters
        topPoint.Insert("//");
        // Move to next line
        topPoint.LineDown(1);
        // Move to the start of the line
        topPoint.StartOfLine();
    }
}
```

Let me describe this simple code in a nutshell (even though code comments can help you to understand what's going on). First we create an instance of the `TextSelection` object to keep the selected text by setting its value to the `ActiveDocument.Selection` property of the DTE. Then we create two objects to keep references to the start point and end point of the selected text. The first object should be of the `EditPoint` type, because we want to use its methods to edit the selected text. The second object can be of the simple `TextPoint` type, because we just want to access its information.

In a `While` loop, we use the `LessThan` method of the `EditPoint` object to traverse through the selected text from the start to the end, and at each step we first inset double slashes to comment the line of code, and then move the active point to the next line and the starting point of that line.

Figure 8-5 shows the result of running this add-in for a piece of code.

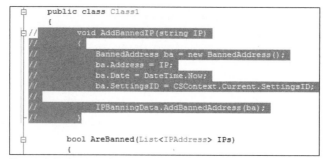

Figure 8-5: Result of commenting a piece of C# code

Inserting a Comment Before Selected Code

For the second example, suppose that you want to insert a line of code comments before the selected text, perhaps to remind yourself to add comments for your code.

The code is presented in Listing 8-4.

Listing 8-4: Inserting a Comment Before Selected Code

```
private void InsertComment()
{
    // Create an instance of the TextSelection for selected text
    TextSelection selectedText =
        this._applicationObject.ActiveDocument.Selection as TextSelection;

    // Create an instance of the EditPoint of the top point of the selected text
    EditPoint topPoint = selectedText.TopPoint.CreateEditPoint();

    // Move to the upper line
    topPoint.LineUp(1);
    // Move to the end of line
    topPoint.EndOfLine();
    // Insert the code comment
    topPoint.Insert("\n// TODO: Insert a code comment");
}
```

First, a `TextSelection` object is created. Then an `EditPoint` object comes into play to refer to the top point. After that, the active point is moved to the end of the preceding line, and finally the code comment is inserted there.

You can see the result in Figure 8-6.

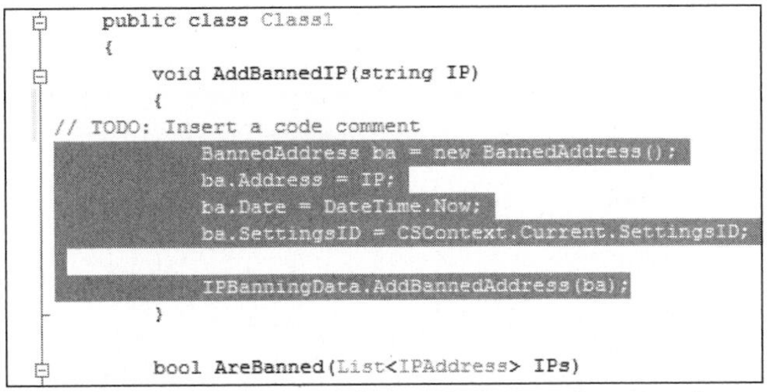

```
public class Class1
{
    void AddBannedIP(string IP)
    {
// TODO: Insert a code comment
        BannedAddress ba = new BannedAddress();
        ba.Address = IP;
        ba.Date = DateTime.Now;
        ba.SettingsID = CSContext.Current.SettingsID;

        IPBanningData.AddBannedAddress(ba);
    }

    bool AreBanned(List<IPAddress> IPs)
```

Figure 8-6: Inserting a comment before the selected code

Adding a Property to the End of the Document

In the third sample, we won't manipulate any selected text. Instead, we'll add a property to the end of a C# code document regardless of the selected text.

Listing 8-5 is the source code of the implementation.

Listing 8-5: Adding a Property to the End of the Document

```
private void AddProperty()
{
    // Create an instance of the TextDocument object
    TextDocument document =
        this._applicationObject.ActiveDocument.Object("TextDocument") as
TextDocument;

    // Create an instance of the EndPoint object
    EditPoint endPoint = document.EndPoint.CreateEditPoint();
    // Move two lines up
    endPoint.LineUp(2);
    // Move to the end of the line
    endPoint.EndOfLine();
    // Insert the property code
    endPoint.Insert("\n public int NewProperty { get; set; } \n");
}
```

This code first creates an instance of the `TextDocument` object by using the `Object` method of the `ActiveDocument` property of the DTE instance. This `TextDocument` object has an `EndPoint` property that enables us to create an instance of the `EditPoint` object, move to two lines earlier, and insert the property code at the end of the line. You move the active point to two lines earlier to insert the code before the end of the class file and namespace. This case assumes that you have a standard formatted C# class code that ends right after the end of the namespace block.

Obviously, this isn't a very professional way to handle this situation, especially for C# code, because you can't guarantee that by moving two lines earlier and inserting the code, you'll reach a valid class. The point was to merely show the main concepts in a simple form.

The output from the preceding code is shown in Figure 8-7.

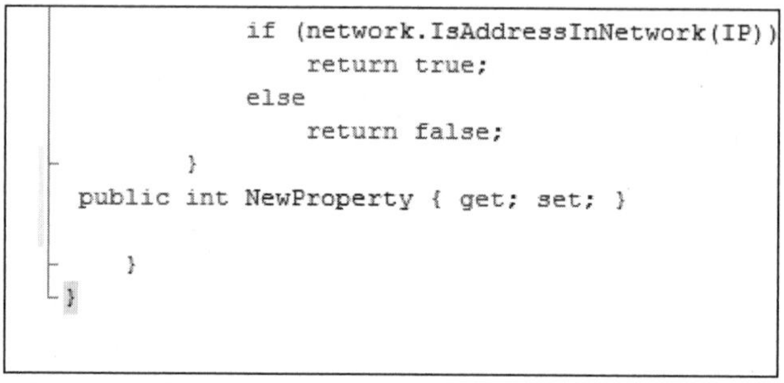

```
                    if (network.IsAddressInNetwork(IP))
                        return true;
                    else
                        return false;
                }
        public int NewProperty { get; set; }


            }
    }
```

Figure 8-7: Adding a property to the end of the document

Deleting the Current Line

The fourth and last sample provides an add-in that deletes the entire current line. You just need to move the cursor to a part of the editor, and the add-in deletes that line automatically.

Listing 8-6 shows the simple code for this sample.

Listing 8-6: Deleting the Current Line

```
private void DeleteCurrentLine()
{
    // Create an instance of the TextDocument object
    TextDocument document =
        this._applicationObject.ActiveDocument.Object("TextDocument") as
    TextDocument;

    // Select the current line
    document.Selection.SelectLine();
    // Delete the selection
    document.Selection.Delete(1);
}
```

After creating an instance of the TextDocument object, you select the current line by calling the SelectLine method of the Selection property of the TextDocument object, and then call the Delete method to delete the selected line.

Figures 8-8 and 8-9 show you how it works.

```
    void AddBannedIP(string IP)
    {
        BannedAddress ba = new BannedAddress();
        ba.Address = IP;
        ba.Date = DateTime.Now;
        ba.SettingsID = CSContext.Current.SettingsID;

        IPBanningData.AddBannedAddress(ba);
    }

    bool AreBanned(List<IPAddress> IPs)
    {
```

Figure 8-8: Code before running the add-in

```
    void AddBannedIP(string IP)
    {
        BannedAddress ba = new BannedAddress();
        ba.Address = IP;
        ba.Date = DateTime.Now;
        ba.SettingsID = CSContext.Current.SettingsID;

    }

    bool AreBanned(List<IPAddress> IPs)
    {
```

Figure 8-9: Code after running the add-in to delete the current line

Summary

Manipulating documents in the editor was the subject of this chapter. Following a brief introduction, you learned about the Documents collection and the Document interface. After that you learned about some related interfaces, such as TextSelection, TextPoint, EditPoint, VirtualPoint, and TextDocument.

After learning about these items, you explored some sample add-ins that should help you understand how to merge and apply all these interfaces to manipulate your codes.

9

Manipulating Code and the Build Process

In Chapter 8 you learned how to manipulate the text in the editors and documents. That was a general case, because you were working with text content without being concerned about its meaning, but what about the programming code?

In Visual Studio you usually write code and don't use it as an editor for text data (who wants to pay for Visual Studio licenses to edit pure text data?!). Therefore, predictably, you need to extend your coding capabilities. This is a common goal of many add-ins for Visual Studio, such as Refactor and ReSharper.

The code model enables you to manipulate programming code and extend Visual Studio to modify it on-the-fly. This part of the automation model provides a set of APIs for working with different pieces of code such as classes and functions. You'll likely agree that it's not logical to get the code as pure text and then apply string manipulation functions to modify it every time you want to change something in your code. This would also be hard to implement (just as string manipulations are hard to implement).

In this chapter, you'll learn all about this and how to manipulate your programming code. While this is the main topic of the chapter, you'll also read about other topics related to building solutions and projects and manipulating your build process. Chapter 21 is dedicated to MSBuild, the Microsoft build engine for custom and automated builds, but things work a bit differently here, and you'll learn how to use the automation model to manipulate your build processes.

In a nutshell, this chapter covers the following:

❑ An introduction to the code model

❑ The CodeModel and FileCodeModel interfaces

❑ Different code element interfaces

❑ How to manipulate the code with code model objects

❑ The SolutionBuild interface

Introduction

The code model represents the programming code in a hierarchical form. This means that it creates a hierarchy of objects for classes that represents namespaces, classes, methods, properties, variables, and so on. Using this structure, you can traverse through your code and manipulate it.

The first interface that you need to care about is the CodeModel interface, and the second one is the FileCodeModel. CodeModel is an interface that enables you to access code elements within a project, and the FileCodeModel interface enables you to access code elements within a project item (a single file).

Both these interfaces work similarly, and the most important property of both is `CodeElements`. `CodeElements` is a property that holds the list of all your code-elements; hierarchy, with different classes (such as namespaces, classes, methods, and properties).

Several types of code elements are available for specific purposes. The CodeElement interface provides the general form of representation of a code element. Along with this interface, some other interfaces are available for special purposes. Following is a short list of common interfaces:

❑ CodeNamespace

❑ CodeClass

❑ CodeFunction

❑ CodeProperty

❑ CodeVariable

❑ CodeEnum

The names will suggest their purpose to you. Figure 9-1 shows the structure for these classes in a schematic form.

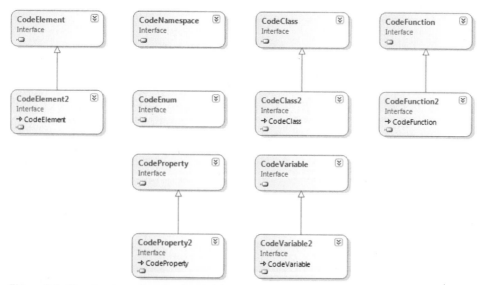

Figure 9-1: The structure of code element types

This figure illustrates that even though you may have assumed that different code-element classes are derived from the base CodeElement interface, that isn't the case; each interface is independent of the others.

Moreover, you can see that most of these interfaces are enhanced in Visual Studio 2005 and have a newer version derived from the original type (indicated by the 2 index at the end).

The list of available code-element classes isn't limited to these few interfaces. There are many more types. Talking about all of them is beyond the scope of this book. You can find them on the MSDN, but another technique to see a quick view of them is to check the vsCMElement enumeration type values. This enumeration type is the type of the `Kind` property of the CodeElement interface. The structure of this enumeration type is shown in Figure 9-2.

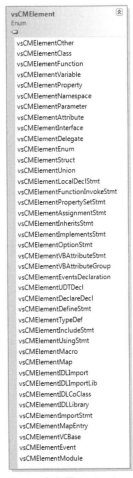

Figure 9-2: The structure of the vsCMElement enumeration type

Code Elements Hierarchy

Now let's take a look at the hierarchy structure of code elements in a sample code. This way you can get a good understanding of the hierarchy, which is a key point in working with the code model — and better than reading several paragraphs of theory.

First consider the simple C# code shown in Listing 9-1.

Listing 9-1: Checking for the Code Element Hierarchy

```csharp
using System;
using System.Collections.Generic;
using System.Text;

namespace WroxProVSX
{
    public class Chapter9
    {
        public int SampleProperty { get; set; }

        public void SampleMethod1(int param1)
        {
            // Do something here
        }

        private int SampleMethod2(int param1, string param2)
        {
            // Do something here
            return 0;
        }
    }
}
```

In the following paragraphs, you'll see the code-element class hierarchy for this code in an output. You may still have some questions when reading this code, but read the rest of the chapter to learn how it all works. For now, just focus on the hierarchy structure.

Listing 9-2 shows the source code of an add-in that I wrote to show this hierarchy. The highlighted code is what you should focus on at the moment, and I'll explain just how it works (I removed the auto-generated code comments for the Visual Studio add-in code template to make things simpler and save space).

Listing 9-2: Add-in Code to Show the Hierarchy of Code Elements

```csharp
using System;
using Extensibility;
using EnvDTE;
using EnvDTE80;
using Microsoft.VisualStudio.CommandBars;
```

```csharp
using System.Resources;
using System.Reflection;
using System.Globalization;
using System.IO;
using System.Text;
using System.Windows.Forms;

namespace ShowCodeElements
{
    public class Connect : IDTExtensibility2, IDTCommandTarget
    {
        public Connect()
        {
        }

        public void OnConnection(object application, ext_ConnectMode connectMode,
object addInInst,
            ref Array custom)
        {
            _applicationObject = (DTE2)application;
            _addInInstance = (AddIn)addInInst;
            if (connectMode == ext_ConnectMode.ext_cm_UISetup)
            {
                object[] contextGUIDS = new object[] { };
                Commands2 commands = (Commands2)_applicationObject.Commands;
                string toolsMenuName;

                try
                {
                    string resourceName;
                    ResourceManager resourceManager = new
ResourceManager("ShowCodeElements.CommandBar",
                        Assembly.GetExecutingAssembly());
                    CultureInfo cultureInfo = new
CultureInfo(_applicationObject.LocaleID);

                    if (cultureInfo.TwoLetterISOLanguageName == "zh")
                    {
                        resourceName = String.Concat(cultureInfo.Name, "Tools");
                    }
                    else
                    {
                        resourceName =
String.Concat(cultureInfo.TwoLetterISOLanguageName, "Tools");
                    }
                    toolsMenuName = resourceManager.GetString(resourceName);
                }
```

(continued)

Listing 9-2 *(continued)*

```
            catch
            {
                toolsMenuName = "Tools";
            }

            Microsoft.VisualStudio.CommandBars.CommandBar menuBarCommandBar =
((Microsoft.VisualStudio.CommandBars.CommandBars)_applicationObject
.CommandBars)["MenuBar"];

            CommandBarControl toolsControl =
menuBarCommandBar.Controls[toolsMenuName];
            CommandBarPopup toolsPopup = (CommandBarPopup)toolsControl;

            try
            {
                Command command = commands.AddNamedCommand2(_addInInstance,
                    "ShowCodeElements", "ShowCodeElements", "Executes the
command for ShowCodeElements",
                    true, 59, ref contextGUIDS,
(int)vsCommandStatus.vsCommandStatusSupported +
                    (int)vsCommandStatus.vsCommandStatusEnabled,
(int)vsCommandStyle.vsCommandStylePictAndText,
                    vsCommandControlType.vsCommandControlTypeButton);

                if ((command != null) && (toolsPopup != null))
                {
                    command.AddControl(toolsPopup.CommandBar, 1);
                }
            }
            catch (System.ArgumentException)
            {
            }
        }
    }

    public void OnDisconnection(ext_DisconnectMode disconnectMode, ref Array
custom)
    {
    }

    public void OnAddInsUpdate(ref Array custom)
    {
    }

    public void OnStartupComplete(ref Array custom)
    {
    }

    public void OnBeginShutdown(ref Array custom)
    {
    }
```

```csharp
        public void QueryStatus(string commandName, vsCommandStatusTextWanted
neededText,
            ref vsCommandStatus status, ref object commandText)
        {
            if (neededText ==
vsCommandStatusTextWanted.vsCommandStatusTextWantedNone)
            {
                if (commandName == "ShowCodeElements.Connect.ShowCodeElements")
                {
                    status =
(vsCommandStatus)vsCommandStatus.vsCommandStatusSupported |
                        vsCommandStatus.vsCommandStatusEnabled;
                    return;
                }
            }
        }

        public void Exec(string commandName, vsCommandExecOption executeOption, ref
object varIn,
            ref object varOut, ref bool handled)
        {
            handled = false;
            if (executeOption == vsCommandExecOption.vsCommandExecOptionDoDefault)
            {
                if (commandName == "ShowCodeElements.Connect.ShowCodeElements")
                {
                    // Get an instance of the FileCodeModel
                    FileCodeModel2 fileCodeModel =
this._applicationObject.ActiveDocument.ProjectItem
.FileCodeModel as FileCodeModel2;

                    // Get an instance of the CodeElements
                    CodeElements elements = fileCodeModel.CodeElements;

                    // Parse the root elements object to the method
                    ShowHierarchy(elements, 0);

                    // Show the output
                    MessageBox.Show(this.textToShow.ToString());

                    handled = true;
                    return;
                }
            }
        }

        private void ShowHierarchy(CodeElements elements, int level)
        {
            // Iterate through all elements available in the passed CodeElements
            foreach (CodeElement element in elements)
```

(continued)

Listing 9-2 *(continued)*

```
        {
            try
            {
                // Add the text to the output string
                AddText(string.Format("{0} ({1})",
                    element.Name, element.Kind), level * 4);

                // Call the method recursively for children elements
                if (element.Children != null)
                    ShowHierarchy(element.Children, level + 1);
            }
            catch
            {
            }
        }
    }

    private void AddText(string text, int indentationLevel)
    {
        // Format the text and add it to the output
        string tempText = text.PadLeft(text.Length + indentationLevel);
        this.textToShow.Append(tempText + "\n");
    }

    private StringBuilder textToShow = new StringBuilder();

    private DTE2 _applicationObject;
    private AddIn _addInInstance;

    }
}
```

Running this add-in for the code presented in Listing 9-1, you get a result like what is shown in Figure 9-3. Note that the indentation presents the level of the hierarchy; element names are shown; and element types are added inside parentheses.

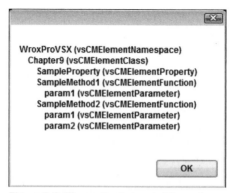

Figure 9-3: The code elements hierarchy for the sample code

Describing the source code of an add-in would be a good sample for this chapter, so let's do that next. This code adds a private variable to the add-in class of type StringBuilder. This variable keeps the output string. Also added are a few lines of code to the Exec method of the add-in (see Listing 9-3).

Listing 9-3: The Exec Method of the Add-in

```csharp
public void Exec(string commandName, vsCommandExecOption executeOption, ref object varIn,
    ref object varOut, ref bool handled)
{
    handled = false;
    if (executeOption == vsCommandExecOption.vsCommandExecOptionDoDefault)
    {
        if (commandName == "ShowCodeElements.Connect.ShowCodeElements")
        {
            // Get an instance of the FileCodeModel
            FileCodeModel2 fileCodeModel =
                this._applicationObject.ActiveDocument.ProjectItem.FileCodeModel
                as FileCodeModel2;

            // Get an instance of the CodeElements
            CodeElements elements = fileCodeModel.CodeElements;

            // Parse the root elements object to the method
            ShowHierarchy(elements, 0);

            // Show the output
            MessageBox.Show(this.textToShow.ToString());

            handled = true;
            return;
        }
    }
}
```

In the Exec method, we first get an instance of the FileCodeModel2 for the currently opened document (which must be a code document such as a class, a module, or an enumeration type). We can get this instance from the FileCodeModel property of the ProjectItem object instance, which can be found in the ActiveDocument property of the DTE.

In the next step, we get an instance of the CodeElements object from the CodeElements property of the FileCodeModel instance. After this, we pass the root CodeElements object to the ShowHierarchy method to generate the output string and finally show the output in a MessageBox.

The ShowHierarchy method is the heart of this add-in (see Listing 9-4).

Listing 9-4: The ShowHierarchy Method

```csharp
private void ShowHierarchy(CodeElements elements, int level)
{
    // Iterate through all elements available in the passed CodeElements
    foreach (CodeElement element in elements)
```

(continued)

Listing 9-4 *(continued)*

```
        {
            try
            {
                // Add the text to the output string
                AddText(string.Format("{0} ({1})",
                    element.Name, element.Kind), level * 4);

                // Call the method recursively for children elements
                if (element.Children != null)
                    ShowHierarchy(element.Children, level + 1);
            }
            catch
            {
            }
        }
    }
```

Here is where we iterate through all `CodeElement` objects in the CodeElements collection and add their names and kinds to the output (with appropriate indentation), and then call the `ShowHierarchy` recursively for each `CodeElement`.

As shown in the code, you nest your code to access the `CodeElement` *properties inside a* try . . . catch *block. This is something that you always need to be careful about, because sometimes, for some code elements, properties may be null and cause exceptions for your application. This usually happens for recursive solutions like this.*

The other part of this implementation logic is the `AddText` method (see Listing 9-5).

Listing 9-5: The AddText Method

```
private void AddText(string text, int indentationLevel)
{
    // Format the text and add it to the output
    string tempText = text.PadLeft(text.Length + indentationLevel);
    this.textToShow.Append(tempText + "\n");
}
```

This code is very simple and the `AddText` method just adds the string to the output with the appropriate indentation level. It uses the `PadLeft` method of type `string` to get this done.

CodeElement

As mentioned previously, the CodeElement interface is the general form of representing a code element. This interface provides some general properties and methods to manipulate a code element.

However, other special forms of code element types provide more specific methods and properties to work with code elements, such as namespaces, classes, and functions.

Discussing all these code element types is beyond the scope of this book and probably isn't necessary anyway, as readers of this book are likely to be experienced developers who can find their way after reading the examples provided in this chapter. However, I'll discuss the CodeElement interface, along with a few common code element types. You can get what you need from these discussions, because the CodeElement logical structure, common properties, and methods are the same in all code element types. The CodeElement is one of the interfaces that is enhanced in Visual Studio 2005, along with CodeElement2.

Typically, all code element types have some properties and methods that enable you to get an instance of the `TextPoint` (and hence `EditPoint` and `VirtualPoint`) object for the start or end of the common parts of the code (for example, header or body). These methods and properties are a common part of the structure of code element types and are helpful when you want to work with or edit a part of the code. Finding the location of a part of the code is hard without these methods and properties.

On the other hand, these code element types provide two properties for the start and end points of their code that are of the TextPoint type, named StartPoint and EndPoint, respectively.

Table 9-1 provides a list of CodeElement2 properties.

Table 9-1: The CodeElement2 Properties

Property	Description
Children	Returns a collection of different `CodeElements` objects contained in this object
Collection	Returns an instance of the `CodeElements` object that is the container of the current `CodeElement` object
DTE	Returns the DTE object instance containing the current `CodeElement` object
ElementID	Returns the string value of an identifier corresponding to the current code element
EndPoint	Returns an instance of the `TextPoint` object for the end point of the code item
Extender	Returns the extender object for the current code element if it exists
ExtenderCATID	Returns the extender category ID for the current object
ExtenderNames	Returns a list of Extender names for the current object
FullName	Returns the fully qualified name of the code element
InfoLocation	Returns some information about the code model
IsCodeType	Determines whether an instance of the `CodeType` object can be created, based on the current object
Kind	Returns an enumeration value of type vsCMElement
Language	Returns the development language for the code element
Name	String value of the name of the current object
ProjectItem	Returns an instance of the `ProjectItem` object corresponding to the current object
StartPoint	Returns an instance of the `TextPoint` object for the start point of the code item

Table 9-2 presents a list of CodeElement2 methods.

Table 9-2: The CodeElement2 Methods

Method	Description
GetEndPoint	Returns an instance of the TextPoint object for the location of the end of the code element
GetStartPoint	Returns an instance of the TextPoint object for the location of the start of the code element
RenameSymbol	Renames the symbol for the current code element to a new value by getting the string value of the new name

The following sections describe a few other common code-element types.

CodeNamespace

The CodeNamespace interface can be considered the container for other code elements, because in the real code the namespace is the container for other code.

You can read a description of CodeNamespace properties in Table 9-3.

Table 9-3: The CodeNamespace Properties

Property	Description
Children	Returns a collection of different CodeElements objects contained in this object
Collection	Returns an instance of the CodeElements object that is the container for the current CodeNamespace object
Comment	The string value of the comment associated with the namespace
DocComment	The string value of the document comment for the namespace
DTE	Returns the DTE object instance containing the current CodeNamespace object
ElementID	Returns the string value of an identifier corresponding to the current code element
EndPoint	Returns an instance of the TextPoint object for the end point of the code item
Extender	Returns the extender object for the current code element if it exists
ExtenderCATID	Returns the extender category ID for the current object
ExtenderNames	Returns a list of Extender names for the current object
FullName	Returns the fully qualified name of the code element

Property	Description
InfoLocation	Returns some information about the code model
IsCodeType	Determines whether an instance of the `CodeType` object can be created based on the current object
Kind	Returns an enumeration value for the vsCMElement type
Language	Returns the development language for the code element
Name	String value of the name of the current object
Parent	Returns the direct parent object of the current object
ProjectItem	Returns an instance of the `ProjectItem` object corresponding to the current object
StartPoint	Returns an instance of the `TextPoint` object for the start point of the code item

Table 9-4 describes the CodeNamespace methods.

Table 9-4: The CodeNamespace Methods

Method	Description
AddClass	Adds a new class to the namespace and returns an instance of the `CodeClass` object for it
AddDelegate	Adds a new delegate to the namespace and returns an instance of the `CodeDelegate` object for it
AddEnum	Adds a new enumerator to the namespace and returns an instance of the `CodeEnum` object for it
AddInterface	Adds a new interface to the namespace and returns an instance of the `CodeInterface` object for it
AddNamespace	Adds a new namespace to the namespace and returns an instance of the `CodeNamespace` object for it
AddStruct	Adds a new structure to the namespace and returns an instance of the `CodeStruct` object for it
GetEndPoint	Returns an instance of the `TextPoint` object for the location of the end of the code element
GetStartPoint	Returns an instance of the `TextPoint` object for the location of the start of the code element

CodeClass

The other type of code-element interface, and probably the most common one, is the CodeClass interface, which underwent an enhancement in Visual Studio 2005 and is now called CodeClass2.

This interface has more properties and methods than the other common code-element types. Its properties are listed in Table 9-5.

Table 9-5: The CodeClass2 Properties

Property	Description
Access	An enumeration value of vsCMAccess type for the access attributes of the code class
Attributes	Returns a collection of all attributes associated with the code class
Bases	Returns a collection of base classes for the code class
Children	Returns a collection of different code elements objects contained in this object
ClassKind	An enumeration value of the vsCMClassKind type for the kind of the class
Collection	Returns an instance of the `CodeElements` object that is the container for the current `CodeNamespace` object
Comment	The string value of the comment associated with the namespace
DataTypeKind	An enumeration value of the vsCMDataTypeKind type for the kind of data type for the class
DerivedTypes	Returns a collection of types derived from the current class
DocComment	The string value of the document comment for the class
DTE	Returns the DTE object instance containing the current `CodeClass` object
EndPoint	Returns an instance of the `TextPoint` object for the end point of the code item
Extender	Returns the extender object for the current code element if it exists
ExtenderCATID	Returns the extender category ID for the current object
ExtenderNames	Returns a list of Extender names for the current object
FullName	Returns the fully qualified name of the code element
ImplementedInterfaces	Returns a collection of interfaces that this class has implemented
InfoLocation	Returns some information about the code model
IsCodeType	Determines whether an instance of the `CodeType` object can be created based on the current object
IsDerivedFrom	Determines whether the class is derived from another type

Property	Description
IsGeneric	Determines whether the class is a generic class
Kind	Returns an enumeration value of the vsCMElement type
Language	Returns the development language for the code element
Members	Returns an instance of the `CodeElements` object for the collection of code elements contained in the class
Name	String value of the name of the current object
Namespace	Returns an instance of the `CodeNamespace` for the namespace containing the current class
Parent	Returns the direct parent object of the current object
PartialClasses	Returns an instance of the `CodeElements` object for the collection of the partial class associated with the current class
Parts	Returns an instance of the `CodeElements` object for the collection of the parts of the current class
ProjectItem	Returns an instance of the `ProjectItem` object corresponding to the current object
StartPoint	Returns an instance of the `TextPoint` object for the start point of the code item

Table 9-6 describes the methods of the CodeClass2 interface.

Table 9-6: The CodeClass2 Methods

Method	Description
AddAttribute	Adds a new attribute to the class and returns an instance of the `CodeAttribute` object for it
AddBase	Adds a new base class to the namespace and returns an instance of the `CodeElement` object for it
AddClass	Adds a new class to the class and returns an instance of the `CodeClass` object for it
AddDelegate	Adds a new delegate to the class and returns an instance of the `CodeDelegate` object for it
AddEnum	Adds a new enumerator to the namespace and returns an instance of the `CodeEnum` object for it

(continued)

Method	Description
AddEvent	Adds a new event to the class and returns an instance of the `CodeEvent` object for it
AddFunction	Adds a new function to the class and returns an instance of the `CodeFunction` object for it
AddImplementedInterface	Adds a new interface to the class and returns an instance of the `CodeInterface` object for it
AddProperty	Adds a new property to the class and returns an instance of the `CodeProperty` object for it
AddStruct	Adds a new structure to the class and returns an instance of the `CodeStruct` object for it
AddVariable	Adds a new variable to the class and returns an instance of the `CodeVariable` object for it
GetEndPoint	Returns an instance of the `TextPoint` object for the location of the end of the code element
GetStartPoint	Returns an instance of the `TextPoint` object for the location of the start of the code element
RemoveBase	Removes a code element from the list of the bases
RemoveInterface	Removes an interface from the list of implemented interfaces
RemoveMember	Removes a code element from the list of the members

CodeFunction

CodeFunction is the last code element type to be covered here. CodeFunction2 is the enhanced version of this interface in Visual Studio 2005.

To learn about CodeFunction2 properties, take a look at Table 9-7.

Table 9-7: The CodeFunction2 Properties

Property	Description
Access	An enumeration value of the vsCMAccess type for the access attributes of the code element
Attributes	Returns a collection of all attributes associated with the function
CanOverride	Determines whether the function can be overridden
Children	Returns a collection of different `CodeElements` objects contained in this object
Collection	Returns an instance of the `CodeElements` object that is the container of the current `CodeFunction` object

Property	Description
Comment	The string value of the comment associated with the function
DocComment	The string value of the document comment for the function
DTE	Returns the DTE object instance containing the current `CodeFunction` object
EndPoint	Returns an instance of the `TextPoint` object for the end point of the code item
Extender	Returns the extender object for the current code element if it exists
ExtenderCATID	Returns the extender category ID for the current object
ExtenderNames	Returns a list of Extender names for the current object
FullName	Returns the fully qualified name of the code element
FunctionKind	An enumeration value of type vsCMFunction for the kind of the function
InfoLocation	Returns some information about the code model
IsCodeType	Determines whether an instance of the `CodeType` object can be created based on the current object
IsGeneric	Determines whether the function is a generic function
IsOverloaded	Determines whether the function is overloaded
IsShared	Determines whether the function is defined as static and thus whether it is specific to the current object or not
Kind	Returns an enumeration value of type vsCMElement
Language	Returns the development language for the code element
MustImplement	Indicates whether the function must be implemented or not. This happens if it's defined as abstract.
Name	String value of the name of the current object
Overloads	Returns an instance of the `ProjectElements` object for the collection of overloads for this function
OverrideKind	An enumeration value of type vsCMOverrideKind for the kind of overriding strategy for the classes derived from the current class
Parameters	Returns an instance of the `CodeElements` object for the list of function parameters
Parent	Returns the direct parent object of the current object
ProjectItem	Returns an instance of the `ProjectItem` object corresponding to the current object
Prototype	Returns a string value of the stub definition for the function
StartPoint	Returns an instance of the `TextPoint` object for the start point of the code item
Type	An instance of the `CodeTypeRef` object that represents the type of the function

CodeFunction2 not only has these properties, but also a few methods, shown in Table 9-8.

Table 9-8: The CodeFunction2 Methods

Method	Description
AddAttribute	Adds a new attribute to the function and returns an instance of the `CodeAttribute` object for it
AddParameter	Adds a new parameter to the namespace and returns an instance of the `CodeParameter` object for it
GetEndPoint	Returns an instance of the `TextPoint` object for the location of the end of the code element
GetStartPoint	Returns an instance of the `TextPoint` object for the location of the start of the code element
RemoveParameter	Removes a parameter from the list of parameters

Code Manipulation Samples

Now that you have a good understanding of the theories of code manipulation, let's explore a few samples to learn how to apply these theories in real-world situations.

Adding a New Class to the Namespace

The first sample that we'll look at occurs when we want to add a new class to a namespace in a code file. Listing 9-6 is the source code of the main method for doing this.

Listing 9-6: Adding a New Class to a Namespace

```
private void AddClass()
{
    // Create an instance of the FileCodeModel
    FileCodeModel2 fileCodeModel =
        this._applicationObject.ActiveDocument.ProjectItem.FileCodeModel
        as FileCodeModel2;

    CodeElements elements = fileCodeModel.CodeElements;

    // Iterate through elements until we find the namespace element
    foreach (CodeElement element in elements)
    {
        if (element.Kind == vsCMElement.vsCMElementNamespace)
        {
```

```
        CodeNamespace ns = element as CodeNamespace;

        ns.AddClass("NewClass", 0, null, null, vsCMAccess.vsCMAccessPublic);

        return;
    }
  }
}
```

The code is simple to understand. After creating an instance of the `FileCodeModel` and getting access to its code elements, I wrote a `foreach` loop to iterate through all the elements in the document. At first glance, you might think that we can simply access the namespace element in the collection by using the zero indexes in it, but that won't work. There are some other code elements for reference statements that fill this index, so it's necessary to iterate through all the code elements and check each one's properties to ensure that the code element is a namespace.

After finding the namespace element, you convert it to a `CodeNamespace` object and call its `AddClass` method to add a new method to the namespace.

At this point it would be useful to take a look at the `AddClass` method in general and its parameters, which will be applicable to almost all the methods of other code element types.

The `AddClass` method gets the name of the class as the first parameter. The second parameter is the position. This parameter specifies the position in the code element where the new element should be added (a class in our case). In our discussion, because code-element collections start at 1 index, 0 inserts the new element at the start of the element. -1 is also an index to insert the element at the end of the code. You can also pass a `CodeElement` object, and in this case the new code element comes right after this element.

The third parameter is the optional `Bases` parameter, which can be set to the collection of base classes for the class to inherit from. You can pass 0, which is the default value, to avoid setting any base class.

The fourth parameter is an optional `ImplementedInterfaces` parameter that can be set to the collection of interfaces to be implemented by the class. You can also set this to 0 as the default value to avoid setting any interface (as I did).

The last parameter is the optional `Access` parameter of the vsCMAccess enumeration type for setting the access level of the new code element. I set it to be a public class.

The preceding discussion is applicable to many method parameters in the code model, so consider it a key part of this topic. Suppose that you have a code like Listing 9-7. Running this add-in for this code, you end up with a code like Listing 9-8.

Listing 9-7: Code to Add a New Class

```
using System;
using System.Collections.Generic;
using System.Text;

namespace WroxProVSX
{
}
```

Listing 9-8: Code after Adding a New Class

```
using System;
using System.Collections.Generic;
using System.Text;

namespace WroxProVSX
{
    public class NewClass
    {
    }
}
```

Adding a Property to a Class

The second example that we'll look at demonstrates how to add a new property to a class. The code is shown in Listing 9-9.

Listing 9-9: Adding a New Property to a Class

```
private void AddProperty()
{
    // Create an instance of the FileCodeModel
    FileCodeModel2 fileCodeModel =
        this._applicationObject.ActiveDocument.ProjectItem.FileCodeModel
        as FileCodeModel2;

    CodeElements elements = fileCodeModel.CodeElements;

    // Iterate through elements until we find the namespace element
    foreach (CodeElement element in elements)
    {
        if (element.Kind == vsCMElement.vsCMElementNamespace)
        {
            // Iterate through child elements until we find the class element
            foreach (CodeElement element2 in element.Children)
            {
                if (element2.Kind == vsCMElement.vsCMElementClass)
                {
                    CodeClass2 currentClass = element2 as CodeClass2;

                    currentClass.AddProperty("NewProperty", "NewProperty",
vsCMTypeRef.vsCMTypeRefInt,
                        0, vsCMAccess.vsCMAccessPublic, null);

                    return;
                }
            }
        }
    }
}
```

This code adds a `foreach` loop to iterate through the code elements in a document and find the namespace element. I then added a second `foreach` loop to loop through the namespace children and find the class. After finding the class code element, I called the `AddProperty` method to add a new property to the class.

Running this add-in results in the code shown in Listing 9-10.

Listing 9-10: Code to Add a New Property

```csharp
using System;
using System.Collections.Generic;
using System.Text;

namespace WroxProVSX
{
    public class Chapter9
    {
    }
}
```

This adds a new property, as shown in Listing 9-11.

Listing 9-11: Code after Adding a New Property

```csharp
using System;
using System.Collections.Generic;
using System.Text;

namespace WroxProVSX
{
    public class Chapter9
    {
        public int NewProperty
        {
            get
            {
                return default(int);
            }
            set
            {
            }
        }
    }
}
```

Builds

The other key aspect of the automation model is the capability to modify the build process in Visual Studio for solutions and projects. This section describes how you can modify the build process.

The main interface for working with the build process is the SolutionBuild interface, which also underwent an enhancement in Visual Studio 2005 and is now SolutionBuild2 (see Figure 9-4).

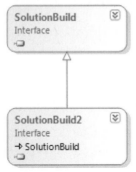

Figure 9-4: The SolutionBuild structure

You can access an instance of this object by using the `SolutionBuild` property of the Solution interface (in Visual Studio 2008 you have to use the Solution3 interface instead).

Table 9-9 lists the properties of the SolutionBuild2 interface.

Table 9-9: The SolutionBuild2 Properties

Property	Description
ActiveConfiguration	Returns an instance of the `SolutionConfiguration` object for the solution configurations
BuildDependencies	Returns an instance of the BuildDependencies collection to apply dependencies between projects
BuildState	Returns an instance of the vsBuildState enumeration value for the state of the build process
DTE	Returns the DTE object in which the current object is located
LastBuildInfo	Returns the number of projects that failed to build
LastPublishInfo	Returns the number of items that are published
Parent	Returns the direct parent object of the current object
PublishState	Returns an instance of the vsPublishState enumeration value for the state of the publishing process
SolutionConfigurations	Returns an instance of the SolutionConfigurations collection
StartupProjects	Specifies the names of the projects that are startup projects for the solution

Table 9-10 describes the methods of the SolutionBuild2 interface.

Table 9-10 The SolutionBuild2 Methods

Method	Description
Build	Builds the whole solution
BuildProject	Builds a specified project
Clean	Deletes all generated files for the previously built projects
Debug	Starts debugging the solution
Deploy	Starts deploying all projects in the solution that are marked to be deployed
DeployProject	Deploys a specified project
Publish	Publishes the solution
PublishProject	Publishes a specified project
Run	Starts running the solution

Building a Solution

The first example is easy. It creates a simple code (see Listing 9-12) to build the current solution. Building a solution is equivalent to choosing the Build Solution item from the Build menu in the Visual Studio IDE.

Listing 9-12: Building the Solution

```
private void Build()
{
    // Get an instance of the SolutionBuild
    SolutionBuild2 build =
        this._applicationObject.Solution.SolutionBuild
        as SolutionBuild2;

    // Build the solution
    build.Build(true);
}
```

After creating an instance of the SolutionBuild2 object, you call its Build method to build the solution. Passing true as a parameter forces it to wait until the build finishes.

Building a Particular Project

You can also build a particular project. This doesn't have an equivalent in the Visual Studio IDE, but it is simple to implement in code (see Listing 9-13). This example builds the first project in the solution.

Listing 9-13: Building a Particular Project

```
private void Build()
{
    // Get an instance of the SolutionBuild
    SolutionBuild2 build =
        this._applicationObject.Solution.SolutionBuild
        as SolutionBuild2;

    // Get an instance of the Project
    Project project =
        this._applicationObject.Solution.Projects.Item(1)
        as Project;

    // Build the project
    build.BuildProject("Release", project.FullName, true);
}
```

After creating the SolutionBuild2 object, you create an instance of the Project object for the first project in the solution. After this, you call the BuildProject method of the SolutionBuild2 object to build the project. This method gets a string value of solution configurations that you set to Release, as well as the unique name of the project and a Boolean parameter that instructs the code to wait until the build finishes before exiting the method.

Summary

Manipulating code and understanding the build process were the two main topics of this chapter. You first read a brief overview of the code model in Visual Studio and the hierarchy structure of code elements. Then you read about different code-element objects and their properties and methods. After that, you looked at some examples that demonstrated how to use these objects.

The second main topic of this chapter was manipulating the build process, and you learned about this at the end of the chapter by exploring the main SolutionBuild interface and two simple examples related to this topic.

10

The User Interface

So far you've just seen how to manipulate some abstract elements — we haven't yet covered anything about the user interface and what end users see. A big part of the automation model, however, is dedicated to manipulating the user interface (also abbreviated as UI for simplicity).

This topic can be grouped in three smaller topics:

❑ **Adding user interface elements to add-ins in order to get user inputs and options and implement the logic behind the add-in.** This makes your add-ins more powerful and user friendly. Interacting with users and responding to their choices make your add-ins professional and enables them to behave in the way that users expect. Up until now, the preceding chapters have just used simple MessageBox dialogs to show any output, because this was a quick and easy way to display information to users, but real life isn't limited to this option, and of course you need to be able to add user interface elements such as Windows Forms and user controls to your add-ins.

❑ **Manipulating the user interface elements in Visual Studio designers.** You also need to be able to access some information about Windows Forms and the controls on them in Visual Studio designers to extend their behavior or change it.

❑ **Working with common Visual Studio windows such as Toolbox, Output, Task List, and Error List.** These are considered separate parts in the automation model, and some APIs are dedicated to working with them. Because these windows are commonly used, it's clear that you need to be able to manipulate them in extensibility scenarios, so you need to know their APIs to some extent.

These main three topics comprise the fundamentals of this chapter, and I cover them one by one by dividing them into smaller subtopics and giving a detailed discussion of each. After reading this chapter, you should have a good understanding of the automation model and writing common add-ins; then, in the next few chapters, you'll learn about some related topics that will help you write more professional add-ins.

Here are the main things we'll cover in this chapter:

❑   How to add different user interface elements to your add-ins

❑   Adding menu items to Visual Studio IDE for your add-ins

❑   Adding toolbar items for your add-ins

❑   How to manipulate Windows Forms and the user controls for them

❑   Working with Visual Studio windows such as the Command window, the Output window, and the Task List.

Let's get started.

Adding User Interface Elements to Add-Ins

Without a good interaction with end users, your add-ins are nothing but some code! Not only does adding user interface elements to your add-ins make them better and easier for users, it also makes them professional and enables you to extend simple behaviors to more complex behaviors, leading to better functionality for your add-ins.

Adding user interface elements to add-ins isn't difficult; in fact, you can achieve it easily through Visual Studio IDE commands and Windows Forms.

In this section, you'll learn how to use both of these to enhance your add-ins.

Adding Elements with Commands

The first option for adding Visual Studio elements to add-ins is using Visual Studio commands. In this case, you define commands, add them to the Visual Studio commands collection, and create a mapping between commands and corresponding Visual Studio IDE elements, including the event logic behind them.

Here are two examples of this approach for adding menu items and toolbars for add-ins.

Adding Menu Items

As you saw in the earlier chapters, when you create a new add-in and configure it to show a menu item, it adds a new menu item to the Tools menu with a smiley icon by default. You can also add new menu items to the Visual Studio IDE with your own event logic for different purposes.

Let me describe this with a very basic example that adds a new menu item to the Tools menu. It uses simple event logic to show a MessageBox. The process of adding a new menu item to the Visual Studio IDE is simple. You've seen it before in the auto-generated template code for new add-ins, but a discussion about it was saved for now.

I created a new add-in for this example, but I didn't check the item specifying that my add-in not show any UI modal in the fourth page of the Add-In Wizard.

Listing 10-1 shows the source code of this add-in. All XML code comments are removed to save space and simplify the code.

Listing 10-1: Adding a New Menu Item for the Add-in

```csharp
using System;
using Extensibility;
using EnvDTE;
using EnvDTE80;
using Microsoft.VisualStudio.CommandBars;
using System.Resources;
using System.Reflection;
using System.Globalization;
using System.Windows.Forms;

namespace AddMenuItems
{
    public class Connect : IDTExtensibility2, IDTCommandTarget
    {
        public Connect()
        {
        }

        public void OnConnection(object application, ext_ConnectMode connectMode,
            object addInInst, ref Array custom)
        {
            _applicationObject = (DTE2)application;
            _addInInstance = (AddIn)addInInst;
            if (connectMode == ext_ConnectMode.ext_cm_UISetup ||
                connectMode == ext_ConnectMode.ext_cm_Startup)
            {
                object[] contextGUIDS = new object[] { };
                Commands2 commands = (Commands2)_applicationObject.Commands;
                string toolsMenuName;

                try
                {
                    //If you would like to move the command to a different menu,
change the word "Tools" to the
                    //  English version of the menu. This code will take the
culture, append on the name of the menu
                    //  then add the command to that menu. You can find a list of
all the top-level menus in the file
                    //  CommandBar.resx.
                    string resourceName;
                    ResourceManager resourceManager = new
ResourceManager("AddMenuItems.CommandBar",
                        Assembly.GetExecutingAssembly());
                    CultureInfo cultureInfo = new
CultureInfo(_applicationObject.LocaleID);

                    if (cultureInfo.TwoLetterISOLanguageName == "zh")
                    {
                        resourceName = String.Concat(cultureInfo.Name, "Tools");
```

(continued)

171

Listing 10-1 *(continued)*

```
                            }
                            else
                            {
                                resourceName =
String.Concat(cultureInfo.TwoLetterISOLanguageName, "Tools");
                            }
                            toolsMenuName = resourceManager.GetString(resourceName);
                        }
                        catch
                        {
                            //We tried to find a localized version of the word Tools, but
one was not found.
                            //  Default to the en-US word, which may work for the current
culture.
                            toolsMenuName = "Tools";
                        }

                        //Place the command on the tools menu.
                        //Find the MenuBar command bar, which is the top-level command bar
holding all the main menu items:
                        Microsoft.VisualStudio.CommandBars.CommandBar menuBarCommandBar =
((Microsoft.VisualStudio.CommandBars.CommandBars)_applicationObject.
CommandBars)["MenuBar"];

                        //Find the Tools command bar on the MenuBar command bar:
                        CommandBarControl toolsControl = menuBarCommandBar.
Controls[toolsMenuName];
                        CommandBarPopup toolsPopup = (CommandBarPopup)toolsControl;

                        //This try/catch block can be duplicated if you wish to add
multiple commands to be handled by your Add-in,
                        //  just make sure you also update the QueryStatus/Exec method to
include the new command names.
                        try
                        {
                            //Add a command to the Commands collection:
                            Command command = commands.AddNamedCommand2(_addInInstance,
"AddMenuItems", "AddMenuItems",
                                "Executes the command for AddMenuItems", true, 59, ref
contextGUIDS,
                                (int)vsCommandStatus.vsCommandStatusSupported +
(int)vsCommandStatus.vsCommandStatusEnabled,
                                (int)vsCommandStyle.vsCommandStylePictAndText,
vsCommandControlType.vsCommandControlTypeButton);

                            //Add a control for the command to the tools menu:
                            if ((command != null) && (toolsPopup != null))
                            {
                                command.AddControl(toolsPopup.CommandBar, 1);
                            }
```

```
                    // Add new command to the Command collection:
                    Command newCommand = commands.AddNamedCommand2(_addInInstance,
"AddMenuItems2", "New Menu Item",
                        "Executes the command for new menu item", true, 59, ref
contextGUIDS,
                        (int)vsCommandStatus.vsCommandStatusSupported +
(int)vsCommandStatus.vsCommandStatusEnabled,
                        (int)vsCommandStyle.vsCommandStylePictAndText,
vsCommandControlType.vsCommandControlTypeButton);

                    if ((newCommand != null) && (toolsPopup != null))
                    {
                        newCommand.AddControl(toolsPopup.CommandBar, 1);
                    }


                }
                catch (System.ArgumentException)
                {
                }
            }
        }

        public void OnDisconnection(ext_DisconnectMode disconnectMode, ref Array
custom)
        {
        }

        public void OnAddInsUpdate(ref Array custom)
        {
        }

        public void OnStartupComplete(ref Array custom)
        {
        }

        public void OnBeginShutdown(ref Array custom)
        {
        }

        public void QueryStatus(string commandName, vsCommandStatusTextWanted
neededText,
            ref vsCommandStatus status, ref object commandText)
        {
            if (neededText == vsCommandStatusTextWanted
.vsCommandStatusTextWantedNone)
            {
                if (commandName == "AddMenuItems.Connect.AddMenuItems")
                {
                    status = (vsCommandStatus)vsCommandStatus.
vsCommandStatusSupported |
                        vsCommandStatus.vsCommandStatusEnabled;
                    return;
                }
```

(continued)

173

Listing 10-1 *(continued)*

```
            else if (commandName == "AddMenuItems.Connect.AddMenuItems2")
            {
                status = (vsCommandStatus)vsCommandStatus
.vsCommandStatusSupported |
                    vsCommandStatus.vsCommandStatusEnabled;
                return;
            }
```

```
        }
    }

    public void Exec(string commandName, vsCommandExecOption executeOption, ref
object varIn,
        ref object varOut, ref bool handled)
    {
        handled = false;
        if (executeOption == vsCommandExecOption.vsCommandExecOptionDoDefault)
        {
            if (commandName == "AddMenuItems.Connect.AddMenuItems")
            {
                handled = true;
                return;
            }
```

```
            else if (commandName == "AddMenuItems.Connect.AddMenuItems2")
            {
                MessageBox.Show("Item Clicked!");
                handled = true;
                return;
            }
```

```
        }
    }

    private DTE2 _applicationObject;
    private AddIn _addInInstance;
    }
}
```

Notice the highlighted code and a few additions to the add-in code template. As you can guess, the process is as simple as creating a new command for the Visual Studio IDE, mapping this command to a menu item, and then handling its events when the command is raised.

To begin, you need to create and add a new command to the IDE (see Listing 10-2).

Listing 10-2: Adding a New Command to the IDE

```
public void OnConnection(object application, ext_ConnectMode connectMode,
    object addInInst, ref Array custom)
{
    _applicationObject = (DTE2)application;
    _addInInstance = (AddIn)addInInst;
```

```
        if (connectMode == ext_ConnectMode.ext_cm_UISetup ||

            connectMode == ext_ConnectMode.ext_cm_Startup)

    {
        object[] contextGUIDS = new object[] { };
        Commands2 commands = (Commands2)_applicationObject.Commands;
        string toolsMenuName;

        try
        {
            //If you would like to move the command to a different menu, change the
word "Tools" to the
            //  English version of the menu. This code will take the culture,
append on the name of the menu
            //  then add the command to that menu. You can find a list of all the
top-level menus in the file
            //  CommandBar.resx.
            string resourceName;
            ResourceManager resourceManager = new
ResourceManager("AddMenuItems.CommandBar",
                    Assembly.GetExecutingAssembly());
            CultureInfo cultureInfo = new CultureInfo(_applicationObject.LocaleID);

            if (cultureInfo.TwoLetterISOLanguageName == "zh")
            {
                resourceName = String.Concat(cultureInfo.Name, "Tools");
            }
            else
            {
                resourceName = String.Concat(cultureInfo.TwoLetterISOLanguageName,
"Tools");
            }
            toolsMenuName = resourceManager.GetString(resourceName);
        }
        catch
        {
            //We tried to find a localized version of the word Tools, but one was
not found.
            //  Default to the en-US word, which may work for the current culture.
            toolsMenuName = "Tools";
        }

        //Place the command on the tools menu.
        //Find the MenuBar command bar, which is the top-level command bar holding
all the main menu items:
        Microsoft.VisualStudio.CommandBars.CommandBar menuBarCommandBar =

((Microsoft.VisualStudio.CommandBars.CommandBars)_applicationObject
.CommandBars)["MenuBar"];

        //Find the Tools command bar on the MenuBar command bar:
        CommandBarControl toolsControl = menuBarCommandBar.Controls[toolsMenuName];
        CommandBarPopup toolsPopup = (CommandBarPopup)toolsControl;
```

(continued)

Listing 10-2 *(continued)*

```
        //This try/catch block can be duplicated if you wish to add multiple
commands to be handled by your Add-in,
        //  just make sure you also update the QueryStatus/Exec method to include
the new command names.
        try
        {
            //Add a command to the Commands collection:
            Command command = commands.AddNamedCommand2(_addInInstance,
"AddMenuItems", "AddMenuItems",
                "Executes the command for AddMenuItems", true, 59, ref
contextGUIDS,
                (int)vsCommandStatus.vsCommandStatusSupported +
(int)vsCommandStatus.vsCommandStatusEnabled,
                (int)vsCommandStyle.vsCommandStylePictAndText,
vsCommandControlType.vsCommandControlTypeButton);

            //Add a control for the command to the tools menu:
            if ((command != null) && (toolsPopup != null))
            {
                command.AddControl(toolsPopup.CommandBar, 1);
            }

            // Add new command to the Command collection:
            Command newCommand = commands.AddNamedCommand2(_addInInstance,
"AddMenuItems2", "New Menu Item",
                "Executes the command for new menu item", true, 59, ref
contextGUIDS,
                (int)vsCommandStatus.vsCommandStatusSupported +
(int)vsCommandStatus.vsCommandStatusEnabled,
                (int)vsCommandStyle.vsCommandStylePictAndText,
vsCommandControlType.vsCommandControlTypeButton);

            if ((newCommand != null) && (toolsPopup != null))
            {
                newCommand.AddControl(toolsPopup.CommandBar, 1);
            }

        }
        catch (System.ArgumentException)
        {
        }
    }
}
```

This code is familiar to you because you've seen it many times before. There are only a few new additions, which simply repeat the existing code with new names to add a new command and menu item. The first change is the addition of a new term for the connect model when a startup is highlighted at the top of the code. After this and within the If case, you can see some code that tries to get the resource name of the Tools menu from the resource files, based on the user's culture. You can replace the Tools menu text with other names to move your item to other menus.

After finding the text value for the Tools menu, you create an instance of the CommandBar object for the menu bar, and instances of CommandBarControl and CommandBarPopup for your Tools menu. In the next step, you create an instance of the Command object by calling the AddNamedCommand2 method of the commands collection in the IDE. This method takes some arguments about the command, adds the command to the command collection, and returns the Command instance. I'll talk about this method in a moment.

After creating an instance of the Command object and adding it to the commands collection, you check to make sure that it's not null and that you have a real Tools menu; then you call the AddControl method of this object instance to map your command with a menu item. This method takes two parameters:

- ❑ **Owner:** An instance of the Microsoft.VisualStudio.CommandBars.CommandBar object where you want to add your command
- ❑ **Position:** The integer value of the index position, starting at 1

The default code has done this job for the Tools menu to create an item, and you can simply modify this code for your needs. In the preceding example, I added a new command to the collection in the same way that the default code does.

Regarding the AddNamedCommand2 method, this method is responsible for creating and adding a new command to the Visual Studio commands collection. It takes several parameters:

- ❑ AddInInstance: The add-in instance for the command
- ❑ Name: The string value of the command name
- ❑ ButtonText: The string value of the button text
- ❑ Tooltip: The string value of the tooltip description for the command
- ❑ MSOButton: Indicates whether the command's button picture is a Microsoft Office picture
- ❑ Bitmap: The identifier of the icon resource
- ❑ ContextUIGUIDs: A SafeArray of GUID values that specify the environment parameters for the command, such as debug or design mode
- ❑ vsCommandStatusValue: Specifies that if the command is disabled, then it should be invisible or gray
- ❑ CommandStyleFlags: A vsCommandStyle enumeration value that controls the UI style of the command
- ❑ ControlType: Determines the control type that is added when the user interface is created

The other change in the add-in code is in the QueryStatus method (see Listing 10-3).

Listing 10-3: Changes in the QueryStatus Method

```
public void QueryStatus(string commandName, vsCommandStatusTextWanted neededText,
    ref vsCommandStatus status, ref object commandText)
```

(continued)

Listing 10-3 *(continued)*

```
    {
        if (neededText == vsCommandStatusTextWanted.vsCommandStatusTextWantedNone)
        {
            if (commandName == "AddMenuItems.Connect.AddMenuItems")
            {
                status = (vsCommandStatus)vsCommandStatus.vsCommandStatusSupported |
                    vsCommandStatus.vsCommandStatusEnabled;
                return;
            }

            else if (commandName == "AddMenuItems.Connect.AddMenuItems2")
            {
                status = (vsCommandStatus)vsCommandStatus.vsCommandStatusSupported |
                    vsCommandStatus.vsCommandStatusEnabled;
                return;
            }

        }
    }
```

The changes are simple: you add a new case for when the command is equal to the newly added command, and then just set the status to the appropriate enumeration value to let Visual Studio knows this command can be executed.

The last change is in the Exec method to handle executing a command (see Listing 10-4).

Listing 10-4: Changes in the Exec Method

```
public void Exec(string commandName, vsCommandExecOption executeOption, ref object
varIn,
    ref object varOut, ref bool handled)
{
    handled = false;
    if (executeOption == vsCommandExecOption.vsCommandExecOptionDoDefault)
    {
        if (commandName == "AddMenuItems.Connect.AddMenuItems")
        {
            handled = true;
            return;
        }

        else if (commandName == "AddMenuItems.Connect.AddMenuItems2")
        {
            MessageBox.Show("Item Clicked!");
            handled = true;
            return;
        }

    }
}
```

In this method, you add code to check whether the executed command is equal to the newly added command, and then show a MessageBox and mark the command as handled.

Figure 10-1 shows the addition of this new menu item to the Tools menu, and Figure 10-2 shows the result of clicking this menu item.

Figure 10-1: Adding a new item to the Tools menu

Figure 10-2: Result of clicking on the new menu item

Adding a Toolbar Item

You can also add a toolbar for your add-ins to the Visual Studio IDE. Like adding menu items, you can do this by writing code.

Before showing you the code, let me outline the main steps that you need to follow to add a toolbar item for your add-ins:

1. Get an instance of one of the command bars in the Visual Studio IDE or create your own.

2. Create a new command in the Visual Studio IDE.

3. Add this command's control to the command bar.

Listing 10-5 shows the source code of an add-in that creates and adds a button to the Visual Studio standard toolbar.

Listing 10-5: Add-in to Add a Button to the Standard Toolbar

```csharp
using System;
using Extensibility;
using EnvDTE;
using EnvDTE80;
using Microsoft.VisualStudio.CommandBars;
using System.Resources;
using System.Reflection;
using System.Globalization;
using System.Windows.Forms;

namespace AddToolbar
{
    public class Connect : IDTExtensibility2, IDTCommandTarget
    {
        public Connect()
        {
        }

        public void OnConnection(object application, ext_ConnectMode connectMode,
object addInInst,
                ref Array custom)
        {
            _applicationObject = (DTE2)application;
            _addInInstance = (AddIn)addInInst;
            if (connectMode == ext_ConnectMode.ext_cm_UISetup ||

                    connectMode == ext_ConnectMode.ext_cm_Startup ||
                    connectMode == ext_ConnectMode.ext_cm_AfterStartup)

            {
                object[] contextGUIDS = new object[] { };
                Commands2 commands = (Commands2)_applicationObject.Commands;
                string toolsMenuName;

                try
                {
                    //If you would like to move the command to a different menu,
change the word "Tools" to the
                    //  English version of the menu. This code will take the
culture, append on the name of the menu
```

```
                    //  then add the command to that menu. You can find a list of
all the top-level menus in the file
                    //   CommandBar.resx.
                    string resourceName;
                    ResourceManager resourceManager = new
ResourceManager("AddToolbar.CommandBar",
                        Assembly.GetExecutingAssembly());
                    CultureInfo cultureInfo = new
CultureInfo(_applicationObject.LocaleID);

                    if (cultureInfo.TwoLetterISOLanguageName == "zh")
                    {
                        resourceName = String.Concat(cultureInfo.Name, "Tools");
                    }
                    else
                    {
                        resourceName =
String.Concat(cultureInfo.TwoLetterISOLanguageName, "Tools");
                    }
                    toolsMenuName = resourceManager.GetString(resourceName);
                }
                catch
                {
                    //We tried to find a localized version of the word Tools, but
one was not found.
                    //  Default to the en-US word, which may work for the current
culture.
                    toolsMenuName = "Tools";
                }

                //Place the command on the tools menu.
                //Find the MenuBar command bar, which is the top-level command bar
holding all the main menu items:
                Microsoft.VisualStudio.CommandBars.CommandBar menuBarCommandBar =

((Microsoft.VisualStudio.CommandBars.CommandBars)_applicationObject
.CommandBars)["MenuBar"];

                //Find the Tools command bar on the MenuBar command bar:
                CommandBarControl toolsControl = menuBarCommandBar
.Controls[toolsMenuName];
                CommandBarPopup toolsPopup = (CommandBarPopup)toolsControl;

                //This try/catch block can be duplicated if you wish to add
multiple commands to be handled by your Add-in,
                //  just make sure you also update the QueryStatus/Exec method to
include the new command names.
                try
                {
                    //Add a command to the Commands collection:
                    Command command = commands.AddNamedCommand2(_addInInstance,
"AddToolbar",
                        "AddToolbar", "Executes the command for AddToolbar", true,
59, ref contextGUIDS,
```

(continued)

Listing 10-5 *(continued)*

```
                        (int)vsCommandStatus.vsCommandStatusSupported +
        (int)vsCommandStatus.vsCommandStatusEnabled,
                        (int)vsCommandStyle.vsCommandStylePictAndText,
        vsCommandControlType.vsCommandControlTypeButton);

                    //Add a control for the command to the tools menu:
                    if ((command != null) && (toolsPopup != null))
                    {
                        command.AddControl(toolsPopup.CommandBar, 1);
                    }


                    // Add Toolbar item
                    CommandBars commandBars = this._applicationObject.CommandBars
        as CommandBars;

                    CommandBar commandBar = commandBars["Standard"];

                    Command command2 = commands.AddNamedCommand2(_addInInstance,
        "AddToolbar2",
                        "Toolbar Item", "New item for toolbar", true, 59, ref
        contextGUIDS,
                        (int)vsCommandStatus.vsCommandStatusSupported +
        (int)vsCommandStatus.vsCommandStatusEnabled,
                        (int)vsCommandStyle.vsCommandStylePictAndText,
        vsCommandControlType.vsCommandControlTypeButton);

                    command2.AddControl(commandBar, 1);


                }
                catch (System.ArgumentException)
                {
                }
            }
        }

        public void OnDisconnection(ext_DisconnectMode disconnectMode, ref Array
    custom)
        {
        }

        public void OnAddInsUpdate(ref Array custom)
        {
        }

        public void OnStartupComplete(ref Array custom)
        {
        }

        public void OnBeginShutdown(ref Array custom)
        {
        }
```

```
        public void QueryStatus(string commandName, vsCommandStatusTextWanted
neededText,
            ref vsCommandStatus status, ref object commandText)
        {
            if (neededText ==
vsCommandStatusTextWanted.vsCommandStatusTextWantedNone)
            {
                if (commandName == "AddToolbar.Connect.AddToolbar")
                {
                    status =
(vsCommandStatus)vsCommandStatus.vsCommandStatusSupported |
                        vsCommandStatus.vsCommandStatusEnabled;
                    return;
                }

                else if (commandName == "AddToolbar.Connect.AddToolbar2")
                {
                    status =
(vsCommandStatus)vsCommandStatus.vsCommandStatusSupported |
                        vsCommandStatus.vsCommandStatusEnabled;
                    return;
                }


            }
        }

        public void Exec(string commandName, vsCommandExecOption executeOption, ref
object varIn,
            ref object varOut, ref bool handled)
        {
            handled = false;
            if (executeOption == vsCommandExecOption.vsCommandExecOptionDoDefault)
            {
                if (commandName == "AddToolbar.Connect.AddToolbar")
                {
                    handled = true;
                    return;
                }

                else if (commandName == "AddToolbar.Connect.AddToolbar2")
                {
                    handled = true;
                    return;
                }


            }
        }

        private DTE2 _applicationObject;
        private AddIn _addInInstance;
    }
}
```

I'll discuss this code next, but I won't cover any more additions to the QueryStatus and Exec methods, as their implementations are similar to what you've seen before. Here I'll just focus on the main code to add the button to the toolbar.

The code for the OnConnection method is presented in Listing 10-6. This method contains the main code implementation to add the button to the toolbar.

Listing 10-6: Adding a New Button to the Toolbar

```
public void OnConnection(object application, ext_ConnectMode connectMode, object
addInInst,
    ref Array custom)
{
    _applicationObject = (DTE2)application;
    _addInInstance = (AddIn)addInInst;
    if (connectMode == ext_ConnectMode.ext_cm_UISetup ||

        connectMode == ext_ConnectMode.ext_cm_Startup ||
        connectMode == ext_ConnectMode.ext_cm_AfterStartup)

    {
        object[] contextGUIDS = new object[] { };
        Commands2 commands = (Commands2)_applicationObject.Commands;
        string toolsMenuName;

        try
        {
            //If you would like to move the command to a different menu, change the
word "Tools" to the
            //  English version of the menu. This code will take the culture,
append on the name of the menu
            //  then add the command to that menu. You can find a list of all the
top-level menus in the file
            //  CommandBar.resx.
            string resourceName;
            ResourceManager resourceManager = new ResourceManager("AddToolbar.
CommandBar",
                Assembly.GetExecutingAssembly());
            CultureInfo cultureInfo = new CultureInfo(_applicationObject.LocaleID);

            if (cultureInfo.TwoLetterISOLanguageName == "zh")
            {
                resourceName = String.Concat(cultureInfo.Name, "Tools");
            }
            else
            {
                resourceName = String.Concat(cultureInfo.TwoLetterISOLanguageName,
"Tools");
            }
            toolsMenuName = resourceManager.GetString(resourceName);
        }
        catch
```

```
        {
                //We tried to find a localized version of the word Tools, but one was
not found.
                //  Default to the en-US word, which may work for the current culture.
                toolsMenuName = "Tools";
        }

        //Place the command on the tools menu.
        //Find the MenuBar command bar, which is the top-level command bar holding
all the main menu items:
        Microsoft.VisualStudio.CommandBars.CommandBar menuBarCommandBar =

((Microsoft.VisualStudio.CommandBars.CommandBars)_applicationObject
.CommandBars)["MenuBar"];

        //Find the Tools command bar on the MenuBar command bar:
        CommandBarControl toolsControl = menuBarCommandBar.Controls[toolsMenuName];
        CommandBarPopup toolsPopup = (CommandBarPopup)toolsControl;

        //This try/catch block can be duplicated if you wish to add multiple
commands to be handled by your Add-in,
        //  just make sure you also update the QueryStatus/Exec method to include
the new command names.
        try
        {
                //Add a command to the Commands collection:
                Command command = commands.AddNamedCommand2(_addInInstance,
"AddToolbar",
                        "AddToolbar", "Executes the command for AddToolbar", true, 59, ref
contextGUIDS,
                        (int)vsCommandStatus.vsCommandStatusSupported +
(int)vsCommandStatus.vsCommandStatusEnabled,
                        (int)vsCommandStyle.vsCommandStylePictAndText,
vsCommandControlType.vsCommandControlTypeButton);

                //Add a control for the command to the tools menu:
                if ((command != null) && (toolsPopup != null))
                {
                        command.AddControl(toolsPopup.CommandBar, 1);
                }
```

```
                // Add Toolbar item
                CommandBars commandBars = this._applicationObject.CommandBars as
CommandBars;

                CommandBar commandBar = commandBars["Standard"];

                Command command2 = commands.AddNamedCommand2(_addInInstance,
"AddToolbar2",
                        "Toolbar Item", "New item for toolbar", true, 59, ref contextGUIDS,
                        (int)vsCommandStatus.vsCommandStatusSupported +
(int)vsCommandStatus.vsCommandStatusEnabled,
```

(continued)

Listing 10-6 *(continued)*

```
              (int)vsCommandStyle.vsCommandStylePictAndText,
   vsCommandControlType.vsCommandControlTypeButton);

          command2.AddControl(commandBar, 1);

      }
      catch (System.ArgumentException)
      {
      }
   }
}
```

In this code, I first checked the connection mode and executed my logic when it was equal to the user interface startup, the startup, or the after startup connection modes. I then created an instance of the `Microsoft.VisualStudio.Commandbars.CommandBars` object for the standard toolbar. Then, as shown in previous examples, I created a new command for my toolbar button and, finally, added this command to the standard toolbar as a button.

Note that I could have done more with this and used some classes such as `CommandBarControl` and `CommandBarButton` to create more enhanced toolbar items, but I wanted to keep the code simple to illustrate the basics of this topic.

Now if I restart the Visual Studio environment, the new button appears on my standard toolbar (see Figure 10-3).

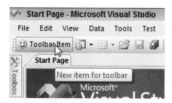

Figure 10-3: Adding a new button to the toolbar

Adding Elements with Windows Forms and Controls

While you can use commands to display some user interface elements to end users, it's also possible to use Windows Forms and control elements to interact with users in order to get their inputs and enable them to modify some options.

The process to display Windows Forms in your add-ins is simple and relies on some common techniques for displaying them in other types of applications. You only need to display dialogs with the appropriate data in them.

Let me give an example that should show you everything you need to begin adding Windows Forms to your add-ins. This example creates an add-in that displays a dialog with a TextBox containing the code selected in the editor; the user can modify it and then copy it automatically to the clipboard.

First, create a new add-in project. After this, you add a new Windows Form to your project with a simple user interface that contains a RichTextBox control and two buttons. The first button copies the text in the RichTextBox to the clipboard, and the second is the Cancel button of the form (see Figure 10-4).

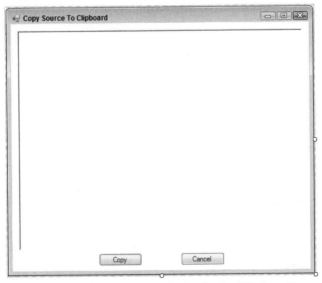

Figure 10-4: The user interface design for the Windows Form

This form has the simple code logic presented in Listing 10-7.

Listing 10-7: Code Logic for the Windows Form

```csharp
using System;
using System.Collections.Generic;
using System.ComponentModel;
using System.Data;
using System.Drawing;
using System.Text;
using System.Windows.Forms;

namespace CopyCodeToClipboard
{
    public partial class Main : Form
    {
        public Main()
        {
            InitializeComponent();
        }

        public string Code { get; set; }
```

(continued)

Listing 10-7 *(continued)*

```
        private void Main_Load(object sender, EventArgs e)
        {
            txtCode.Text = this.Code;
        }


        private void btnCopy_Click(object sender, EventArgs e)
        {
            Clipboard.Clear();
            Clipboard.SetText(txtCode.Text);
        }

    }
}
```

Focus on the highlighted code. The form has a string Code property that holds the code text. In the load event of the form, the text of the RichTextBox is set to this property. The btnCopy button simply clears the clipboard and copies the content of the RichTextBox to it.

Later, you add the Code property of this form to the selected code in the Visual Studio editor and then show the form dialog.

Now it's time to write the add-in code (see Listing 10-8).

Listing 10-8: Add-in to Copy the Selected Code to the Clipboard

```
using System;
using Extensibility;
using EnvDTE;
using EnvDTE80;
using Microsoft.VisualStudio.CommandBars;
using System.Resources;
using System.Reflection;
using System.Globalization;

namespace CopyCodeToClipboard
{
    public class Connect : IDTExtensibility2, IDTCommandTarget
    {
        public Connect()
        {
        }

        public void OnConnection(object application, ext_ConnectMode connectMode,
object addInInst,
            ref Array custom)
        {
            _applicationObject = (DTE2)application;
            _addInInstance = (AddIn)addInInst;
            if (connectMode == ext_ConnectMode.ext_cm_UISetup)
            {
```

```csharp
object[] contextGUIDS = new object[] { };
Commands2 commands = (Commands2)_applicationObject.Commands;
string toolsMenuName;

try
{
    //If you would like to move the command to a different menu,
    change the word "Tools" to the
    //  English version of the menu. This code will take the
    culture, append on the name of the menu
    //  then add the command to that menu. You can find a list of
    all the top-level menus in the file
    //  CommandBar.resx.
    string resourceName;
    ResourceManager resourceManager = new
ResourceManager("CopyCodeToClipboard.CommandBar",
        Assembly.GetExecutingAssembly());
    CultureInfo cultureInfo = new
CultureInfo(_applicationObject.LocaleID);

    if (cultureInfo.TwoLetterISOLanguageName == "zh")
    {
        resourceName = String.Concat(cultureInfo.Name, "Tools");
    }
    else
    {
        resourceName =
String.Concat(cultureInfo.TwoLetterISOLanguageName, "Tools");
    }
    toolsMenuName = resourceManager.GetString(resourceName);
}
catch
{
    //We tried to find a localized version of the word Tools, but
    one was not found.
    //  Default to the en-US word, which may work for the current
    culture.
    toolsMenuName = "Tools";
}

//Place the command on the tools menu.
//Find the MenuBar command bar, which is the top-level command bar
holding all the main menu items:
Microsoft.VisualStudio.CommandBars.CommandBar menuBarCommandBar =
((Microsoft.VisualStudio.CommandBars.CommandBars)_applicationObject
.CommandBars)["MenuBar"];

//Find the Tools command bar on the MenuBar command bar:
CommandBarControl toolsControl = menuBarCommandBar
.Controls[toolsMenuName];
CommandBarPopup toolsPopup = (CommandBarPopup)toolsControl;

//This try/catch block can be duplicated if you wish to add
```

(continued)

Listing 10-8 *(continued)*

```
multiple commands to be handled by your Add-in,
                // just make sure you also update the QueryStatus/Exec method to
include the new command names.
                try
                {
                    //Add a command to the Commands collection:
                    Command command = commands.AddNamedCommand2(_addInInstance,
"CopyCodeToClipboard",
                        "CopyCodeToClipboard", "Executes the command for
CopyCodeToClipboard", true, 59,
                        ref contextGUIDS,
(int)vsCommandStatus.vsCommandStatusSupported +
                        (int)vsCommandStatus.vsCommandStatusEnabled,
(int)vsCommandStyle.vsCommandStylePictAndText,
                        vsCommandControlType.vsCommandControlTypeButton);

                    //Add a control for the command to the tools menu:
                    if ((command != null) && (toolsPopup != null))
                    {
                        command.AddControl(toolsPopup.CommandBar, 1);
                    }
                }
                catch (System.ArgumentException)
                {
                }
            }
        }

        public void OnDisconnection(ext_DisconnectMode disconnectMode, ref Array
custom)
        {
        }

        public void OnAddInsUpdate(ref Array custom)
        {
        }

        public void OnStartupComplete(ref Array custom)
        {
        }

        public void OnBeginShutdown(ref Array custom)
        {
        }

        public void QueryStatus(string commandName, vsCommandStatusTextWanted
neededText,
            ref vsCommandStatus status, ref object commandText)
        {
            if (neededText ==
vsCommandStatusTextWanted.vsCommandStatusTextWantedNone)
            {
                if (commandName ==
```

```
"CopyCodeToClipboard.Connect.CopyCodeToClipboard")
                {
                        status =
(vsCommandStatus)vsCommandStatus.vsCommandStatusSupported |
                        vsCommandStatus.vsCommandStatusEnabled;
                        return;
                }
            }
        }

        public void Exec(string commandName, vsCommandExecOption executeOption, ref
object varIn,
            ref object varOut, ref bool handled)
        {
            handled = false;
            if (executeOption == vsCommandExecOption.vsCommandExecOptionDoDefault)
            {
                if (commandName ==
"CopyCodeToClipboard.Connect.CopyCodeToClipboard")
                {

                        ShowDialog();


                        handled = true;
                        return;
                }
            }
        }

        private void ShowDialog()
        {
            Main frmMain = new Main();

            TextSelection selection =
this._applicationObject.ActiveDocument.Selection
                    as TextSelection;

            frmMain.Code = selection.Text;
            frmMain.ShowDialog();
        }

        private DTE2 _applicationObject;
        private AddIn _addInInstance;
    }
}
```

In the preceding code, you insert a ShowDialog method call in the Exec method to handle all code logic to load the Windows Form and show data.

In the ShowDialog method, you create an instance of the Main form (your Windows Form) and an instance of the TextSelection object for the selected text. Then you set the Code property of your form to the selected code and show the window.

If you run this add-in for selected text in the Visual Studio editor, you can see a result like what is shown in Figure 10-5.

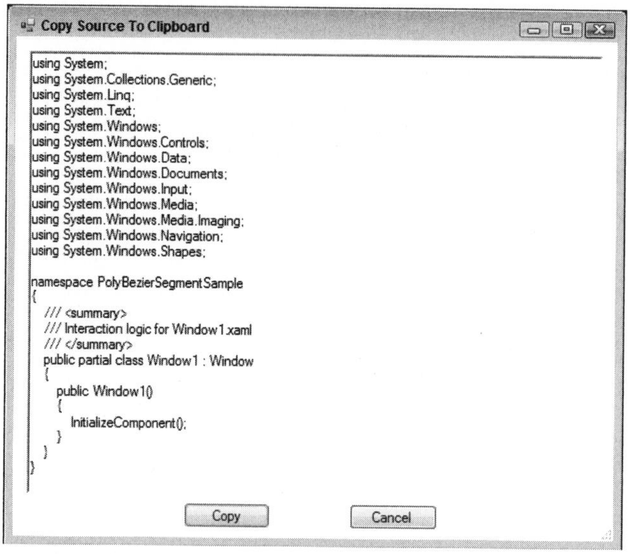

Figure 10-5: Copying selected text to the clipboard

Manipulating User Interface Elements

The other aspect of working with the user interface is manipulating Windows Forms and controls on them via the automation model. Usually you create and work with Windows Forms with the Windows Form designer or programming codes, but here I want to show you how to automate these tasks in order to manipulate them.

This topic is vast and beyond the scope of a single chapter, but fortunately it's easy to follow if you understand the principles. I assume here that readers are experienced developers, so I won't bother you with long and unnecessary discussions. Instead, I'll just demonstrate the principles in a detailed example; you'll know what to do after that.

Suppose that you have a clean Windows Forms application that has a default Form1 Windows Form and want to manipulate this form. You already know how to create a Windows Form project on-the-fly from Chapter 7, based on project templates, and how to add new project items to it. Combining that knowledge with what you see here, you can create a fully automated process of creating a project, adding items to it, and then modifying these items.

Suppose that you want to add a `TextBox` and a `Button` control to a Windows Form on-the-fly via an add-in. Listing 10-9 shows the source code of the add-in to do this.

Listing 10-9: Add-in for a TextBox and Button on a Windows Form

```csharp
using System;
using Extensibility;
using EnvDTE;
using EnvDTE80;
using Microsoft.VisualStudio.CommandBars;
using System.Resources;
using System.Reflection;
using System.Globalization;

using System.Windows.Forms;
using System.ComponentModel;
using System.ComponentModel.Design;


namespace WinFormSample
{
    public class Connect : IDTExtensibility2, IDTCommandTarget
    {
        public Connect()
        {
        }

        public void OnConnection(object application, ext_ConnectMode connectMode, object addInInst,
            ref Array custom)
        {
            _applicationObject = (DTE2)application;
            _addInInstance = (AddIn)addInInst;
            if (connectMode == ext_ConnectMode.ext_cm_UISetup)
            {
                object[] contextGUIDS = new object[] { };
                Commands2 commands = (Commands2)_applicationObject.Commands;
                string toolsMenuName;

                try
                {
                    //If you would like to move the command to a different menu,
change the word "Tools" to the
                    //  English version of the menu. This code will take the
culture, append on the name of the menu
                    //  then add the command to that menu. You can find a list of
all the top-level menus in the file
                    //  CommandBar.resx.
                    string resourceName;
                    ResourceManager resourceManager = new
ResourceManager("WinFormSample.CommandBar",
                        Assembly.GetExecutingAssembly());
                    CultureInfo cultureInfo = new
CultureInfo(_applicationObject.LocaleID);

                    if (cultureInfo.TwoLetterISOLanguageName == "zh")
```

(continued)

Listing 10-9 *(continued)*

```
            {
                resourceName = String.Concat(cultureInfo.Name, "Tools");
            }
            else
            {
                resourceName =
String.Concat(cultureInfo.TwoLetterISOLanguageName, "Tools");
            }
            toolsMenuName = resourceManager.GetString(resourceName);
        }
        catch
        {
            //We tried to find a localized version of the word Tools, but
one was not found.
            //  Default to the en-US word, which may work for the current
culture.
            toolsMenuName = "Tools";
        }

        //Place the command on the tools menu.
        //Find the MenuBar command bar, which is the top-level command bar
holding all the main menu items:
            Microsoft.VisualStudio.CommandBars.CommandBar menuBarCommandBar =
((Microsoft.VisualStudio.CommandBars.CommandBars)_applicationObject
.CommandBars)["MenuBar"];

        //Find the Tools command bar on the MenuBar command bar:
            CommandBarControl toolsControl = menuBarCommandBar.
Controls[toolsMenuName];
            CommandBarPopup toolsPopup = (CommandBarPopup)toolsControl;

        //This try/catch block can be duplicated if you wish to add
multiple commands to be handled by your Add-in,
            //  just make sure you also update the QueryStatus/Exec method to
include the new command names.
            try
            {
                //Add a command to the Commands collection:
                Command command = commands.AddNamedCommand2(_addInInstance,
"WinFormSample", "WinFormSample",
                    "Executes the command for WinFormSample", true, 59, ref
contextGUIDS,
                    (int)vsCommandStatus.vsCommandStatusSupported +
(int)vsCommandStatus.vsCommandStatusEnabled,
                    (int)vsCommandStyle.vsCommandStylePictAndText,
vsCommandControlType.vsCommandControlTypeButton);

                //Add a control for the command to the tools menu:
                if ((command != null) && (toolsPopup != null))
                {
                    command.AddControl(toolsPopup.CommandBar, 1);
                }
```

```
                }
                catch (System.ArgumentException)
                {
                    //If we are here, then the exception is probably because a
command with that name
                    //  already exists. If so there is no need to recreate the
command and we can
                    //  safely ignore the exception.
                }
            }
        }

        public void OnDisconnection(ext_DisconnectMode disconnectMode, ref Array
custom)
        {
        }

        public void OnAddInsUpdate(ref Array custom)
        {
        }

        public void OnStartupComplete(ref Array custom)
        {
        }

        public void OnBeginShutdown(ref Array custom)
        {
        }

        public void QueryStatus(string commandName, vsCommandStatusTextWanted
neededText,
            ref vsCommandStatus status, ref object commandText)
        {
            if (neededText ==
vsCommandStatusTextWanted.vsCommandStatusTextWantedNone)
            {
                if (commandName == "WinFormSample.Connect.WinFormSample")
                {
                    status =
(vsCommandStatus)vsCommandStatus.vsCommandStatusSupported |
                        vsCommandStatus.vsCommandStatusEnabled;
                    return;
                }
            }
        }

        public void Exec(string commandName, vsCommandExecOption executeOption, ref
object varIn,
            ref object varOut, ref bool handled)
        {
            handled = false;
            if (executeOption == vsCommandExecOption.vsCommandExecOptionDoDefault)
            {
                if (commandName == "WinFormSample.Connect.WinFormSample")
                {
```

(continued)

195

Listing 10-9 *(continued)*

```
                    AddControls();


                handled = true;
                return;
            }
        }
    }

        private void AddControls()
        {
            // Create a designer host
            IDesignerHost designerHost =
this._applicationObject.ActiveWindow.Object
                as IDesignerHost;

            // Create a Button
            IComponent button = designerHost.CreateComponent
                (designerHost.GetType("System.Windows.Forms.Button"));

            // Create a TextBox
            IComponent textbox = designerHost.CreateComponent
                (designerHost.GetType("System.Windows.Forms.TextBox"));

            // Create an instance of the PropertyDescriptor
            PropertyDescriptor descriptor =
TypeDescriptor.GetProperties(button)["Parent"];

            // Add controls to form
            descriptor.SetValue(button, designerHost.RootComponent);
            descriptor.SetValue(textbox, designerHost.RootComponent);
        }

        private DTE2 _applicationObject;
        private AddIn _addInInstance;
    }
}
```

In this code, the AddControl method does the main job of adding the TextBox and Button to the form.

This example assumes that you have a Windows Forms project open, and that it has a Form1 item that is open and active in design mode. I could have written code to automatically load this item, but I wanted to keep the code simple.

In this method, you first create an object instance of the IDesignerHost interface for the currently active window in which your form resides. This designer host is where you can apply your changes, and it provides some methods and properties to work with form items.

In the next step, you create two instances of the IComponent object by passing types of Button and TextBox controls. In fact, these two objects represent your button and text box.

Now that you have a `Button` and a `TextBox`, you need to access their parent form and insert your controls on it. You can do this via a `PropertyDescriptor` object that can be set to the `Parent` property of either the `Button` or `TextBox` control.

The last step is to call the `SetValue` method of the `PropertyDescriptor` object to add controls to the root component (form) of the designer host.

Now when you open a Windows Forms project and default Form1 item and run this add-in, a button and a text box will be added to the form designer, as shown in Figure 10-6.

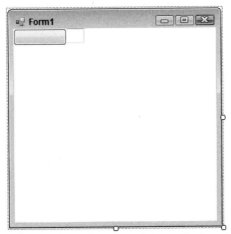

Figure 10-6: Adding controls to a Windows Form

Moving forward, let's look at the case where you want to modify some properties for this button and text box in your add-ins.

Suppose that you want to update the button and set its `Text` property, move it to a new location, update the text box and resize it, and then move it to a new location as well.

Listing 10-10 shows the updated version of the `AddControl` method to reflect these changes.

Listing 10-10: Updating Some Control Properties

```
private void AddControls()
{
    // Create a designer host
    IDesignerHost designerHost = this._applicationObject.ActiveWindow.Object
        as IDesignerHost;

    // Create a Button
    IComponent button = designerHost.CreateComponent
        (designerHost.GetType("System.Windows.Forms.Button"));

    // Create a TextBox
    IComponent textbox = designerHost.CreateComponent
        (designerHost.GetType("System.Windows.Forms.TextBox"));
```

(continued)

Listing 10-10 *(continued)*

```
    // Create an instance of the PropertyDescriptor
    PropertyDescriptor descriptor = TypeDescriptor.GetProperties(button)["Parent"];

    // Add controls to form
    descriptor.SetValue(button, designerHost.RootComponent);
    descriptor.SetValue(textbox, designerHost.RootComponent);


    // Update Button properties
    PropertyDescriptorCollection buttonDescriptorCollection =
        TypeDescriptor.GetProperties(button);

    // Set the Text property of the Button
    PropertyDescriptor buttonTextDescriptor =
        buttonDescriptorCollection["Text"];

    buttonTextDescriptor.SetValue(button, "Button");

    // Change the Location of the Button
    PropertyDescriptor buttonLocationDescriptor =
        buttonDescriptorCollection["Location"];

    Point buttonLocation = new Point(15, 40);

    buttonLocationDescriptor.SetValue(button, buttonLocation);

    // Update TextBox properties
    PropertyDescriptorCollection textboxDescriptorCollection =
        TypeDescriptor.GetProperties(textbox);

    // Resize the TextBox
    PropertyDescriptor textboxSizeDescriptor =
        textboxDescriptorCollection["Size"];

    Size textboxSize = new Size(150, 20);

    textboxSizeDescriptor.SetValue(textbox, textboxSize);

    // Change the Location of the TextBox
    PropertyDescriptor textboxLocationDescriptor =
        textboxDescriptorCollection["Location"];

    Point textboxLocation = new Point(80, 92);

    textboxLocationDescriptor.SetValue(textbox, textboxLocation);

}
```

Actually, here you repeat the same programming task four times: twice for Button properties and twice for TextBox properties, so knowing one of them would be sufficient.

The process to set a property of a control is simple. First, don't forget to add a reference to the System. Drawing namespace. You need to create a `PropertyDescriptorCollection` object that keeps all properties for a component (a control in our case). Then you create a `PropertyDescriptor` object for the property that you're going to set. The last step is to call the `SetValue` method of this `PropertyDescriptor` object to set the property. Do this four times for your controls to set their properties.

Figure 10-7 shows the result of these changes.

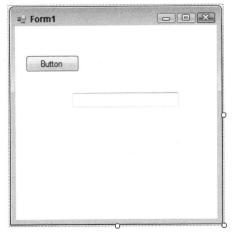

Figure 10-7: Setting properties of controls in forms

You should now have a good background on this topic. There are many more things to learn if you're interested, and you can continue on your own once you know the principles. You can actually consider this topic a part of Windows Forms programming, not Visual Studio extensibility, because we're just using classes from other namespaces.

Manipulating Visual Studio Windows

The last major topic that I'm going to discuss is manipulating some common Visual Studio Windows. The automation model provides some APIs to work with these windows, such as the following:

❑   Command window

❑   Error List

❑   Output window

❑   Solution Explorer

❑   Task List

❑   ToolBox

You can access object instances related to these windows via the `DTE2.ToolWindows` property. The following subsections cover each of these windows.

Command Window

The CommandWindow interface represents the Command window in the automation model and provides a few properties and methods to work with it.

Table 10-1 lists the properties of the CommandWindow interface.

Table 10-1: The CommandWindow Properties

Property	Description
DTE	Returns the DTE object instance where this CommandWindow object is located
Parent	Returns the direct parent object for the CommandWindow object
TextDocument	Returns an instance of the TextDocument object representing the text in the Command window

Table 10-2 lists the methods of this interface.

Table 10-2: The CommandWindow Methods

Method	Description
Clear	Clears the content of the window
OutputString	Writes a string to the window
SendInput	Sends a line of the input to the window

As an example, Listing 10-11 clears the Command window and writes a string to it. The CommandWindowSample method is called from the Exec method in the add-in.

Listing 10-11: Working with the Command Window

```
private void CommandWindowSample()
{
    this._applicationObject.ToolWindows.CommandWindow.Clear();

    this._applicationObject.ToolWindows.CommandWindow.OutputString
        ("Wrox Professional Visual Studio Extensibility");
}
```

Figure 10-8 shows the output of this code.

200

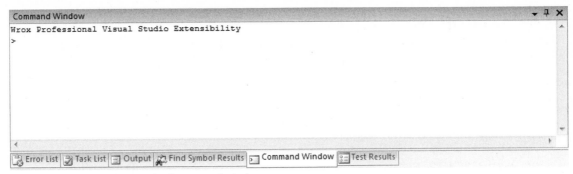

Figure 10-8: Writing text to the **Command window**

Error List

The ErrorList interface represents the Error List window in the automation model. In order to work with this window, you need to deal with its properties, which are described in Table 10-3.

Table 10-3: The ErrorList Properties

Property	Description
DTE	Returns the DTE object instance where this ErrorList object is located
ErrorItems	Returns an instance of the ErrorItems collection that contains a list of ErrorItem objects for each error item. This enables you to access information about individual error items.
Parent	Returns the direct parent object for the ErrorList object
SelectedItems	Returns an object as a list of selected items in the window
ShowErrors	Determines whether the errors should be displayed in the Error List window
ShowMessages	Determines whether the messages should be displayed in the Error List window
ShowWarnings	Determines whether the warnings should be displayed in the Error List window

Listing 10-12 is an example that shows how to use this interface. It excludes messages and warnings from the Error List window and shows the filename in which the first error item is located in a MessageBox.

Listing 10-12: Working with Error List Window

```
private void ErrorListSample()
{
    this._applicationObject.ToolWindows.ErrorList.ShowMessages = false;
    this._applicationObject.ToolWindows.ErrorList.ShowWarnings = false;

    MessageBox.Show(string.Format("First item's file name: {0}",

    this._applicationObject.ToolWindows.ErrorList.ErrorItems.Item(1).FileName));
}
```

The output is shown in Figure 10-9 and Figure 10-10.

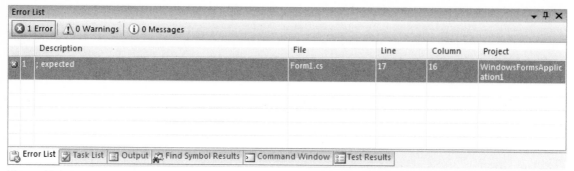

Figure 10-9: Excluding messages and warnings from the Error List window

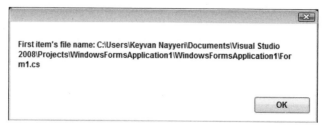

Figure 10-10: Showing the filename of the first error in the list

Output Window

You can work with Output window via the OutputWindow interface in the automation model, which provides the four properties listed in Table 10-4.

Table 10-4: The OutputWindow Properties

Property	Description
ActivePane	Returns an instance of the OutputWindowPane object for the latest active pane in output window
DTE	Returns the DTE object instance where this OutputWindow object is located
OutputWindowPanes	Returns an instance of the OutputWindowPanes for the collection of all panes in the window
Parent	Returns the direct parent object for the OutputWindow object

Solution Explorer

The SolutionExplorer property of the DTE.ToolWindows object is of type UIHierarchy. This type is used in Visual Studio IDE to represent hierarchical tool windows such as Solution Explorer, Server Explorer, and Macro Explorer.

This interface provides some properties and methods to work with the tree of items in these windows and simplifies your work.

You can read about the properties of this interface in Table 10-5.

Table 10-5: The <UIHierarchy> Properties

Property	Description
DTE	Returns the DTE object instance where this UIHierarchy object is located
Parent	Returns the direct parent object for the UIHierarchy object
SelectedItems	Returns a collection of selected items in the hierarchy
UIHierarchyItems	Returns a collection of all items in the hierarchy

The methods of this interface are listed in Table 10-6.

Table 10-6: The <UIHierarchy> Methods

Method	Description
DoDefaultAction	Performs the default action associated with the hierarchy. This is similar to double-clicking on the item or pressing Enter.
GetItem	Returns an item for the specified path
SelectDown	Selects the item right after the currently selected item
SelectUp	Selects the item right before the currently selected item

Task List

The TaskList interface is the next type that helps you work with the Task List window, and it has five properties (listed in Table 10-7).

Table 10-7: The TaskList Properties

Property	Description
DefaultCommentToken	Returns the default string that you can use to add tasks to the list
DTE	Returns the DTE object instance where this `TaskList` object is located
Parent	Returns the direct parent object for the `TaskList` object
SelectedItems	Returns a collection of selected task items in the list
TaskItems	Returns an instance of the `TaskItems` object for the collection of all task items in the list

There are also some related objects for working with the Task List window, such as `TaskItems`, `TaskItem`, and `TaskListEvents`. They are not covered here, as they have a simple structure and you can understand them quickly.

As a very simple example, Listing 10-13 shows the code to add a new task to the list on-the-fly. It simply calls the `Add` method of the `TaskItems` object to add a new item.

Listing 10-13: Adding a New Task to the Task List Window

```
private void TaskListSample()
{
    this._applicationObject.ToolWindows.TaskList.TaskItems.Add(" ", " ", "New Task",
        vsTaskPriority.vsTaskPriorityMedium, vsTaskIcon.vsTaskIconComment,
        true, "", 8, true, true);
}
```

The result is shown in Figure 10-11. Note that the task that is added from the add-in appears in the Add-ins and Macros list by default.

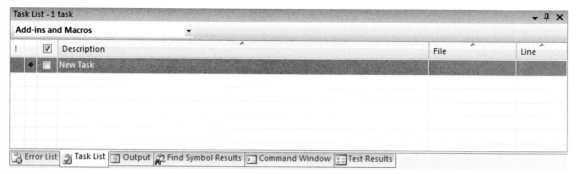

Figure 10-11: Adding a new task to the Task List

ToolBox

The last window is the ToolBox, and it has an associated ToolBox interface in the automation model to represent it with the four properties listed in Table 10-8.

Table 10-8: The ToolBox Properties

Property	Description
ActiveTab	Returns an instance of the ToolBoxTab object for the currently selected item in the ToolBox
DTE	Returns the DTE object instance where this ToolBox object is located
Parent	Returns the direct parent object for the ToolBox object
ToolBoxTabs	Returns an instance of the ToolBoxTabs object for the collection of items in the ToolBox

Summary

This chapter covered three major topics related to the user interface: adding user interface elements to your add-ins, manipulating Windows Forms elements, and manipulating the main Visual Studio windows.

First we talked about adding add-in command items to menus and toolbars, and then we explored adding Windows Forms to add-ins to display user interface elements.

After that, we addressed the second major topic of the chapter: manipulating Windows Forms in the designer and how to add controls to forms and set their properties.

The last topic was Visual Studio windows and how to manipulate them. Here we looked at six main windows in the IDE: the Command window, the Error List, Output window, Solution Explorer, the Task List, and the Toolbox.

11

Tools Options Page

All good professional software has options for configuration, and tools that enable users to customize the application. You're already familiar with options menu items in many applications and no doubt always head there to change the behavior of an application. We need the same capability for Visual Studio add-ins, because when it comes to real-world scenarios, we need to enable our end users to configure the add-in based on their requirements and get the best performance from it.

However, because Visual Studio is our host application when writing add-ins, it doesn't seem like a good idea to create a separate options page for our add-ins and implement a lot of code to display — possibly creating add-ins inconsistent with the environment.

In Visual Studio, an excellent options page is located in the Tools menu — one that enables you to configure Visual Studio behavior. All the extensions to Visual Studio use this page for their configuration. Add-ins aren't an exception, and it's strongly recommended that you make your options a part of the options page in Visual Studio in order to maintain consistency.

This chapter shows you how to create and customize a page in the Options dialog for your add-ins in order to make it configurable. Included in this chapter are the following:

❑   A quick overview of how to create a Tools Options page for add-ins

❑   How to implement an options page for an add-in

❑   How to configure an add-in to use the options page

This isn't a broad or complicated topic, so you can learn it quickly, and then easily apply its content in real-world scenarios.

Background

If you go to the Tools ⇨ Options dialog in the Visual Studio environment, you can find a list of categories and subcategories in the left pane that provides options for different aspects of Visual Studio. For example, Figure 11-1 shows the Options dialog page for the Themes subcategory of the Workflow Designer category, which is responsible for providing options for Windows Workflow Designer themes.

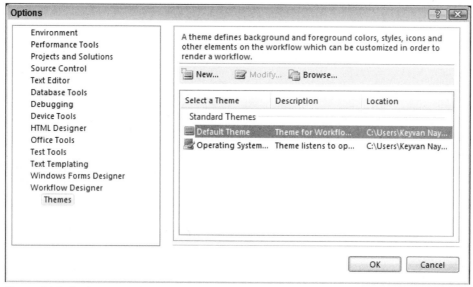

Figure 11-1: Options page for Workflow Designer

Implementing such an options page for Visual Studio extensions (add-ins in our case) is an easy task, which you'll learn in this chapter. Then you can apply your knowledge to create options pages for other extension types, such as VSPackages. Here I'll just focus on add-ins and implementing an options page for them.

You need to follow two main steps to create an options page for an add-in:

1. Implement the EnvDTE.IDTToolsOptionsPage interface in a class.
2. Configure your .AddIn file to use this class.

Previously, the process of creating the custom options page was harder, as you needed to work with ActiveX controls and registry keys, but you no longer need to deal with such things. Instead, you can work with XML files and easily configure your add-ins.

Implementing the Options Page

Implementing the options page is as easy as creating a custom user control and adding your own logic to it, and then implementing the IDTToolsOptionsPage interface for it.

The following sections describe this process step by step using a sample add-in that includes an options page for user-defined configurations. As usual, I first create an add-in project but without adding any custom code implementation for it.

Creating a User Control

First, you need to create a user control for your options page user interface. This custom user control will be inserted in the Options dialog, so you need to consider its size in order to achieve a uniform look for your options page.

You can create this user control either by adding a user control to your add-in project or by creating a Windows Forms Controls Library project, and then referencing it in your .AddIn file configuration. The first approach is more common because it makes deployment easier.

After creating my add-in project, I add a new user control to it and name it OptionsPage, to reflect its purpose. I then set its size to 380 × 160 to display better in the Options dialog.

Suppose I wanted to create a file path for the user to store some information. In that case, I would add a Label and a TextBox to the user control to collect the user's input (see Figure 11-2). Note that it would be better to use a dialog to allow the user to choose the path easily — but here I want to keep things simple and focus on the task at hand.

Figure 11-2: The user control structure

Now that I have created my user interface, I can go to the next step: implementing my logic for the options page.

Implementing the IDTToolsOptionsPage Interface

The next step, and the main step, is implementing logic to deal with the user control that you created, thus bringing it to life.

Visual Studio needs a class that implements the EnvDTE.IDTToolsOptionsPage interface so it will be considered as the options page via the .AddIn configuration file. You need to implement this interface in your user control in order to apply your logic to the code.

The IDTToolsOptionsPage interface has five methods of implementation, which are listed and described in Table 11-1.

Table 11-1: The IDTToolsOptionsPage Methods

Method	Description
GetProperties	Returns an object representing properties for the options page
OnAfterCreated	Occurs after an options page is created
OnCancel	Occurs when the user clicks the Cancel button
OnHelp	Occurs when the user clicks the Help button
OnOk	Occurs when the user clicks the OK button

Now if I implement the IDTToolsOptionsPage interface without adding any code to my user control, it should look like what is shown in Listing 11-1.

Listing 11-1: Initial Implementation of the IDTToolsOptionsPage Interface

```
using System;
using System.Collections.Generic;
using System.ComponentModel;
using System.Drawing;
using System.Data;
using System.Text;
using System.Windows.Forms;

using EnvDTE;

namespace OptionsPageSample
{
    public partial class OptionsPage : UserControl, IDTToolsOptionsPage
    {
        public OptionsPage()
        {
            InitializeComponent();
        }

        #region IDTToolsOptionsPage Members

        public void GetProperties(ref object PropertiesObject)
        {
            throw new NotImplementedException();
        }

        public void OnAfterCreated(DTE DTEObject)
        {
            throw new NotImplementedException();
        }
```

```
        public void OnCancel()
        {
            throw new NotImplementedException();
        }

        public void OnHelp()
        {
            throw new NotImplementedException();
        }

        public void OnOK()
        {
            throw new NotImplementedException();
        }

        #endregion
    }
}
```

Before following the implementation, I need to define a class to hold the options page properties to be used in conjunction with the GetProperties method.

As there is only one string property for the path that I need, I define a new class and name it PageProperties, with a single string property, as shown in Listing 11-2.

Listing 11-2: OptionsPageSample

```
using System;
using System.Collections.Generic;
using System.Text;
using System.Runtime.InteropServices;

namespace OptionsPageSample
{
    [ComVisible(true)]
    [ClassInterface(ClassInterfaceType.AutoDual)]
    public class PageProperties
    {
        public string PathProperty
        {
            get
            {
                return OptionsPage.GetValue();
            }
            set
            {
                OptionsPage.SetValue(value);
            }
        }
    }
}
```

For now, don't worry about the `OptionsPage.GetValue` and `OptionsPage.SetValue` method calls. They're discussed later in the chapter.

As you can see, this class is marked with two attributes that make it COM-visible and define its interface type.

Let's get back to the OptionsPage implementation. Now I need to add code logic for the IDTToolsOptionsPage interface methods. Before doing this, I create a static instance of the newly created `PageProperties` class in my `OptionsPage` class to keep properties. After this, I add some codes to my class, as shown in Listing 11-3.

Listing 11-3: Add-in Implementation for IDTToolsOptionsPage Methods

```
using System;
using System.Collections.Generic;
using System.ComponentModel;
using System.Drawing;
using System.Data;
using System.Text;
using System.Windows.Forms;
using EnvDTE;

namespace OptionsPageSample
{
    public partial class OptionsPage : UserControl, IDTToolsOptionsPage
    {
        static PageProperties properties = new PageProperties();

        public OptionsPage()
        {
            InitializeComponent();
        }

        #region IDTToolsOptionsPage Members

        public void GetProperties(ref object PropertiesObject)
        {
            PropertiesObject = properties;
        }

        public void OnAfterCreated(DTE DTEObject)
        {
            this.txtPath.Text = GetValue();
        }

        public void OnCancel()
        {
        }

        public void OnHelp()
```

```
        {
            MessageBox.Show("Help can be displayed here!");
        }

        public void OnOK()
        {
            SetValue(txtPath.Text);
        }

        #endregion
    }
}
```

In the `GetProperties` method I set the parameter that is passed by reference to the internal static instance of my `PageProperties` class.

In the `OnAfterCreated` method I set the `Text` property of my TextBox to what is returned from the `GetValue` method. `GetValue` is a helper method, discussed in a moment, that retrieves the path string value from the registry.

In the `OnCancel` method I haven't inserted any logic because I don't need it, but you can add your own logic to be executed before closing the options page. On the other hand, in the `OnHelp` method, I just show a MessageBox for simplicity. However, you can do even more — for example, create an instance of a help form and show it to the user.

In the last method, `OnOK`, I called the helper `SetValue` method, which gets a string parameter to store that parameter in the registry, and I also passed the `Text` property of the TextBox.

I'm almost done with the code. I just need to implement two helper methods: `SetValue` and `GetValue`. These two methods are responsible for storing and retrieving, respectively, the string value of the path to or from the registry keys. Using registry keys for this purpose is a common technique, but you can write your own code to use different storage systems, such as the file system, for this purpose.

Listing 11-4 shows the code for the `SetValue` method.

Listing 11-4: SetValue Method

```
public static void SetValue(string value)
{
    string registryValue;

    RegistryKey registryKey = Registry.CurrentUser.OpenSubKey
        (@"SOFTWARE\Microsoft\VisualStudio\9.0", true);
    if (!string.IsNullOrEmpty(value))
        registryValue = value;
    else
        registryValue = "0";

    registryKey.SetValue("PathPropertyForOptionsPage",
        registryValue, RegistryValueKind.String);
}
```

The preceding code created a RegistryKey object in order to gain access to an appropriate registry key. It then calls the SetValue method to store the path value in the registry.

Listing 11-5 is the code for the GetValue method.

Listing 11-5: GetValue Method

```
public static string GetValue()
{
    RegistryKey registryKey = Registry.CurrentUser.OpenSubKey
        (@"SOFTWARE\Microsoft\VisualStudio\9.0", false);

    string registryValue = (string)registryKey.GetValue
        ("PathPropertyForOptionsPage", "0");

    if (registryValue == "0")
        return string.Empty;

    return registryValue;
}
```

In this code I created an instance of the RegistryKey object again, but this time to retrieve the path string. I used the same registry path and name to get access to the stored information, and then called the GetValue method of the RegistryKey to load the path string and return it.

Applying all these changes to the OptionsPage class, the final code looks like Listing 11-6.

Listing 11-6: Final OptionsPage Code

```
using System;
using System.Collections.Generic;
using System.ComponentModel;
using System.Drawing;
using System.Data;
using System.Text;
using System.Windows.Forms;
using EnvDTE;

using Microsoft.Win32;

namespace OptionsPageSample
{
    public partial class OptionsPage : UserControl, IDTToolsOptionsPage
    {
        static PageProperties properties = new PageProperties();

        public OptionsPage()
        {
            InitializeComponent();
        }

        #region IDTToolsOptionsPage Members

        public void GetProperties(ref object PropertiesObject)
```

```
{
    PropertiesObject = properties;
}

public void OnAfterCreated(DTE DTEObject)
{
    this.txtPath.Text = GetValue();
}

public void OnCancel()
{
}

public void OnHelp()
{
    MessageBox.Show("Help can be displayed here!");
}

public void OnOK()
{
    SetValue(txtPath.Text);
}

#endregion

#region Helper methods

public static void SetValue(string value)
{
    string registryValue;

    RegistryKey registryKey = Registry.CurrentUser.OpenSubKey
        (@"SOFTWARE\Microsoft\VisualStudio\9.0", true);
    if (!string.IsNullOrEmpty(value))
        registryValue = value;
    else
        registryValue = "0";

    registryKey.SetValue("PathPropertyForOptionsPage",
        registryValue, RegistryValueKind.String);
}

public static string GetValue()
{
    RegistryKey registryKey = Registry.CurrentUser.OpenSubKey
        (@"SOFTWARE\Microsoft\VisualStudio\9.0", false);

    string registryValue = (string)registryKey.GetValue
        ("PathPropertyForOptionsPage", "0");

    if (registryValue == "0")
```

(continued)

Listing 11-6 *(continued)*

```
                return string.Empty;

        return registryValue;
    }

        #endregion
    }
}
```

That completes the code implementation for the options page, but before configuring an add-in to use this code, I need to modify the add-in to apply this information.

Listing 11-7 shows the code for my add-in after adding simple logic to store a string value in a file at the specified path in the options page.

Listing 11-7: Add-in Implementation

```
using System;
using Extensibility;
using EnvDTE;
using EnvDTE80;
using Microsoft.VisualStudio.CommandBars;
using System.Resources;
using System.Reflection;
using System.Globalization;

using System.IO;

namespace OptionsPageSample
{
    public class Connect : IDTExtensibility2, IDTCommandTarget
    {
        public Connect()
        {
        }

        public void OnConnection(object application, ext_ConnectMode connectMode,
            object addInInst, ref Array custom)
        {
            _applicationObject = (DTE2)application;
            _addInInstance = (AddIn)addInInst;
            if (connectMode == ext_ConnectMode.ext_cm_UISetup)
            {
                object[] contextGUIDS = new object[] { };
                Commands2 commands = (Commands2)_applicationObject.Commands;
                string toolsMenuName;

                try
                {
                    string resourceName;
                    ResourceManager resourceManager = new
ResourceManager("OptionsPageSample.CommandBar",
```

```
                                Assembly.GetExecutingAssembly());
                        CultureInfo cultureInfo = new
CultureInfo(_applicationObject.LocaleID);

                        if (cultureInfo.TwoLetterISOLanguageName == "zh")
                        {
                            resourceName = String.Concat(cultureInfo.Name, "Tools");
                        }
                        else
                        {
                            resourceName =
String.Concat(cultureInfo.TwoLetterISOLanguageName, "Tools");
                        }
                        toolsMenuName = resourceManager.GetString(resourceName);
                    }
                    catch
                    {
                        toolsMenuName = "Tools";
                    }

                    Microsoft.VisualStudio.CommandBars.CommandBar menuBarCommandBar =
((Microsoft.VisualStudio.CommandBars.CommandBars)_applicationObject
.CommandBars)["MenuBar"];

                    CommandBarControl toolsControl =
menuBarCommandBar.Controls[toolsMenuName];
                    CommandBarPopup toolsPopup = (CommandBarPopup)toolsControl;

                    try
                    {
                        Command command = commands.AddNamedCommand2(_addInInstance,
                            "OptionsPageSample", "OptionsPageSample",
                            "Executes the command for OptionsPageSample", true, 59,
                            ref contextGUIDS, (int)vsCommandStatus.
vsCommandStatusSupported +
                                (int)vsCommandStatus.vsCommandStatusEnabled,
                                (int)vsCommandStyle.vsCommandStylePictAndText,
                                vsCommandControlType.vsCommandControlTypeButton);

                        if ((command != null) && (toolsPopup != null))
                        {
                            command.AddControl(toolsPopup.CommandBar, 1);
                        }
                    }
                    catch (System.ArgumentException)
                    {
                    }
                }
            }

        public void OnDisconnection(ext_DisconnectMode disconnectMode, ref Array
custom)
```

(continued)

Listing 11-7 *(continued)*

```
        {
        }

        public void OnAddInsUpdate(ref Array custom)
        {
        }

        public void OnStartupComplete(ref Array custom)
        {
        }

        public void OnBeginShutdown(ref Array custom)
        {
        }

        public void QueryStatus(string commandName, vsCommandStatusTextWanted
neededText,
            ref vsCommandStatus status, ref object commandText)
        {
            if (neededText ==
vsCommandStatusTextWanted.vsCommandStatusTextWantedNone)
            {
                if (commandName == "OptionsPageSample.Connect.OptionsPageSample")
                {
                    status =
(vsCommandStatus)vsCommandStatus.vsCommandStatusSupported
                        | vsCommandStatus.vsCommandStatusEnabled;
                    return;
                }
            }
        }

        public void Exec(string commandName, vsCommandExecOption executeOption,
            ref object varIn, ref object varOut, ref bool handled)
        {
            handled = false;
            if (executeOption == vsCommandExecOption.vsCommandExecOptionDoDefault)
            {
                if (commandName == "OptionsPageSample.Connect.OptionsPageSample")
                {
                    StoreData();

                    handled = true;
                    return;
                }
            }
        }

        private void StoreData()
        {
            string path = OptionsPage.GetValue();
```

```
        if (!string.IsNullOrEmpty(path))
            File.WriteAllText(OptionsPage.GetValue(),
    "This is a sample text to be stored at the specified path!");
        }


        private DTE2 _applicationObject;
        private AddIn _addInInstance;
    }
}
```

In the next section, you'll learn how to configure your add-in to use the created options page.

Configuring the Add-In

In Chapter 6, in the discussion about .AddIn file structure, I briefly introduced the
<ToolsOptionsPage> element as one of optional children elements of the root <Extensibility>
element. I noted that this element can be used to configure an add-in to have a Tools Options page.

This section elaborates on that element and describes how you can configure your .AddIn files to use it.
You already know the structure of the <ToolsOptionsPage> element and its possible children elements
and attributes, so I won't rehash that here.

Listing 11-8 shows the .AddIn file configuration that enables the add-in to use the Tools Options page
created earlier.

Listing 11-8: .AddIn Configuration for the Tools Options Page

```
<?xml version="1.0" encoding="UTF-16" standalone="no"?>
<Extensibility xmlns="http://schemas.microsoft.com/AutomationExtensibility">
  <HostApplication>
    <Name>Microsoft Visual Studio Macros</Name>
    <Version>9.0</Version>
  </HostApplication>
  <HostApplication>
    <Name>Microsoft Visual Studio</Name>
    <Version>9.0</Version>
  </HostApplication>
  <Addin>
    <FriendlyName>Options Page Sample</FriendlyName>
    <Description>
      A sample add-in for Options dialog page.
    </Description>
    <AboutBoxDetails>
      For more information about , see the  website at\r\nhttp://www.wrox.com
    </AboutBoxDetails>
    <AboutIconData>
      <!-- This section is removed to save the space -->
    </AboutIconData>
```

(continued)

Listing 11-8 *(continued)*

```
      <Assembly>OptionsPageSample.dll</Assembly>
      <FullClassName>OptionsPageSample.Connect</FullClassName>
      <LoadBehavior>1</LoadBehavior>
      <CommandPreload>1</CommandPreload>
      <CommandLineSafe>0</CommandLineSafe>
    </Addin>

    <ToolsOptionsPage>
      <Category Name="Sample Category">
        <SubCategory Name="Sample Subcategory">
          <Assembly>OptionsPageSample.dll</Assembly>
          <FullClassName>OptionsPageSample.OptionsPage</FullClassName>
        </SubCategory>
      </Category>
    </ToolsOptionsPage>
```

```
  </Extensibility>
```

In the preceding example code, I just used the assembly name and full class name of my add-in and the `OptionsPage` class to configure the add-in.

After building and deploying the add-in, and then returning to the Tools Options dialog, notice the addition of Sample Category and Sample Subcategory in the left pane, and the options page in the right pane (see Figure 11-3).

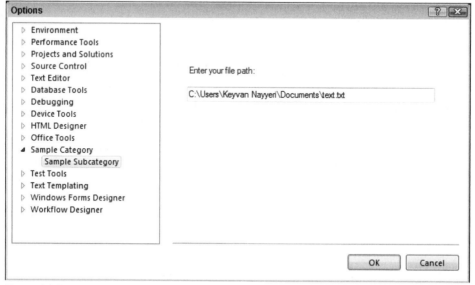

Figure 11-3: Tools Options page for the add-in

If I set the value of the path and click the OK button, then this value will be stored in registry keys and I can see or modify it again whenever I open this dialog. If I click the Cancel button, then it closes the dialog without doing anything. If I click on the question mark button at the top right corner of the dialog, it shows the MessageBox that I wrote in my code (see Figure 11-4).

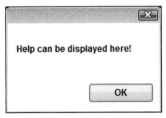

Figure 11-4: Help can be displayed for the Tools Options page.

If you click the OK button, the specified path will be stored in the registry and you can view this change in the Registry Editor (see Figure 11-5).

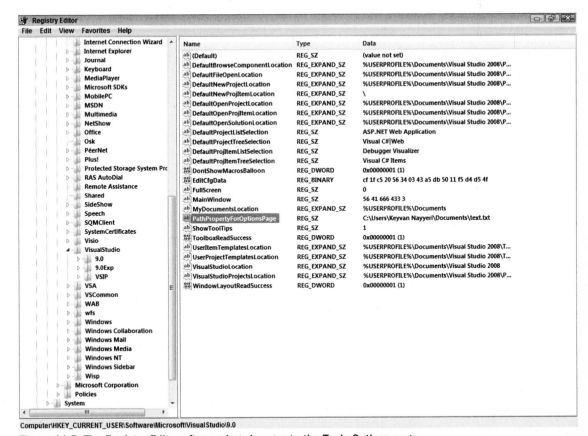

Figure 11-5: The Registry Editor after saving changes to the Tools Options page

If I run this add-in, then it creates a new text file at the specified path in the Tools Options page and stores a text value in it (see Figure 11-6).

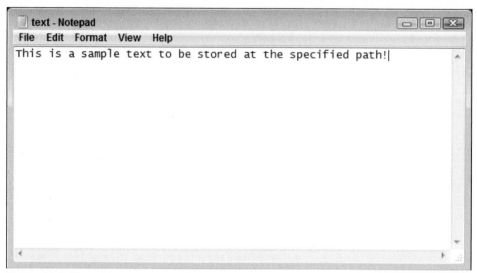

Figure 11-6: The add-in stores the text in the specified file.

As a complement to this section, let me point out that Visual Studio has a set of tokens for .AddIn files. When it first loads, it looks for all .AddIn files and replaces these tokens with their corresponding paths on the system. You can find these tokens in the Tools ⇨ Options page by navigating to the Environment category and the Add-in/Macros Security subcategory. You can use these tokens to simplify the process of deploying your add-ins.

Summary

Having a Tools Options page for your extensions helps users configure them easily and makes your extensions look more professional. In this chapter you learned how to create a Tools Options page for your add-ins, which of course is applicable to other extension types.

You also looked at the two major steps you need to take in order to create an options page, including implementing the IDTToolsOptionsPage interface in your custom user controls and configuring your .AddIn files to use this implementation. This was illustrated with a step-by-step guide and an example.

12

Debugging and Testing Add-Ins

Debugging and testing are two of the main stages in software development that all developers have encountered many times in their programming life. Almost all software has bugs and exceptions that need to be debugged and solved before deployment. You already know these principles from software development textbooks so it isn't necessary to go over the importance of debugging and testing.

What I want to say here, however, is that writing add-ins is no exception to this principle: You need to debug and test your add-ins before deploying them as well. In this case it's even more important, because a simple bug or exception in an add-in can prevent the whole environment from working, even though the structure of Visual Studio and its mechanism to load and manage add-ins try avoid this and run add-ins in a way that can't damage the IDE. However, debugging, exception handling, and testing your add-ins is still mandatory.

If you've written an add-in, how can you test it to make sure it works fine? How can you debug an exception to determine the source of the problem? How can you handle an exception in an appropriate exception-handling mechanism to avoid any problem for the add-in?

All these topics are important for you as a developer, and this chapter aims to teach you how to achieve these goals — how to debug your add-ins, how to handle exceptions, and how to test add-ins before deployment to ensure that they work.

Normally you debug your .NET applications that are DLL files in the Visual Studio IDE with several debugging options. You can do this easily in the same environment, but add-ins are a little different, and some specific techniques should be applied to debug them. You probably would agree that it's not logical to write an add-in and deploy it to see how it works before writing a lot of code to show exceptions in the user interface. This would be a very time-consuming task. The importance of this chapter is that it teaches you how to apply specific techniques to debug your add-ins easily in a shorter amount of time, even though these techniques should be a part of an experienced .NET developer's knowledge of debugging with Visual Studio.

The following list highlights the main topics that you'll encounter in this chapter:

❑ A brief description of debugging and testing add-ins

❑ How to debug add-ins

❑ How to handle errors and exceptions

❑ How to test your add-ins

You should read this chapter carefully because it can help you a lot when developing add-ins.

Background

Unfortunately, the process of debugging an add-in isn't as easy as debugging normal types of .NET applications in Visual Studio, so this chapter will teach you some tips and tricks for doing it.

The difficulty stems from the fact that add-ins can't be loaded by Visual Studio as source code packages and must be compiled into DLL files, with the DLL files then loaded by Visual Studio. However, after loading, you can't access these DLL files because they're locked! That means you can't debug them easily and go back and forth in your code to find the source of a problem.

In order to debug an add-in, you need to be able to start another instance of Visual Studio on-the-fly, which loads your add-in and allows you to debug your code.

The process of debugging an add-in has been made easier since Visual Studio 2005, but it's still different from other debugging methods and a little harder. Nonetheless, in the following sections, you'll learn how to do just that.

The other main topic is handling errors and exceptions in add-in codes. This is very critical, and you have to be careful about it because a simple exception can cause many headaches for anyone attempting to use your add-in. It may even force them to disable your add-in and stop using it. You also learn in the following sections about exception handling in add-in codes.

The last major topic is about testing your add-ins before deployment to ensure that they work as expected. I'll show you some useful techniques, including some unit testing code for testing your code and ensuring its correctness for all inputs and cases. Note, however, you need to have a background in unit testing in order to do unit tests on your add-ins.

Debugging

To debug an add-in you need to start another instance of the Visual Studio IDE when your add-in project is set to start in debug mode. In this case, you can run your add-in in the second IDE and use Visual Studio debugging techniques in the first IDE to see what's going on with your code in the second instance.

By default, the Visual Studio Add-in Wizard generates an add-in project that is configured to start the second instance when you choose to start your project in Debug mode. This process applies some changes to your project configuration to let you debug your add-in easily.

However, for various reasons you may need to configure your add-in project to start the second instance of the Visual Studio IDE manually, so I'll describe that process first. Begin by creating a new add-in project with the Visual Studio Add-in Wizard (as described in Chapter 5). After you've completed the wizard successfully and created an add-in project, right-click the add-in project's name in the Solution Explorer and choose Properties (alternatively, you can access project properties from menus or any other way that you know). Now choose the Debug item from the left to see how this project is configured for debugging (see Figure 12-1).

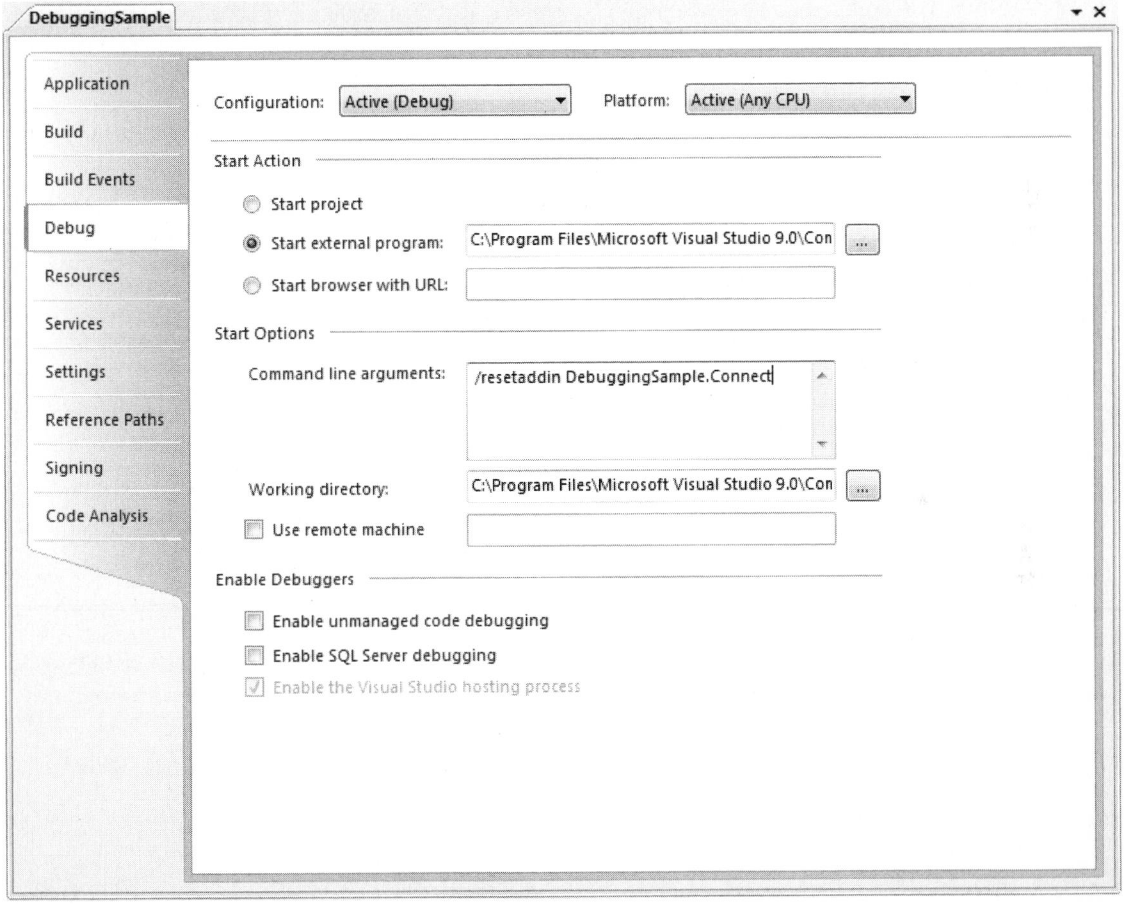

Figure 12-1: Debug properties for an add-in project

You need to have an external program launched when you start your add-in project in debug mode, so choose the appropriate Start Action item, which is "Start external program." Then set it to the path of the Visual Studio launcher path (devenv.exe).

The other change is to pass appropriate command-line arguments when launching the IDE, so you need to add some arguments to the "Command line arguments" text box of the Start Options section. These changes restart your add-in whenever you start the add-in in debug mode:

```
/resetaddin DebuggingSample.Connect
```

After you have these settings, when you start your project in debug mode (by clicking on the appropriate buttons or menu items or pressing F5), a second instance of the Visual Studio IDE is loaded with your add-in, and you can debug your add-in in this IDE.

This is the default behavior, but I prefer to customize this process to use a better environment for my debugging purposes. There is an *experimental hive IDE* for Visual Studio that can be installed when you install the Visual Studio SDK on your machine. This experimental hive is very similar to the original Visual Studio IDE and is suitable for debugging purposes. It comes in handy when you're debugging VSPackages (described in Chapter 18). Figure 12-2 shows the Visual Studio experimental hive in its default mode. You'll notice the similarity between the main IDE and the experimental hive.

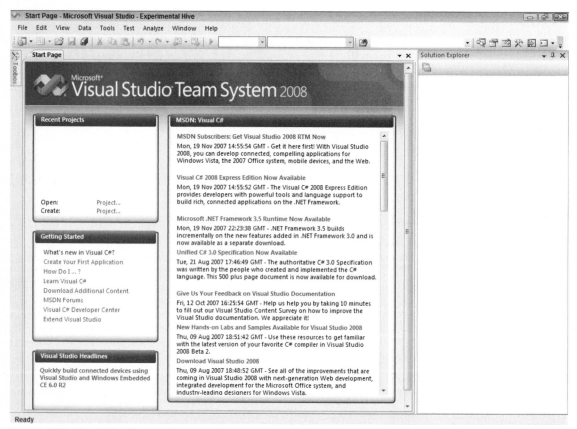

Figure 12-2: Visual Studio experimental hive

I got this idea from VSPackages and so far have had good experiences with it and can recommend it to you as well. However, in order to use the experimental hive, you must configure your add-in project manually and tweak the settings described earlier.

You can load the Visual Studio experimental hive by passing command-line arguments to the Visual Studio IDE launcher, so you don't need to change the path of the external program that you want to use for debugging your add-in, and you only need to add two command-line arguments. The final command-line arguments should look like the following:

```
/resetaddin DebuggingSample.Connect

/rootSuffix Exp /RANU
```

These changes are shown in Figure 12-3.

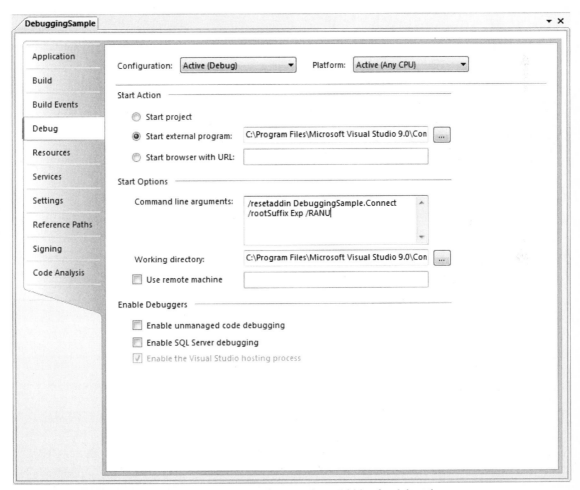

Figure 12-3: Configuring the add-in project to use the experimental hive for debugging

Now you know how to configure your project to be able to debug your add-in. Let's take a look at a sample debugging scenario to get familiar with the debugging process.

For debugging purposes, I've written the sample add-in shown in Listing 12-1. This add-in doesn't do anything except request, in an InputBox, a file path from the user. It then saves a text string into the file at the specified path.

Listing 12-1: Sample Add-in for Debugging

```
using System;
using Extensibility;
using EnvDTE;
using EnvDTE80;
using Microsoft.VisualStudio.CommandBars;
using System.Resources;
using System.Reflection;
using System.Globalization;
using System.Windows.Forms;

using Microsoft.VisualBasic;
using System.IO;

namespace DebuggingSample
{
    public class Connect : IDTExtensibility2, IDTCommandTarget
    {
        public Connect()
        {
        }

        public void OnConnection(object application, ext_ConnectMode connectMode,
            object addInInst, ref Array custom)
        {
            _applicationObject = (DTE2)application;
            _addInInstance = (AddIn)addInInst;
            if (connectMode == ext_ConnectMode.ext_cm_UISetup)
            {
                object[] contextGUIDS = new object[] { };
                Commands2 commands = (Commands2)_applicationObject.Commands;
                string toolsMenuName;

                try
                {
                    string resourceName;
                    ResourceManager resourceManager = new
ResourceManager("DebuggingSample.CommandBar",
                        Assembly.GetExecutingAssembly());
                    CultureInfo cultureInfo = new
CultureInfo(_applicationObject.LocaleID);

                    if (cultureInfo.TwoLetterISOLanguageName == "zh")
                    {
                        resourceName = String.Concat(cultureInfo.Name, "Tools");
                    }
```

```
                    else
                    {

resourceName = String.Concat(cultureInfo.TwoLetterISOLanguageName, "Tools");
                    }
                    toolsMenuName = resourceManager.GetString(resourceName);
                }
                catch
                {
                    toolsMenuName = "Tools";
                }

                Microsoft.VisualStudio.CommandBars.CommandBar menuBarCommandBar =
((Microsoft.VisualStudio.CommandBars.CommandBars)_applicationObject.
CommandBars)["MenuBar"];

                CommandBarControl toolsControl = menuBarCommandBar.
Controls[toolsMenuName];
                CommandBarPopup toolsPopup = (CommandBarPopup)toolsControl;

                try
                {
                    Command command = commands.AddNamedCommand2(_addInInstance,
"DebuggingSample",
 "DebuggingSample", "Executes the command for DebuggingSample",
                        true, 59, ref contextGUIDS,
(int)vsCommandStatus.vsCommandStatusSupported +
                        (int)vsCommandStatus.vsCommandStatusEnabled,
(int)vsCommandStyle.vsCommandStylePictAndText,
                        vsCommandControlType.vsCommandControlTypeButton);

                    if ((command != null) && (toolsPopup != null))
                    {
                        command.AddControl(toolsPopup.CommandBar, 1);
                    }
                }
                catch (System.ArgumentException)
                {
                }
            }
        }

        public void OnDisconnection(ext_DisconnectMode disconnectMode, ref Array
custom)
        {
        }

        public void OnAddInsUpdate(ref Array custom)
        {
        }

        public void OnStartupComplete(ref Array custom)
```

(continued)

Listing 12-1 *(continued)*

```
        {
        }

        public void OnBeginShutdown(ref Array custom)
        {
        }

        public void QueryStatus(string commandName, vsCommandStatusTextWanted
neededText,
            ref vsCommandStatus status, ref object commandText)
        {
            if (neededText == vsCommandStatusTextWanted.
vsCommandStatusTextWantedNone)
            {
                if (commandName == "DebuggingSample.Connect.DebuggingSample")
                {
                    status = (vsCommandStatus)vsCommandStatus.
vsCommandStatusSupported |
                        vsCommandStatus.vsCommandStatusEnabled;
                    return;
                }
            }
        }

        public void Exec(string commandName, vsCommandExecOption executeOption, ref
object varIn,
            ref object varOut, ref bool handled)
        {
            handled = false;
            if (executeOption == vsCommandExecOption.vsCommandExecOptionDoDefault)
            {
                if (commandName == "DebuggingSample.Connect.DebuggingSample")
                {
                    WriteToFile();

                    handled = true;
                    return;
                }
            }
        }

        private void WriteToFile()
        {
            string path = Interaction.InputBox
                ("Enter path:", "Path", "Enter your file path here", 300, 400);

            File.WriteAllText(path, "Sample text!");
        }

        private DTE2 _applicationObject;
        private AddIn _addInInstance;
    }
}
```

To begin, start this add-in in debug mode in the experimental hive and run it, but don't change the default value in the InputBox from what is shown in Figure 12-4.

Figure 12-4: Leave the InputBox as is, without any changes.

Obviously, in this case you have entered an invalid path and you wouldn't expect the add-in to work. However, the add-in doesn't throw any exception — it just doesn't work (as expected). How can you determine why it couldn't work?

Let's work around this by putting a breakpoint before the line that stores data to the text file to determine the value of the path variable. (I'm assuming here that you're an experienced developer and already know how to debug a code by finding some possible reasons for the bug.) This step is shown in Figure 12-5.

```
private void WriteToFile()
{
    string path = Interaction.InputBox
        ("Enter path:", "Path", "Enter your file path here", 300, 400);

    File.WriteAllText(path, "Sample text!");
}

private DTE2 _applicationObject;
private AddIn _addInInstance;
```

Figure 12-5: Insert a breakpoint to debug the code.

Now you can run the add-in in debug mode and leave the InputBox without any change to reach the breakpoint. At this point you can use several debugging options, such as visualizers, the Locals window, or the Watch window, to monitor the values of variables. As shown in Figure 12-6, you can see that the value of the path property is invalid for a path, and can change your code to handle this exception easily.

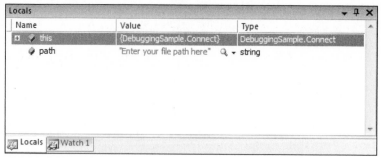

Figure 12-6: You can use the Locals window to monitor the value of variables.

When you build an add-in project and restart the Visual Studio IDE to load the project again and follow your development, you'll probably get an error when trying to build and start the add-in project. The error message will indicate that the add-in DLL file is in use by other processes. To work around this, simply disable the add-in from working for the current instance of the Visual Studio IDE, and then begin working on your code. I use a post-build command-line event for the add-in project to copy my add-in DLL and .AddIn file to the appropriate path and debug my add-ins easily.

Exception Handling

There are no special instructions regarding exception and error handling in add-ins, but you need to know that Visual Studio doesn't throw exceptions, so they won't be shown to end users. In other words, if there is an exception in your add-in somewhere, then Visual Studio keeps working and doesn't show any exception — but most likely the add-in won't work as expected.

Listing 12-2 shows the updated code for the `WriteToFile` method provided in Listing 12-1 to add exception handling logic.

Listing 12-2: A Work-around to Handle the Exception

```
private void WriteToFile()
{
    string path = Interaction.InputBox
        ("Enter path:", "Path", "Enter your file path here", 300, 400);

    try
    {
        File.WriteAllText(path, "Sample text!");
    }
    catch (UnauthorizedAccessException ex)
    {
        // Exception handled
    }
}
```

Obviously, this handles the exception, but it's useless because it doesn't do anything that Visual Studio doesn't do itself. Nonetheless, you can use these exception-handling mechanisms to log events and exceptions somewhere and then view them later in order to solve exceptions in your add-in. This makes your add-in more professional and helps you diagnose and deal with reported bugs when your add-ins are in the hands of users.

For example, Listing 12-3 updates the code in Listing 12-2 to log the exception in the system Event Log (don't forget to add a reference to the System.Diagnostics namespace).

Listing 12-3: Logging the Exception to the Event Log

```
private void WriteToFile()
{
    string path = Interaction.InputBox
        ("Enter path:", "Path", "Enter your file path here", 300, 400);

    try
    {
        File.WriteAllText(path, "Sample text!");
    }
    catch (UnauthorizedAccessException ex)
    {
        EventLog.WriteEntry("Sample Add-in", ex.ToString(),
            EventLogEntryType.Error);
    }
}
```

Unit Testing

Test-driven development (also known as TDD) has become a very common way to develop software. In this case, you develop your software based on tests and try to write several tests to ensure that your code works.

Part of test-driven development is unit testing, whereby you write programming codes to test different units of your code to ensure that smaller pieces work as expected before putting these pieces together to build your software. There are two approaches for testing: test first and test last. In this former case, you develop an application from the base using unit tests; in the latter technique you use architecture-driven methods to develop the software, and then test your code after that.

One of the great benefits of automated unit testing is the confidence it provides you to guarantee the integrity of your code. It can also help you test your code in smaller units, especially in critical cases that you think might cause problems for your application.

Some editions of Visual Studio 2005 supported unit-testing features out of the box, but Visual Studio 2008 supports these features for more commercial editions. Moreover, these features are enhanced in Visual Studio 2008. You can also find several unit-testing applications that are available commercially or free online. I've listed some well-known unit-testing tools in Appendix A.

If you don't know about test-driven development and unit testing or your knowledge isn't very deep, I strongly recommend that you learn more about them, as they're going to be increasingly important and common in the near future.

A detailed discussion of test-driven development and unit testing is beyond the scope of this book (they're even beyond the scope of a single book), so we won't get into much more detail about them here. Instead, I provide a simple example to demonstrate the idea.

Suppose that you have a simple add-in that shows a MessageBox, and you want to restrict when this add-in can run to times after 6:00. The code for this add-in is presented in Listing 12-4. Notice the additions to the QueryStatus method.

Listing 12-4: Sample Add-in for Testing

```csharp
using System;
using Extensibility;
using EnvDTE;
using EnvDTE80;
using Microsoft.VisualStudio.CommandBars;
using System.Resources;
using System.Reflection;
using System.Globalization;

using System.Windows.Forms;

namespace TestingSample
{
    public class Connect : IDTExtensibility2, IDTCommandTarget
    {
        public Connect()
        {
        }

        public void OnConnection(object application, ext_ConnectMode connectMode,
            object addInInst, ref Array custom)
        {
            _applicationObject = (DTE2)application;
            _addInInstance = (AddIn)addInInst;
            if (connectMode == ext_ConnectMode.ext_cm_UISetup)
            {
                object[] contextGUIDS = new object[] { };
                Commands2 commands = (Commands2)_applicationObject.Commands;
                string toolsMenuName;

                try
                {
                    string resourceName;
                    ResourceManager resourceManager = new
ResourceManager("TestingSample.CommandBar",
                        Assembly.GetExecutingAssembly());
                    CultureInfo cultureInfo = new
CultureInfo(_applicationObject.LocaleID);

                    if (cultureInfo.TwoLetterISOLanguageName == "zh")
```

```
                {
                    resourceName = String.Concat(cultureInfo.Name, "Tools");
                }
                else
                {
                    resourceName =
String.Concat(cultureInfo.TwoLetterISOLanguageName, "Tools");
                }
                toolsMenuName = resourceManager.GetString(resourceName);
            }
            catch
            {
                toolsMenuName = "Tools";
            }

            Microsoft.VisualStudio.CommandBars.CommandBar menuBarCommandBar =
((Microsoft.VisualStudio.CommandBars.CommandBars)_applicationObject
.CommandBars)["MenuBar"];

            CommandBarControl toolsControl = menuBarCommandBar
.Controls[toolsMenuName];
            CommandBarPopup toolsPopup = (CommandBarPopup)toolsControl;

            try
            {
                Command command = commands.AddNamedCommand2(_addInInstance,
"TestingSample",
                    "TestingSample", "Executes the command for TestingSample",
true, 59,
                     ref contextGUIDS,
(int)vsCommandStatus.vsCommandStatusSupported +
                        (int)vsCommandStatus.vsCommandStatusEnabled,
                        (int)vsCommandStyle.vsCommandStylePictAndText,
                        vsCommandControlType.vsCommandControlTypeButton);

                if ((command != null) && (toolsPopup != null))
                {
                    command.AddControl(toolsPopup.CommandBar, 1);
                }
            }
            catch (System.ArgumentException)
            {
            }
        }
    }

    public void OnDisconnection(ext_DisconnectMode disconnectMode, ref Array
custom)
    {
    }

    public void OnAddInsUpdate(ref Array custom)
```

(continued)

Listing 12-4 *(continued)*

```csharp
        {
        }

        public void OnStartupComplete(ref Array custom)
        {
        }

        public void OnBeginShutdown(ref Array custom)
        {
        }

        public void QueryStatus(string commandName, vsCommandStatusTextWanted
neededText,
            ref vsCommandStatus status, ref object commandText)
        {
            if (neededText ==
vsCommandStatusTextWanted.vsCommandStatusTextWantedNone)
            {
                if (commandName == "TestingSample.Connect.TestingSample")
                {
                    if (CanRunAddIn())
                    {
                        status =
(vsCommandStatus)vsCommandStatus.vsCommandStatusSupported |
                            vsCommandStatus.vsCommandStatusEnabled;
                        return;
                    }
                }
            }
        }

        public void Exec(string commandName, vsCommandExecOption executeOption,
            ref object varIn, ref object varOut, ref bool handled)
        {
            handled = false;
            if (executeOption == vsCommandExecOption.vsCommandExecOptionDoDefault)
            {
                if (commandName == "TestingSample.Connect.TestingSample")
                {
                    ShowMessage();

                    handled = true;
                    return;
                }
            }
        }

        private void ShowMessage()
        {
```

```
                    MessageBox.Show("Wrox Professional Visual Studio Extensibility");
        }

        private bool CanRunAddIn()
        {
            if (DateTime.Now.Hour >= 6)
                return true;
            return false;
        }

        private DTE2 _applicationObject;
        private AddIn _addInInstance;
    }
}
```

Now suppose that you want to test the QueryStatus method to make sure that it works as expected. To do this, you create a new Visual Studio unit-test project and add a test method to test your QueryStatus method. The code for this test class is shown in Listing 12-5.

Listing 12-5: Class to Test the Add-in

```
using TestingSample;
using Microsoft.VisualStudio.TestTools.UnitTesting;
using EnvDTE;
using System;

namespace UnitTestAddIn
{


    /// <summary>
    ///This is a test class for ConnectTest and is intended
    ///to contain all ConnectTest Unit Tests
    ///</summary>
    [TestClass()]
    public class ConnectTest
    {

        private TestContext testContextInstance;

        /// <summary>
        ///Gets or sets the test context which provides
        ///information about and functionality for the current test run.
        ///</summary>
        public TestContext TestContext
        {
            get
            {
                return testContextInstance;
            }
```

(continued)

Listing 12-5 *(continued)*

```csharp
            set
            {
                testContextInstance = value;
            }
        }

        /// <summary>
        /// A test for QueryStatus
        /// </summary>
        [TestMethod()]
        public void QueryStatusTest()
        {
            Connect target = new Connect();

            string commandName = "TestingSample.Connect.TestingSample";

            vsCommandStatusTextWanted neededText =
                vsCommandStatusTextWanted.vsCommandStatusTextWantedNone;

            vsCommandStatus status = new vsCommandStatus();
            vsCommandStatus statusExpected = new vsCommandStatus();

            if (DateTime.Now.Hour >= 6)
                statusExpected =
        (vsCommandStatus)vsCommandStatus.vsCommandStatusSupported
                    | vsCommandStatus.vsCommandStatusEnabled;

            object commandText = null;

            target.QueryStatus(commandName, neededText, ref status, ref
    commandText);

            Assert.AreEqual(statusExpected, status);
        }
    }
}
```

Let's walk through the preceding example. You want to test whether the `QueryStatus` method works as expected. This means that you expect it to return a specific value for the `status` parameter based on the time when the add-in is running. Therefore, you expect a value for the `status` parameter that is passed by reference, and you need to check its value after running the `QueryStatus` method with the value that you expect.

With this background information, after creating a new instance of the `Connect` class, you pass the appropriate values for the `commandName` and `neededText` parameters, and then create two variables as `status` and `statusExpected`.

After that, you set the `statusExpected` value based on the time; and after that, you call the `QueryStatus` by passing the `status` variable by reference. After running the method, you check the equality of `status` and `statusExpected` to ensure that this method is working as expected.

Now if you run this test, it can pass successfully (see Figure 12-7).

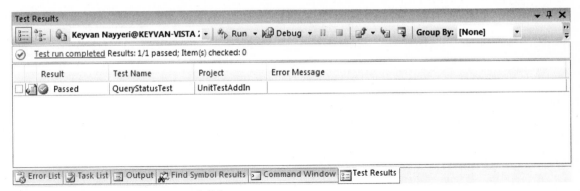

Figure 12-7: The test passes successfully!

Summary

Debugging and testing are two main stages of developing any software, and both are covered in this chapter for add-ins. First you learned how to configure your add-in projects for debugging and looked at an example of debugging. Then you read a short description of error and exception handling in add-ins, and finally you learned about unit testing for add-ins, using a simple example add-in.

13

Deploying Add-Ins

Generally, the last stage of developing an add-in is deploying it and enabling users to install and apply it easily. Deployment is an important stage of software development, and important enough to warrant its own chapter.

The process of deploying an add-in on a user's machine isn't complicated, and you can do it easily. For the machine on which you develop the add-in, Visual Studio does the job and deploys the add-in for the IDE, but for other machines you need to copy necessary files to appropriate paths to enable the add-in on those machines.

Add-ins are COM components, and previously they had to be registered on all machines that wanted to host them; otherwise, they didn't work. Now, however, you can simply copy two files to appropriate paths to enable them. For this task, .AddIn files come into play and do the job for you, configuring the add-in to work with the Visual Studio IDE easily.

You need to have an appropriate Visual Studio version installed on the machine. For example, if you have written an add-in for Visual Studio 2008 with newly added APIs to its automation model and have configured its .AddIn file to use the Visual Studio 2008 IDE as the application host, then it's not possible to install this add-in on machines with Visual Studio 2005 installed.

Deploying an add-in isn't hard to do manually, but it's been simplified by Windows Installer packages that automatically copy files on-the-fly.

In this chapter you'll read about the following:

- ❑ Steps required to deploy an add-in
- ❑ Where to copy required files to
- ❑ Using Windows Installer to deploy an add-in
- ❑ How to use the Visual Studio Content Installer tool to simplify deployment
- ❑ The Add-in Manager dialog

After reading this chapter, you'll know everything necessary to work with the automation model and create add-ins from start to finish. In Chapter 14, you'll learn how to localize your add-ins as well.

An Overview of the Deployment Process

The process of deploying an add-in is straightforward. This process was harder in the past when you had to register the add-in COM component on the machine in the registry and copy some files to appropriate paths, but now you don't need to worry about such tasks.

After writing your add-in, and debugging and testing it to make sure it works as expected on your development machine, you need to build it. After a successful build, you need to ensure that the .AddIn file that configures the add-in to work with the IDE is ready. You can find a detailed discussion about this file in Chapter 6.

When all these things are done successfully, you'll have the two files necessary to deploy an add-in:

❏   The add-in's DLL file, which contains all the code and logic for it

❏   The .AddIn file, which configures the add-in to work with the Visual Studio IDE

Both of these files need to be copied to appropriate paths on the target machines in order to deploy add-ins. This procedure varies depending on your Windows version and your Visual Studio installation paths.

The add-in installation path for the current user is the Addins folder, located in the Visual Studio 2008 folder in the Documents folder of the current user (or the My Documents folder for Windows XP and 2003 users). In fact, this path can be represented as "[*PersonalFolder*]\Visual Studio 2008\Addins."

> *This installation path is for Visual Studio 2008 add-ins. If you're going to install an add-in for Visual Studio 2005, for example, then you need to replace the Visual Studio 2008 folder with Visual Studio 2005. In addition, if the Addins folder doesn't exist, then you can create it manually.*

Windows Installer

One of the options you have to simplify the deployment process is to use a Windows Installer to copy files to appropriate paths. Before looking at this option, however, consider the following very simple example add-in to deploy.

This sample add-in just updates the text in the IDE status bar. The code for this add-in is presented in Listing 13-1.

Listing 13-1: Add-in to Update the Status Bar Text

```
using System;
using Extensibility;
using EnvDTE;
using EnvDTE80;
using Microsoft.VisualStudio.CommandBars;
```

```
using System.Resources;
using System.Reflection;
using System.Globalization;

namespace DeploymentSample
{
    public class Connect : IDTExtensibility2, IDTCommandTarget
    {
        public Connect()
        {
        }

        public void OnConnection(object application, ext_ConnectMode connectMode,
            object addInInst, ref Array custom)
        {
            _applicationObject = (DTE2)application;
            _addInInstance = (AddIn)addInInst;
            if (connectMode == ext_ConnectMode.ext_cm_UISetup)
            {
                object[] contextGUIDS = new object[] { };
                Commands2 commands = (Commands2)_applicationObject.Commands;
                string toolsMenuName;

                try
                {
                    string resourceName;
                    ResourceManager resourceManager = new
ResourceManager("DeploymentSample.CommandBar",
                        Assembly.GetExecutingAssembly());
                    CultureInfo cultureInfo = new
CultureInfo(_applicationObject.LocaleID);

                    if (cultureInfo.TwoLetterISOLanguageName == "zh")
                    {
                        resourceName = String.Concat(cultureInfo.Name, "Tools");
                    }
                    else
                    {
                        resourceName =
String.Concat(cultureInfo.TwoLetterISOLanguageName, "Tools");
                    }
                    toolsMenuName = resourceManager.GetString(resourceName);
                }
                catch
                {
                    toolsMenuName = "Tools";
                }

                Microsoft.VisualStudio.CommandBars.CommandBar menuBarCommandBar =
                    ((Microsoft.VisualStudio.CommandBars.CommandBars)
_applicationObject.CommandBars)["MenuBar"];

                CommandBarControl toolsControl =
menuBarCommandBar.Controls[toolsMenuName];
```

(continued)

Listing 13-1 *(continued)*

```csharp
            CommandBarPopup toolsPopup = (CommandBarPopup)toolsControl;

            try
            {
                Command command = commands.AddNamedCommand2(_addInInstance,
"DeploymentSample",
                    "DeploymentSample", "Executes the command for
DeploymentSample", true, 59,
                    ref contextGUIDS,
(int)vsCommandStatus.vsCommandStatusSupported +
                    (int)vsCommandStatus.vsCommandStatusEnabled,
(int)vsCommandStyle.vsCommandStylePictAndText,
                    vsCommandControlType.vsCommandControlTypeButton);

                if ((command != null) && (toolsPopup != null))
                {
                    command.AddControl(toolsPopup.CommandBar, 1);
                }
            }
            catch (System.ArgumentException)
            {
            }
        }
    }

    public void OnDisconnection(ext_DisconnectMode disconnectMode, ref Array
custom)
    {
    }

    public void OnAddInsUpdate(ref Array custom)
    {
    }

    public void OnStartupComplete(ref Array custom)
    {
    }

    public void OnBeginShutdown(ref Array custom)
    {
    }

    public void QueryStatus(string commandName, vsCommandStatusTextWanted
neededText,
        ref vsCommandStatus status, ref object commandText)
    {
        if (neededText ==
vsCommandStatusTextWanted.vsCommandStatusTextWantedNone)
        {
            if (commandName == "DeploymentSample.Connect.DeploymentSample")
            {
                status =
(vsCommandStatus)vsCommandStatus.vsCommandStatusSupported |
```

```
                        vsCommandStatus.vsCommandStatusEnabled;
                    return;
                }
            }
        }

        public void Exec(string commandName, vsCommandExecOption executeOption, ref
object varIn,
            ref object varOut, ref bool handled)
        {
            handled = false;
            if (executeOption == vsCommandExecOption.vsCommandExecOptionDoDefault)
            {
                if (commandName == "DeploymentSample.Connect.DeploymentSample")
                {
                    UpdateStatus();

                    handled = true;
                    return;
                }
            }
        }

        private void UpdateStatus()
        {
            this._applicationObject.StatusBar.Text =
    "Professional Visual Studio Extensibility";
        }

        private DTE2 _applicationObject;
        private AddIn _addInInstance;
    }
}
```

The output of this add-in is shown in Figure 13-1.

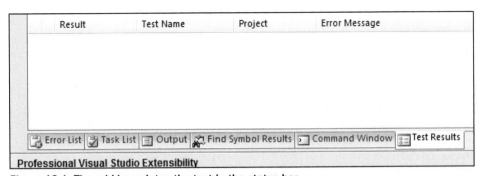

Figure 13-1: The add-in updates the text in the status bar.

Now you can create a Windows Installer to deploy this add-in automatically. To do so, add a new Setup project to your solution (see Figure 13-2).

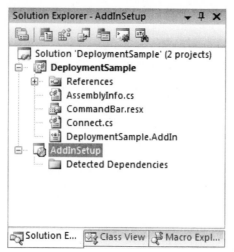

Figure 13-2: Add a Setup project to the solution.

After creating the Setup project, you need to set its Project Output to your add-in project by right-clicking on the setup project name and choosing Add ⇨ Project Output. Here, choose the Primary Output option for the add-in project chosen in the Project drop-down list (see Figure 13-3).

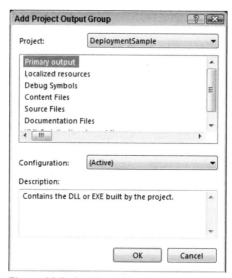

Figure 13-3: Set the project output.

After choosing these, you can click the OK button to add the output to the Setup project. This adds any required dependencies to the project as well (see Figure 13-4).

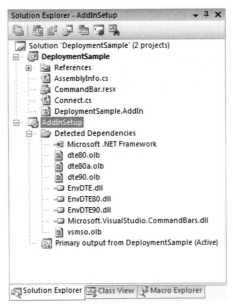

Figure 13-4: Project output is added to the setup.

The next step is to deploy the add-in files to the appropriate path on the user's machine. To do this, you first open the File System view of the user's machine and right-click on the root node to choose Add Special Folder ⇨ Custom Folder. Then you choose a name for the folder (such as "AddIns Folder").

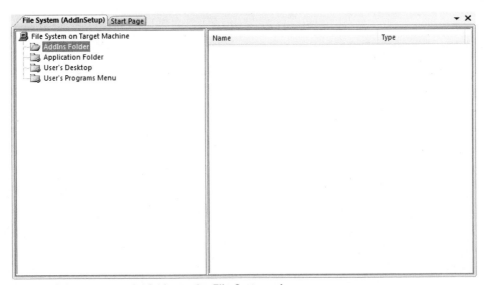

Figure 13-5: Add a special folder to the File System view.

After this, you set the `DefaultLocation` property of this folder in the Properties window to "[*PersonalFolder*]\Visual Studio 2008\Addins" (for Visual Studio 2008). This action deploys everything in the newly created folder to the Addins folder.

Now you add a file and an assembly to this folder by right-clicking in the right pane and choosing Add ⇨ File and Add ⇨ Assembly. Shown in Figure 13-6 are my add-in assembly and .AddIn files.

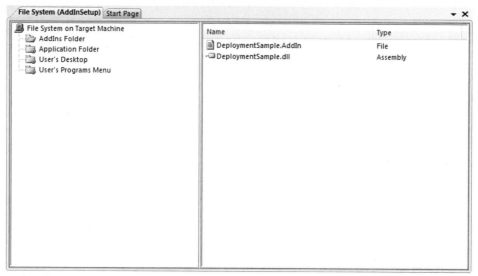

Figure 13-6: Add a file and an assembly to the Setup project.

We're almost done with this Setup project, but you can add some properties, such as author name, description, manufacturer, and title, to the add-in project via its Properties window.

After building your projects in the right order, you have a Setup project that can deploy your add-in automatically (see Figure 13-7).

Figure 13-7: Add-in setup starts

After finishing this setup, the add-in is available in your Visual Studio IDE. Later, if desired, you can also uninstall this add-in from the machine, just as you would other programs.

Visual Studio Content Installer

Using a Windows Installer is an excellent and easy way to deploy add-ins and many other types of Visual Studio extensions, but it can be even simpler for both the developer and the user.

Craig Skibo, a former member of the Visual Studio Ecosystem team, has done a great job of creating a general content installer for Visual Studio extensions that enables you have a dedicated Windows Installer for Visual Studio content. This installer simplifies the process of creating and deploying add-ins for developers, and makes the add-in easier to use for users. It saves you the effort of deploying files to appropriate places because it knows where to deploy them. All you need do is define the extension type you're going to deploy and the list of files; the installer does the rest for you.

Operation of this content installer is based on a single XML file, which has a special structure defined by its schema. This content installer can be used to deploy the following types of items:

❑ Add-ins

❑ Code snippets

❑ Visual Studio templates

❑ Toolbox controls

❑ Macros

Here are the simple steps you need to take in order to deploy an add-in:

1. Create your add-in and ensure that it works properly.

2. Create an XML file to define the content installer and give it a .vscontent extension.

3. Create a ZIP package of your add-in files and the .vscontent file and rename its extension to .vsi.

That's all you need; and after creating the .vsi file, you can simply click on it and run the Windows Content Installer to deploy your add-in or other extensions.

Here I want to discuss the XML structure of VSContent file definitions. This XML file has an XML namespace that must be set to `http://schemas.microsoft.com/developer/vscontent/2005`. It has a root `<Content>` element that doesn't have any attributes, it but can have six possible elements:

❑ `<Attributes>`: Can contain one or more `<Attribute>` elements that specify a combination of name-value pairs for additional information about the content, such as the project type for a Visual Studio template

❑ `<ContentVersion>`: This is a string value of the content version that always must be set to 1.0 or 2.0. The 1.0 is for Visual Studio 2005 content and the 2.0 is for Visual Studio 2008.

❑ `<Description>`: String value of a description about the content

❑ `<DisplayName>`: String value of a display name for the content

❑   `<FileContentType>`: Specifies the content type, such as Addin, Code Snippet, VSTemplate, Toolbox Control, and Macro Project

❑   `<FileName>`: String value of the filename, which is inserted in the package to deploy. `<Content>` can contain one or more `<FileName>` elements.

Listing 13-2 shows the XML content of my VSContent file for deploying the sample add-in provided in Listing 13-2.

Listing 13-2: VSContent to Deploy the Add-in

```xml
<?xml version="1.0" encoding="utf-8"?>
<VSContent xmlns="http://schemas.microsoft.com/developer/vscontent/2005">
  <Content>
    <ContentVersion>2.0</ContentVersion>
    <Description>Sample package for VS Content Installer.</Description>
    <DisplayName>Sample VS Content Installer</DisplayName>
    <FileContentType>Addin</FileContentType>
    <FileName>DeploymentSample.dll</FileName>
    <FileName>DeploymentSample.addin</FileName>
  </Content>
</VSContent>
```

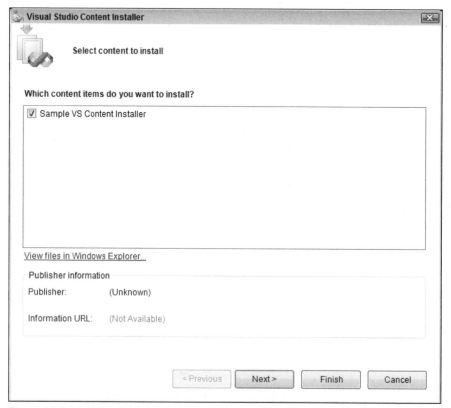

Figure 13-8: The Visual Studio Content Installer appears.

Now I can save this file with a .vscontent extension, named appropriately to something like Deployment. vscontent, and then copy my add-in assembly and .AddIn files in the same path as this file. After selecting these three files and adding them to a ZIP archive, I rename the ZIP archive to have a .vsi extension to turn it into a Visual Studio Content Installer. Windows automatically changes the icon of this file and considers it a special type, so when you click on it the content installer appears (see Figure 13-8).

From this page you can select which items to install and/or view the files in Windows Explorer before installation. When you click the Next button, Windows alerts you that your content file has not been signed and may be harmful (see Figure 13-9). You can trust this package and choose Yes.

Figure 13-9: Windows alerts you about the security of the content.

In the next page, you're ready to begin installation by clicking the Finish button (see Figure 13-10).

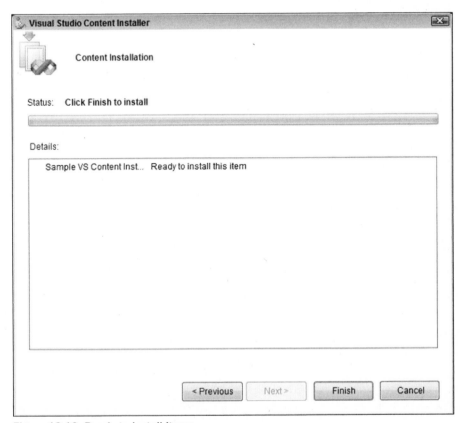

Figure 13-10: Ready to install items

Finally, it installs all the items for you and displays the status report, as shown in Figure 13-11.

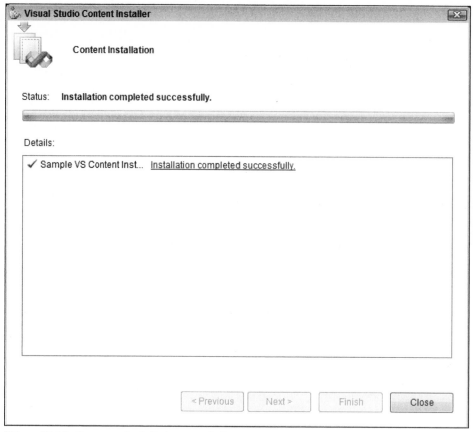

Figure 13-11: Items are installed successfully.

This installer copies files to appropriate paths based on the content type that you defined in your VSContent file. This automatically installs the add-in for you.

You're not limited to deploying a single content item with this installer; you can define multiple <Content> *elements with different content types for installation by this tool.*

Add-In Manager

The last major topic discussed in this chapter is the Add-in Manager window, which is accessible via the Tools ⇨ Add-in Manager menu item in the Visual Studio IDE. The same window can be found for the Macros IDE in the same menu.

This dialog is shown in Figure 13-12.

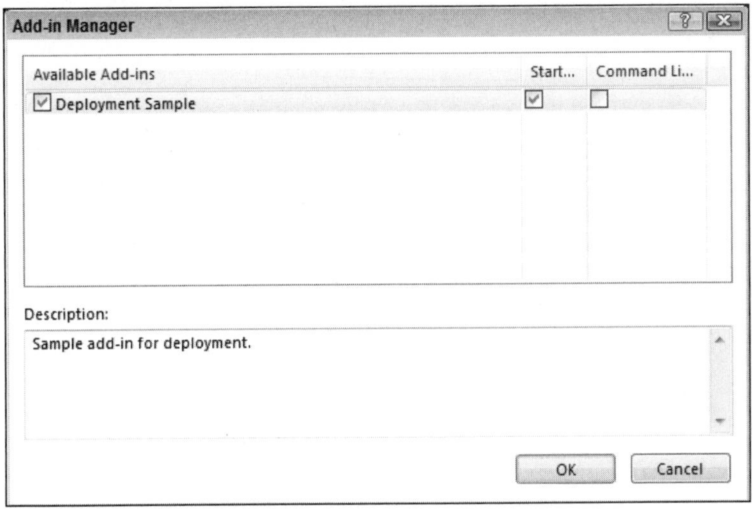

Figure 13-12: Add-in Manager window

The Add-in Manager window helps you to enable or disable available add-ins in the Visual Studio environment. Visual Studio loads all add-ins that it can find and adds them to this dialog. You can check or uncheck them in order to enable or disable them from loading in the environment. The two columns on the right can be used to enable or disable add-ins from starting with the environment startup or loading from the command line. There is also a text description about each add-in that you can define in your .AddIn files.

Summary

This chapter described the final step of the add-in development process: deployment. It began with a quick overview of things you need to do to deploy an add-in, and then demonstrated how to use Setup projects to apply Windows Installer and automatically deploy your add-ins.

The third topic was the Visual Studio Content Installer, which makes this process even simpler. At the end, you had a short introduction to the Add-in Manager in the Visual Studio IDE.

14

Localizing Add-Ins

In previous chapters you learned about different topics connected to add-in development. You also learned important aspects of the automation model and Development Tools Extensibility (DTE). Before leaving the topic of add-ins, however, it would be useful to cover a topic that may be a concern for some developers — localization and internationalization of add-ins.

You need to deal with this topic in the following two cases:

❑ If you're a developer who develops native applications for a particular culture

❑ If you're developing a professional multilingual add-in for several cultures

Localization of .NET applications is a broad topic involving several techniques. For add-ins, the most important concern regards text values that appear in the Visual Studio IDE for end users and that need to be localized for the specific culture.

In this chapter you'll learn about localization of add-ins and how to target different cultures in your add-in user interface. The topics explored in this chapter include the following:

❑ What is localization and what are its goals?

❑ How to use embedded resources in .NET applications

❑ How to use embedded resources to localize an add-in

As a developer, you may not be interested in localization, or think you need to know about it. Nonetheless, it's worth taking a brief look at the topic to learn about the use of resources in add-ins — you may one day find you need to use them in your projects.

What Is Localization?

Before moving forward, let me point out that when I use the term "culture," it has a technical meaning in .NET programming; it reflects a set of native properties for a country or culture such as language, calendar, currency, and alphabet.

The main goal of localization is to replace all culture-specific elements in the user interface with their native corresponding values. The localization process of different cultures may be different, but almost all cultures share some techniques for such tasks as translating the user interface text values and calendars.

In general, the main goal of localization is to ensure that an application works well for another culture.

Internationalization and Localization

Regarding software, the terms internationalization and localization are sometimes misused.

Internationalization is the process of providing all the means necessary to correctly display some culture-specific properties to end users. An example would be making sure that a Persian piece of text can be rendered in a browser without any problems.

Localization is the process of retrieving information and managing the software workflow so that the culture-specific information is actually displayed.

Here's a simple example: Suppose you want to render the Italian text "Ciao Mondo" for end users in an ASP.NET application. Internationalization makes sure that this text can be rendered in the browsers of cultures that don't use the Roman alphabet. Localization enables retrieving this text to show it in the browser.

In this chapter, we'll be talking about localization, and will leave internationalization to the upper levels of the .NET Framework and Windows. You probably won't have any problem rendering your culture-specific information in Visual Studio extensions.

From one point of view, we can split languages into two groups: left-to-right languages (also known as LTR) such as English, Italian, Spanish, French, and many other western languages, and right-to-left languages (RTL) such as Persian and Arabic.

In .NET, especially after the .NET Framework 2.0, Microsoft introduced several features to enable easier localization of different types of applications. In .NET, new classes have been added to represent almost all cultures around the world, with their different properties. For add-ins, however, our big concern is storing and retrieving culture-specific information; you can learn other aspects of localization from general .NET books.

In .NET, the preferred way to store and retrieve culture-specific text values is through resources. *Resources* are a set of different item types that can be embedded into .NET assemblies to be retrieved later. Almost all file types can be stored in resources, including strings, images, and videos.

Embedded Resources

You often need to use different types of resources in your applications — such things as text values, images, videos, and JavaScript files. One option would be storing these resources in their native format in separate files and deploying them with the application, but this wouldn't always be a good choice.

You probably don't want to deploy many files with your application. Even if you could, it would be hard to manage retrieving them for use. Visual Studio add-ins provide a good example. You need to deploy two files for an add-in — its assembly file and its .AddIn configuration file. Deploying more files on an add-in user's machine would be possible but could raise problems of consistency and would make your code more complicated.

Resources are a good way to handle such situations. These resources contain different types of data that can be embedded into .NET assemblies. Actually, .NET uses a built-in mechanism to encode data and insert it into assemblies. This may make your assemblies larger, but it's a good way to keep your projects simple and clean.

> It's common among .NET developers to label these types of resources embedded resources, to differentiate them from the more general term "resources."

You can turn a project item to an embedded resource by marking it in its Properties window and setting its Build Action property to Embedded Resource (see Figure 14-1).

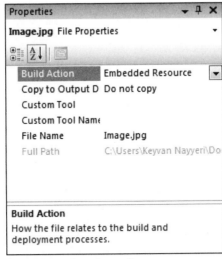

Figure 14-1: Marking a file as an embedded resource

Later you can retrieve the information about this file using the properties and methods of an `Assembly` class instance, which is located in System.Reflection.

For example, suppose that you have a console application and want to open a Windows Form in it in order to show an image. This image is embedded in the assembly.

First, you design a form with a `PictureBox` control on it to show the image. This form has simple code, shown in Listing 14-1.

Listing 14-1: Windows Form Code to Display the Image

```csharp
using System;
using System.Collections.Generic;
using System.ComponentModel;
using System.Data;
using System.Drawing;
using System.Linq;
using System.Text;
using System.Windows.Forms;

namespace EmbeddedResourceSample
{
    public partial class DisplayImage : Form
    {
        public DisplayImage()
        {
            InitializeComponent();
        }

        public Image ImageToDisplay { get; set; }

        private void DisplayImage_Load(object sender, EventArgs e)
        {
            pictureBox.Image = this.ImageToDisplay;
        }
    }
}
```

The console application code is presented in Listing 14-2.

Listing 14-2: Console Application to Load the Image and Display the Form

```csharp
using System;
using System.Collections.Generic;
using System.Linq;
using System.Text;
using System.Reflection;
using System.IO;
using System.Drawing;

namespace EmbeddedResourceSample
{
    class Program
    {
        static void Main(string[] args)
```

```
    {
        // Load the assembly
        Assembly assembly = Assembly.GetExecutingAssembly();

        // Get the stream of the image from the assembly
        Stream stream = assembly.GetManifestResourceStream
            ("EmbeddedResourceSample.Image.jpg");

        // Convert the stream to an Image instance
        Image image = Image.FromStream(stream);

        // Display the form and image on it
        DisplayImage form = new DisplayImage();
        form.ImageToDisplay = image;

        form.ShowDialog();
    }
  }
}
```

The preceding code first creates an instance of the Assembly class, and then passes the image name to its GetManifestResourceStream in order to get the stream value of the image. It then converts this stream to an image and displays the form. The output is shown in Figure 14-2.

Figure 14-2: Displaying the embedded image

The other type of embedded resource is the resource file that is available in projects. You can add it to your projects like other project items. These files have .resx extensions. Actually, these files are a general container for several types of embedded resources, such as strings, images, icons, and audio files. Resource files keep the list of resources as an XML file behind the scenes.

I can add a new resource item and name it Texts, and then open it to add a new string item to its collection. Resource files have a collection of required name-value pairs as well as optional comment items for string resources. When you change the resource type from the top left corner list to something else (such as images), the resource will change its display to be appropriate for that type of resource. However, as shown in Figure 14-3, here I've just used a string resource and added it to the list for my form title.

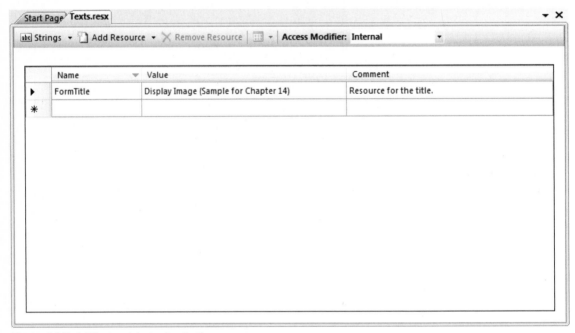

Figure 14-3: Adding a string value to the resource

Next, I update the code to provide the correct form title when it loads (see Listing 14-3).

Listing 14-3: Updating the Title When the Form Loads

```
private void DisplayImage_Load(object sender, EventArgs e)
{
    // Get the ResourceManager instance
    ResourceManager resources = new ResourceManager
        ("EmbeddedResourceSample.Texts", Assembly.GetExecutingAssembly());

    // Retrieve the text
    this.Text = resources.GetString("FormTitle");

    pictureBox.Image = this.ImageToDisplay;
}
```

Here I created an instance of the `ResourceManager` object, located in the System.Resources namespace, by passing the name of the resource file and the instance of my assembly. Then I called its `GetString` method by passing the name of the string resource to retrieve its value. Figure 14-4 shows the output after this change.

Figure 14-4: Output after updating the title using string resources

Obviously, this was a quick overview of embedded resources in .NET, meant only to introduce you to them, in case you don't already know the principles. Their use is vital to any developer who works on Visual Studio extensions, especially add-ins. As you probably guessed, embedded resources are used for localization of add-ins, and you'll read more about this in the next section.

Using Embedded Resources to Localize Add-Ins

The best way to localize Visual Studio add-ins is by using embedded resources. By default, Visual Studio generates an embedded resource for your add-in projects after executing the Add-in Wizard. This embedded resource is named CommandBar.resx. It contains some default string values for localization of command-bar information for common cultures, and you have already seen the auto-generated code for add-ins that retrieves some information for command bars from this resource.

You can follow this process and add your localization string values to add-in projects and retrieve them to localize the user interface for your users. Let's look at a very simple example to help explain the process. This example demonstrates an add-in that just shows a Windows Form to the end user and nothing else. This Windows Form contains two labels that show the current time and a text message. I want to localize this add-in to retrieve the title of the form and the text for these two labels from the embedded resources based on the user's culture. If the user's culture is Farsi (the culture for Persian speakers), then it shows appropriate messages; otherwise, it uses general English strings.

To do this, first I add a new resource file to my add-in project and name it Localization, and then add some string resources to it as shown in Figure 14-5.

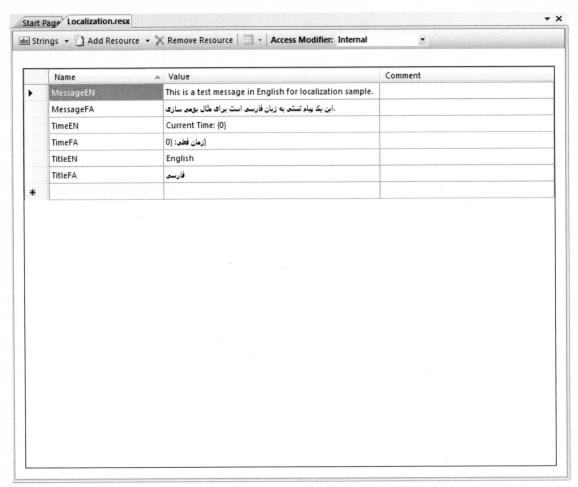

Figure 14-5: Resource file to localize the add-in

Listing 14-4 shows the source code of this add-in, which tries to create an instance of my Windows Form and show it.

Listing 14-4: Add-in to Be Localized

```
using System;
using Extensibility;
using EnvDTE;
using EnvDTE80;
using Microsoft.VisualStudio.CommandBars;
using System.Resources;
using System.Reflection;
using System.Globalization;

using System.Windows.Forms;

namespace LocalizationSample
```

```
{
    public class Connect : IDTExtensibility2, IDTCommandTarget
    {
        public Connect()
        {
        }

        public void OnConnection(object application, ext_ConnectMode connectMode,
            object addInInst, ref Array custom)
        {
            _applicationObject = (DTE2)application;
            _addInInstance = (AddIn)addInInst;
            if (connectMode == ext_ConnectMode.ext_cm_UISetup)
            {
                object[] contextGUIDS = new object[] { };
                Commands2 commands = (Commands2)_applicationObject.Commands;
                string toolsMenuName;

                try
                {
                    string resourceName;
                    ResourceManager resourceManager = new
ResourceManager("LocalizationSample.CommandBar",
                        Assembly.GetExecutingAssembly());
                    CultureInfo cultureInfo = new
CultureInfo(_applicationObject.LocaleID);

                    if (cultureInfo.TwoLetterISOLanguageName == "zh")
                    {
                        System.Globalization.CultureInfo parentCultureInfo =
                            cultureInfo.Parent;
                        resourceName = String.Concat(parentCultureInfo.Name,
"Tools");
                    }
                    else
                    {
                        resourceName =
String.Concat(cultureInfo.TwoLetterISOLanguageName, "Tools");
                    }
                    toolsMenuName = resourceManager.GetString(resourceName);
                }
                catch
                {
                    toolsMenuName = "Tools";
                }

                Microsoft.VisualStudio.CommandBars.CommandBar menuBarCommandBar =
                    ((Microsoft.VisualStudio.CommandBars.CommandBars)
                    _applicationObject.CommandBars)["MenuBar"];

                CommandBarControl toolsControl =
menuBarCommandBar.Controls[toolsMenuName];
```

(continued)

Listing 14-4 *(continued)*

```
                CommandBarPopup toolsPopup = (CommandBarPopup)toolsControl;

                try
                {
                    Command command = commands.AddNamedCommand2(_addInInstance,
                        "LocalizationSample", "LocalizationSample", "Executes the
command for LocalizationSample", true, 59, ref contextGUIDS, (int)vsCommandStatus
.vsCommandStatusSupported + (int)vsCommandStatus.vsCommandStatusEnabled,
(int)vsCommandStyle.vsCommandStylePictAndText, vsCommandControlType.
vsCommandControlTypeButton);

                    if ((command != null) && (toolsPopup != null))
                    {
                        command.AddControl(toolsPopup.CommandBar, 1);
                    }
                }
                catch (System.ArgumentException)
                {
                }
            }
        }

        public void OnDisconnection(ext_DisconnectMode disconnectMode,
            ref Array custom)
        {
        }

        public void OnAddInsUpdate(ref Array custom)
        {
        }

        public void OnStartupComplete(ref Array custom)
        {
        }

        public void OnBeginShutdown(ref Array custom)
        {
        }

        public void QueryStatus(string commandName, vsCommandStatusTextWanted
neededText,
            ref vsCommandStatus status, ref object commandText)
        {
            if (neededText ==
vsCommandStatusTextWanted.vsCommandStatusTextWantedNone)
            {
                if (commandName == "LocalizationSample.Connect.LocalizationSample")
                {
                    status =
(vsCommandStatus)vsCommandStatus.vsCommandStatusSupported |
```

```
                              vsCommandStatus.vsCommandStatusEnabled;
                    return;
                }
            }
        }

        public void Exec(string commandName, vsCommandExecOption executeOption,
            ref object varIn, ref object varOut, ref bool handled)
        {
            handled = false;
            if (executeOption == vsCommandExecOption.vsCommandExecOptionDoDefault)
            {
                if (commandName == "LocalizationSample.Connect.LocalizationSample")
                {
                    frmMain form = new frmMain();
                    if (CultureInfo.CurrentCulture.Name == "fa-IR")
                        form.RightToLeft = RightToLeft.Yes;
                    form.ShowDialog();

                    handled = true;
                    return;
                }
            }
        }
        private DTE2 _applicationObject;
        private AddIn _addInInstance;
    }
}
```

This code should be easy to read and understand so it isn't described it in detail.

Listing 14-5 shows the source code for my Windows Form. It indicates appropriate values to the end user based on his or her culture.

Listing 14-5: Windows Form Source Code

```
using System;
using System.Collections.Generic;
using System.ComponentModel;
using System.Data;
using System.Drawing;
using System.Text;
using System.Windows.Forms;
using System.Resources;
using System.Reflection;
using System.Globalization;


namespace LocalizationSample
{
    public partial class frmMain : Form
    {
        public frmMain()
```

(continued)

Listing 14-5 *(continued)*

```
    {
        InitializeComponent();
    }

    private void frmMain_Load(object sender, EventArgs e)
    {
        LocalizeForm();
    }

    private void LocalizeForm()
    {
        // Set the current culture
        string strCulture = "EN";
        if (CultureInfo.CurrentCulture.Name == "fa-IR")
            strCulture = "FA";

        // Create the ResourceManager instance
        ResourceManager resources = new ResourceManager
            ("LocalizationSample.Localization",
            Assembly.GetExecutingAssembly());

        // Set the form title
        this.Text = resources.GetString("Title" + strCulture);

        // Set the lblTime text
        lblTime.Text = string.Format(resources.GetString("Time" + strCulture),
            DateTime.Now.ToString());

        // Set the lblMessage text
        lblMessage.Text = resources.GetString("Message" + strCulture);
    }
  }
}
```

The main logic is inserted in the `LocalizeForm` method. Here I use a helper `strCulture` variable to simplify my code and set it to the appropriate culture to be used. Then I create a `ResourceManager` object in order to retrieve the string values from the resource. After that, three string values are set to appropriate values from my resource file, based on the culture.

For example, if users have Farsi as their default format and culture, then they'll see Farsi text, as shown in Figure 14-6.

Figure 14-6: Farsi output

If users have anything else as their culture, then English values will be displayed, as shown in Figure 14-7.

Figure 14-7: General English output

Further Localization

This hasn't begun to cover everything that can be said about localization, but it does explain the main point. Translation of text values is the most common part of localization in applications. However, you may need to use local calendars and currency values for your applications as well. In this case, the System.Globalization namespace and its classes provide everything that you need to do that easily. This is a general .NET topic beyond the scope of this chapter, but you can learn about it easily from online resources and tutorials.

In addition to these common steps in localization, RTL languages include an extra step to change the direction of user interface elements in a left-to-right document so that it's right to left (like what I did in its simplest form in my example). This may be hard in some cases, requiring you to do some extra work. This topic is also related to Windows Forms and user interface design. Fortunately, Microsoft has provided great features in Windows Forms to convert texts into right to left.

Summary

This chapter covered localization, especially the translation of add-ins. Localization may be a task that you need to do for your add-ins from time to time, even if you don't frequently deal with other cultures. Aside from this, you'll always need to work with embedded resources for your add-ins, so this chapter should be useful in both cases.

After getting a short introduction to the concept of localization, you learned about embedded resources and how to use them in .NET applications to embed different types of items, including string values, into your assemblies. After that, you learned about localization of add-ins with embedded string resources. Finally, you read a short overview of some extra steps that you may need to follow to localize your add-ins.

15

Visual Studio Shell

You probably already know that Visual Studio has a rich IDE with many great elements. These elements of the IDE and user interface are common in other applications, and they can be helpful for any developer. The great features of Visual Studio toolbars, Explorer windows, or tabular structure are common in today's user interfaces.

This part of the book describes some other options for extending Visual Studio in different ways. The first of these options is Visual Studio Shell. Visual Studio Shell (described in this chapter) enables you to bring Visual Studio IDE elements to your own applications.

There are several benefits of having such a capability:

❑ You can begin building an IDE for your applications from a starting point. Even if your requirements are very different from what is provided by VS Shell, it's still worthwhile because it saves you some extra work.

❑ You can be sure of the power and correctness of what you're using. The Visual Studio IDE has been a well-known and very popular IDE for many years; hence, you can trust it more than any other IDE.

❑ The Visual Studio IDE has most of the common elements in today's interfaces. For example, tabular structure among toolbars is common among user interfaces, and Visual Studio has provided these elements out of the box.

Beside these benefits for your own applications, with Visual Studio Shell you can create custom language IDEs for new development languages, or you can build your own designers. This is provided by the integrated mode of Visual Studio Shell, which is actually another name for the VSPackages described in Chapter 18.

In addition to the integrated mode, there is something new, called *isolated mode,* which is a part of Visual Studio Shell and is added to the Visual Studio SDK in its newest version (2008). This addition is also considered one of the main new features of Visual Studio 2008.

In this chapter you'll learn about the following topics related to Visual Studio Shell and how to use it:

❑ The concept of Visual Studio Shell and its applications

❑ Integrated mode and isolated mode and their differences

❑ How to use Visual Studio isolated mode to extend Visual Studio

❑ How to customize an isolated IDE

❑ How to deploy an isolated IDE

Please note that this chapter isn't a full discussion about Visual Studio Shell — in my opinion, a separate book should be written about this broad topic. Here I'll just provide a short introduction and a quick overview outlining the basic principles of Visual Studio Shell. Unfortunately, currently there isn't any book available about Visual Studio Shell, and online documentation isn't rich enough to help you easily find more details about it. It is hoped that there will be more documentation from Microsoft, along with articles and tutorials from community members, in the near future. The good news is that there are some good open-source projects that are actually showcases for Visual Studio Shell, and you can take a look at their source code to learn many things.

In this chapter I'll use the Visual C++ language for developing my Visual Studio Shell isolated applications, because presently this language is the only one that has a project template for Visual Studio Shell isolated mode development. The integrated mode of Visual Studio Shell is covered in Chapter 18, so here I'll just give an introduction to it and describe its differences from isolated mode.

What Is Visual Studio Shell?

Before Visual Studio 2008, Microsoft provided the capability to use Visual Studio IDE elements in integrated applications as a part of something called Premier Partner Edition. This is actually the previous version of the Visual Studio Shell integrated mode that you'll see in a moment. These applications could use the same instances of Visual Studio on a machine to integrate something external with the Visual Studio IDE. Included was a set of references that you could use in other applications in order to apply Visual Studio user interface elements to your applications and build your applications with VS IDE elements.

The Visual Studio Shell was completely correlated with the installation of Visual Studio, so you couldn't use it without having Visual Studio installed on a machine. This was a big limitation, and as a result only Microsoft could use this technology in some of its products.

A good example of the use of Visual Studio Shell is in Microsoft SQL Server 2005. The IDE for some parts of SQL Server 2005 is based on Visual Studio Shell. For example, if you open the SQL Server 2005 Management Studio (see Figure 15-1) and compare its structure with the Visual Studio IDE (see Figure 15-2), you can see the similarities between these two IDEs.

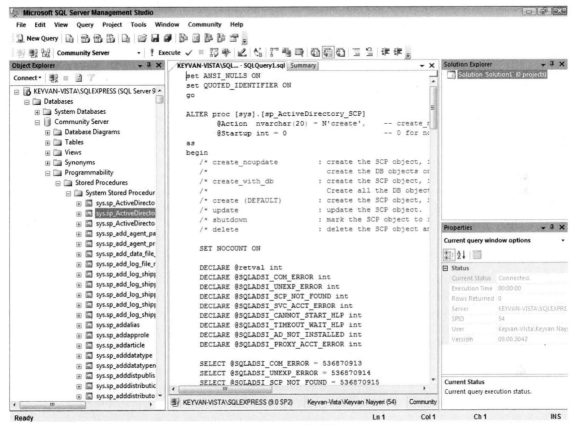

Figure 15-1: Microsoft SQL Server 2005 Management Studio IDE

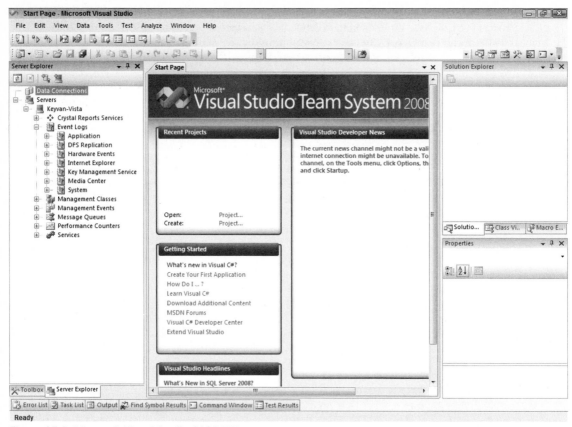

Figure 15-2: Microsoft Visual Studio 2008 IDE

If you take a close look at what is included after installation of Microsoft SQL Server 2005, you'll notice that there are many parts of Visual Studio 2005.

For Visual Studio 2008, Microsoft began thinking about a way around requiring installation of Visual Studio in order to use Visual Studio Shell. The result was a new mode for Visual Studio Shell called *isolated mode*. (The previous mode was *integrated mode,* whereby you could only use Visual Studio Shell by installing Visual Studio.)

Visual Studio Packages and Visual Studio Shell integrated applications are the same, and integrated mode is just another name to describe the relationship between VSPackages and VS Shell. VSPackages are described in Chapter 18 in more detail, which explains how they use the Visual Studio Shell API to work.

Microsoft has released two redistributable packages for the integrated and isolated modes of Visual Studio Shell. These enable you to run your Visual Studio Shell IDEs without needing to install the Visual Studio IDE, which was the main drawback of Premier Partner Edition.

The other prerequisite for your Visual Studio Shell applications is the .NET Framework 3.5. The redistributable packages mentioned above also contain necessary files for the .NET Framework 3.5, and work with it. You just need to add these prerequisite packages to your setup projects in order to deploy them on a user's machine.

Before giving a short description about the integrated and isolated modes of Visual Studio Shell, let's take a look at the concept of Visual Studio *stubs* and the way you run Visual Studio IDE instances.

Every time you run an instance of one of the Visual Studio editions, you're actually running a stub .exe file with a specific AppId for that edition of Visual Studio. This means that the Visual Studio Standard Edition has a specific AppId, and Visual Studio Team Suite has a different AppId.

Stubs enable users to differentiate between different versions of Visual Studio. Using stubs, the Visual Studio team was able to add to a list of core features. The Standard edition adds some extra features to this core, the Professional edition adds new features to the Standard edition, and so forth.

Visual Studio Shell provides a list of the features of the Visual Studio IDE that you can use in your isolated or integrated mode applications, and these features are enabled for you. This list is available online at `http://msdn2.microsoft.com/en-us/vstudio/bb856491.aspx`. Even though you're limited to using these features, you'll find that this list covers almost everything in the Visual Studio IDE for you, so you don't need to worry about being limited.

In addition to this list of features for both isolated and integrated modes, there are also specific lists of features for the two modes that are more detailed than the aforementioned general list.

Integrated Mode

As mentioned in the previous section, the integrated mode of Visual Studio Shell helps you create an integrated IDE with Visual Studio elements in order to integrate external technologies with VS. For example, if you want to integrate a new development tool with Visual Studio, then integrated mode is the best choice for you. Team Explorer, which is a client for Visual Studio Team Foundation Server source control, is integrated with Visual Studio through the integrated mode of Visual Studio Shell.

If you take a closer look at the components installed with the Visual Studio 2008 Team Explorer setup, you'll notice that the Visual Studio 2008 Shell integrated mode package is one of them (see Figure 15-3).

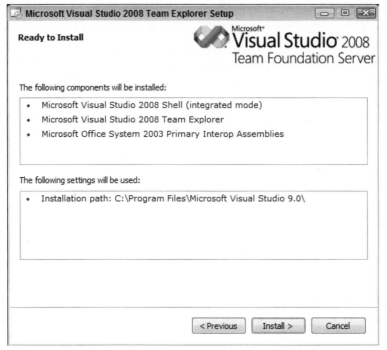

Figure 15-3: Team Explorer setup installs VS Shell integrated mode

Team Explorer adds an Explorer window to the VS IDE to navigate between different projects and repositories on source control and work items related to them. It also adds separate windows for Pending Changes items and viewing work items, so you can see that integrated mode is able to add several windows inside the Visual Studio IDE with a custom implementation and provide a similar look and feel.

In integrated mode, you run your applications based on the same instances of Visual Studio installed on a machine and actually run them in the same stub (with the same AppId) of an available Visual Studio IDE. In other words, you don't create a new IDE; you can develop based on an existing IDE.

Developing within the integrated mode of Visual Studio Shell is a broad topic, so there is a dedicated chapter for this subject later (Chapter 18). The remainder of this chapter concentrates on the new isolated mode.

Isolated Mode

The isolated mode of Visual Studio Shell is completely new and is an addition to and a main feature of Visual Studio 2008. Isolated mode enables you to create your own applications with a user interface similar to Visual Studio, one that consists of customized elements of the Visual Studio IDE.

For example, you can create a customized splash screen, Toolbox, Solution Explorer, or Task List and then use these customized elements in your application. For example, suppose that you're going to write a Unified Modeling Language (UML) tool. You can use the Toolbox to provide various UML diagrams based on different groups, and Solution Explorer as a way to navigate between different parts of a project. You can use the Properties window as a tool to show different properties of a diagram or item.

You can also put your UML designer at the center of the screen to enable users to design their own UML diagrams. Clearly, Visual Studio can be a very good starting point for you.

Isolated mode is independent from the installation of Visual Studio, so you can apply it easily in your applications; you just need to install the Visual Studio Isolated Model redistributable package.

With isolated mode, you create independent IDEs with their own stubs. Moreover, you can enable some extensibility features for these IDEs, just as you can with the Visual Studio IDE. You can use add-ins and packages in your Visual Studio Shell IDEs to enable extensibility for them.

Currently, there are some open-source projects, hosted on CodePlex and written by Microsoft developers or third-party companies, that showcase Visual Studio Shell isolated mode. These can be helpful examples for anyone getting started with isolated IDEs.

One of these projects is AddOn Studio for World of Warcraft (WoW), written by two Microsoft developers and available at `www.codeplex.com/WarcraftAddOnStudio`. This IDE brings the Visual Studio experience to building World of Warcraft game add-ons. AddOn Studio has a custom designer, an editor, IntelliSense, and some other customizations to implement this functionality. Figure 15-4 shows a view of this IDE.

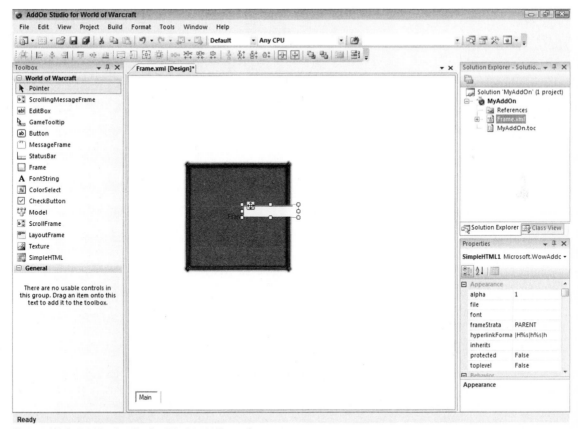

Figure 15-4: AddOn Studio for World of Warcraft

Another such project is IronPython Studio, written by Clarius Consulting, a company that is very active in the area of VS Extensions. This IDE, available at `www.codeplex.com/IronPythonStudio`, is actually an IDE for Python developers who want to develop Python applications for .NET. An IronPython sample is included in the Visual Studio SDK, and IronPython Studio is built on top of this example.

Figure 15-5 shows this IDE when developing an IronPython application.

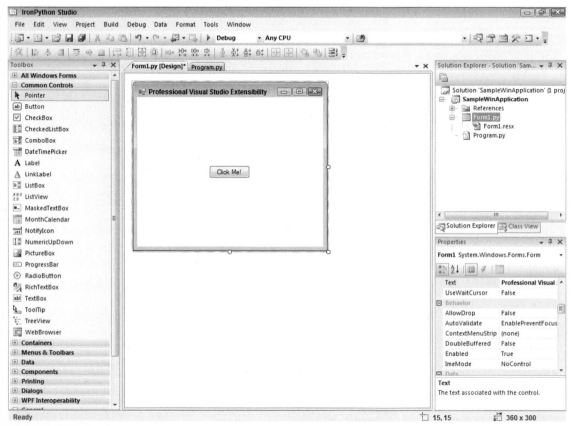

Figure 15-5: IronPython Studio

The last project I want to introduce here is Storyboard Designer — another open-source project written by Clarius Consulting and available at `www.codeplex.com/storyboarddesigner`. This IDE enables developers to design storyboards based on existing controls and designers. It has a domain-specific language in its core and has a custom project and item template.

Figure 15-6 shows this IDE when designing a storyboard diagram.

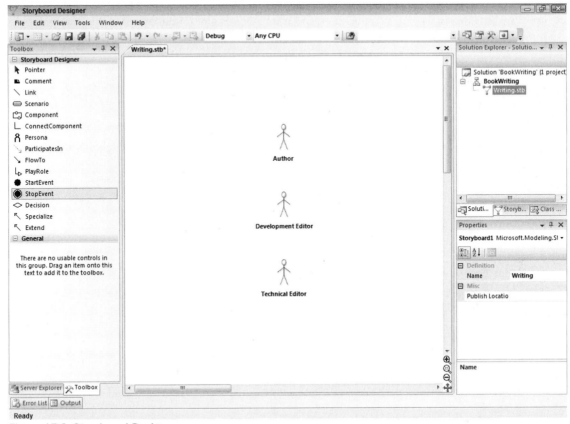

Figure 15-6: Storyboard Designer

I strongly recommend that you use these three samples (as well as any other samples that come along after publication of this book) to learn about VS Shell isolated mode.

A Working Example

I think the best way to learn about the purpose and applications of Visual Studio Shell is to see it in action. To that end, this section provides a sample Visual Studio Shell isolated IDE and describes the process step by step, including some minor customizations to demonstrate how it works.

Of course, this example doesn't show everything about Visual Studio Shell, but as mentioned earlier, VS Shell is a new and wide topic and still has a long way to go to become familiar to developers. It isn't something that can be covered in a single chapter or even a few chapters.

Creating the Project

Obviously, the first step is to create a new project. As with other projects in Visual Studio, you need to open the New Project dialog. Navigate to the Extensibility node and choose the Visual Studio Shell project template (see Figure 15-7).

> *You need to run your Visual Studio IDE as the Administrator user when you're creating a new Visual Studio Shell project; otherwise, you'll encounter problems when running your isolated IDE. To run your Visual Studio IDE as Administrator, simply right-click on its icon and choose the Run as Administrator option in the right-click menu.*

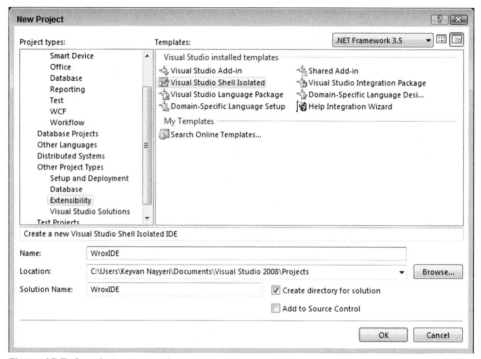

Figure 15-7: Creating a new project

Surprised? Yes, it generates Visual C++ code, because currently Visual Studio Shell is only supported by this language.

What Is There Already?

After creating the project, Visual Studio generates some code for you and creates two projects. The first has the same name that you chose, and the second appends a "UI" suffix. This latter project is responsible for managing the user interface side of things for your isolated IDE.

Figure 15-8 shows the structure of the projects generated by Visual Studio for you.

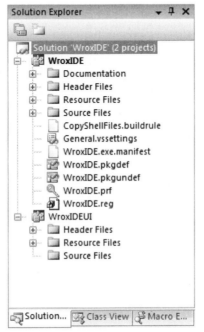

Figure 15-8: The structure of Visual Studio Shell solutions

These two projects contain some files that build your isolated IDE. In the main project, which is also set to be the startup project, there is a folder containing simple documentation about isolated mode. This documentation, which is an HTML file, is opened when you create your project (see Figure 15-9).

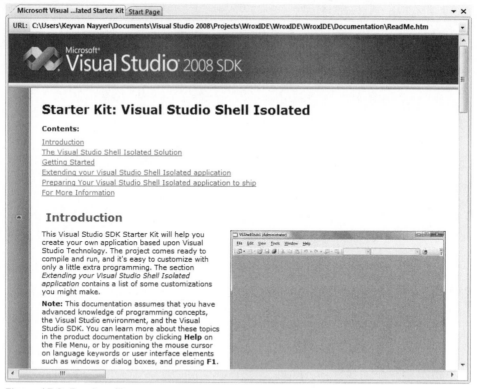

Figure 15-9: Readme file

Also included are some header files for your project, as well as some resource files for configurations, icons, and strings, and some source files for your project. All these files are grouped in separate folders. Some main files for your project are located in the root as well.

In the root you can see a `CopyShellFiles.buildrule` file that defines build rules for your package. There is also a Visual Studio settings file, which is actually an XML file named `General.vssettings`. This can be used to customize your IDE settings.

In addition to these files are two package definition files named `WroxIDE.pkgdef` and `WroxIDE.pkgundef` that declare registry settings for your IDE for installation and uninstallation, respectively.

`WroxIDE.prf` is a PICSRules file that can be installed into the Content Adviser of Internet Explorer, and `WroxIDE.reg` is a registry file that contains all registry settings, which you can merge into the registry of the user's machine in your setup projects.

In the user interface project are three folders that contain header files, resource files, and maybe source files. This code, as is, can be run to load a very simple uncustomized IDE. If you press F5 to run this project, a white splash screen appears, showing your loaded isolated IDE. This IDE, shown in Figure 15-10, looks similar to a clean Visual Studio IDE.

Figure 15-10: The initial isolated IDE

If you take a deeper look at the project properties, you'll notice that there is a pre-build event for the project that builds the project and registers it in the registry. Here is the pre-build event:

```
md "$(OutDir)\PackagesToLoad"
md "$(OutDir)\Profiles"
copy /Y "$(ProjectDir)CurrentSettings.vssettings"
       "$(OutDir)\Profiles\CurrentSettings.vssettings"
copy /Y "$(ProjectDir)$(ProjectName).exe.config" "$(OutDir)"
copy /Y "$(ProjectDir)Splash.bmp" "$(OutDir)"
copy /Y "$(ProjectDir)$(ProjectName).ico" "$(OutDir)"
copy /Y "$(ProjectDir)$(ProjectName).prf" "$(OutDir)\$(ProjectName).prf"
```

This event copies some files such as your IDE settings, the PRF file, and others to appropriate paths. Keep in mind that the entry point of your isolated IDE is a source file named WroxIDE.cpp (this name varies, of course, according to your project's name). The source code of this file is shown in Listing 15-1.

Listing 15-1: Source Code of the Isolated IDE

```
#include "stdafx.h"
#include "WroxIDE.h"

#define MAX_LOADSTRING 100

typedef int (__cdecl *STARTFCN)(LPSTR, LPWSTR, int,
                                            GUID *, WCHAR *pszSettings);
typedef int (__cdecl *SETUPFCN)(LPSTR, LPWSTR, GUID *);
typedef int (__cdecl *REMOVEFCN)(LPSTR, LPWSTR);

void ShowNoComponentError(HINSTANCE hInstance)
{
 WCHAR szErrorString[1000];
 WCHAR szCaption[1000];
 LoadStringW(hInstance, IDS_ERR_MSG_FATAL, szErrorString, 1000);
 LoadStringW(hInstance, IDS_ERR_FATAL_CAPTION, szCaption, 1000);

 MessageBoxW(NULL, szErrorString, szCaption, MB_OK|MB_ICONERROR);
}

// Helper function to convert a unicode string to an ANSI one
static char* W2A(const wchar_t* pwsz)
{
 if (NULL == pwsz)
        return NULL;

 // Get the size of the buffer needed to store the converted string.
 int ret = WideCharToMultiByte(CP_ACP, 0, pwsz, -1,
        NULL, 0, NULL, NULL);
 if (0 == ret)
 {
        return NULL;
 }

 // Get the size of the buffer.
 int bufferSize = ret + 1;
 if (bufferSize < ret)
        return NULL;

 // Allocate the buffer.
 char* ansiBuffer = new char[bufferSize];
 if (NULL == ansiBuffer)
        return NULL;

 if (0 == WideCharToMultiByte(CP_ACP, 0, pwsz, -1, ansiBuffer,
        bufferSize, NULL, NULL))
 {
        delete [] ansiBuffer;
        return NULL;
 }
```

```
    return ansiBuffer;
}

int APIENTRY _tWinMain(HINSTANCE hInstance, HINSTANCE hPrevInstance,
                                LPTSTR lpCmdLine, int nCmdShow)
{
UNREFERENCED_PARAMETER(hPrevInstance);
UNREFERENCED_PARAMETER(lpCmdLine);

int nRetVal = -1;
WCHAR szExeFilePath[MAX_PATH];
HKEY hKeyAppEnv90Hive = NULL;

if(RegOpenKeyExW(HKEY_LOCAL_MACHINE, L"Software\\Microsoft\\AppEnv\\9.0",
        0, KEY_READ, &hKeyAppEnv90Hive) == ERROR_SUCCESS)
{
        DWORD dwType;
        DWORD dwSize = MAX_PATH;
        RegQueryValueExW(hKeyAppEnv90Hive, L"AppenvStubDLLInstallPath",
            NULL, &dwType, (LPBYTE)szExeFilePath, &dwSize);
        RegCloseKey(hKeyAppEnv90Hive);
}

if(GetFileAttributesW(szExeFilePath) == INVALID_FILE_ATTRIBUTES)
{
        //If we cannot find it at a registered location, then try
        // in the same directory as the application
        GetModuleFileNameW(NULL, szExeFilePath, MAX_PATH);
        WCHAR *pszStartOfFileName = wcsrchr(szExeFilePath, '\\');
        if(!pszStartOfFileName)
        {
                return -1;
        }
        *pszStartOfFileName = 0;
        wcscat_s(szExeFilePath, MAX_PATH, L"\\appenvstub.dll");

        if(GetFileAttributesW(szExeFilePath) == INVALID_FILE_ATTRIBUTES)
        {
                //If the file cannot be found in the same directory as the
                // calling exe, then error out.
                ShowNoComponentError(hInstance);
                return -1;
        }
}

HMODULE hModStubDLL = LoadLibraryW(szExeFilePath);
if(!hModStubDLL)
{
        ShowNoComponentError(hInstance);
        return -1;
}

//Check to see if the /setup arg was passed. If so, then call the Setup method
//      to prepare the registry for the AppID.
```

(continued)

283

Listing 15-1 *(continued)*

```
int nArgs = 0;
bool fDoSetup = false;
bool fDoRemove = false;
LPWSTR *szArglist = CommandLineToArgvW(GetCommandLineW(), &nArgs);
for(int i = 0 ; i < nArgs ; i++)
{
        if(_wcsicmp(szArglist[i], L"/setup") == 0)
        {
                fDoSetup = true;
        }
        if(_wcsicmp(szArglist[i], L"/remove") == 0)
        {
                fDoRemove = true;
        }
}
LocalFree(szArglist);

if(fDoSetup && fDoRemove)
{
    //Cannot have both /setup and /remove on the command line at the same time.
     return -1;
}


if(fDoSetup)
{
        WCHAR szExeFilePath[MAX_PATH];

        SETUPFCN Setup = (SETUPFCN)GetProcAddress(hModStubDLL, "Setup");
        if(!Setup)
        {
                ShowNoComponentError(hInstance);
                return -1;
        }

        nRetVal = Setup(W2A(lpCmdLine),
                L"WroxIDE_4ccb9bea-95e7-47ca-83af-ae750a5e7f28", NULL);

        //Store the path to this program in the registry.
        // This is necessary in the event that a service pack
        //  is released for Visual Studio Shell Isolated,
        // or if an update to a package and corresponding
        //  pkgdef file is released. If this information
        // is removed, then updating for these changes may
        //  not be possible.
        const wchar_t* szRegKeyPath =
                L"Software\\Microsoft\\AppEnv\\9.0\\Apps\\WroxIDE_4ccb9bea-95e7-
47ca-83af-ae750a5e7f28";

        GetModuleFileNameW(NULL, szExeFilePath, MAX_PATH);
```

```
                    HKEY hRegKeyExeFilePath = NULL;
                    if(RegCreateKeyExW(HKEY_LOCAL_MACHINE, szRegKeyPath,
                            0, NULL, REG_OPTION_NON_VOLATILE, KEY_READ|KEY_WRITE, NULL,
                            &hRegKeyExeFilePath, NULL) == ERROR_SUCCESS)
                    {
                            RegSetValueExW(hRegKeyExeFilePath, L"StubExePath",
                                    NULL, REG_SZ, (LPBYTE)szExeFilePath,
                                    (wcslen(szExeFilePath)+1)*sizeof(WCHAR));
                            RegCloseKey(hRegKeyExeFilePath);
                    }
            }
            else if(fDoRemove)
            {
                    REMOVEFCN Remove = (REMOVEFCN)GetProcAddress(hModStubDLL, "Remove");
                    if(!Remove)
                    {
                            ShowNoComponentError(hInstance);
                            return -1;
                    }

                    nRetVal = Remove(W2A(lpCmdLine),
                            L"WroxIDE_4ccb9bea-95e7-47ca-83af-ae750a5e7f28");
            }
            else
            {
                    STARTFCN Start = (STARTFCN)GetProcAddress(hModStubDLL, "Start");
                    if(!Start)
                    {
                            ShowNoComponentError(hInstance);
                            return -1;
                    }

                    nRetVal = Start(W2A(lpCmdLine),
                            L"WroxIDE_4ccb9bea-95e7-47ca-83af-ae750a5e7f28",
                            nCmdShow, NULL, NULL);
            }

            FreeLibrary(hModStubDLL);

            return nRetVal;
    }
```

The code in Listing 15-1 is where your IDE manages its setup process, with three switches for setup, remove, and start. The Visual Studio SDK deploys a DLL named AppEnvStup.dll that provides three operations: Setup, Remove, and Start. This tool is used in the code in order to apply these operations.

Using the Setup operation, you can set up your IDEs, and this operation along with the code in Listing 15-1 does the job of registering your IDE in the registry. If you run your IDE and open your registry editor for the "HKEY_LOCAL_MACHINE\SOFTWARE\Microsoft\AppEnv\9.0\Apps\" path, you then can find registry information for your IDE (see Figure 15-11). As you see, your isolated IDE has its own AppId, indicating that it has its own stub and runs independently from Visual Studio.

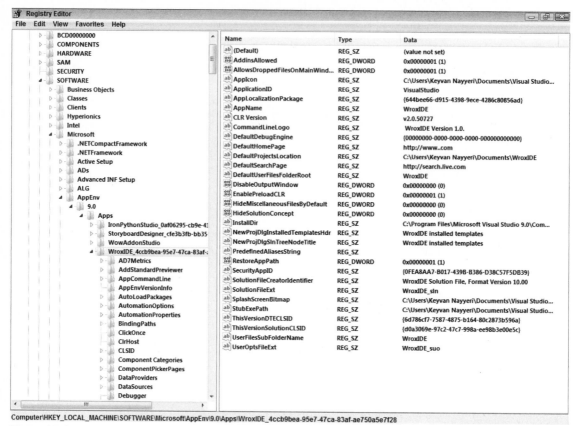

Figure 15-11: Registry editor for the isolated IDE

Each isolated IDE has its own hive, and the name of this hive is built from the name of the stub and a GUID. The following line is where you define this name in your code:

```
nRetVal = Setup(W2A(lpCmdLine), L"WroxIDE_4ccb9bea-95e7-47ca-83af-ae750a5e7f28",
NULL);
```

There is a file with a .pkgdef extension located in your main project (for my sample, it's WroxIDE.pkgdef). This text file, which is actually a registry editor file, is the main place where you can customize your IDE, and it works like a configuration file for the isolated IDE. If you open this file, you can see that it contains a list of values for specific properties, such as SplashScreenBitmap, AppName, and AppIcon. You can change these values to customize your IDE.

For example, I can change the value of AppName to Wrox IDE (to add a space in the default name) and rebuild my project to change the name of my IDE and hence its title (see Figure 15-12).

You often will need to rebuild your project to include changes, because the build events must apply such changes to the registry.

Figure 15-12: Changing the name of the IDE

Changing the Splash Screen

Suppose I want to replace the default white splash screen with a new customized splash screen carrying the Wrox Press logo. To do this, I open my WroxIDE.pkgdef file and change the value of the SplashScreenBitmap to $RootFolder$\WroxSplash.bmp, which is the relative path of my new splash screen image.

Now I rebuild my project and run the IDE to see the new splash screen, as shown in Figure 15-13.

Figure 15-13: New splash screen for the isolated IDE

You can see that Visual Studio has added the text "Powered by Visual Studio" to the bottom, right corner of the splash screen.

Removing Elements

Besides WroxIDE.pkgdef, which adds registry keys and values to the registry, there is a WroxIDE.pkgundef file that can remove some keys and values and actually uninstall them. This file is empty by default, but you can add some registry keys, and by using this file you can remove some elements from the IDE.

For example, I can add the following text to WroxIDE.pkgundef in order to remove my Class View window:

```
//Server Explorer
[$RootKey$\ToolWindows\{C9C0AE26-AA77-11d2-B3F0-0000F87570EE}]
```

Now if I open my IDE, the Class View window is removed (compare Figure 15-14 with Figure 15-12). Note that this window is listed in the View menu and you can click on it, but nothing happens.

Figure 15-14: The Class View window is removed.

Disabling Elements

Generally, you can remove different elements as described in the previous section, but you can also keep them and disable them according to your needs. As you saw, removing an element doesn't exclude it from all the menus, it just removes the element itself, but disabling an element excludes it from all menus and the IDE.

You can disable an element by opening a .vsct file located in the Resource Files folder of your user interface project. For my sample, I have to open the `WroxIDEUI.vsct` file located in the WroxIDEUI project. This XML configuration file, called a command table file, contains a list of commented elements that are grouped in a structure. Actually, this list contains all available commands in your IDE.

If you uncomment each element, then its corresponding user interface element will be excluded from your IDE.

For example, I can uncomment the `<Define name="No_WindowListCommand"/>` and `<Define name="No_ShellPkg_ToolWindows_CommandWindow"/>` elements to exclude the list of windows in the IDE and Command Window (see Figure 15-15 and Figure 15-16).

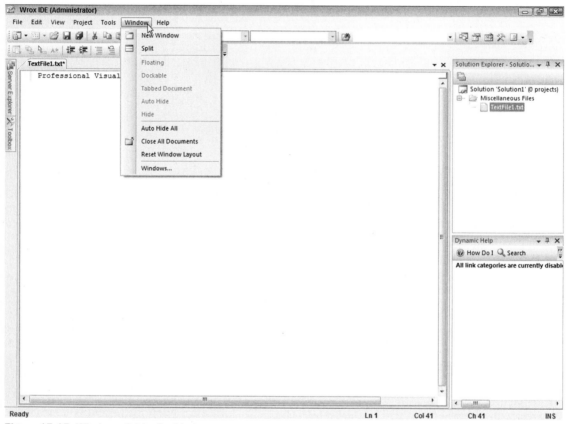

Figure 15-15: Windows list is disabled

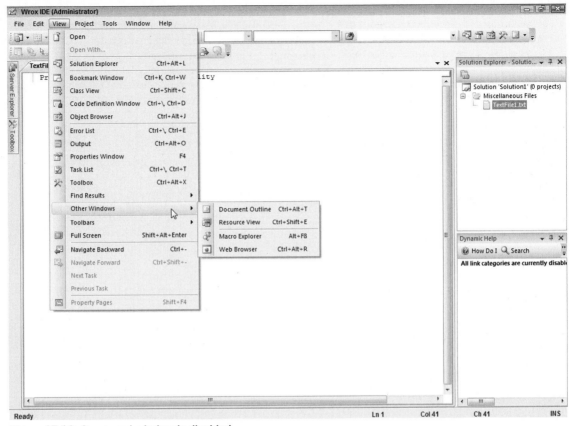

Figure 15-16: Command window is disabled

Deployment

To deploy a Visual Studio Shell isolated IDE, you need to create a setup project that deploys your IDE along with the VS Shell isolated mode redistributable package, and add appropriate registry values to the registry by borrowing them from the WroxIDE.reg file generated by Visual Studio. You simply can import this file to the user's registry settings in your setup project and use it (the same process is described for deploying VSPackages in Chapter 18, and you can read about it there).

Before doing this, however, you need to get a Shell Load Key (SLK) from the VSIP members' site (http://vsipmembers.com) to use for your VS Shell IDE when you want to deploy your IDE to the end user's machine.

When you're developing your IDE on a local machine, Visual Studio obtains a Developer Load Key (DLK) for the IDE, so you don't need to worry about this.

To obtain a Shell Load Key (SLK) from the VSIP members' site, you get some information about your isolated IDE and enter it on the site, after which you get the key. This information is available in the `WroxIDE.pkgdef` file. Specifically, you need to get the `ThisVersionDTECLSID`, `AppName`, and `Productversion` values and enter them on the site.

After obtaining your SLK, open the resource file for your IDE, located in the Resource Files folder. For my IDE it's `WroxIDE.rc`. Here, you need to open the string table and set the caption for `IDS_SLKSTRING` (see Figure 15-17).

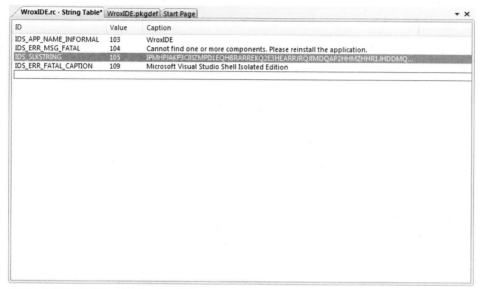

Figure 15-17: Set the SLK for the IDE.

After this, you can build your setup project as described previously to simplify the process of deploying your isolated IDEs.

Additional Information

This was just a quick overview and an introduction. Before finishing the chapter, I'd like to point out some other information that may be helpful to you. An isolated IDE is a completely independent IDE and works like an instance of the Visual Studio IDE. As a result, almost all extensibility options for Visual Studio are applicable to isolated IDEs. This means that you can build add-ins, VSPackages, or project and item templates for your IDEs and customize them.

When you install an isolated IDE, it creates a folder with the same name as your IDE in your personal documents folder (this folder is "Documents" in Windows Vista and "My Documents" in Windows XP or 2003). This is the storage path for your projects; it also has the same folders as Visual Studio, and you can build and deploy your project and item templates into the Templates subfolder. In Chapter 20 you'll learn how to create project and item templates.

The same is true for add-ins or packages; you can build add-ins and packages for an isolated IDE in a way similar to the method you use in the Visual Studio IDE to create add-ins and VSPackages. However, I don't get into details here because that would duplicate other chapters of this book.

Summary

Talking comprehensively about Visual Studio Shell in a single chapter isn't possible, but I've tried to give you an introduction and a quick overview of the Visual Studio Shell integrated and isolated modes, as well as their goals and applications. You can read a more detailed discussion about integrated mode in Chapter 18.

This chapter focused on isolated mode and included an example with a few minor customizations to familiarize you with this completely new mode.

16

Domain-Specific Language Tools

The concept of domain-specific languages (DSLs) is something general in the software development world and isn't specifically .NET-related. In recent years, we've been dealing with a lot of domain-specific languages in our daily development and can cite many instances of them. For example, an instance of a domain-specific language is a class diagram designer. The first section of this chapter introduces the concept of domain-specific languages, so don't worry if you don't have a good understanding of them yet.

In Visual Studio we don't need to deal with domain-specific languages directly in order to design and create them, because Microsoft has created some tools for us already. Created by members of the Visual Studio Ecosystem team, these tools, known as Domain-Specific Language Tools (or simply DSL Tools), help developers build domain-specific languages easier and faster, and are a part of the Visual Studio SDK. Therefore, you must have the Visual Studio SDK installed to enjoy the benefits of these tools and to use the sample source code of this chapter.

The team that was creating DSL tools at Microsoft was known as the DSL Tools team, but some months before the release of Visual Studio 2008 this team joined the Visual Studio Extensibility team in order to centralize their work on the Visual Studio Ecosystem Team better.

The topic of domain-specific languages, and domain-specific language tools, for that matter, is beyond the scope of a single chapter. Here, as in Chapter 15, covering Visual Studio Shell isolated mode, I'll just give a short introduction and a quick overview of the main topics. For readers who wish to know more about DSL tools, check out the unique book *Domain-Specific Development with Visual Studio DSL Tools,* written by four members of the DSL Tools team at Microsoft.

In this chapter you'll read about the following major topics:

❑   What is a domain-specific language (DSL)?

❑   How to create a DSL in Visual Studio

❑   Basic concepts in DSL

❑   What the generated solution for the DSL contains

❑   An overview of DSL tools in Visual Studio

DSL tools, along with Visual Studio Shell, are two features of the Visual Studio 2008 SDK that offer a lot of new material to discover. Even though DSL tools were a part of the Visual Studio 2005 SDK, in Visual Studio 2008 they're more closely integrated with Visual Studio Extensibility features than in the past.

Introducing Domain-Specific Languages

A domain-specific language (DSL) is a programming language designed for a specific purpose. It is the opposite of the normal general-purpose programming languages that we know.

Normal programming languages (such as Basic, C, C++, and Java) are designed for general purposes and can be used to implement logic to achieve various tasks. Conversely, a DSL is a programming language that does a specific job, and it's called domain-specific because it's just that: specific to its domain. Domain-specific languages are a part of language-oriented programming, whereby you build specific languages to achieve different tasks in a software system.

A DSL may be a visual diagramming language or a textual language, but in either case a DSL doesn't have definitions for low-level API programming, such as accessing file system storage. Regular expressions are an instance of a domain-specific languages, as is the famous Generic Eclipse Modeling System written for Eclipse. In general, the initial definition of a domain-specific language as one created for a specific task is the best way to understand the concept of the DSL.

When we speak of domain-specific languages, we can't forget the close relationship between the concepts of a DSL and software factories. Software factories enable easier, faster, and cheaper development of software via visual programming languages, and domain-specific languages simplify the process of development by automating its steps. A great book on this topic is *Software Factories: Assembling Applications with Patterns, Models, Frameworks, and Tools* (Wiley, 2004).

If you're interested in the topic of domain-specific languages and want to learn more about them, I would strongly recommend you read *The Definitive ANTLR Reference: Building Domain-Specific Languages* (O'Reilly, 2007).

Domain-Specific Languages in Visual Studio

When it comes to Visual Studio and .NET, Microsoft has provided a set of built-in tools in the Visual Studio SDK to work with domain-specific languages. These have been a part of the Visual Studio SDK since Visual Studio 2005 and are improved in the Visual Studio 2008 SDK.

These tools are rich enough to enable you to build a DSL easily and with the best features. The combination of these tools with the power of the .NET Framework gives the best of both worlds in creating a DSL. Using the .NET Framework's Base Class Library to work with low-level APIs fills the gap left by not having low-level API access in general.

A domain-specific language can be created with the following versions of Visual Studio 2008 (the same editions of Visual Studio 2005 can also be used):

- ❑ Visual Studio 2008 Professional Edition
- ❑ Visual Studio 2008 Team Edition for Software Architects
- ❑ Visual Studio 2008 Team Edition for Software Developers
- ❑ Visual Studio 2008 Team Edition for Software Testers
- ❑ Visual Studio 2008 Team Suite

You can deploy a domain-specific language to these editions, plus the Visual Studio 2008 Standard Edition. This means that it's only with the Professional Edition that you can't create a DSL.

The rest of this chapter provides a short overview of the process for creating a simple DSL with Visual Studio 2008. In addition, it describes key concepts about DSL tools by walking through a sample Family Tree DSL included in the Visual Studio SDK.

Creating a Domain-Specific Language Solution

In order to create a DSL solution in Visual Studio, open the New Project dialog, go to Extensibility node, choose the Domain-Specific Language Designer project template, and then pick a name for your project (see Figure 16-1).

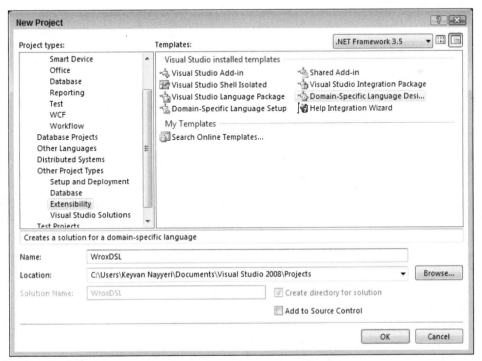

Figure 16-1: Create a new project for a domain-specific language.

Domain-Specific Language Designer Wizard

At this point, the Domain-Specific Language Designer Wizard appears. It has five steps (the last one being a summary of the previous steps). On the left side, you can choose different steps and edit them, and on the right side you can configure each step.

The first step is choosing your solution settings (see Figure 16-2). First, select a template for your domain-specific language from four available templates (Class Diagrams, Component Models, Minimal Language, and Task Flow). You'll learn more about these four templates in the next subsection, but for now just choose the Minimal Language template. Next, choose a name for your DSL. By default, this name is the same as your project name.

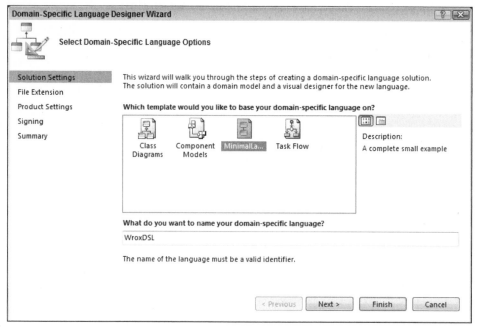

Figure 16-2: Solution Settings step

In the second step (see Figure 16-3) you need to choose a file extension and icon for your DSL. After choosing the extension, Visual Studio lists any other applications that may be registered to handle the extension. This enables you to avoid using such extensions. You can also unregister an extension from other applications in order to register it for your DSL.

If you don't want the default icon provided by Visual Studio, you can choose a different one for your files.

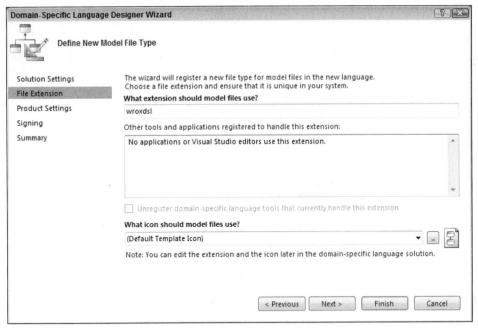

Figure 16-3: File Extension step

The third step is choosing some product settings for your DSL, such as product name, company name, and a default root namespace for projects (see Figure 16-4).

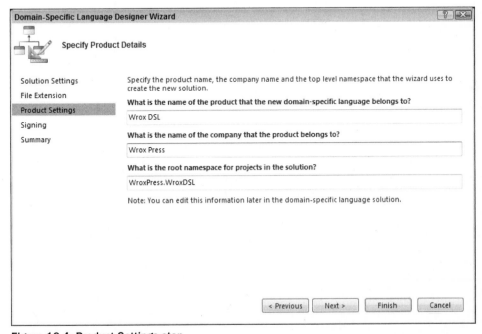

Figure 16-4: Product Settings step

The fourth step is signing your assembly (see Figure 16-5). You can create a new strong-name key file or use an existing file.

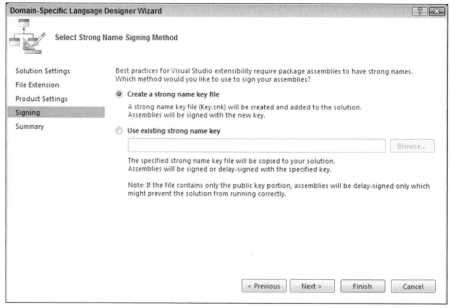

Figure 16-5: Signing step

The last step presents a summary of what you've chosen in the previous steps (see Figure 16-6).

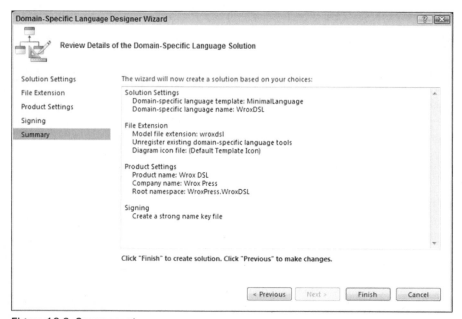

Figure 16-6: Summary step

After you click the Finish button, Visual Studio creates a new solution with two projects in it and starts transforming some text templates (check the Output window). The following sections describe the generated solution and its elements, as well as different ways you can customize this code.

Domain-Specific Language Solution Templates

In the first step of the Domain-Specific Language Designer wizard, you had to choose among four available templates for your domain-specific language. You can use these four templates as starting points for your DSL. Each of these templates generates default code that saves you a lot of time and effort. The following list describes each template so you know what it does:

❑ **Class Diagrams:** This is very similar to the class diagrams and tools that you see in UML tools and in Visual Studio class diagrams. This template provides a set of classes and entities with relationships between them and their properties. This template is suitable for scenarios in which you want to deal with the relationship between entities, as it helps you create classes with a list of their properties in a box.

❑ **Component Models:** This is suitable when you want to use a port for an entity because it provides a port shape that you can add to an entity to define a relationship in the model.

❑ **Minimal Language:** This is an "otherwise" template. You can use this template if you can't find a suitable template among the other three. It creates a DSL with one class and one relationship, as box and line.

❑ **Task Flow:** This template provides a set of geometric shapes and lines to create workflows and sequences. Obviously, it's suitable for workflow sequences.

Basic Concepts

You should understand some basic concepts when working with a DSL in Visual Studio. These concepts relate to the Visual Studio DSL designer that I'll describe shortly. Figure 16-7 shows the Visual Studio IDE when working on a DSL. This figure shows the main elements of the Visual Studio IDE that you use while working with DSL tools.

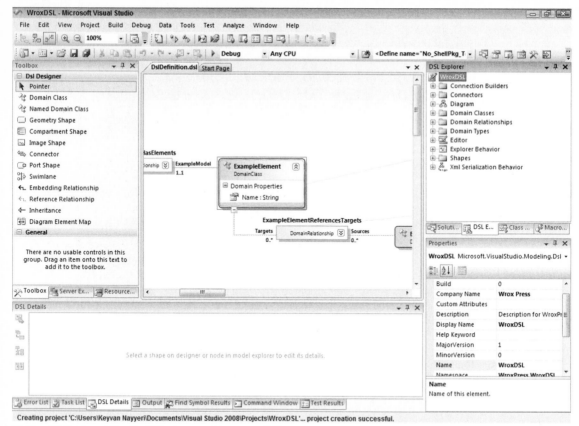

Figure 16-7: Visual Studio IDE when working on a DSL

On the left side is a Toolbox window with appropriate items for working with domain-specific languages. In the center is the DSL designer where you can design your domain-specific language. At the top, right corner, DSL Explorer is available as a tool to explore DSL projects and elements. In the bottom, right corner is the Properties window for DSL items, and in the bottom of the IDE is the DSL Details window, which shows details of each DSL element.

Now it's time to address those basic concepts that you need to know, which you may already be aware of. The following section offers a short overview/review.

Domain Model

A domain model is actually the definition of a domain-specific language. A domain model contains domain classes and the relationships between them. With these two types of elements, we define our DSL and enable users to use these elements in their models.

Figure 16-8 shows a domain model for book publishing. You can see two domain classes (Book and Author) and a relationship between them. As in real life, a book can have one or more authors, which is specified at the end of the relationship line.

Figure 16-8: A domain model

Our main job as DSL designers is to create the domain model; our users can use the domain model instance.

Model

A model is an instance of the domain model or an instance of the domain-specific language and what the end user does with it. It contains instances of classes and relationships and their properties, which users can use in their code.

Figure 16-9 shows the model for the aforementioned domain model. It contains a Wrox Pro VSX book instance that has a single author (Keyvan Nayyeri), and a Wrox Pro Community Server book that has four authors (Wyatt Preul, Keyvan Nayyeri, Jose Lema, and Jim Martin). These are two models for the domain model.

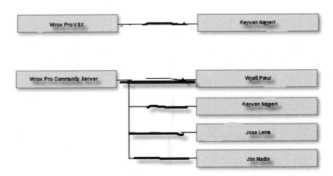

Figure 16-9: Model instance

Domain Relationship

As shown earlier, a domain model consists of relationships between classes. There are two general types of relationships in DSL:

❑ **Embedding relationship:** An embedding relationship is one in which you embed the elements of the target class in the source class. These elements are shown in the Properties window for the source class. As a rule, all elements in a DSL must be the target of an embedding relationship, and only the root element in the DSL is an exception.

❑ **Reference relationship:** In this type of relationship, elements of the source class reference the elements of target elements and do not embed them. Referenced elements may appear in the Properties window for the element, rather than in the DSL Explorer Window.

Domain relationships have roles and multiplicities. The roles of a relationship appear on the top right and top left sides of the relationship diagram.

Multiplicities specify the possible types of relationships in the domain and are similar to multiplicities for relationships between tables in relational databases. You can have one-to-one, one-to-many, zero-to-one, and zero-to-many relationships. The multiplicity of relationships appears in the bottom left and bottom right sides of relationship diagrams.

Figure 16-10 shows an example.

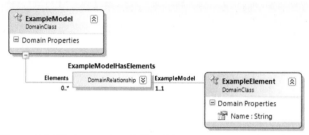

Figure 16-10: A sample relationship between two domain classes

In this figure, you can see that there are two domain classes (ExampleModel and ExampleElement) and a relationship between them. The ExampleElement has a domain property called Name.

The relationship specifies that "Example Model Has Element." At two sides, there are roles and multiplicities at the top and bottom of the relationship lines. An ExampleModel instance can be in relationship with zero or more ExampleElement instances, and an ExampleElement instance can be in relationship with only one ExampleModel.

Anatomy of a Domain-Specific Language Solution

After running the Domain-Specific Language Designer Wizard, Visual Studio generates two projects for you: a DSL project that has definitions for the DSL, and a VSPackage project that creates a VSPackage for your DSL.

The first project, the DSL project, contains some folders that hold generated codes and resources (images and icons). Besides these, there is a main file with a .dsl extension named DslDefinition.dsl, which is the main definition file for your domain-specific language. When you open this file, the Visual Studio DSL designer opens its content in a designer and you can customize the default-generated DSL.

In fact, this class is an XML file that contains all definitions as XML elements and attributes. This XML gets its schema from a specific XML namespace:

```
http://schemas.microsoft.com/VisualStudio/2005/DslTools/DslDefinitionModel
```

If you open this file in an XML editor, you can view its content easily. However, I haven't included the content of this file here.

The second project is a VSPackage. VSPackages are covered in detail in Chapter 18. Visual Studio deploys your DSL in a VSPackage to be used by Visual Studio easily. This VSPackage project contains appropriate files for this VSPackage, including project item templates for C# and the Visual Basic language for your DSL, as well as a set of commands and some generated code files.

An Overview of the Domain-Specific Language Tools

Now let's familiarize ourselves with the default domain-specific language tools in Visual Studio by taking a look at the Family Tree DSL sample included in the Visual Studio SDK.

This DSL looks like what is shown in Figure 16-11.

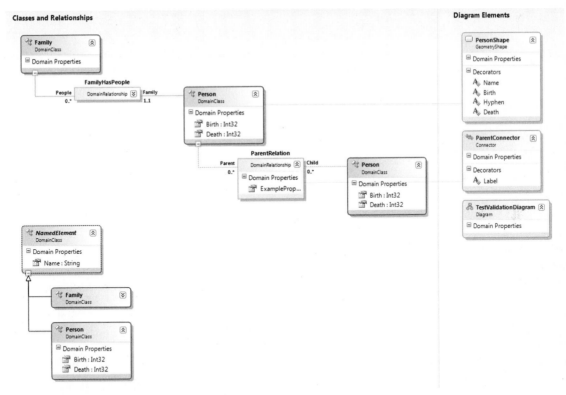

Figure 16-11: The final DSL

Let me describe this DSL briefly. The root domain model is a family. The family has some members, people, and these people have relationships with other people. For example, someone may be a parent of another. These concepts are reflected in the two classes in this DSL: `Family` (the root domain model) and `Person`.

Regarding these concepts, there are two relationships between these two classes as well. One of them is between a family and a person; this is an embedded relationship, and a family can have a relationship with zero or more people; but a person has a relationship with one family. There is also another relationship in which a person can be in relation to another person, just as one can be a parent to a child or the child of a parent.

When you build your DSL, you need to transform your text templates before testing or debugging your DSL. To do this, click the Transform All Templates button on top of the Solution Explorer (see Figure 16-12).

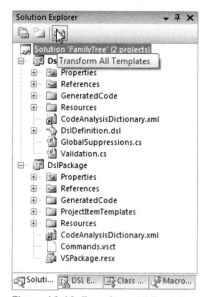

Figure 16-12: Transform All Templates

This results in a security warning dialog notifying you that this action may harm your computer (see Figure 16-13). However, you can consider me (indeed, Microsoft) as a trusted source in this case, and click the OK button to transform your text templates (notice the output in the Output window).

Figure 16-13: Security warning

Now you can test or debug your DSL. To test your DSL, start it without debugging (Ctrl + F5); to debug it, start it with debugging (F5).

In both cases, the Visual Studio Experimental Hive loads, which contains a project named Debugging that includes the following items:

❑   `Test.fdsl`: A test designer for the DSL

❑   `FamilyTreeReport.tt`: Test template report file for the C# language

❑   `FamilyTreeReportVB`: Test template report file for the VB language

❑   `TestValidationSchema.xsd`: The XSD schema for the DSL

You should have some files with similar names and structures. If you open the DSL designer by opening the Test.fdsl file, then you can see appropriate Toolbox items in the Toolbox (see Figure 16-14).

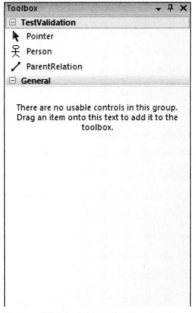

Figure 16-14: Added Toolbox items

You can drag and drop these items to the designer to create an instance of the DSL (see Figure 16-15).

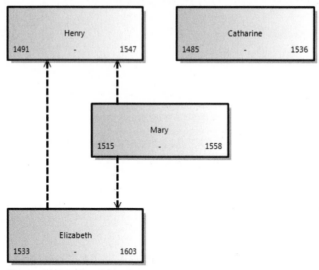

Figure 16-15: Use DSL elements in the designer.

If you choose items in the designer, you can check their properties in the Properties window and see the properties that you designed (see Figure 16-16).

Figure 16-16: Properties are listed in the Properties window.

There are several ways to deal with DSL tools in Visual Studio via designer and programming code, in order to add elements and relationships and the logic behind the elements. However, that's a discussion for another book, as it would require more background than we have space or time for.

However, as an example of dealing with DSL tools programmatically, I'll show you how to add validation logic behind your elements to ensure that they receive valid values. For example, suppose you want to ensure that your users choose a valid value for the `Birth` and `Death` properties.

To add validation to the domain model for Family Tree, first you need to decide when you want to validate the model. You can choose from a few options. To set this, open your DslDefinition.dsl file and DSL Explorer. Then expand the Editor node and choose the Validation item (see Figure 16-17).

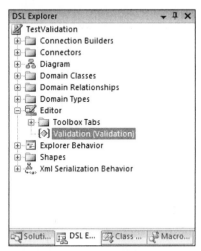

Figure 16-17: Select validation for a DSL

Now check out the Properties window (see Figure 16-18).

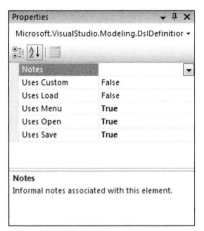

Figure 16-18: Properties window for validation

Here you have the following options:

- ❑ **Custom:** You can invoke validation from your custom code.

- ❑ **Load:** You can invoke validation when the user loads a model.

- ❑ **Menu:** You can invoke validation when the user chooses the Validate menu option.

- ❑ **Open:** You can invoke validation when the user opens a model.

- ❑ **Save:** You can invoke validation when the user saves a model.

For Family Tree, three items are selected by default (Menu, Open, and Save).

To add a validation to a DSL, you need to add a partial class with the same name and namespace as the class you're going to validate. For example, in Family Tree there is a Validation file in the root that contains partial `Person` and `ParentRelation` classes to validate `Person` and `ParentRelation` classes.

Code for this file is presented in Listing 16-1.

Listing 16-1: Code for the Validation File

```
using System;
using System.Collections.Generic;
using System.Text;
using System.Collections.ObjectModel;
using Microsoft.VisualStudio.Modeling.Validation;

namespace Fabrikam.Dsl.TestValidation
{
    [ValidationState(ValidationState.Enabled)]
    public partial class Person
    {
        [ValidationMethod(ValidationCategories.Open |
                          ValidationCategories.Save |
                          ValidationCategories.Menu)]
        public void ValidateDates(ValidationContext context)
        {
            if (context == null)
                throw new global::System.ArgumentNullException("context");

            if (this.Birth > this.Death)
            {
                context.LogError("Death must be after Birth",
                    "FamilyPersonDateError", this);
            }
        }

        [ValidationMethod(ValidationCategories.Open |
                ValidationCategories.Save |
                ValidationCategories.Menu)]
        public void ValidateParentBirth(ValidationContext context)
        {
            foreach (Person parent in this.Parent)
```

```
            {
                if (this.Birth <= parent.Birth)
                {
                    context.LogError("Birth must be after Parent's birth",
                        "FamilyParentBirthError", this, parent);
                }
            }
        }
    }

    [ValidationState(ValidationState.Enabled)]
    public partial class ParentRelation
    {

        [ValidationMethod(ValidationCategories.Open |
                          ValidationCategories.Save |
                          ValidationCategories.Menu)]
        public void ValidateParentDeath(ValidationContext context)
        {
            if (context == null)
                throw new global::System.ArgumentNullException("context");
            if (this.Parent.Death + 1 < this.Child.Birth)
            {
                context.LogError
                    ("Child must not be born later than a year after parent's
death",
                    "FamilyParentRelationDeathDateError", this);
            }
        }

    }
}
```

These partial classes have the same name and namespace as the domain class we want to validate. The ValidationState attribute that is set to Enabled guarantees that validation will occur for all methods in the class.

In addition to this attribute are three validation methods in these classes, marked with the ValidationMethod attribute. This attribute gets some arguments that are similar to the items that you can choose for validation of your domain model. These methods get a ValidationContext parameter and have their own logic for validation. If validation fails, then they use the ValidationContext .LogError method in order to notify Visual Studio about the error. This method shows an error in the Error List window and activates specified elements if a user chooses the item in the list.

These three methods (in two separate classes) validate against three situations that are naturally impossible. First, we ensure that the person's death date is later than the birth date. Next, we verify that the birth date of a person is later than the birth date of his or her parent. Finally, because a person cannot possibly be born later than a year after the parent's death, we make sure that the birth date of a person is earlier than the death date of the parent plus one year.

If you open the DSL designer for Family Tree and create a domain with some invalid data, then you can see that VS shows an error in an Error List window. For example, opening the `Test.free` file reveals an error immediately (see Figure 16-19). This is because the birth date for Mary is before the birth date for Elizabeth, who is the parent.

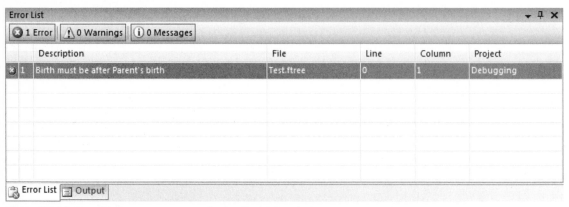

Figure 16-19: A validation error appears in the Error List window.

This example highlights just one of several aspects of DSL tools in Visual Studio to show you the basic idea. You can do whatever you can do with designer via programming code and add your logic behind a DSL.

Visual Studio creates a VSPackage for your DSL along with project templates that you can use to create new projects based on your DSL. VSPackages are covered in detail in Chapter 18.

To deploy a DSL you can use Domain-Specific Language Setup projects. A project template for these projects is available in the Extensibility node in the New Project dialog.

Summary

This chapter introduced you to the broad topic of domain-specific languages and presented a quick overview of the process of creating DSLs in Visual Studio, including the basic concepts related to them.

Next, you learned how to create a solution to build a DSL in Visual Studio and learned about basic concepts involving DSLs. Finally, you learned how to customize the generated solution for your DSL in Visual Studio and test it.

Domain-specific languages are a fascinating topic and you can find out more about this well-documented area if you are interested. However, you may not need a DSL for your daily work because it targets a particular area.

17

Extending the Debugger

Debugging is a main step in software development that gets a lot of time from developers during the software development process. You should solve bugs and exceptions in your applications before shipping them to customers — otherwise, obviously, these applications fail.

Debugging is a process to find and fix bugs in software or reduce the number of bugs. We expect a program to do what it was designed to do. If it doesn't, then we know there is a problem with it. This problem may have several sources. Problems that are related to software development can be grouped as bugs and exceptions. Bugs occur frequently and are more important than exceptions, because they can stop a program from working completely, whereas exceptions just stop it in some special cases. Fixing and reducing the number of bugs is a main process in the software world. You can find numerous references about debugging in general, and about debugging for specific technologies and development tools. Also available are various debugging tools designed to make debugging easier.

In the .NET world, many debugging mechanisms are provided out of the box, and these features are part of Visual Studio. Thanks to several debugging features in Visual Studio, you can debug a .NET application in a reasonable amount of time and with good results. Some of the important debugging features in Visual Studio include the following:

❑ Breakpoints

❑ Attach to process

❑ Visualizers

❑ Watch window

❑ Error List window

Beginning with Visual Studio 2008 and the .NET Framework 3.5, Microsoft began sharing the source code of the .NET Framework to enable developers to debug their applications more easily. Now when your application stops at some point and you need to know what's going on behind the scenes in order to solve the problem, you can do this by looking at the source code of the .NET Framework.

Debugging consists of the following steps:

❑ Recognizing that a bug exists

❑ Locating the source code that causes the bug

❑ Finding the reason for the bug

❑ Finding a fix for the bug and applying this fix

❑ Testing to ensure that the bug is fixed

Obviously, Visual Studio can't help you find a reason or a fix for the bug, but its debugging features can help you in the first two steps to recognize the bug and find its source. Debugging concepts and debugging techniques, in the .NET world and Visual Studio, are considered separate topics, and a full treatment of both are beyond the scope of this book. Many excellent books address these two topics, but here I assume that you have a background in debugging and Visual Studio debugging features.

As debugging is an important aspect of Visual Studio, Microsoft has spent a great deal of time providing extensibility options for Visual Studio debugging features. This chapter discusses these extensibility options in detail and helps you extend VS debugging features for your needs.

This chapter covers the following main topics:

❑ Different ways to extend Visual Studio debugging features

❑ The concept of type proxies and how to write them

❑ The concept and usage of visualizers and how to build, test, and deploy them

The chapter also includes a sample visualizer to clearly demonstrate these concepts.

How to Extend the Debugger

Among the debugging features in Visual Studio, some features are extensible and represent an important aspect of Visual Studio extensibility. The main part of this extensibility involves showing the value, visually, of different properties of a variable. There are two ways to accomplish this:

❑ Type proxy

❑ Visualizer

With a type proxy, you can display a custom list of properties for a variable in the Watch window. This is helpful because it enables you to have fewer property items in the Watch window. That way, you can focus on just those properties that you need to check.

As its name implies, with a visualizer you can show the content of a variable in a visual manner. For example, you can show the content of a bitmap as an image. By default, Visual Studio shows the properties of a variable one by one, based on some built-in visualizers for system types.

Visual Studio includes visualizers for common types in Visual Studio, but sometimes they're not exactly what you need in order to see the content of a property, such as when you want to monitor the content of a stream (the example that you saw in Chapter 3) or when you want to monitor the content of an image.

These two examples are two common ones to extend your debugger and make the job easier. In the rest of this chapter, you'll read more about them and how to build, test, and deploy them, using examples.

Type Proxy

A type proxy, as its name suggests, is a proxy for types. It acts as a converter that takes a class type and provides a new type, which you can use in order to debug your variables.

In other words, type proxy is a class that filters the properties of an original type to enable us to see those special properties in the Watch window.

Type proxies offer several advantages:

❏ You can quickly find properties that you'd like to watch.

❏ You have a simpler and cleaner Watch window.

❏ You can change the value that is shown in the debugger window based on your needs.

Normally, a Watch window displays a list of all properties for a type, as well as properties for its parent class or classes (if it's a derived class), plus properties of any type used in a hierarchical manner. For example, if TypeA is a type derived from TypeB, then all properties of TypeB are shown to end users when they view the Watch window for TypeA. Conversely, if TypeC and TypeD are two types for two properties of TypeA, then all properties for these two types will be displayed in the Watch window for TypeA. You see how complicated a Watch window can be.

Consider Figure 17-1, which shows the Watch window for the common System.Web.HttpResponse type. As you see, it's not easy to quickly find the value of a specific property in this window. Note that this covers a small part of the properties for this type in the Watch window.

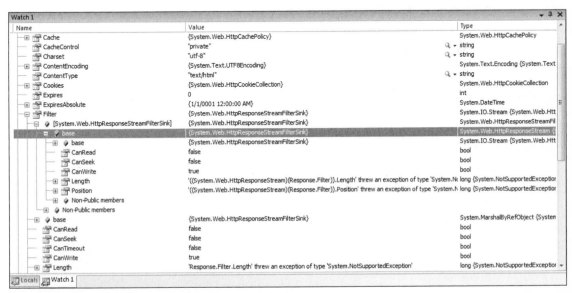

Figure 17-1: Watch window for the **HttpResponse** type

In the next section, you'll learn how to write your own type proxies to avoid such windows.

How to Write a Type Proxy

Suppose that you have a class for soldiers. This class contains some common properties for first name, last name, birth date, degree, and military rank. It also has a property that keeps a generic Dictionary with the names of different military tests and the point to which soldiers have gotten on that test.

The implementation of this class is presented in Listing 17-1.

Listing 17-1: Initial Soldier Class

```
using System;
using System.Collections.Generic;
using System.Linq;
using System.Text;

namespace TypeProxySample
{
    public class Soldier
    {
        public Soldier(string firstName, string lastName)
        {
            this.FirstName = firstName;
            this.LastName = lastName;
        }

        // First Name
        private string firstName;

        public string FirstName
        {
            get { return firstName; }
            set { firstName = value; }
        }

        // Last Name
        private string lastName;

        public string LastName
        {
            get { return lastName; }
            set { lastName = value; }
        }

        // Birth Date
        private DateTime birthDate;

        public DateTime BirthDate
```

```
        {
            get { return birthDate; }
            set { birthDate = value; }
        }

        // Degree
        private string degree;

        public string Degree
        {
            get { return degree; }
            set { degree = value; }
        }

        // Military Rank
        private string rank;

        public string Rank
        {
            get { return rank; }
            set { rank = value; }
        }

        // Test and Points
        private Dictionary<string, int> points = new Dictionary<string, int>();

        public Dictionary<string, int> Points
        {
            get { return points; }
            set { points = value; }
        }
    }
}
```

You can create this class in a console application in order to be able to test your codes easier. Then you write a code for your console program to monitor the property values of an instance of this class in the Watch window (see Listing 17-2).

Listing 17-2: Console Code to Monitor the Values of `soldier` Class Properties

```
using System;
using System.Collections.Generic;
using System.Linq;
using System.Text;

namespace TypeProxySample
{
    class Program
    {
        static void Main(string[] args)
```

(continued)

Listing 17-2 *(continued)*

```
        {
            Console.Title = "Type Proxy Example";

            Soldier soldier = new Soldier("Keyvan", "Nayyeri");
            soldier.BirthDate = DateTime.Parse("October 11, 1984");
            soldier.Degree = "BS";
            soldier.Rank = "Second LT";

            soldier.Points.Add("Shooting", 96);
            soldier.Points.Add("Running", 82);
            soldier.Points.Add("Climbing", 90);

            Console.WriteLine(string.Format("{0} {1}", soldier.FirstName,
                soldier.LastName));

            Console.ReadLine();
        }
    }
}
```

Here you put a breakpoint on the last line of the code and run your application (see Figure 17-2). When it reaches this breakpoint, right-click on the name of the `Soldier` variable and choose the Add to Watch option to see the values of the properties for this variable in the Watch window.

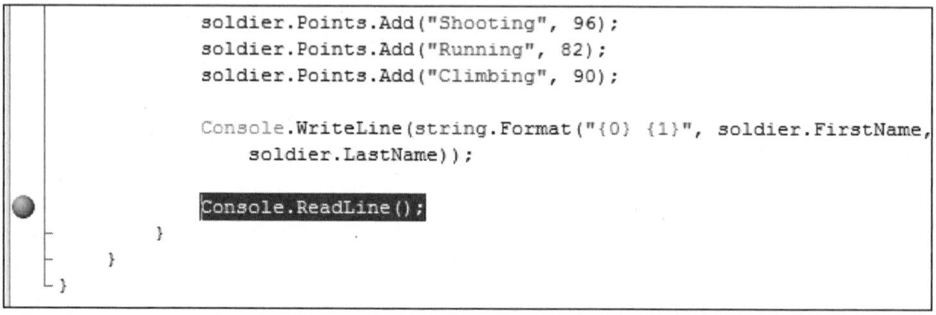

```
            soldier.Points.Add("Shooting", 96);
            soldier.Points.Add("Running", 82);
            soldier.Points.Add("Climbing", 90);

            Console.WriteLine(string.Format("{0} {1}", soldier.FirstName,
                soldier.LastName));

            Console.ReadLine();
        }
    }
}
```

Figure 17-2: Insert a breakpoint to monitor properties of the Soldier class.

Figure 17-3 shows the Watch window for this variable. At this point, you may be asking why we use a type proxy for something this simple. Yes, it's simple, but I don't want to get more complicated at the moment. The example is just to introduce concepts more easily.

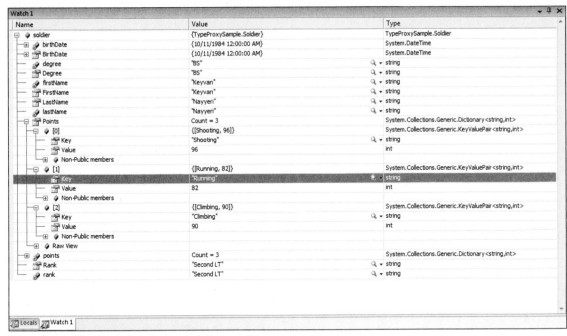

Watch 1		▾ ♯ ✕
Name	Value	Type
⊟ ◈ soldier	{TypeProxySample.Soldier}	TypeProxySample.Soldier
⊕ 🔩 birthDate	{10/11/1984 12:00:00 AM}	System.DateTime
⊕ 🔩 BirthDate	{10/11/1984 12:00:00 AM}	System.DateTime
🔩 degree	"BS"	🔍 ▾ string
🔩 Degree	"BS"	🔍 ▾ string
🔩 firstName	"Keyvan"	🔍 ▾ string
🔩 FirstName	"Keyvan"	🔍 ▾ string
🔩 LastName	"Nayyeri"	🔍 ▾ string
🔩 lastName	"Nayyeri"	🔍 ▾ string
⊟ 🔩 Points	Count = 3	System.Collections.Generic.Dictionary<string,int>
⊟ ◈ [0]	{[Shooting, 96]}	System.Collections.Generic.KeyValuePair<string,int>
🔩 Key	"Shooting"	🔍 ▾ string
🔩 Value	96	int
⊕ ◈ Non-Public members		
⊟ ◈ [1]	{[Running, 82]}	System.Collections.Generic.KeyValuePair<string,int>
🔩 Key	"Running"	✦ ▾ string
🔩 Value	82	int
⊕ ◈ Non-Public members		
⊟ ◈ [2]	{[Climbing, 90]}	System.Collections.Generic.KeyValuePair<string,int>
🔩 Key	"Climbing"	🔍 ▾ string
🔩 Value	90	int
⊕ ◈ Non-Public members		
⊕ ◈ Raw View		
⊕ 🔩 points	Count = 3	System.Collections.Generic.Dictionary<string,int>
🔩 Rank	"Second LT"	🔍 ▾ string
🔩 rank	"Second LT"	🔍 ▾ string

| 🔲 Locals 🔲 Watch 1 | |

Figure 17-3: Watch window for the Soldier variable

Now suppose that you're interested in viewing the values for some properties in a different way, as follows:

❑   Show a soldier's full name, rather than first and last names separately.

❑   Show the soldier's age, rather than the birth date.

❑   Show the Points collection in linear form, rather than a collection form. This means that you want to see items in this collection in one line as a string that shows the name of tests and their corresponding point.

To accomplish these things, you can use a type proxy to change the display of the property in the debugger window. Before continuing the discussion, however, it would be useful to consider some principles about type proxies.

A type proxy is nothing but a class. This class has a public constructor that gets an instance of a type. We want to use this type proxy to change the display of its properties. The type proxy class has some read-only properties, and it is these properties that we want to display in the Watch window. However, the code logic behind these properties is something that we have to write in order to change the display of the original type's properties.

Knowing these principles, you create a new internal class for your type proxy and name it `SoldierTypeProxy`. (I chose internal scope because I just want to use this code for internal purposes and debugging my application.) The code for `SoldierTypeProxy` is shown in Listing 17-3.

Listing 17-3: `SoldierTypeProxy` Class

```csharp
using System;
using System.Collections.Generic;
using System.Linq;
using System.Text;
using System.Collections.Specialized;

namespace TypeProxySample
{
    internal class SoldierTypeProxy
    {
        private Soldier soldier;

        public SoldierTypeProxy(Soldier soldier)
        {
            this.soldier = soldier;
        }

        public string Name
        {
            get
            {
                return string.Format("{0} {1}",
                    this.soldier.FirstName, this.soldier.LastName);
            }
        }

        public int Age
        {
            get
            {
                int difference = DateTime.Now.Year - this.soldier.BirthDate.Year;

                if (DateTime.Now.Month < this.soldier.BirthDate.Month ||
                    (DateTime.Now.Month == this.soldier.BirthDate.Month &&
                    DateTime.Now.Day < this.soldier.BirthDate.Day))
                    difference--;

                return difference;
            }
        }

        public string Degree
        {
            get
```

```
        {
            return this.soldier.Degree;
        }
    }

    public string MilitaryRank
    {
        get
        {
            return this.soldier.Rank;
        }
    }

    public string Points
    {
        get
        {
            List<string> items = new List<string>();

            foreach (KeyValuePair<string, int> pair in this.soldier.Points)
            {
                items.Add(string.Format("{0} : {1}", pair.Key, pair.Value));
            }

            return string.Join(" | ", (String[])items.ToArray());
        }
    }
}
}
```

To implement the aforementioned changes in the display of property values, you first add a simple string manipulation code to the Name property to show the soldier's full name, rather than first and last name. The second change is implemented by adding an Age property and simple code to calculate the year difference between the current year and the year when the soldier was born.

The last change is in the Points property, where a list of strings is used to keep the combination of test names and their corresponding points. In the end, a simple join on an array of strings generates what you need.

To connect the original class to this type proxy, you go back to the Soldier class, where you need to make two changes:

❑ Add a reference to the System.Diagnostics namespace to have access to the DebuggerTypeProxy attribute.

❑ Add a DebuggerTypeProxy attribute to your class and pass the type name of your type proxy to it as an argument.

The final code for the `Soldier` class is presented in Listing 17-4.

Listing 17-4: Final Code for the `Soldier` Class

```csharp
using System;
using System.Collections.Generic;
using System.Linq;
using System.Text;
using System.Diagnostics;

namespace TypeProxySample
{
    [DebuggerTypeProxy(typeof(SoldierTypeProxy))]
    public class Soldier
    {
        public Soldier(string firstName, string lastName)
        {
            this.FirstName = firstName;
            this.LastName = lastName;
        }

        // First Name
        private string firstName;

        public string FirstName
        {
            get { return firstName; }
            set { firstName = value; }
        }

        // Last Name
        private string lastName;

        public string LastName
        {
            get { return lastName; }
            set { lastName = value; }
        }

        // Birth Date
        private DateTime birthDate;

        public DateTime BirthDate
        {
            get { return birthDate; }
            set { birthDate = value; }
        }

        // Degree
        private string degree;

        public string Degree
        {
            get { return degree; }
```

```
        set { degree = value; }
    }

    // Military Rank
    private string rank;

    public string Rank
    {
        get { return rank; }
        set { rank = value; }
    }

    // Test and Points
    private Dictionary<string, int> points = new Dictionary<string, int>();

    public Dictionary<string, int> Points
    {
        get { return points; }
        set { points = value; }
    }
    }
}
```

At this point, you can run the code in Listing 17-2 to see the new Watch window for your `Soldier` variable (see Figure 17-4).

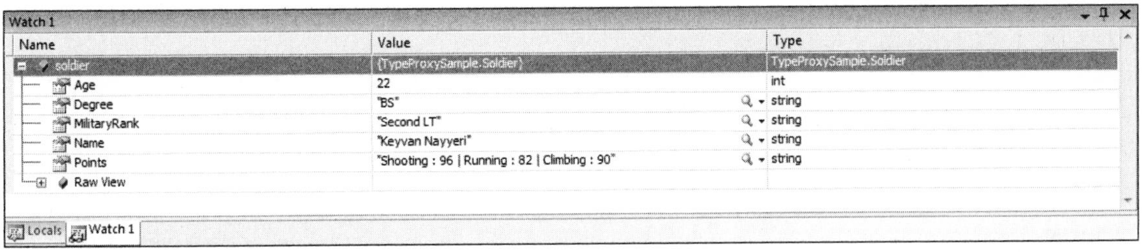

Figure 17-4: New Watch window for the `Soldier` variable with a type proxy

Behind the scenes, Visual Studio passes the current object instance of the `Soldier` class to the `SoldierTypeProxy` as a constructor and then shows all properties for the instance of `SoldierTypeProxy` in the Watch window.

That's it! Clearly, it's easy to write type proxies.

One point to note about the type proxy is the Raw View item in the Watch window when you use a type proxy (refer to Figure 17-4). This enables you to see the original view of the Watch window for a type. If you expand this item, then the original view of the Watch window opens up as its child (see Figure 17-5).

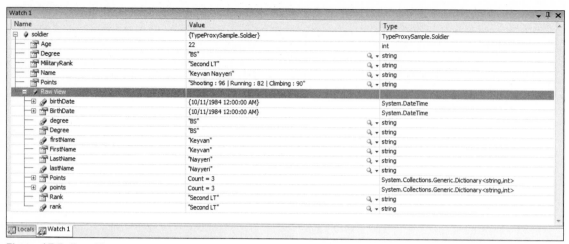

Figure 17-5: Raw View

Additional Points

The previous section described the main points about the type proxy and creating your own type proxies, but knowing a few more details about type proxies can improve them. These points concern two attributes that enable you to have a customized debugger: DebuggerDisplay and DebuggerBrowsable.

DebuggerDisplay

This attribute can be used to control how a class, property, or field is displayed in the debugger Output window. It requires an argument of the string type specifying what must be displayed in the value column for end users. This string can contain braces. Values between braces are evaluated as parameter, field, or method.

Sometimes you override the ToString method of the object class for your own classes. By default, Visual Studio uses the name of a type to display it in debugger windows, but if you have done this then it uses the result of the ToString method. If you use a DebuggerDisplay attribute on a type that has already overridden the ToString method, then Visual Studio will use the text defined by the DebuggerDisplay attribute.

You can use this attribute with several arguments that customize the way a variable is displayed in the debugger. I provide some common examples in the sample for this section. Before taking a look at this sample, note that you can use the DebuggerDisplay attribute for your original class and its properties and/or your type proxy class. This attribute is independent of the type proxy and can be used with any class, property, or field to change its display in the debugger Output window.

At this point, you can modify the sample codes from the previous section to show some common applications of the DebuggerDisplay attribute. The modified code of Listing 17-4 is shown in Listing 17-5.

Listing 17-5: Modified Code for the soldier **Class with** DebuggerDisplay

```
using System;
using System.Collections.Generic;
using System.Linq;
using System.Text;
using System.Diagnostics;

namespace TypeProxySample
{
    [DebuggerTypeProxy(typeof(SoldierTypeProxy))]
    [DebuggerDisplay("Soldier Type Proxy")]
    public class Soldier
    {
        public Soldier(string firstName, string lastName)
        {
            this.FirstName = firstName;
            this.LastName = lastName;
        }

        // First Name
        private string firstName;

        public string FirstName
        {
            get { return firstName; }
            set { firstName = value; }
        }

        // Last Name
        private string lastName;

        public string LastName
        {
            get { return lastName; }
            set { lastName = value; }
        }

        // Birth Date
        private DateTime birthDate;

        public DateTime BirthDate
        {
            get { return birthDate; }
            set { birthDate = value; }
        }

        // Degree
```

(continued)

Listing 17-5 *(continued)*

```
            private string degree;

            public string Degree
            {
                get { return degree; }
                set { degree = value; }
            }

            // Military Rank
            private string rank;

            public string Rank
            {
                get { return rank; }
                set { rank = value; }
            }

            // Test and Points
            private Dictionary<string, int> points = new Dictionary<string, int>();

            public Dictionary<string, int> Points
            {
                get { return points; }
                set { points = value; }
            }
        }
    }
```

Note that there is only one change in this code: the addition of the DebuggerDisplay attribute for the class, which changes the string value shown in the Value column of the Watch window. You can't add this property to class properties because it won't take effect. You must use a type proxy, which doesn't let the properties be shown normally in the Watch window. Of course, it takes effect in the Raw Header view.

Now you can go to the type proxy class and modify it. A modified version of Listing 17-3 is presented in Listing 17-6.

Listing 17-6: Modified Code for the SoldierTypeProxy **Class with** DebuggerDisplay

```
using System;
using System.Collections.Generic;
using System.Linq;
using System.Text;
using System.Collections.Specialized;
using System.Diagnostics;

namespace TypeProxySample
{
```

```
internal class SoldierTypeProxy
{
    private Soldier soldier;

    public SoldierTypeProxy(Soldier soldier)
    {
        this.soldier = soldier;
    }

    [DebuggerDisplay("Full Name = {Name}")]
    public string Name
    {
        get
        {
            return string.Format("{0} {1}",
                this.soldier.FirstName, this.soldier.LastName);
        }
    }

    [DebuggerDisplay("Soldier's Age = {Age}")]
    public int Age
    {
        get
        {
            int difference = DateTime.Now.Year - this.soldier.BirthDate.Year;

            if (DateTime.Now.Month < this.soldier.BirthDate.Month ||
                (DateTime.Now.Month == this.soldier.BirthDate.Month &&
                DateTime.Now.Day < this.soldier.BirthDate.Day))
                difference--;

            return difference;
        }
    }

    [DebuggerDisplay("Degree = {Degree}")]
    public string Degree
    {
        get
        {
            return this.soldier.Degree;
        }
    }

    [DebuggerDisplay("Military Rank = {MilitaryRank}")]
    public string MilitaryRank
    {
        get
        {
            return this.soldier.Rank;
        }
    }
```

(continued)

Listing 17-6 *(continued)*

```
            [DebuggerDisplay("Test Name and Points = {Points}")]

    public string Points
    {
        get
        {
            List<string> items = new List<string>();

            foreach (KeyValuePair<string, int> pair in this.soldier.Points)
            {
                items.Add(string.Format("{0} : {1}", pair.Key, pair.Value));
            }

            return string.Join(" | ", (String[])items.ToArray());
        }
    }
}
}
```

Obviously, the first step is to add a reference to the System.Diagnostics namespace, because DebuggerDisplay is a member of this namespace. The next change is the addition of the DebuggerDisplay attribute for properties.

After running the code again, Figure 17-6 shows how DebuggerDisplay has affected the Watch window.

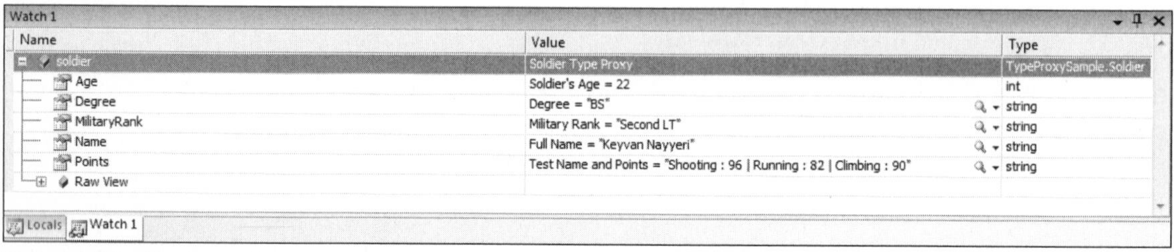

Figure 17-6: Watch window for the **Soldier** variable with **DebuggerDisplay**

DebuggerBrowsable

DebuggerBrowsable is another attribute that can be used to control how a member is displayed in the Watch window. This class is a sealed class; you can't inherit other classes from it. DebuggerBrowsable can be added to fields and properties.

DebuggerBrowsable is only available in C#; and unlike previous attributes (DebuggerTypeProxy and DebuggerDisplay), you can't use it in Visual Basic.

DebuggerBrowsable gets an argument of the DebuggerBrowsableState enumerator type. This enumerator has three values, described in Table 17-1.

Table 17-1 DebuggerBrowsableState Enumerator

Value	Description
Collapsed	The default value, this specifies that a member must be displayed but not expanded
Never	Completely removes a field or property from the debugger window so it doesn't show up
RootHidden	A member doesn't show up in the debugger window but its objects must be displayed (for array and collection types)

For example, you can go back to the original state of your console application and exclude the type proxy from your project to see the original view of the Watch window for your `Soldier` variable, and then modify the `Soldier` class to use the `DebuggerBrowsable` attribute. Listing 17-7 is a modified version of Listing 17-1 with the `DebuggerBrowsable` attribute.

Listing 17-7: Modified Code for the `Soldier` Class with `DebuggerBrowsable`

```
using System;
using System.Collections.Generic;
using System.Linq;
using System.Text;
using System.Diagnostics;

namespace TypeProxySample
{
    public class Soldier
    {
        public Soldier(string firstName, string lastName)
        {
            this.FirstName = firstName;
            this.LastName = lastName;
        }

        // First Name
        private string firstName;

        public string FirstName
        {
            get { return firstName; }
            set { firstName = value; }
        }

        // Last Name
        private string lastName;

        public string LastName
        {
            get { return lastName; }
```

(continued)

Listing 17-7 *(continued)*

```csharp
            set { lastName = value; }
        }

        // Birth Date
        private DateTime birthDate;

        [DebuggerBrowsable(DebuggerBrowsableState.Collapsed)]
        public DateTime BirthDate
        {
            get { return birthDate; }
            set { birthDate = value; }
        }

        // Degree
        private string degree;

        [DebuggerBrowsable(DebuggerBrowsableState.Never)]
        public string Degree
        {
            get { return degree; }
            set { degree = value; }
        }

        // Military Rank
        private string rank;

        public string Rank
        {
            get { return rank; }
            set { rank = value; }
        }

        // Test and Points
        private Dictionary<string, int> points = new Dictionary<string, int>();

        [DebuggerBrowsable(DebuggerBrowsableState.RootHidden)]
        public Dictionary<string, int> Points
        {
            get { return points; }
            set { points = value; }
        }
    }
}
```

The preceding code adds three `DebuggerBrowsable` attributes with different arguments. First, it adds the `Collapsed` value to the `BirthDate` property, which is the default behavior and doesn't change anything. The second change was for the `Degree` property, where the `Never` value is used to hide this property from the debugger window. Finally, the `RootHidden` value for the `Points` property removes the root value from the debugger window but keeps its items in the list.

Running your console application, you would get the new Watch window shown in Figure 17-7.

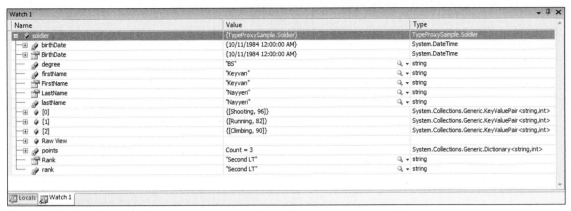

Figure 17-7: Watch window for the `Soldier` variable with `DebuggerBrowsable`

Visualizers

Introduced with the release of Visual Studio 2005, Visualizers are a well-known extensibility option in Visual Studio. They are improved in Visual Studio 2008, but their technical details haven't changed.

As the name suggests, a visualizer is a tool that visualizes the property values for a variable. It helps you see the content of a variable at runtime in a visual manner when you move the mouse over the name of the variable or when you choose it from the debugger window.

Let's look at an example. Listing 17-8 shows a console application that loads the content of an XML file into an `XmlDocument` variable and writes it in the console window.

Listing 17-8: Console Application to Test the XML Visualizer

```
using System;
using System.Collections.Generic;
using System.Linq;
using System.Text;
using System.Xml;
using System.IO;

namespace XmlVisualizerTest
{
    class Program
    {
        static void Main(string[] args)
        {
            Console.Title = "Xml Visualizer";

            XmlDocument xml = new XmlDocument();
```

(continued)

Listing 17-8 *(continued)*

```
            xml.LoadXml(File.ReadAllText("Editors.xml"));

            Console.WriteLine(xml.InnerXml);

            Console.ReadLine();
        }
    }
}
```

Figure 17-8 shows the insertion of a breakpoint to the last line of code to pause the runtime when it reaches this point.

```
        Console.Title = "Xml Visualizer";

        XmlDocument xml = new XmlDocument();
        xml.LoadXml(File.ReadAllText("Editors.xml"));

        Console.WriteLine(xml.InnerXml);

        Console.ReadLine();
    }
}
```

Figure 17-8: Insert a breakpoint to pause the runtime.

At this point, I run the application to reach the breakpoint. When it reaches this point, I can move the cursor on the name of the `xml` variable and a general visualizer for this variable appears, as shown in Figure 17-9.

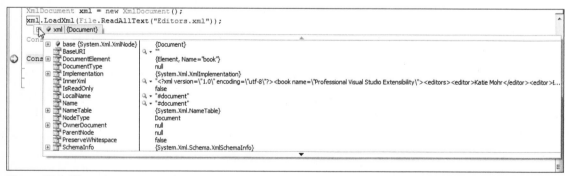

Figure 17-9: Move the mouse to the variable name to see the visualizer.

I scroll down the list of properties to find the `InnerXml` property, and then click on the arrow next to the lens icon and choose the XML Visualizer item from the list to see the content of my XML file in an XML visualizer (see Figure 17-10).

Figure 17-10: XML visualizer

This is an example of a built-in visualizer in Visual Studio. Many built-in visualizers are available in Visual Studio for common types, but sometimes you need to write your own visualizers for other types. In the following sections, you'll learn how to write a visualizer and then test and deploy it.

In addition to these visualizers, many third-party visualizers, written by community members, are available for different types. Some of the better-known ones are listed in Appendix A.

Writing a Visualizer

Technically, a visualizer is nothing but a class that is derived from the `DialogDebuggerVisualizer` base class. Visualizers have a code template that is provided as an item template in Visual Studio.

To write a visualizer, you need to create a Class Library project and add a new item to it. From the Add New Item dialog, choose the Debugger Visualizer item and enter a name for your visualizer (see Figure 17-11). This is just a name for your code. Later, you can set the visualizer name to display to end users in the user interface.

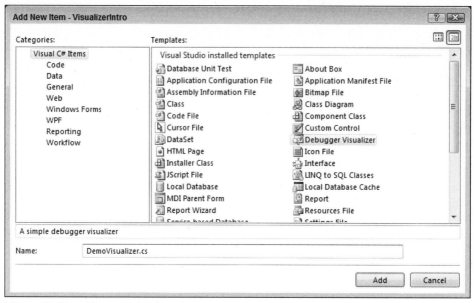

Figure 17-11: Add a new visualizer item to the project.

This adds a new class to the project, derived from the `DialogDebuggerVisualizer` base class, with a code template similar to what is shown in Listing 17-9. It also adds references to appropriate assemblies such as Microsoft.VisualStudio.DebuggerVisualizers, System.Drawing, and System.Windows.Forms.

Listing 17-9: Code Template for a Visualizer

```
using Microsoft.VisualStudio.DebuggerVisualizers;
using System;
using System.Collections.Generic;
using System.Linq;
using System.Windows.Forms;

namespace VisualizerIntro
{
    // TODO: Add the following to SomeType's definition to see this visualizer when
    debugging instances of SomeType:
    //
    //   [DebuggerVisualizer(typeof(DemoVisualizer))]
    //   [Serializable]
    //   public class SomeType
    //   {
    //    ...
    //   }
    //
    /// <summary>
```

```
        /// A Visualizer for SomeType.
        /// </summary>
        public class DemoVisualizer : DialogDebuggerVisualizer
        {
            protected override void Show(IDialogVisualizerService windowService,
IVisualizerObjectProvider objectProvider)
            {
                // TODO: Get the object to display a visualizer for.
                //       Cast the result of objectProvider.GetObject()
                //       to the type of the object being visualized.
                object data = (object)objectProvider.GetObject();

                // TODO: Display your view of the object.
                //       Replace displayForm with your own custom Form or Control.
                using (Form displayForm = new Form())
                {
                    displayForm.Text = data.ToString();
                    windowService.ShowDialog(displayForm);
                }
            }

            // TODO: Add the following to your testing code to test the visualizer:
            //
            //     DemoVisualizer.TestShowVisualizer(new SomeType());
            //
            /// <summary>
            /// Tests the visualizer by hosting it outside of the debugger.
            /// </summary>
            /// <param name="objectToVisualize">The object to display in the
    visualizer.</param>
            public static void TestShowVisualizer(object objectToVisualize)
            {
                VisualizerDevelopmentHost visualizerHost = new
VisualizerDevelopmentHost(objectToVisualize, typeof(DemoVisualizer));
                visualizerHost.ShowVisualizer();
            }
        }
    }
```

As you see, this template consists of definitions for two methods:

❑   `Show()`: This method, overridden from the base class, is the main place to implement your logic for the visualizer. It has two parameters of type `IDialogVisualizerService` and `IVisualizerObjectProvider`. You can use the first object to get access to Windows services and display user interface elements for your visualizer. Use the second object to get access to passed objects to this visualizer.

❑   `TestShowVisualizer()`: This static method gets an object and tries to show its content with a visualizer. This method is helpful for test purposes, and you can use it to test your visualizer easily and quickly.

The `IVisualizerObjectProvider` parameter of the `Show` method helps you work with your object's data. You can use it to change the data on-the-fly and then return this data to the main program. Table 17-2 describes the important methods of this interface.

Table 17-2: IVisualizerObjectProvider Methods

Method	Description
GetData	Returns a `Stream` of the object that is being visualized
GetObject	Returns the object that is being visualized
ReplaceData	Replaces the current object that is being visualized with the `Stream` that is passed to it
ReplaceObject	Replaces the current object that is being visualized with the object that is passed to it
TransferData	Returns the object data `Stream` to the debuggee. You must call this method after replacing your data `Stream`.
TransferObject	Returns the object to the debuggee. You must call this method after replacing your object.

This interface also has an `IsObjectReplaceable` Boolean property that specifies whether the currently visualized object is replaceable or not.

To implement a visualizer, you need to get the `Object` variable from the parameters of the `Show` method, create a windows form to show the variable content in the way that you want, and then display the form with the window's service parameters.

A simple example helps to demonstrate these theories. This example is a visualizer that displays the content of a list of `Soldier` objects (introduced earlier in Listing 17-1) in a `DataGridView` to enable users to debug the code easier.

As mentioned before, the first step is to create a Class Library project and add a Debugger Visualizer item to it. Before beginning the main implementation of the visualizer, mark your `Soldier` class as `Serializable`.

> *As a general rule, you can use a visualizer only for serializable types. That is, if you try to visualize a type that is not serializable, you get a runtime error whether this type is a built-in .NET type or a custom type you have created yourself. For example, you can't visualize the `Button` control in Windows Presentation Foundation because it's not serializable.*

This is a requirement for any type that you want to visualize; otherwise, you get a runtime error. Here, you also remove the `Points` property from the class for simplicity, resulting in the `Soldier` class shown in Listing 17-10.

Listing 17-10: New `Soldier` Class Marked as Serializable

```csharp
using System;
using System.Collections.Generic;
using System.Linq;
using System.Text;

namespace ListViewVisualizer
{
    [Serializable()]
    public class Soldier
    {
        public Soldier(string firstName, string lastName)
        {
            this.FirstName = firstName;
            this.LastName = lastName;
        }

        // First Name
        private string firstName;

        public string FirstName
        {
            get { return firstName; }
            set { firstName = value; }
        }

        // Last Name
        private string lastName;

        public string LastName
        {
            get { return lastName; }
            set { lastName = value; }
        }

        // Birth Date
        private DateTime birthDate;

        public DateTime BirthDate
        {
            get { return birthDate; }
            set { birthDate = value; }
        }

        // Degree
        private string degree;

        public string Degree
        {
            get { return degree; }
            set { degree = value; }
```

(continued)

Listing 17-10 *(continued)*

```
        }

        // Military Rank
        private string rank;

        public string Rank
        {
            get { return rank; }
            set { rank = value; }
        }
    }
}
```

Now you can change the auto-generated code for the visualizer to something like the code presented in Listing 17-11.

Listing 17-11: Code for the Visualizer

```
using Microsoft.VisualStudio.DebuggerVisualizers;
using System;
using System.Collections.Generic;
using System.Linq;
using System.Windows.Forms;

namespace ListViewVisualizer
{
    /// <summary>
    /// A Visualizer for Soldier.
    /// </summary>
    public class ListViewVisualizer : DialogDebuggerVisualizer
    {
        protected override void Show(IDialogVisualizerService windowService,
            IVisualizerObjectProvider objectProvider)
        {
            List<Soldier> data = (List<Soldier>)objectProvider.GetObject();

            using (Viewer displayForm = new Viewer())
            {
                displayForm.InternalDataSource = data;
                windowService.ShowDialog(displayForm);
            }
        }

        /// <summary>
        /// Tests the visualizer by hosting it outside of the debugger.
        /// </summary>
        /// <param name="objectToVisualize">The object to display in the
        visualizer.</param>
        public static void TestShowVisualizer(object objectToVisualize)
        {
            VisualizerDevelopmentHost visualizerHost =
                new VisualizerDevelopmentHost(objectToVisualize,
        typeof(ListViewVisualizer));
```

```
                    visualizerHost.ShowVisualizer();
                }
            }
        }
```

This code first replaces the general Object type with the type that you want to visualize (list of Soldier objects) and keeps its content in the data variable by calling objectProvider.GetObject and converting the result to your type. Then you use a form to show your data in its DataGridView control. Here it is named Viewer.

Viewer is a window form that I added to the project. It contains a DataGridView control to show my data. This form has a property to keep data items and simple logic in its Load event to bind DataGridView to data (see Listing 17-12).

Listing 17-12: Viewer Form Code

```csharp
using System;
using System.Collections.Generic;
using System.ComponentModel;
using System.Data;
using System.Drawing;
using System.Linq;
using System.Text;
using System.Windows.Forms;

namespace ListViewVisualizer
{
    public partial class Viewer : Form
    {
        public Viewer()
        {
            InitializeComponent();
        }

        private List<Soldier> internalDataSource;

        public List<Soldier> InternalDataSource
        {
            get
            {
                return this.internalDataSource;
            }
            set
            {
                this.internalDataSource = value;
            }
        }

        private void Viewer_Load(object sender, EventArgs e)
        {
            dataGridView.DataSource = this.internalDataSource;
            dataGridView.Refresh();
        }
    }
}
```

At this point, we're done with the main code for the visualizer. We don't need to touch the TestShowVisualizer method because it does its job automatically. In the next section, you'll learn how to test a visualizer with this method.

Testing a Visualizer

Now that we have a visualizer, we can test it with the handy TestShowVisualizer method, which gets an object as a parameter and visualizes this object. All we need to do is write code that creates a list of Soldier objects and passes it to this method.

You can do this by adding a new console application to the solution. Add a reference to the visualizer project in order to be able to call the TestShowVisualizer method from there. You also need to add a reference to Microsoft.VisualStudio.DebuggerVisualizers; otherwise, you'll get a runtime error.

The simple code in Listing 17-13 tests the new visualizer.

Listing 17-13: Testing the Visualizer

```csharp
using System;
using System.Collections.Generic;
using System.Linq;
using System.Text;
using ListViewVisualizer;

namespace TestListVisualizer
{
    class Program
    {
        static void Main(string[] args)
        {
            Console.Title = "Test List<Soldier> Visualizer";

            List<Soldier> soldiers = new List<Soldier>();

            Soldier soldier1 = new Soldier("Keyvan", "Nayyeri");
            soldier1.BirthDate = DateTime.Parse("October 11, 1984");
            soldier1.Degree = "BS";
            soldier1.Rank = "Second LT";
            soldiers.Add(soldier1);

            Soldier soldier2 = new Soldier("John", "Smith");
            soldier2.BirthDate = DateTime.Parse("January 22, 1980");
            soldier2.Degree = "MS";
            soldier2.Rank = "First LT";
            soldiers.Add(soldier2);

            Soldier soldier3 = new Soldier("Gary", "Stevens");
            soldier3.BirthDate = DateTime.Parse("April 1, 1982");
            soldier3.Degree = "BS";
```

```
                    soldier3.Rank = "Second LT";
                    soldiers.Add(soldier3);


                    ListViewVisualizer.ListViewVisualizer.TestShowVisualizer(soldiers);

                    Console.ReadLine();
                }
            }
        }
```

After running this code, you would get the result shown in Figure 17-12.

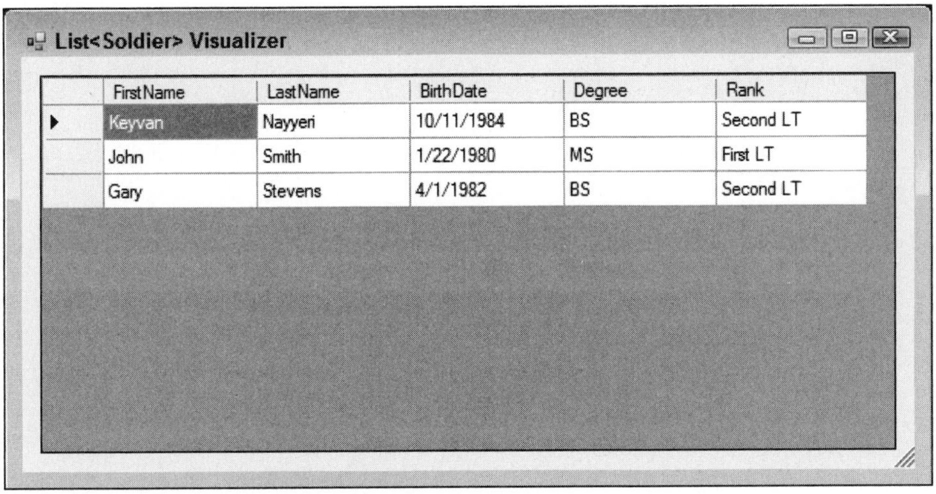

Figure 17-12: Result of testing the visualizer

Deploying a Visualizer

The purpose of deploying a visualizer is to make it available for a current user of the system or to enable all users to use the specified type in all their codes. This deployment is relatively easy.

First, you need to add an assembly attribute to your visualizer class. This attribute has a DebuggerVisualizer attribute (which can be found in the System.Diagnostics namespace). It has three arguments:

❏   Type of the visualizer class

❏   Target type of the visualizer

❏   Test description of the visualizer

With these points in mind, you can update the visualizer code (see Listing 17-14).

Listing 17-14: Making the Visualizer Ready for Deployment

```csharp
using Microsoft.VisualStudio.DebuggerVisualizers;
using System;
using System.Collections.Generic;
using System.Linq;
using System.Windows.Forms;
using System.Diagnostics;

namespace ListViewVisualizer
{
    /// <summary>
    /// A Visualizer for Soldier.
    /// </summary>
    [assembly: DebuggerVisualizer(typeof(ListViewVisualizer),
        Target = typeof(Soldier),
        Description = "List<Soldier> Visualizer")]
    public class ListViewVisualizer : DialogDebuggerVisualizer
    {
        protected override void Show(IDialogVisualizerService windowService,
            IVisualizerObjectProvider objectProvider)
        {
            List<Soldier> data = (List<Soldier>)objectProvider.GetObject();

            using (Viewer displayForm = new Viewer())
            {
                displayForm.InternalDataSource = data;
                windowService.ShowDialog(displayForm);
            }
        }

        /// <summary>
        /// Tests the visualizer by hosting it outside of the debugger.
        /// </summary>
        /// <param name="objectToVisualize">The object to display in the
        visualizer.</param>
        public static void TestShowVisualizer(object objectToVisualize)
        {
            VisualizerDevelopmentHost visualizerHost =
                new VisualizerDevelopmentHost(objectToVisualize,
        typeof(ListViewVisualizer));
            visualizerHost.ShowVisualizer();
        }
    }
}
```

After compiling this class into an assembly, you can use the assembly for deployment. You have two options for deployment:

❑ **Deploy for current user only:** Copy the assembly to [Personal Documents Folder]\Visual Studio 2008\Visualizers.

❑ **Deploy for all users on the system:** Copy the assembly to [Program Files Folder]\Microsoft Visual Studio 9.0\Common7\Packages\Debugger\Visualizers.

After deploying your visualizer and restarting the Visual Studio IDE, you can use this visualizer in your code. You can also create windows installers that automate the deployment process in order to offer professional deployment packages.

Assigning a Visualizer to Your Types

When you're creating your own types, you can connect the type to a specific visualizer. In this case, whenever you try to visualize this type, Visual Studio uses the specified visualizer.

You can assign a visualizer to your types by adding a `DebuggerVisualizer` attribute to your class. This attribute gets an argument that is the type of visualizer that you want to assign to your type.

Listing 17-15 shows how this is applied to the example.

Listing 17-15: Assigning a Visualizer to a Type

```csharp
using System;
using System.Collections.Generic;
using System.Linq;
using System.Text;
using System.Diagnostics;

namespace ListViewVisualizer
{
    [DebuggerVisualizer(typeof(ListViewVisualizer))]
    [Serializable()]
    public class Soldier
    {
        public Soldier(string firstName, string lastName)
        {
            this.FirstName = firstName;
            this.LastName = lastName;
        }

        // First Name
        private string firstName;

        public string FirstName
        {
            get { return firstName; }
            set { firstName = value; }
        }

        // Last Name
        private string lastName;

        public string LastName
        {
            get { return lastName; }
            set { lastName = value; }
        }

        // Birth Date
```

(continued)

Listing 17-15 *(continued)*

```csharp
        private DateTime birthDate;

        public DateTime BirthDate
        {
            get { return birthDate; }
            set { birthDate = value; }
        }

        // Degree
        private string degree;

        public string Degree
        {
            get { return degree; }
            set { degree = value; }
        }

        // Military Rank
        private string rank;

        public string Rank
        {
            get { return rank; }
            set { rank = value; }
        }
    }
}
```

Sample Bitmap Visualizer

An image visualizer is a common type of visualizer. To finish this chapter, I'll create a new visualizer with the code presented in Listing 17-16 to visualize a bitmap type.

Listing 17-16: Bitmap Visualizer

```csharp
using Microsoft.VisualStudio.DebuggerVisualizers;
using System;
using System.Collections.Generic;
using System.Linq;
using System.Windows.Forms;
using System.Drawing;

namespace ImageVisualizer
{
    /// <summary>
    /// A Visualizer for Bitmap.
    /// </summary>
    public class BitmapVisualizer : DialogDebuggerVisualizer
    {
        protected override void Show(IDialogVisualizerService windowService,
            IVisualizerObjectProvider objectProvider)
        {
```

```
        Bitmap data = (Bitmap)objectProvider.GetObject();

        using (ImageViewer displayForm = new ImageViewer())
        {
            displayForm.internalImage = data;
            windowService.ShowDialog(displayForm);
        }
    }

    /// <summary>
    /// Tests the visualizer by hosting it outside of the debugger.
    /// </summary>
    /// <param name="objectToVisualize">The object to display in the
visualizer.</param>
    public static void TestShowVisualizer(object objectToVisualize)
    {
        VisualizerDevelopmentHost visualizerHost =
            new VisualizerDevelopmentHost(objectToVisualize,
typeof(BitmapVisualizer));
        visualizerHost.ShowVisualizer();
    }
  }
}
```

This implementation applies another form named `ImageViewer` in order to view the image. This form has a property that holds the bitmap data and displays this data in a `PictureBox` control when the form loads (see Listing 17-17).

Listing 17-17: `ImageViewer` Form Code

```
using System;
using System.Collections.Generic;
using System.ComponentModel;
using System.Data;
using System.Drawing;
using System.Linq;
using System.Text;
using System.Windows.Forms;

namespace ImageVisualizer
{
    public partial class ImageViewer : Form
    {
        public ImageViewer()
        {
            InitializeComponent();
        }

        public Bitmap internalImage { get; set; }

        private void ImageViewer_Load(object sender, EventArgs e)
        {
            pictureBox.Image = this.internalImage;
            this.Width = pictureBox.Width = this.internalImage.Width + 15;
```

(continued)

Listing 17-17 *(continued)*

```
            this.Height = pictureBox.Height = this.internalImage.Height + 35;
        }
    }
}
```

The code implementation is straightforward. After assigning the content of the `internalImage` property to the `PictureBox` control, it resizes the `PictureBox` and form to have the same size as the image.

With the code in Listing 17-18, I can test my visualizer.

Listing 17-18: Testing the Image Visualizer

```
using System;
using System.Collections.Generic;
using System.Linq;
using System.Text;
using System.Drawing;

namespace TestImageVisualizer
{
    class Program
    {
        static void Main(string[] args)
        {
            Bitmap image = (Bitmap)Image.FromFile("Image.gif");
            ImageVisualizer.BitmapVisualizer.TestShowVisualizer(image);
        }
    }
}
```

You can see the result in Figure 17-13.

Figure 17-13: Image visualizer

Like other samples in this chapter, you can download the source package to see the code.

Summary

A key part of the development process is debugging. This chapter focused on extending the debugger and debugging features in Visual Studio. You learned how to extend the basic debugging features in order to simplify your debugging process. After learning about all the ways you can extend debugging features, you learned about type proxies and visualizers and how to write them. You also learned how to test and deploy a visualizer, and finally saw a sample visualizer in action.

18

VSPackages

Along with macros, add-ins, and visualizers, a VSPackage is a common way to extend Visual Studio. It is also the most powerful way to do it. Internal teams at Microsoft use VSPackages to create many built-in features in Visual Studio. With VSPackages, you can have complete integration between your code and Visual Studio, something that can't be achieved with any other extensibility option.

VSPackages open doors to you with many APIs, enabling you to add custom functionality to Visual Studio, as add-ins do. However, VSPackages can give you many more capabilities to create custom packages and extend Visual Studio than are possible with add-ins. Using VSPackages, you can add your own functionality and features to Visual Studio, including your very own tool windows, designers, editors, and commands.

Note that VSPackages are the same as Visual Studio Shell integrated packages. We looked at Visual Studio Shell isolated mode in Chapter 15. Here we cover VSPackages and Visual Studio Shell integrated mode, which are the same thing. This chapter uses the term VSPackage because it's more common and familiar for this purpose. If you read Chapter 15, then you have a good understanding of Visual Studio Shell integrated mode, and hence VSPackages.

A good example of this deep integration with the help of a VSPackage is IronPython, a language that's integrated with Visual Studio through a VSPackage that helps Python programmers write their programs for .NET with .NET Framework classes and APIs but in Python syntax.

VSPackage is also known as the Visual Studio Integration Package (VSIP) interface, and it's actually a COM component. You can work with VSPackages directly by writing all code from the base, but this isn't so easy. Therefore, Microsoft has provided a rich set of ready-to-go project templates, wizards, and code samples in the Visual Studio SDK for working with VSPackages and creating them easily.

Throughout this chapter, you'll use these tools and code templates — so installing the Visual Studio SDK is mandatory for reading this chapter. Once you install the Visual Studio SDK, it adds some sample codes and project templates for Visual Studio extensibility options. There's also a project template for VSPackages.

Specifically, this chapter covers the following topics:

❑ The concept of VSPackages and their application

❑ The anatomy of a VSPackage

❑ VSPackage Wizard in Visual Studio

❑ Developing a VSPackage with programming codes

❑ Testing a VSPackage

❑ Deploying a VSPackage

Before beginning, note that the topic of VSPackages is completely correlated with COM programming and .NET interoperability with COM components. This topic is broader than one chapter can possibly cover and warrants a deeper discussion, which should be considered a part of advanced topics in Visual Studio extensibility. This chapter provides a good introduction, including some background, and avoids detailed topics.

In fact, Microsoft's documentation and other resources for VSPackages aren't currently very rich, and this chapter may be the only printed resource you'll find about VSPackage development. Many developers prefer to use other extensibility options to achieve their goals because VSPackages are harder to use and develop.

What Is a VSPackage?

Many readers of this book are likely to have no background in Visual Studio extensibility, and especially in VSPackages. Even if you have this background, you may have a wrong or partial understanding of VSPackages. Therefore, this section provides a short introduction to VSPackages, including their applications and capabilities. After reading this section, not only will you know what a VSPackage is, you'll also know what can and can't be achieved with VSPackages.

First of all, as is obvious from its name, a VSPackage is a package, or module, related to Visual Studio. Compare the name VSPackage to VSMacro (which is commonly known as "macro" and is described in Chapter 22). VSPackage contains some extra functionality that integrates with Visual Studio. It is another extensibility option that can be developed with a rich set of Visual Studio APIs in lower levels than add-ins or macros.

Typically, a VSPackage includes some general groups of extensions:

❑ User interface elements

❑ Projects

❑ Services

❑ Designers

❑ Editors

A VSPackage can contain one or more of these extensions in order to add some extra functionality to Visual Studio. With VSPackages, you can have a completely integrated extension with the same look and feel as other components.

For example, suppose you want to create an integrated IDE for developing a new .NET language that you've created (you can name it Keyvan#!). Obviously, this language needs good support in an editor, as well as some command-line instructions and a toolbar window. It also may need some project templates that can't be achieved with a VSPackage (see Chapter 20). The best approach to implement this scenario is a VSPackage that creates a toolbar, command, and editor for your language. With this approach, you can extend Visual Studio much more than with any other extensibility options, and ultimately you have an integrated language with Visual Studio.

As mentioned earlier, compared with other extensibility options, VSPackages are harder to develop, but they give you more tools to customize or extend the VS IDE.

The Anatomy of a VSPackage

This section provides a short overview of the technical anatomy of VSPackages; then we'll get into technical details about them. A VSPackage is just a COM object, and it implements the IVsPackage interface in the core. In Visual Studio 2005, the Managed Package Framework (MPF) was introduced, so you no longer need to implement this interface or even know about it, because this framework provides a base class from which you need to inherit.

This class is `Package` (see Figure 18-1), which is a part of the Visual Studio Shell namespace (described in Chapter 15).

In this chapter we'll use this base class to develop our VSPackages. The `Package` base class implements several interfaces, including the following:

- ❑ IVsPackage
- ❑ IServiceProvider
- ❑ IOleCommandTarget
- ❑ IVsPersistSolutionOpts
- ❑ IServiceContainer
- ❑ System.IServiceProvider
- ❑ IVsUserSettings
- ❑ IVsUserSettingsMigration
- ❑ IVsToolWindowFactory

Each of these interfaces enables you to access some APIs for developing your VSPackage. They also help you work with many aspects of Visual Studio to extend it.

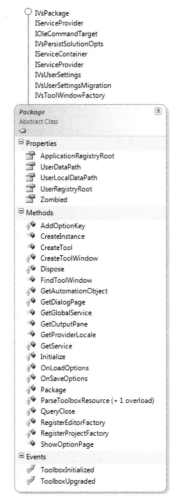

Figure 18-1: `Package` base class

A wizard creates VSPackage code templates for you automatically. This wizard creates some code files, configuration files, resource files, and other elements, and you just need to develop your code based on these templates and files. In addition to the VSPackage project itself, there's a Visual Studio unit-test project that you can use to test your VSPackages.

VSPackages can be developed with Visual C++, Visual C#, and Visual Basic. Before Visual Studio 2008, you were limited to Visual C++ and Visual C#, but in Visual Studio 2008, Microsoft did an excellent job of bringing extensibility to the Visual Basic language and including samples in the SDK. When using Visual C# or Visual Basic as your language, there's a one-to-one mapping between your classes and objects with Visual C++ codes. Actually, your C# codes are very similar to Visual C++ codes in this case.

VSPackages need a Package Load Key (PLK) in order to load on machines. You don't need to be too concerned about this on your machine when you're developing a VSPackage because the key is generated automatically and loads up easily. For deploying and transferring your VSPackage to other machines, however, you need to spend some time on this. This topic is covered later in this chapter when we discuss VSPackage deployment.

You can also configure your VSPackage to work with a minimum edition of Visual Studio. For example, you can configure it to work with Visual Studio Professional and later editions.

Building a VSPackage

This section describes how to build VSPackages with the Visual Studio Integration Package Wizard, and includes development code. I'll begin with the wizard, which makes the process easier, and then discuss development details of VSPackages.

Before starting this topic, note that you need to have the Visual Studio 2008 SDK installed on your machine in order to see and use some options in this chapter.

Visual Studio Integration Package Wizard

In order to create a new VSPackage project (a Visual Studio Shell integration package), open the New Project dialog, and choose Extensibility from the left pane and the Visual Studio Integration Package from the right pane, as shown in Figure 18-2. This template (along some other templates) appears here if you have the Visual Studio SDK installed.

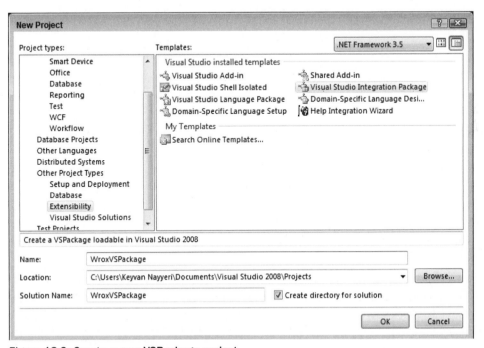

Figure 18-2: Create a new VSPackage project.

After creating this project, the Visual Studio Integration Package Wizard appears, enabling you to create some code templates for your VSPackage based on your needs (see Figure 18-3). The initial page of this wizard doesn't require any input; it merely contains some information about the wizard itself.

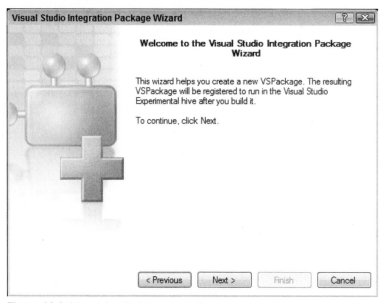

Figure 18-3: Visual Studio Integration Package Wizard

After continuing to the next page, you'll see the first dialog of this wizard, from which you can choose a development language for your VSPackage (see Figure 18-4). Three options are available: Visual C++, Visual C#, and the newly added Visual Basic. If you select either Visual C# or Visual Basic (as I do in the example), then you have to choose whether you want to generate a new key file and sign your assembly with it, or whether you want to use an existing key file for the assembly signing. You'll learn more about the purpose of this key file later in the chapter.

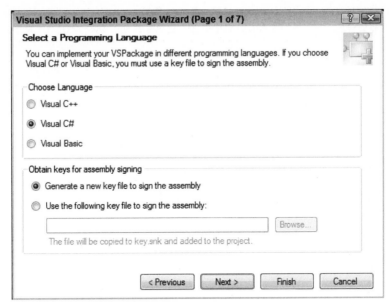

Figure 18-4: Page 1 of the Integration Package Wizard

Figure 18-5 shows the second page of the wizard, where you can enter some general information about your VSPackage, such as company name, package name, version, minimum Visual Studio edition to use for the VSPackage, and a detailed description about the package. You can also choose an icon for your VSPackage here.

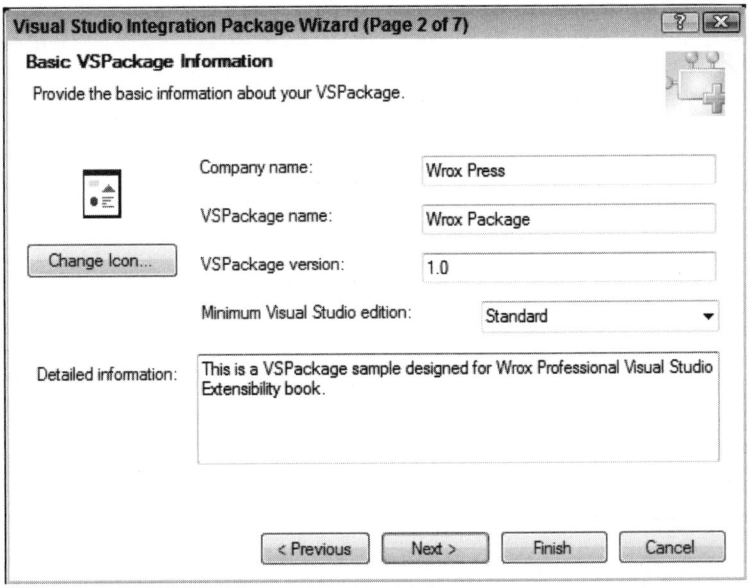

Figure 18-5: Page 2 of the Integration Package wizard

From the third page, shown in Figure 18-6, you can choose which additional functionalities you want to add to your VSPackage. You can add a menu command, a tool window, and a custom editor to your VSPackage. In Figure 18-6, all these options are selected.

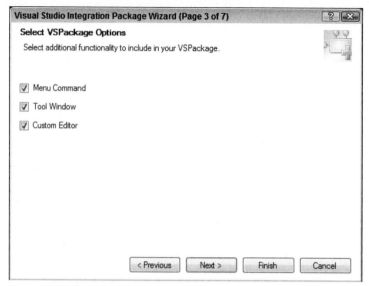

Figure 18-6: Page 3 of the Integration Package wizard

At this point, you may finish and exit the wizard or continue to other pages. After this, the pages vary based on your selections on page 3.

Page 4 presents the options for a command window. You can choose a command name and command ID for your command window, as shown in Figure 18-7.

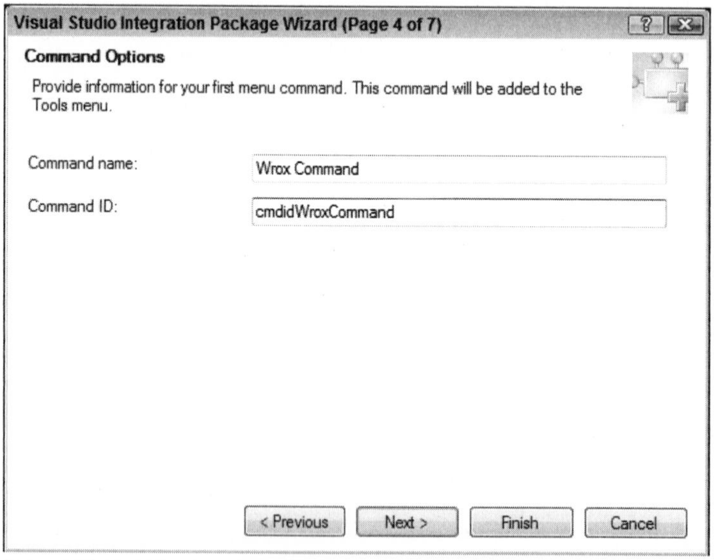

Figure 18-7: Page 4 of the Integration Package Wizard

On page 5 (see Figure 18-8), as on page 4, you can set some options for your tool window, such as window name and command ID.

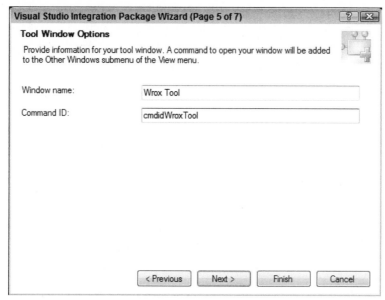

Figure 18-8: Page 5 of the Integration Package Wizard

Page 6 is where you can configure some options for your editors, such as a name, a file extension, and a default filename. You can also choose an icon for your editor from here, as shown in Figure 18-9.

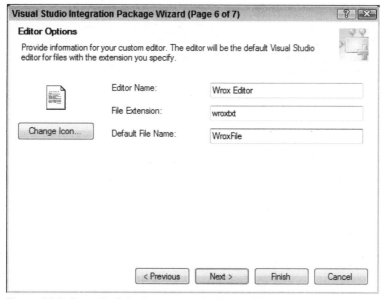

Figure 18-9: Page 6 of the Integration Package Wizard

Use the last page, page 7, to indicate whether or not you'd like to have an integrated test and a Unit Test project for your package (see Figure 18-10). These projects are a kind of Visual Studio unit-testing facility that enables you to test your VSPackage. This is a new option for developers in the Visual Studio 2008 SDK. You'll learn more about these test projects later.

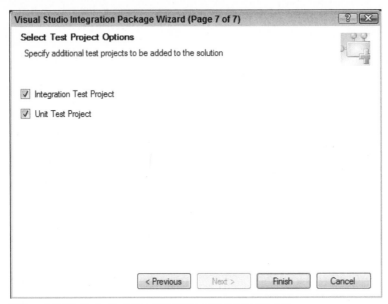

Figure 18-10: Page 7 of the Integration Package Wizard

After clicking Finish, Visual Studio generates any necessary projects and some code templates for you. In the following sections, you'll learn how to develop your VSPackage based on these templates.

At this point, Visual Studio has created some code, and you can test this VSPackage to see what's added to your VS IDE without writing even one line. These codes just show some MessageBoxes and write some text values to trace.

If you start this project, it shows up as a new Visual Studio IDE, similar to the original one in the experimental hive, but if you click on some menus and choose some items, you can see a few changes in this IDE.

First, choose Help ➪ About Microsoft Visual Studio to see the addition of your package to the list of packages (see Figure 18-11).

Now choose the Tools menu. There you see a new item named Wrox Command (see Figure 18-12). When you click on this item, you get a MessageBox that comes from the default code for this command.

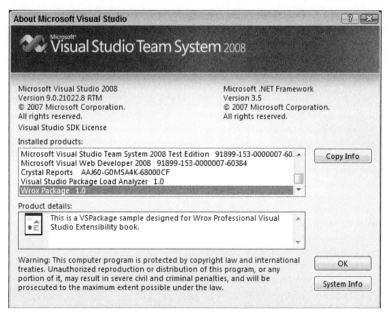

Figure 18-11: **Package** is added to the list of packages.

Figure 18-12: A new item on the Tools menu

You can also go to View ➪ Other Windows to see the addition of the Wrox Tool window (see Figure 18-13), which brings up a new toolbar for your package (see Figure 18-14).

	Bookmark Window	Ctrl+W, B
	Command Window	Ctrl+W, A
	Wrox Tool	
	Document Outline	Ctrl+W, U
	Object Test Bench	
	Property Manager	
	Resource View	Ctrl+W, R
	Macro Explorer	Alt+F8
	Start Page	
	Web Browser	Ctrl+W, W
	Performance Explorer	
	Code Metrics Results	

Figure 18-13: Addition of the Wrox Tool window

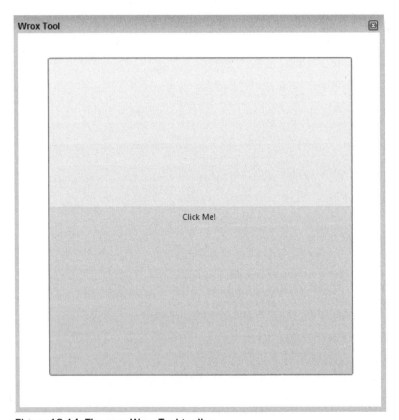

Wrox Tool

Click Me!

Figure 18-14: The new Wrox Tool toolbar

The WroxVSPackageToolbar is also added to the View ⇨ Toolbars menu, as shown in Figure 18-15.

Figure 18-15:
WroxVSPackageToolbar is
added to the Toolbars menu.

Now choose File ⇨ New ⇨ File to create a new file. Wrox Editor Files is a new item in the left pane, and you can create a new file for the Wrox editor template (Figure 18-16).

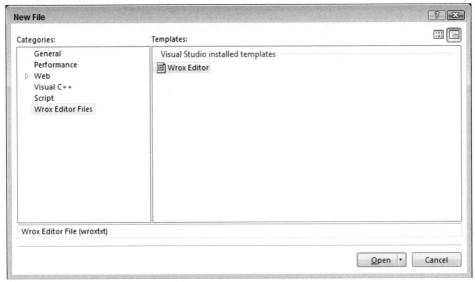

Figure 18-16: Create a new Wrox Editor file.

Finally, this loads an editor, along with its toolbar, for you. This is your package editor (see Figure 18-17).

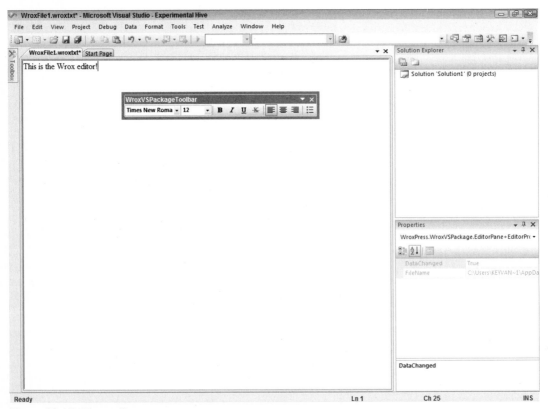

Figure 18-17: Wrox editor

You now should have a good understanding of a VSPackage and its power. Next, let's look at some technical details.

Developing a VSPackage

The wizard creates three projects: WroxVSPackage, WroxVSPackage_IntegrationTestProject, and WroxVSPackage UnitTestProject. The first one is the main project for developing the VSPackage, and the second and third projects are for unit-testing purposes. For now, ignore the test projects and just focus on the WroxVSPackage project.

In the WroxVSPackage, some references have been added to the project automatically, and there are two folders, as well as some code files, resource files, and controls. In the Resources folder, you can find some icons and bitmap images for your VSPackage; in the Templates folder are some text templates for your editor package.

The root of the project holds different files: class files, component files, user controls, resource files, and an assembly key. These files can be grouped into four categories based on their relationship to different parts of the VSPackage:

❑   VSPackage functionality in general

❑   Command menu

❑   Tool window

❑   Editor

Table 18-1 lists of all these files, with a short description of each. Note that based on your choices in the wizard, you may have fewer files than these.

Table 18-1: List of Files in a VSPackage Project

File	Description
EditorFactory.cs	A factory to create the editor object
EditorPane.cs	Hosts the editor and manages the handling of commands for the editor and some other operations for the editor
EditorTextBox.cs	The textbox component for the editor
GlobalSuppressions.cs	The file to be used by Code Analysis tools in Visual Studio to maintain SuppressMessage attributes
Guids.cs	A static class that contains a set of GUIDs related to different parts of the package
IEditor.cs	A COM interface for the editor
MyControl	A user control for the package toolbar
MyEditor	A user control for the package editor

(continued)

File	Description
MyToolWindow.cs	A class that manages the toolbar window of the package and loads its interface
NativeMethods.cs	A class containing definitions for all methods that you want to import
PkgCmdID.cs	A static class that holds a set of command IDs for the package
Resources.resx	A resource file for different pieces of the package
VSMacroRecorder.cs	A class that manages the macro recorder logic for the package
VSPackage.resx	A resource file containing resource definitions for VSPackage information that you entered in the VSPackage Wizard
WroxVSPackagePackage.cs	The main class for the package you derive from the `Package` base class

The following sections explore each of the four general groups of components that play a role in a VSPackage and explain how to develop your VSPackage from these codes.

Before looking at the following code, please note that you'll see some long source codes around VSPackages that may be unfamiliar to you, especially if you don't have a strong background in COM programming. Because of numerous code comments and attributes, these codes may seem very complicated, but I removed many of these code comments in order to keep things simple and save space.

Don't worry about these codes, because you won't have a lot to do with them. Nonetheless, I'll show you how to work with them just to avoid confusion later. Recall that VSPackages are a little harder to work with than other extensibility options in Visual Studio because they're correlated with COM programming and lower APIs.

Package

The main class file that defines the VSPackage is WroxVSPackagePackage.cs, where your package class is derived from the `Package` base class (see Figure 18-18).

Figure 18-18: `Package` class diagram

First take a look at the code in Listing 18-1 (some XML code comments are removed to save space).

Listing 18-1: Package Class Code

```
using System;
using System.Diagnostics;
using System.Globalization;
using System.Runtime.InteropServices;
using System.ComponentModel.Design;
using Microsoft.Win32;
using Microsoft.VisualStudio.Shell.Interop;
using Microsoft.VisualStudio.OLE.Interop;
using Microsoft.VisualStudio.Shell;

namespace WroxPress.WroxVSPackage
{
    // This attribute tells the registration utility (regpkg.exe) that this class
needs
    // to be registered as package.
    [PackageRegistration(UseManagedResourcesOnly = true)]
    // A Visual Studio component can be registered under different regitry roots;
    // for instance when you debug your package you want to register it in the
    // experimental hive. This attribute specifies the registry root to use if
    // no one is provided to regpkg.exe with the /root switch.
    [DefaultRegistryRoot("Software\\Microsoft\\VisualStudio\\9.0")]
    // This attribute is used to register the informations needed to
    // show the this package
    // in the Help/About dialog of Visual Studio.
    [InstalledProductRegistration(false, "#110", "#112", "1.0", IconResourceID =
400)]
    // In order be loaded inside Visual Studio in a machine that has not the
    // VS SDK installed,
    // package needs to have a valid load key (it can be requested at
    // http://msdn.microsoft.com/vstudio/extend/). This attributes tells the
    // shell that this package has a load key embedded in its resources.
    [ProvideLoadKey("Standard", "1.0", "Wrox Package", "Wrox Press", 1)]
    // This attribute is needed to let the shell know that this package exposes
    // some menus.
    [ProvideMenuResource(1000, 1)]
    // This attribute registers a tool window exposed by this package.
    [ProvideToolWindow(typeof(MyToolWindow))]
    [ProvideEditorExtension(typeof(EditorFactory), ".wroxtxt", 50,
            ProjectGuid = "{A2FE74E1-B743-11d0-AE1A-00A0C90FFFC3}",
            TemplateDir = "..\\..\\Templates",
            NameResourceID = 105,
            DefaultName = "Wrox Package")]
    [ProvideKeyBindingTable(GuidList.guidWroxVSPackageEditorFactoryString, 102)]
    [ProvideEditorLogicalView(typeof(EditorFactory),
        "{7651a703-06e5-11d1-8ebd-00a0c90f26ea}")]
    [Guid(GuidList.guidWroxVSPackagePkgString)]
    public sealed class WroxVSPackagePackage : Package
```

(continued)

Listing 18-1 *(continued)*

```
    {
        public WroxVSPackagePackage()
        {
            Trace.WriteLine(string.Format(CultureInfo.CurrentCulture,
                "Entering constructor for: {0}", this.ToString()));
        }

        private void ShowToolWindow(object sender, EventArgs e)
        {
            // Get the instance number 0 of this tool window. This window
            // is single instance so this instance is actually the only one.
            // The last flag is set to true so that if the tool window does
            // not exists it will be created.
            ToolWindowPane window = this.FindToolWindow(typeof(MyToolWindow), 0,
true);
            if ((null == window) || (null == window.Frame))
            {
                throw new NotSupportedException(Resources.CanNotCreateWindow);
            }
            IVsWindowFrame windowFrame = (IVsWindowFrame)window.Frame;
            Microsoft.VisualStudio.ErrorHandler.ThrowOnFailure(windowFrame.Show());
        }


        // Overriden Package Implementation
        #region Package Members

        protected override void Initialize()
        {
            Trace.WriteLine(string.Format(CultureInfo.CurrentCulture,
                "Entering Initialize() of: {0}", this.ToString()));
            base.Initialize();

            //Create Editor Factory. Note that the base Package class will
            // call Dispose on it.
            base.RegisterEditorFactory(new EditorFactory(this));

            // Add our command handlers for menu (commands must exist in
            // the .vsct file)
            OleMenuCommandService mcs = GetService(typeof(IMenuCommandService))
                as OleMenuCommandService;
            if (null != mcs)
            {
                // Create the command for the menu item.
                CommandID menuCommandID = new CommandID
                    (GuidList.guidWroxVSPackageCmdSet,
                    (int)PkgCmdIDList.cmdidWroxCommand);
                MenuCommand menuItem = new MenuCommand
                    (MenuItemCallback, menuCommandID);
                mcs.AddCommand(menuItem);
                // Create the command for the tool window
                CommandID toolwndCommandID = new CommandID
```

```
                    (GuidList.guidWroxVSPackageCmdSet,
                    (int)PkgCmdIDList.cmdidWroxTool);
            MenuCommand menuToolWin = new MenuCommand
                    (ShowToolWindow, toolwndCommandID);
            mcs.AddCommand(menuToolWin);
        }
    }
    #endregion

    private void MenuItemCallback(object sender, EventArgs e)
    {
        // Show a Message Box to prove we were here
        IVsUIShell uiShell = (IVsUIShell)GetService(typeof(SVsUIShell));
        Guid clsid = Guid.Empty;
        int result;
        Microsoft.VisualStudio.ErrorHandler.ThrowOnFailure(uiShell
.ShowMessageBox(
                    0,
                    ref clsid,
                    "Wrox Package",
                    string.Format(CultureInfo.CurrentCulture,
                    "Inside {0}.MenuItemCallback()", this.ToString()),
                    string.Empty,
                    0,
                    OLEMSGBUTTON.OLEMSGBUTTON_OK,
                    OLEMSGDEFBUTTON.OLEMSGDEFBUTTON_FIRST,
                    OLEMSGICON.OLEMSGICON_INFO,
                    0,          // false
                    out result));
        }

    }
}
```

This class is a sealed class that derives from the `Package` base class and has several attributes that define how it should be registered in the registry. It also has tool window and editor classes assigned to it. These attributes are described in Table 18-2.

Table 18-2: VSPackage Class Attributes

Attribute	Description
PackageRegistration	This marks this class as the `Package` class, which tells the registration tool that the current class should be registered as the `Package` class.
DefaultRegistryRoot	This attribute specifies the default registration root for the package. The default value registers the package in the experimental hive.
InstalledProductRegistration	Here you set the information that is shown to users in the Help ⇨ About Microsoft Visual Studio menu.

(continued)

Attribute	Description
ProvideLoadKey	This specifies that the VSPackage has a load key embedded in it and provides some general information about the package. You learn more about this key and deployment of VSPackages later in the chapter.
ProvideMenuResource	This tells the Visual Studio Shell that the package has some menu resources.
ProvideToolWindow	Registers a tool window for the package
ProvideEditorExtension	Declares an editor with a unique GUID, default extension, default name, and other properties
ProvideKeyBindingTable	This specifies some information, such as a unique GUID for the binding table.
ProvideEditorLogicalView	Sets the type name of the editor factory and assigns a unique GUID for logical view
Guid	This attribute assigns a unique GUID value to the package class. Each VSPackage must have a unique GUID in order to work.

The VSPackage class contains four methods. One is the public constructor. Another is an overridden method from the base class (Initialize). The other two are just some additions to it. Table 18-3 gives a brief description of these methods.

Table 18-3: VSPackage Class Methods

Method	Description
WroxVSPackage	This public constructor of the package doesn't do anything by default (except writing something to trace), but you can add your code for any special purposes when the class is being created.
ShowToolWindow	The menu item for the tool window is associated with this method, and it's called whenever the user clicks this menu item. The logic inside this method shows the tool window to the end user.
Initialize	This is an overridden method from the Package base class for initialization of the package. It contains some code logic to assign different pieces of the package to it, such as tool window, command, and editor.
MenuItemCallback	This method executes whenever a user clicks a menu item. By default, it just shows a message to end users.

Here I omit some classes such as GuidList, NativeMethods, PkgCmdIDList, and VSMacroRecorder that are related to the VSPackage's functionality because they can complicate the discussion, and you won't typically care much about them anyway.

Tool Window

A user control and a class make the main part of VSPackage logic for a tool window. MyControl is where you can design the look and feel of your tool window, and the MyToolWindow class is where you implement the logic to load this control.

MyControl is a simple user control that has a Button control only. The code behind this button simply shows a message box to users.

However, MyToolWindow is a class derived from the ToolWindowPane abstract base class (see Figure 18-19) and is responsible for loading and showing the control in the tool window.

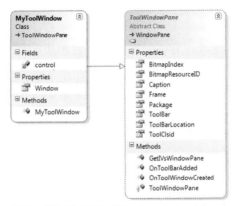

Figure 18-19: MyToolWindow derived from ToolWindowPane

Presented in Listing 18-2, MyToolWindow has a field to contain the user control. It also has a public constructor where it creates this control. It overrides the Window property from the base class and converts the control to IWin32Window and returns it. This class also has a Guid attribute that assigns a unique GUID to it.

Listing 18-2: MyToolWindow Class

```
using System;
using System.Collections;
using System.ComponentModel;
using System.Drawing;
using System.Data;
using System.Windows.Forms;
using System.Runtime.InteropServices;
using Microsoft.VisualStudio.Shell.Interop;
```

(continued)

Listing 18-2 *(continued)*

```
using Microsoft.VisualStudio.Shell;

namespace WroxPress.WroxVSPackage
{
    [Guid("5c7a60c7-c8b1-4809-aafd-76c9cb462229")]
    public class MyToolWindow : ToolWindowPane
    {
        // This is the user control hosted by the tool window; it is exposed
        // to the base class using the Window property. Note that, even if
        // this class implements IDispose, we are not calling Dispose on this
        // object. This is because ToolWindowPane calls Dispose on the object
        // returned by the Window property.
        private MyControl control;

        public MyToolWindow() :
            base(null)
        {
            // Set the window title reading it from the resources.
            this.Caption = Resources.ToolWindowTitle;
            // Set the image that will appear on the tab of the window frame
            // when docked with an other window
            // The resource ID correspond to the one defined in the resx file
            // while the Index is the offset in the bitmap strip. Each image in
            // the strip being 16x16.
            this.BitmapResourceID = 301;
            this.BitmapIndex = 1;


            control = new MyControl();
        }

        override public IWin32Window Window
        {
            get
            {
                return (IWin32Window)control;
            }
        }

    }
}
```

You can add your controls and write logic to handle different events in the control in order to build your tool window.

Editor

Some classes, components, and controls make the package editor for you, such as `EditorFactory`, `EditorPane`, `EditorTextBox`, and `IEditor`, along with the `MyEditor` control.

The package editor is an extended version of the `RichTextBox` control that is implemented in the `EditorTextBox` component. There are numerous codes in classes related to this editor to implement the logic for editor and macro recording operations. A full discussion of these classes is beyond the scope of this chapter, so I'm omitting details here. Just be aware that for your VSPackages, you may need to change these codes or add new codes to them, but by default you have a full-featured editor to use.

The Initialize method in the VSPackage class creates an instance of EditorFactory and registers it. The structure of the EditorFactory class is shown in Figure 18-20. This class implements the IVsEditorFactory and IDisposable interfaces.

Figure 18-20:
EditorFactory class
structure

EditorFactory itself does the job of using the EditorPane class to load the editor. EditorPane has logic to load the MyEditor control where the Editor control is added.

Listing 18-3 shows the code for the EditorFactory class.

Listing 18-3: EditorFactory Class

```
using System;
using System.Diagnostics;
using System.Globalization;
using System.Runtime.InteropServices;
using System.Security.Permissions;
using Microsoft.VisualStudio;
using Microsoft.VisualStudio.Shell.Interop;
```

(continued)

Listing 18-3 *(continued)*

```csharp
using Microsoft.VisualStudio.Shell;

using IOleServiceProvider = Microsoft.VisualStudio.OLE.Interop.IServiceProvider;

namespace WroxPress.WroxVSPackage
{
    [Guid(GuidList.guidWroxVSPackageEditorFactoryString)]
    public sealed class EditorFactory : IVsEditorFactory, IDisposable
    {
        private WroxVSPackagePackage editorPackage;
        private ServiceProvider vsServiceProvider;


        public EditorFactory(WroxVSPackagePackage package)
        {
            Trace.WriteLine(string.Format(CultureInfo.CurrentCulture,
                "Entering {0} constructor", this.ToString()));

            this.editorPackage = package;
        }

        public void Dispose()
        {
            if (vsServiceProvider != null)
            {
                vsServiceProvider.Dispose();
            }
        }

        #region IVsEditorFactory Members

        public int SetSite(Microsoft.VisualStudio.OLE.Interop.IServiceProvider psp)
        {
            vsServiceProvider = new ServiceProvider(psp);
            return VSConstants.S_OK;
        }

        public object GetService(Type serviceType)
        {
            return vsServiceProvider.GetService(serviceType);
        }


        public int MapLogicalView(ref Guid rguidLogicalView,
            out string pbstrPhysicalView)
        {
            pbstrPhysicalView = null;    // initialize out parameter

            // we support only a single physical view
            if (VSConstants.LOGVIEWID_Primary == rguidLogicalView)
                return VSConstants.S_OK;        // primary view uses NULL as
pbstrPhysicalView
            else
```

```
                    return VSConstants.E_NOTIMPL;     // you must return E_NOTIMPL for any
unrecognized rguidLogicalView values
        }

        public int Close()
        {
            return VSConstants.S_OK;
        }

        [SecurityPermission(SecurityAction.Demand, Flags =
            SecurityPermissionFlag.UnmanagedCode)]
        public int CreateEditorInstance(
                        uint grfCreateDoc,
                        string pszMkDocument,
                        string pszPhysicalView,
                        IVsHierarchy pvHier,
                        uint itemid,
                        System.IntPtr punkDocDataExisting,
                        out System.IntPtr ppunkDocView,
                        out System.IntPtr ppunkDocData,
                        out string pbstrEditorCaption,
                        out Guid pguidCmdUI,
                        out int pgrfCDW)
        {
            Trace.WriteLine(string.Format(CultureInfo.CurrentCulture,
                "Entering {0} CreateEditorInstace()", this.ToString()));

            // Initialize to null
            ppunkDocView = IntPtr.Zero;
            ppunkDocData = IntPtr.Zero;
            pguidCmdUI = GuidList.guidWroxVSPackageEditorFactory;
            pgrfCDW = 0;
            pbstrEditorCaption = null;

            // Validate inputs
            if ((grfCreateDoc & (VSConstants.CEF_OPENFILE |
                VSConstants.CEF_SILENT)) == 0)
            {
                return VSConstants.E_INVALIDARG;
            }
            if (punkDocDataExisting != IntPtr.Zero)
            {
                return VSConstants.VS_E_INCOMPATIBLEDOCDATA;
            }

            // Create the Document (editor)
            EditorPane NewEditor = new EditorPane(editorPackage);
            ppunkDocView = Marshal.GetIUnknownForObject(NewEditor);
            ppunkDocData = Marshal.GetIUnknownForObject(NewEditor);
            pbstrEditorCaption = "";
            return VSConstants.S_OK;
        }

        #endregion
    }
}
```

In this code, `CreateEditorInstance` is the main method that creates an instance of the editor from `EditorPane` and loads it. This function is called with a set of parameters, some of which are `out` parameters that return various values to the caller code. This way, it returns some objects to define the `Editor` object and its caption text.

Also included are some text templates for the package editor in the Templates folder that define the default font type, size, and other layout properties of the editor.

Resources in VSPackage

In addition to programming classes, components, controls, and other files, a VSPackage contains some resources such as localization resources, bitmap images, and icons.

Resources.resx is a resource file that contains string values for a tool window. It can be used to keep string values for any new part of the VSPackage. VSPackage.resx is another resource file that is used to keep string values for VSPackage. You enter this information in the Visual Studio Integration Package Wizard. VSPackage code will use .NET APIs to refer to these resources in order to display text values to end users. You can use these resources for localization of your VSPackages as well.

Also in the Resources folder are some bitmap and icon images that are used in your VSPackage. You can add your own images here for use later in your VSPackage.

For example, suppose I want to localize the text for a button in a toolbar window in the Persian (Farsi) language and show it to end users. This button is located inside the `MyControl` user control.

To do this, I first open the Resources.resx file, add a new resource item for my localized text, name it `ClickMeFarsi`, and assign the Persian translation to it (see Figure 18-21).

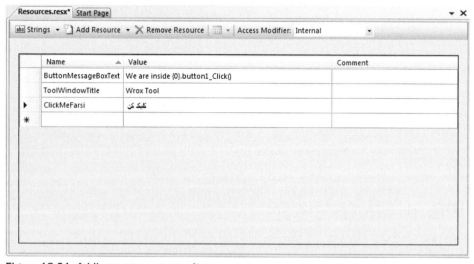

Figure 18-21: Adding a new resource item

Now I go to `MyControl` and add a line of code to its `Load` event in order to assign this text resource to the `Text` property of the button (see Listing 18-4).

Listing 18-4: Localizing the Text Property of the Button

```
private void MyControl_Load(object sender, EventArgs e)
{
    this.button1.Text = Resources.ResourceManager.GetString("ClickMeFarsi");
}
```

The result is shown in Figure 18-22.

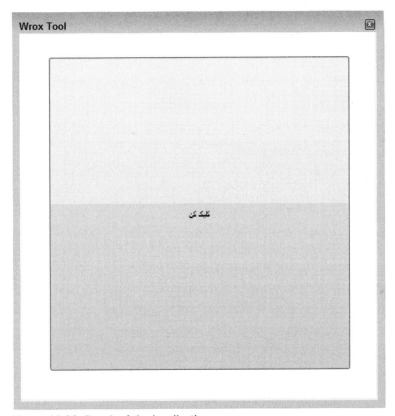

Figure 18-22: Result of the localization

Testing a VSPackage

Test-driven development, the main competitor for architecture-driven development, has become a common way to develop software systems. *Unit testing,* a key part of test-driven development, refers to writing a bit of programming code in order to test other programming code. In this case, some tools (known as unit-testing tools for a specific platform) provide APIs that enable you to create instances of your code and compare your expected results with actual results of a code. Details of test-driven development and unit testing are not covered here, as they require separate books of their own.

However, it is recommended that you familiarize yourself with these development processes, as they are becoming increasingly common in the software world.

Growing numbers of unit-testing fans in the software world and especially in the .NET community have led to the addition of unit-testing features in Visual Studio 2005 for Team Suite Edition. In Visual Studio 2008, Microsoft enhanced these features and ported them into the professional edition as well. There are also some community projects for the same purposes that provide free or commercial tools for test-driven development and unit testing. Some of these tools are listed in Appendix A.

Visual Studio 2008 includes a new option for your VSPackages that enables you to test them with two unit-testing projects. As you saw, one can choose to generate these projects in the last step of the Visual Studio Integration Package Wizard. These unit-testing projects generate all the necessary code to unit-test default code for a VSPackage, and you can use this starting point to test your VSPackage easily.

You can generate two unit-testing projects. One of them is an Integration Test project that targets testing the integration of VSPackage and its elements in general, and the other is a Unit Test project that targets testing separate parts of the package, such as its editor, menu items, or the tool window.

Listing 18-5 shows the source code of a test class, `PackageTest`, which is a test class in the Integration Test project. It contains a test method to determine whether the VSPackage is loaded successfully.

Listing 18-5: PackageTest Test Class

```
using System;
using System.Text;
using System.Collections.Generic;
using System.Linq;
using Microsoft.VisualStudio.TestTools.UnitTesting;
using Microsoft.VSSDK.Tools.VsIdeTesting;
using Microsoft.VisualStudio.Shell.Interop;
using Microsoft.VisualStudio.Shell;
using EnvDTE;

namespace IntegrationTestProject
{
    /// <summary>
    /// Integration test for package validation
    /// </summary>
    [TestClass]
    public class PackageTest
    {
        private delegate void ThreadInvoker();

        private TestContext testContextInstance;

        /// <summary>
        ///Gets or sets the test context which provides
        ///information about and functionality for the current test run.
        ///</summary>
```

```
        public TestContext TestContext
        {
            get
            {
                return testContextInstance;
            }
            set
            {
                testContextInstance = value;
            }
        }

        [TestMethod]
        [HostType("VS IDE")]
        public void PackageLoadTest()
        {
            UIThreadInvoker.Invoke((ThreadInvoker)delegate()
            {

                //Get the Shell Service
                IVsShell shellService =
                    VsIdeTestHostContext.ServiceProvider.GetService
                    (typeof(SVsShell)) as IVsShell;
                Assert.IsNotNull(shellService);

                //Validate package load
                IVSPackage package;
                Guid packageGuid = new Guid
                    (WroxPress.WroxVSPackage.GuidList.guidWroxVSPackagePkgString);
                Assert.IsTrue(0 == shellService.LoadPackage
                    (ref packageGuid, out package));
                Assert.IsNotNull(package, "Package failed to load");

            });
        }
    }
}
```

In this code, some parts are responsible for loading the test context for current test iteration. Because they're not related to our discussion and shouldn't change here, we don't need to concern ourselves with them. The main part of the code is the PackageLoadTest method where you test your VSPackage.

This test method uses the Visual Studio IDE as its host and applies the UIThreadInvoker.Invoke method (which is a part of the Visual Studio integration test library) to test the UI thread. In the main logic, it first creates an instance of Visual Studio Shell Service, and then tests whether this object is null.

In the next step, it creates an IVsPackage object and passes this object to the LoadPackage method of shellService in order to assign it a value. It also tests this to ensure that the LoadPackage method has invoked successfully.

The last step ensures that the IVsPackage object is not null. In other words, it confirms that the package loaded successfully. Now if I run this test and everything is OK, then my code should pass this test successfully (see Figure 18-23).

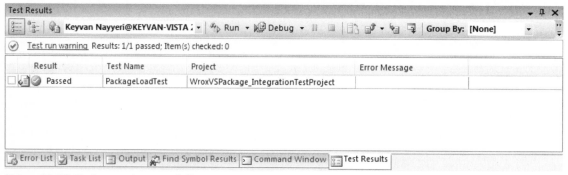

Figure 18-23: Test passed successfully

Deploying a VSPackage

Deployment and installation of a VSPackage are a bit harder than a normal .NET application. Installing a VSPackage requires two prerequisites:

❑ The DLL file of the VSPackage

❑ A Package Load Key (PLK)

You can get the DLL file after building your VSPackage, but to obtain a Package Load Key (PLK) you need to go to www.vsipmembers.com, create an account, and then enter information about your VSPackage, such as its GUID. Later in the process of deploying your VSPackage, you'll need this PLK.

There are two options for installing a VSPackage, manually or with an installer. Both are described in the following sections.

Deploying a VSPackage Manually

Manual installation of a VSPackage is as simple as registering its assembly. Suppose you have built your VSPackage successfully and have a DLL file for it.

Previously, the process of manually installing a VSPackage was harder — you had to generate a registry file for your VSPackage and then run it. In Visual Studio 2008 and after the introduction of the Visual Studio Shell, Microsoft has made this simpler.

After building your VSPackage project, Visual Studio generates a file with the same name as your VSPackage project and with a .pkgdef extension. This file is actually a registry file, but its extension is reserved for Visual Studio Shell definition files. This is the equivalent of the registry file that you had to write yourself before.

You can register this file in order to install the VSPackage on your Visual Studio IDE. For the example presented here, I can do this either by double-clicking on the file or by running the following command:

```
regedit /s WroxVSPackage.pkgdef
```

After registering my assembly, I can load my Visual Studio IDE and see my VSPackage added to it.

Here's the important point: This package can load on my machine successfully because I have Visual Studio SDK installed, but what about other machines? Usually I can't observe this, but I can simply check it by running my Visual Studio IDE with the following command:

```
devenv /novsip
```

The /novsip switch simply runs the VS IDE with VS extensibility features disabled, which comes in handy in some cases. Now if I click on my command items in IDE, I get the error shown in Figure 18-24.

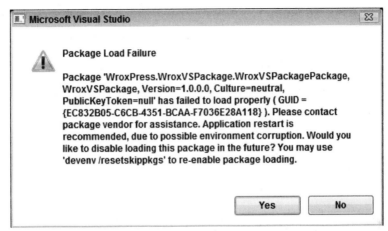

Figure 18-24: Error when registering a VSPackage without a PLK

The error occurs because I haven't specified a Package Load Key (PLK) for my VSPackage yet. To do this, I go first to www.vsipmembers.com and get a PLK related to my package information. Then I open my VSPackage project and WroxVSPackagePackage.cs file. Here, I mainly focus on the `ProvideLoadKey` attribute (see Listing 18-6).

Listing 18-6: ProvideLoadKey Attribute in the `package` Class

```csharp
using System;
using System.Diagnostics;
using System.Globalization;
using System.Runtime.InteropServices;
using System.ComponentModel.Design;
using Microsoft.Win32;
using Microsoft.VisualStudio.Shell.Interop;
using Microsoft.VisualStudio.OLE.Interop;
```

(continued)

Listing 18-6 *(continued)*

```csharp
using Microsoft.VisualStudio.Shell;

namespace WroxPress.WroxVSPackage
{
    // This attribute tells the registration utility (regpkg.exe) that this class needs
    // to be registered as package.
    [PackageRegistration(UseManagedResourcesOnly = true)]
    // A Visual Studio component can be registered under different regitry roots;
    // for instance when you debug your package you want to register it in the
    // experimental hive. This attribute specifies the registry root to use if
    // no one is provided to regpkg.exe with the /root switch.
    [DefaultRegistryRoot("Software\\Microsoft\\VisualStudio\\9.0")]
    // This attribute is used to register the informations needed to
    // show the this package
    // in the Help/About dialog of Visual Studio.
    [InstalledProductRegistration(false, "#110", "#112", "1.0", IconResourceID =
400)]
    // In order be loaded inside Visual Studio in a machine that has not the
    // VS SDK installed,
    // package needs to have a valid load key (it can be requested at
    // http://msdn.microsoft.com/vstudio/extend/). This attributes tells the
    // shell that this package has a load key embedded in its resources.
    [ProvideLoadKey("Standard", "1.0", "Wrox Package", "Wrox Press", 1)]
    // This attribute is needed to let the shell know that this package exposes
    // some menus.
    [ProvideMenuResource(1000, 1)]
    // This attribute registers a tool window exposed by this package.
    [ProvideToolWindow(typeof(MyToolWindow))]
    [ProvideEditorExtension(typeof(EditorFactory), ".wroxtxt", 50,
            ProjectGuid = "{A2FE74E1-B743-11d0-AE1A-00A0C90FFFC3}",
            TemplateDir = "..\\..\\Templates",
            NameResourceID = 105,
            DefaultName = "Wrox Package")]
    [ProvideKeyBindingTable(GuidList.guidWroxVSPackageEditorFactoryString, 102)]
    [ProvideEditorLogicalView(typeof(EditorFactory),
        "{7651a703-06e5-11d1-8ebd-00a0c90f26ea}")]
    [Guid(GuidList.guidWroxVSPackagePkgString)]
    public sealed class WroxVSPackagePackage : Package
    {
        public WroxVSPackagePackage()
        {
            Trace.WriteLine(string.Format(CultureInfo.CurrentCulture,
                "Entering constructor for: {0}", this.ToString()));
        }

        private void ShowToolWindow(object sender, EventArgs e)
        {
            // Get the instance number 0 of this tool window. This window
            // is single instance so this instance is actually the only one.
            // The last flag is set to true so that if the tool window does
```

```
            // not exists it will be created.
            ToolWindowPane window = this.FindToolWindow(typeof(MyToolWindow), 0,
true);

            if ((null == window) || (null == window.Frame))
            {
                throw new NotSupportedException(Resources.CanNotCreateWindow);
            }
            IVsWindowFrame windowFrame = (IVsWindowFrame)window.Frame;
            Microsoft.VisualStudio.ErrorHandler.ThrowOnFailure(windowFrame.Show());
        }


        // Overriden Package Implementation
        #region Package Members

        protected override void Initialize()
        {
            Trace.WriteLine(string.Format(CultureInfo.CurrentCulture,
                "Entering Initialize() of: {0}", this.ToString()));
            base.Initialize();

            //Create Editor Factory. Note that the base Package class will
            // call Dispose on it.
            base.RegisterEditorFactory(new EditorFactory(this));

            // Add our command handlers for menu (commands must exist in
            // the .vsct file)
            OleMenuCommandService mcs = GetService(typeof(IMenuCommandService))
                as OleMenuCommandService;
            if (null != mcs)
            {
                // Create the command for the menu item.
                CommandID menuCommandID = new CommandID
                    (GuidList.guidWroxVSPackageCmdSet,
                    (int)PkgCmdIDList.cmdidWroxCommand);
                MenuCommand menuItem = new MenuCommand
                    (MenuItemCallback, menuCommandID);
                mcs.AddCommand(menuItem);
                // Create the command for the tool window
                CommandID toolwndCommandID = new CommandID
                    (GuidList.guidWroxVSPackageCmdSet,
                    (int)PkgCmdIDList.cmdidWroxTool);
                MenuCommand menuToolWin = new MenuCommand
                    (ShowToolWindow, toolwndCommandID);
                mcs.AddCommand(menuToolWin);
            }
        }
        #endregion

        private void MenuItemCallback(object sender, EventArgs e)
        {
            // Show a Message Box to prove we were here
            IVsUIShell uiShell = (IVsUIShell)GetService(typeof(SVsUIShell));
```

(continued)

Listing 18-6 *(continued)*

```
            Guid clsid = Guid.Empty;
            int result;
            Microsoft.VisualStudio.ErrorHandler.ThrowOnFailure(uiShell
    .ShowMessageBox(
                    0,
                    ref clsid,
                    "Wrox Package",
                    string.Format(CultureInfo.CurrentCulture,
                    "Inside {0}.MenuItemCallback()", this.ToString()),
                    string.Empty,
                    0,
                    OLEMSGBUTTON.OLEMSGBUTTON_OK,
                    OLEMSGDEFBUTTON.OLEMSGDEFBUTTON_FIRST,
                    OLEMSGICON.OLEMSGICON_INFO,
                    0,          // false
                    out result));
        }


    }
}
```

The `ProvideLoadKey` attribute gets five arguments:

❑ `minimumEdition`: The string value of the minimum Visual Studio edition that can use this package

❑ `productVersion`: The string value of the version of the package

❑ `productName`: The string value of the package name

❑ `companyName`: The string value of the company name

❑ `resourceId`: The short value of a resource ID corresponding to the value of Package Load Key (PLK)

You enter the first four values to obtain a PLK and then add this value to the VSPackage.resx resource file. The PLK value is generated based on these parameters.

Therefore, I open the VSPackage.resx file and add a new resource with 1 as its ID, and then paste my Package Load Key to its Value field (see Figure 18-25).

Now I can rebuild my solution and register my WroxVSPackage.pkgdef file again, and then restart the Visual Studio IDE with the `/novsip` switch to confirm that it can load my package without the Visual Studio SDK installed.

Deploying a VSPackage with an Installer

To deploy a VSPackage with an installer, you need, as with other software packages, to create a Setup project and set its project output to your VSPackage project. This adds any necessary dependencies for you, but all these referenced assemblies are available on a machine with Visual Studio installed, so I exclude them to avoid further problems (see Figure 18-26).

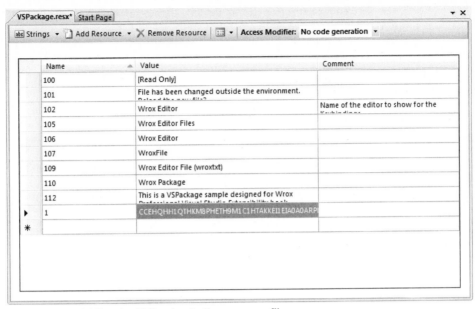

Figure 18-25: Adding the PLK value to the resource file

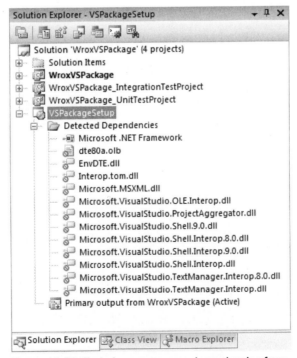

Figure 18-26: Exclude unnecessary dependencies from
the Setup project.

Next, you right-click on the Setup project and choose View ⇨ Registry in order to view the registry for the destination machine. Then right-click on the root item in the left tree (registry tree) and choose Import. In the opening dialog, browse for the package definition file that Visual Studio has generated for you before and import it.

Now expand the left tree (registry) to see what is added there (see Figure 18-27).

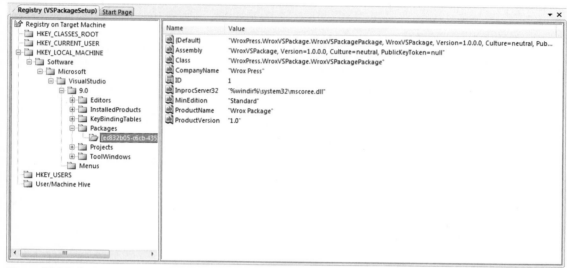

Figure 18-27: Registry of the end user

The rest of the process is registering the VSPackage assembly on the user's machine. This is fairly easy so I ignore it here (but you need to register the assembly in order to be able to run your VSPackage). After registering the assembly on the user's machine and running the registry file, users should be able to use your VSPackage.

Package Load Analyzer

In Visual Studio you have access to Package Load Analyzer tool via the Tools ⇨ Package Load Analyzer menu item. Note that in Windows Vista you need to run your IDE as administrator in order to use this tool.

This tool lists all available packages in the IDE and enables you to analyze them from two views: Plk Verification and Dependency Verification.

Plk Verification verifies the Package Load Analyzer for packages, and Dependency Verification verifies whether dependencies for a package are available. Moreover, this tool highlights in green any package that is running in the IDE, thus letting you know whether a package is running.

Figure 18-28 shows my Package Load Analyzer before registering my VSPackage, when I was running my IDE as a normal user in Vista.

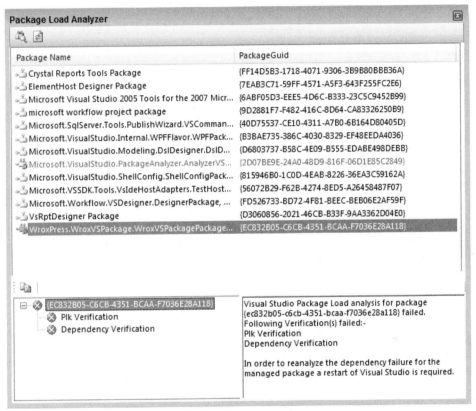

Figure 18-28: Package Load Analyzer tool before registering the package

Figure 18-29 shows the Package Load Analyzer tool after registering the package and running my IDE as administrator.

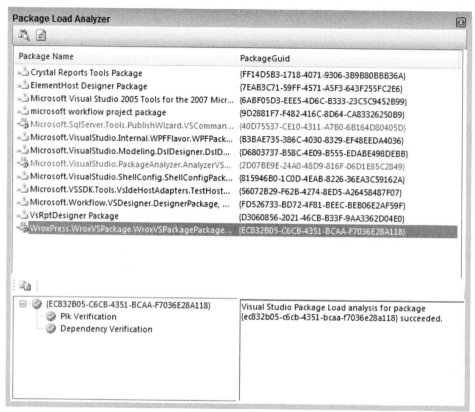

Figure 18-29: Load Analyzer tool after registering the package

Summary

This chapter served as an introduction to VSPackages and provided a general overview of their main elements and development. After a brief section on VSPackages and their application, you explored its anatomy. After that, you learned how to build a VSPackage with the VSPackage Wizard and development code. You also learned about the main elements of a VSPackage. At the end, you read about testing your VSPackages and deploying them manually or with an installer. Of course, this has been just a general discussion about VSPackages. You can learn much more about them if you are interested.

19

Code Snippets

As noted in the introduction of this book, one of the main goals of extending software is saving the time of users by relieving them from some repetitive tasks — in fact, this is probably the main goal.

The most repetitive task in Visual Studio is coding, isn't it? When you think about it, coding itself consists of several repetitive tasks, such as writing casing statements, loops, properties, and fields. Therefore, automating these repetitive tasks is a common goal for developers.

Code snippets were first introduced in Visual Studio 2005 as one of its main new features. Code snippets enable you to declare a template of code and then use it as many times as you like in your applications by replacing some placeholders with appropriate names and types.

In Visual Studio 2008, code snippets are enhanced, and there are also new code snippets. These new snippets cover some new technologies, such as Windows Presentation Foundation (WPF) and Windows Workflow Foundation (WF or WWF), as in the code snippet for dependency properties.

Code snippets are related to a specific language. This means that each language has its own code snippets, and a code snippet belongs to one and only one development language (i.e., VB or C#).

Code snippets are handy tools for coders and can save you a great deal of time. The purpose of this chapter is to teach you what you need to know about code snippets, and the following topics are covered:

❑   The concept of the code snippet and its applications

❑   The anatomy of a code snippet

❑   How to build a code snippet

❑   The XML structure of a code snippet and its elements and attributes

❑   How to manage your code snippets

What Is a Code Snippet?

The concept of a code snippet and its applications will be familiar to .NET developers because code snippets have been used widely in recent years after the release of Visual Studio 2005. For those who aren't familiar with them, this section provides a general overview.

A code snippet is a block of code template that can be inserted in different programming codes for a development language. You can replace its variable names and types in order to get a block of real programming code.

For example, suppose that you want to write a common `for` loop in C#. Here are the steps that you need to follow to get this done:

1.   Type **for** followed by open parentheses, insert a type for your indexer, and then the name of your indexer variable following a semicolon.

2.   Add your case statement and another semicolon, and finally a statement to increase or decrease your indexer value or another operation.

3.   Put your logic for the loop inside its body.

You know that this is one of most common tasks in coding a program, not only in C# but also in all other programming languages. To simplify this repetitive task, .NET provides two major ways. The first way is older and uses specific macros to generate a template. This technique has some drawbacks:

❑   Writing a macro for this purpose isn't easy or fast (compared to code snippets).

❑   Running a macro isn't easy (compared to code snippets).

❑   Macros aren't easily customizable. This means that you can't change the variable names and types easily.

Because of these drawbacks, Microsoft decided to provide a better solution to simplify these repetitive tasks, and the result was what you saw in Visual Studio 2005 — code snippets for different languages. Code snippets solve those drawbacks; they are easier to write and run, and are easily customizable.

In Visual Studio 2008, code snippets are enhanced; and a collection of new common code snippets has been added to Visual Studio and .NET development languages.

For example, let me show you a code snippet for the `for` loop mentioned earlier. In Visual Studio, there is a code snippet for integer `for` loops that iterates through a block of code from an integer indexer with zero as the initial value to an upper bound variable. On each iteration the indexer is increased by one.

Suppose that you're writing code similar to what is shown in Listing 19-1.

Listing 19-1: Code Sample Using a `for` Code Snippet

```
static void Main(string[] args)
{
    Console.Title = "Code Snippet Sample";

    int upperBound = 5;

    string[] names = new string[upperBound];

    // Iterate through array and add name values

    Console.ReadLine();
}
```

As noted in the code comments, somewhere in this code you want to iterate through the names array, add new values to it, and write these values to the console.

Using a code snippet for loops, you can simplify the code here. You simply type **for** where you want to put your `for` loop, in order to select the code-snippet item for the `for` loop from IntelliSense (see Figure 19-1). Then you press the Tab key twice in order to produce the code template shown in Figure 19-2.

Note that you can choose a code snippet from IntelliSense either by clicking on its name (or choosing it and then pressing the Tab key), or by writing its shortcut and pressing the Tab key twice.

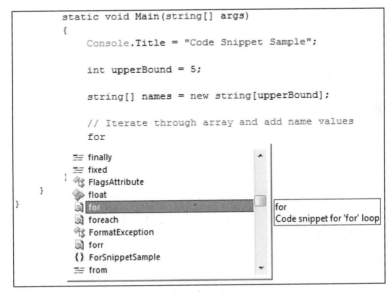

Figure 19-1: Inserting a `for` code snippet

```
static void Main(string[] args)
{
    Console.Title = "Code Snippet Sample";

    int upperBound = 5;

    string[] names = new string[upperBound];

    // Iterate through array and add name values
    for (int i = 0; i < length; i++)
    {

    }

    Console.ReadLine();
}
}
}
```

Figure 19-2: The added **for** code snippet

Now you can simply walk through some placeholders in this code snippet that are highlighted on the screen in green and easily change the name of the indexer variable and upper bound variable. After that, you write some simple code logic for the loop and finish with something like what is shown in Listing 19-2.

Listing 19-2: Final Code after Using the Code Snippet

```
static void Main(string[] args)
{
    Console.Title = "Code Snippet Sample";

    int upperBound = 5;

    string[] names = new string[upperBound];

    // Iterate through array and add name values
    for (int index = 0; index < upperBound; index++)
    {
        Console.WriteLine(string.Format("Enter name #{0}", index + 1));
        names[index] = Console.ReadLine();
        Console.Clear();
    }

    Console.ReadLine();
}
```

There are also code snippets for reverse `for` loops, casing statements, properties, interfaces, and MessageBoxes.

Code snippets are related to a specific development language. This means that you can't use a C# code snippet in Visual Basic or vice versa. Therefore, the list of code snippets for each programming language is different. Generally, Visual Basic has more code snippets than C#.

Visual Studio supports code snippets for Visual C#, Visual Basic, and XML.

The Anatomy of a Code Snippet

What is a code snippet from a technical point of view?

A code snippet is an XML document that holds a code template, as well as definitions for code literals and objects. Code snippet files should be stored with .snippet extensions in order to be recognized as code snippets. A single code snippet file can contain more than one code snippet.

You can use an XML template to create code snippets easily. You can either copy and paste this template or write it manually yourself. The template is actually a collection of some common elements in a code-snippet document.

For example, take a look at Listing 19-3.

Listing 19-3: Sample Code Snippet to Insert a Code Comment

```xml
<?xml version="1.0" encoding="utf-8" ?>
<CodeSnippets xmlns="http://schemas.microsoft.com/VisualStudio/2005/CodeSnippet">
  <CodeSnippet Format="1.0.0">
    <Header>
      <Title>Sample Code Snippet</Title>
      <Shortcut>scsk</Shortcut>
      <Author>Keyvan Nayyeri</Author>
    </Header>
    <Snippet>
      <Code Language="CSharp">
        <![CDATA[
        // This is a simple code comment
        ]]>
      </Code>
    </Snippet>
  </CodeSnippet>
</CodeSnippets>
```

This code snippet is very simple; it just inserts a code comment in the code. However, let's look at some important elements of this snippet.

As you see, this code snippet starts with an XML declaration element; then it has a root <CodeSnippets> element, which holds all code snippet declarations in a file. It also has an XML namespace attribute, which points to a specific namespace dedicated to Visual Studio code snippets.

This root <CodeSnippets> element can contain one or more <CodeSnippet> elements. Each <CodeSnippet> element holds the definition for one code snippet. This is why you can declare many code snippets in a single .snippet file.

A `<CodeSnippet>` element consists of two main parts:

❑ `<Header>`: This contains some general information about the code snippet such as version, title, shortcut, and author.

❑ `<Snippet>`: This contains the definition codes, templates, and elements of the snippet.

Next you'll learn how to build a code snippet and examine all the elements and attributes of a code snippet file in detail.

How to Build a Code Snippet

Building a code snippet is a straightforward task. You just need to create an XML file based on the snippet schema with some elements and attributes.

The first step is to create an XML file and write your snippet implementation in it. When you want to save an XML file in Visual Studio, you can choose from several options, which enables you to store it in different XML derivations. One of these is a code snippet (.snippet extension). When you want to save this XML file, you can choose this extension from the Save As type drop-down list, shown as the Snippet Files (*.snippet) item in Figure 19-3.

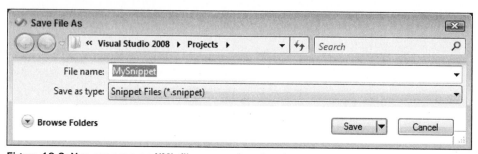

Figure 19-3: You can save an XML file as a code snippet.

The other step you should take before writing your snippet is to add the XML namespace for code snippets to this XML file. To do this, you need to add a `<CodeSnippets>` element to your XML file and then add an `xmlns` attribute with `http://schemas.microsoft.com/VisualStudio/2005/CodeSnippet` as its value.

At this point, the initial code for your code snippet looks like what is shown in Listing 19-4.

Listing 19-4: Initial Code for a Code Snippet

```xml
<?xml version="1.0" encoding="utf-8"?>
<CodeSnippets xmlns="http://schemas.microsoft.com/VisualStudio/2005/CodeSnippet">

</CodeSnippets>
```

Not only does this mark your XML file as a code snippet, it also enables you to get help from Visual Studio IntelliSense when writing your code snippet (see Figure 19-4). This is good, because you can easily see all appropriate elements and attributes for a code snippet, along with a description.

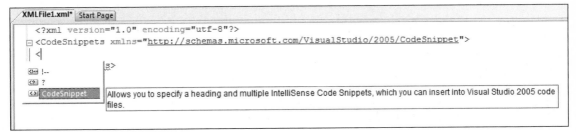

Figure 19-4: IntelliSense helps you write a code snippet easily.

Note that when you have an empty code snippet file (with the root <CodeSnippets> element and without any <CodeSnippet> element embedded within it), you get an XML warning, as shown in Figure 19-5. This warning appears because the code snippet schema expects at least one <CodeSnippet> element embedded within the <CodeSnippets> root element. It shows this warning until you add a <CodeSnippet> element there.

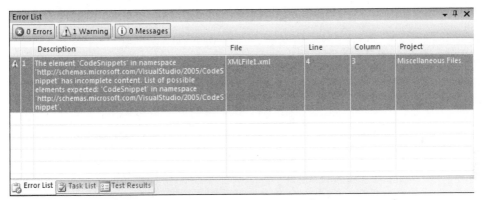

Figure 19-5: An XML warning appears if no CodeSnippet element appears in a code-snippet file.

Code-Snippet Elements and Attributes

This section describes all the elements and attributes available in a code-snippet XML document.

As mentioned before, the root element is <CodeSnippets>, which can have an xmlns attribute for an XML namespace that must refer to http://schemas.microsoft.com/VisualStudio/2005/ CodeSnippet for a code snippet.

The root <CodeSnippets> element can contain one or more <CodeSnippet> elements and nothing else.

The <CodeSnippet> element itself must contain a Format attribute. This required attribute is the only attribute of the <CodeSnippet> element. It specifies the version of the code snippet.

This element also has two required child elements: `<Header>` and `<Snippet>`. The order of these two elements is important and must not change.

Listing 19-5 shows the sample code snippet after the addition of these elements and attributes.

Listing 19-5: Sample Code Snippet after Adding Header and Snippet Elements

```xml
<?xml version="1.0" encoding="utf-8"?>
<CodeSnippets xmlns="http://schemas.microsoft.com/VisualStudio/2005/CodeSnippet">
  <CodeSnippet Format="1.0">
    <Header>

    </Header>
    <Snippet>

    </Snippet>
  </CodeSnippet>
</CodeSnippets>
```

<Header> Element

The `<Header>` element is where you add some general information about your code snippet. It doesn't have any attributes, but it can contain some elements, as described in Table 19-1. Note that some of these elements are optional.

Table 19-1: Sub-elements of the Header Element

Element	Description
Author	This specifies the name of the author and related information.
Description	A text description of the snippet
HelpUrl	A link to online help for the snippet
Keywords	This element is a container for `<Keyword>` elements. Each `<Keyword>` element defines a keyword that can be used by Visual Studio to represent and add keywords via providers.
Shortcut	A text value for a snippet shortcut. This is the text that appears in the IntelliSense, and can be used to insert the snippet in code.
SnippetTypes	This element can contain one or more `<SnippetType>` elements. A `<SnippetType>` element can have one of three values: Expansion, SurroundsWith, or Refactoring. A `<SnippetType>` can be used to specify where a code snippet can be inserted. If you don't set a `<SnippetType>`, then your snippet can be inserted anywhere in the code. If you set the `<SnippetType>` to Expansion, then the snippet can be placed at the cursor. If you set the value to SurroundsWith, then the snippet can be placed around a selected piece of code.
Title	The string title of the code snippet. This is what users see in Visual Studio as the name of the code snippet.

Listing 19-6 shows the source code of the sample snippet after adding some new elements to the `<Header>` element.

Listing 19-6: Sample Snippet after Adding New Sub-elements to the `Header` Element

```xml
<?xml version="1.0" encoding="utf-8"?>
<CodeSnippets xmlns="http://schemas.microsoft.com/VisualStudio/2005/CodeSnippet">
  <CodeSnippet Format="1.0">
    <Header>

        <Author>Keyvan Nayyeri (http://nayyeri.net)</Author>
        <Description>
          Sample code snippet designed for Wrox Pro VS Add-ins and Extensions book
        </Description>
        <HelpUrl>http://www.wrox.com</HelpUrl>
        <Keywords>
          <Keyword>Wrox</Keyword>
          <Keyword>Book</Keyword>
          <Keyword>Sample</Keyword>
        </Keywords>
        <Shortcut>WroxSnippet</Shortcut>
        <Title>Wrox Sample Code Snippet</Title>

    </Header>
    <Snippet>

    </Snippet>
  </CodeSnippet>
</CodeSnippets>
```

This code adds some properties to the snippet, such as author name, a description, a help link, some keywords, a shortcut, and a title.

<Snippet> Element

The other child of the `<CodeSnippet>` element is `<Snippet>`, where you implement your code template, among other things related to the snippet itself. This element doesn't have any attribute but has four sub-elements, which are described in the following sections.

<Code> Element

You can insert the code template for your code snippet in the `<code>` element. This element can have three attributes:

❑ `Delimiter`: The delimiter should be used as a placeholder for literals and objects in the code template. The default value is the dollar sign ($). Later you'll see how it's used.

❑ `Kind`: This specifies the type of code snippet you're going to define in the code element.

❑ `Language`: This is the only required attribute for the `<code>` element. It specifies the language related to this code snippet. Possible values are `VB`, `CSharp`, `VJSharp`, and `XML`.

Inside your <code> element, you can insert the code template that should be used for the snippet. This code template is very similar to normal programming codes but it includes some placeholders for parameters that should be changed in the code by the end user. Listing 19-7 updates the sample with a code template that declares an Add function.

Listing 19-7: Sample Code Snippet after Adding the Code Template

```xml
<?xml version="1.0" encoding="utf-8"?>
<CodeSnippets xmlns="http://schemas.microsoft.com/VisualStudio/2005/CodeSnippet">
  <CodeSnippet Format="1.0">
    <Header>
      <Author>Keyvan Nayyeri (http://nayyeri.net)</Author>
      <Description>
        Sample code snippet designed for Wrox Pro VS Add-ins and Extensions book
      </Description>
      <HelpUrl>http://www.wrox.com</HelpUrl>
      <Keywords>
        <Keyword>Wrox</Keyword>
        <Keyword>Book</Keyword>
        <Keyword>Sample</Keyword>
      </Keywords>
      <Shortcut>WroxSnippet</Shortcut>
      <Title>Wrox Sample Code Snippet</Title>
    </Header>
    <Snippet>

      <Code Language="CSharp">
        <![CDATA[
        private $type$ Add($type$ $parameterName1$, $type$ $parameterName2$)
        {
            return $result$;
        }
        ]]>
      </Code>

    </Snippet>
  </CodeSnippet>
</CodeSnippets>
```

Let's take a closer look at the preceding code. First, I created a <code> element with the Language attribute set to CSharp in order to write a code snippet for C#.

After that, I embedded my code template inside a CDATA section of XML code. Usually developers do this when writing a code snippet, because code templates may have some special characters that break the well-formed structure of the code snippet XML document.

My code template is simple; it defines an Add function template. There are four placeholders: for return type and parameter types, as well as two parameter names and a return parameter name or value. As the names of return-type literals and parameter types are similar, they produce the same type, which is what I want here.

In the next section, you'll read more about literals and how to declare them in a code snippet.

\<Declarations> Element

You can specify the literals and objects you use in your code template in the \<Declarations> element. This element doesn't have any attributes but it can contain one or more \<Literal> or \<Object> elements.

The \<Literal> element can be used to specify a literal part of a template that can be edited by the user. It can function as a placeholder for pieces of code such as strings, numeric values, and variables. The \<Object> element can be used to declare objects in the code template.

Both these elements share the same attributes and child elements. They both have an `Editable` attribute that specifies whether the literal or object should be editable after you insert a code.

Table 19-2 briefly describes the child elements of \<Literal> and \<Object> elements. They share the same sub-elements.

Table 19-2: Sub-elements of \<Literal> and \<Object> Elements

Element	Description
Default	Specifies the default value for the literal or object
Function	Specifies a function that can be executed when the literal or object receives the focus in Visual Studio
ID	Specifies the identifier of the literal or object. This is what you use in the code template.
Tooltip	Specifies a text description about the literal or object that can be displayed to users
Type	Specifies the type of object

Listing 19-8 shows the updated version of the sample snippet.

Listing 19-8: Sample Code Snippet after Adding the Declarations Element

```xml
<?xml version="1.0" encoding="utf-8"?>
<CodeSnippets xmlns="http://schemas.microsoft.com/VisualStudio/2005/CodeSnippet">
  <CodeSnippet Format="1.0">
    <Header>
      <Author>Keyvan Nayyeri (http://nayyeri.net)</Author>
      <Description>
        Sample code snippet designed for Wrox Pro VS Add-ins and Extensions book
      </Description>
      <HelpUrl>http://www.wrox.com</HelpUrl>
      <Keywords>
        <Keyword>Wrox</Keyword>
        <Keyword>Book</Keyword>
```

(continued)

Listing 19-8 *(continued)*

```xml
            <Keyword>Sample</Keyword>
          </Keywords>
          <Shortcut>WroxSnippet</Shortcut>
          <Title>Wrox Sample Code Snippet</Title>
        </Header>
      <Snippet>
        <Code Language="CSharp">
          <![CDATA[
          private $type$ Add($type$ $parameterName1$, $type$ $parameterName2$)
          {
              return $result$;
          }
          ]]>
        </Code>

          <Declarations>
            <Literal>
              <ID>type</ID>
              <ToolTip>Type for parameters and result.</ToolTip>
              <Default>int</Default>
            </Literal>
            <Literal>
              <ID>parameterName1</ID>
              <ToolTip>Name of first parameter.</ToolTip>
              <Default>number1</Default>
            </Literal>
            <Literal>
              <ID>parameterName2</ID>
              <ToolTip>Name of second parameter.</ToolTip>
              <Default>number2</Default>
            </Literal>
            <Literal>
              <ID>result</ID>
              <ToolTip>Result value.</ToolTip>
              <Default>0</Default>
            </Literal>
          </Declarations>

      </Snippet>
    </CodeSnippet>
  </CodeSnippets>
```

In this code I added four declarations for literals in my code snippet. All of them have `<ID>`, `<ToolTip>`, and `<Default>` elements to declare. These are all the literals that I used in my code template previously.

<Imports> Element

Using the `<Imports>` element, you can define some namespaces that should be added to your code when the code snippet is being added to it.

The `<Imports>` element has no attributes but can hold one or more `<Import>` elements. Each `<Import>` element can contain a `<Namespace>` element, which keeps the string value of the namespace.

This element is supported only for Visual Basic projects and can't be used with C# projects.

<References> Element

Using the `<References>` element, you can add references to assemblies when the code snippet is being added to the code.

`<References>` doesn't have any attributes but it does have one or more `<Reference>` elements. Each `<Reference>` element can have an `<Assembly>` and `<URL>` element. An `<Assembly>` element contains either the friendly name of the assembly to be referenced or its strong name. A `<URL>` element can be set to a link that provides more information about the assembly.

Like the `<Imports>` element, `<References>` can be used only with Visual Basic projects.

Now that I've written a simple code snippet, I can test it. For now, I'll ignore the process to import my .snippet file to Visual Studio and just show you the test result.

If I open a project and begin writing code, at some point I can select my code snippet and it will appear in IntelliSense (see Figure 19-6).

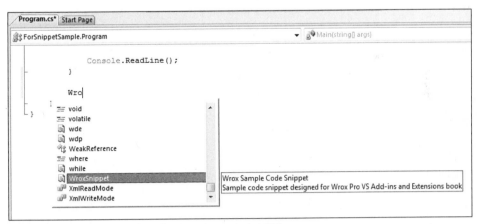

Figure 19-6: A sample code snippet appears in IntelliSense.

Now if I put the snippet in my code, it adds a code template, which you can see in Figure 19-7.

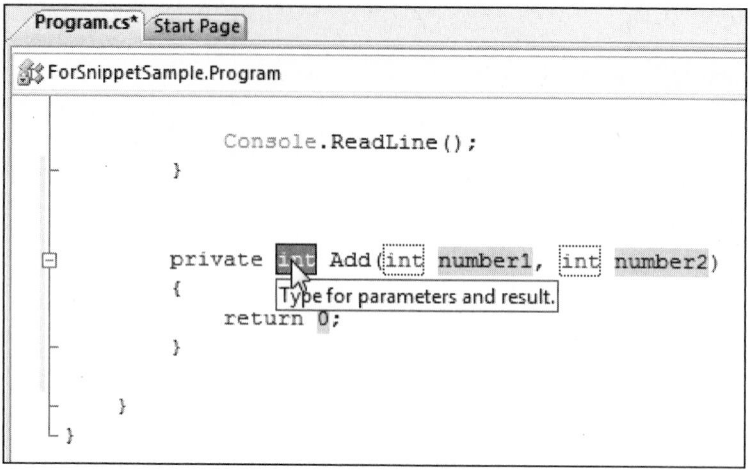

Figure 19-7: Adding a code template to the code

Code-Snippet Functions

This section is included to point out some code-snippet functions that may come in handy in some scenarios. Some snippet functions are available in Visual Studio. These functions enable you to have code-sensitive snippets and generate your snippet values based on your code.

You can't use `<Imports>` and `<References>` elements in C# code snippets, but there's good news here nonetheless. The code-snippet functions described in Table 19-3 are limited to the C# language only.

You saw the `<Function>` element of `<Literal>` and `<Object>` elements in the previous section. You can set this element to a function name. These functions are a part of Visual Studio. Some examples of these code-snippet functions are `ClassName`, `SimpleTypeName`, and `GenerateSwitchCases`, which are described in Table 19-3.

Table 19-3: C# Code-Snippet Functions

Function	Description
GenerateSwitchCases (EnumerationLiteral)	Creates a switch casing statement based on the values of an enumeration type. This enumeration type must be passed as an EnumerationLiteral parameter. It can be a reference to an enumeration literal or an enumeration type.
ClassName	Returns the name of container class for the code snippet
SimpleTypeName (TypeName)	Returns the TypeName parameter in its simplest form in the context

When you use these functions in the `<function>` element of a `<Literal>` or `<Object>`, after inserting the code snippet in the code, Visual Studio runs these functions whenever the focus is placed on that literal or object, and replaces its value with the result of these functions.

Listing 19-9 shows an example of the `ClassName` code-snippet function.

Listing 19-9: Example of the `ClassName` Code-Snippet Function

```xml
<?xml version="1.0" encoding="utf-8"?>
<CodeSnippets xmlns="http://schemas.microsoft.com/VisualStudio/2005/CodeSnippet">
  <CodeSnippet Format="1.0">
    <Header>
      <Author>Keyvan Nayyeri (http://nayyeri.net)</Author>
      <Description>
        Sample code snippet for snippet functions
      </Description>
      <HelpUrl>http://www.wrox.com</HelpUrl>
      <Keywords>
        <Keyword>Wrox</Keyword>
        <Keyword>Book</Keyword>
        <Keyword>Sample</Keyword>
      </Keywords>
      <Shortcut>SnippetFunctionSample</Shortcut>
      <Title>Code Snippet Function Sample</Title>
    </Header>
    <Snippet>
      <Code Language="CSharp">
        <![CDATA[
        using System;
        using System.Collections.Generic;
        using System.Linq;
        using System.Text;

        namespace $namespace$
        {
            public class $className$
            {
                public $className$()
                {
                }
            }
        }

        ]]>
      </Code>
      <Declarations>
        <Literal>
          <ID>namespace</ID>
          <ToolTip>Namespace.</ToolTip>
          <Default>Wrox</Default>
        </Literal>
        <Literal>
          <ID>className</ID>
```

(continued)

Listing 19-9 *(continued)*

```
            <ToolTip>Class type name.</ToolTip>
            <Function>ClassName()</Function>
        </Literal>
      </Declarations>
    </Snippet>
  </CodeSnippet>
</CodeSnippets>
```

This code uses the `ClassName` function to replace the public-constructor name with the class name.

When I import this snippet to Visual Studio, use it in my code to generate an empty class, and type the name of the class, it automatically uses this name for the public-constructor name as well (see Figure 19-8).

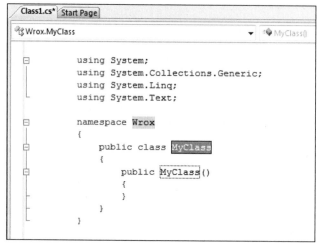

Figure 19-8: Result of using the `ClassName` code-snippet function

Additional Points

Some points related to code snippets are worth mentioning here. One point is about naming your literals and objects in a code snippet. Like all other programming codes, you should always try to choose meaningful and related names for them in order to make your code snippets more readable for others — and even yourself!

It's also recommended that you choose `<ToolTip>` elements for your literals and objects to help the users of your snippet know what a literal or object is doing.

The last point is about inserting multiple code snippets in a single .snippet file. This is technically possible. Simply put your `<CodeSnippet>` element for each code snippet under other `<CodeSnippet>` elements. For example, Listing 19-10 contains two examples from previous sections in one code snippet file.

Listing 19-10: Multiple Code Snippets in a Single Code-Snippet File

```xml
<?xml version="1.0" encoding="utf-8"?>
<CodeSnippets xmlns="http://schemas.microsoft.com/VisualStudio/2005/CodeSnippet">
  <!-- First Code Snippet -->
  <CodeSnippet Format="1.0">
    <Header>
      <Author>Keyvan Nayyeri (http://nayyeri.net)</Author>
      <Description>
        Sample code snippet designed for Wrox Pro VS Add-ins and Extensions book
      </Description>
      <HelpUrl>http://www.wrox.com</HelpUrl>
      <Keywords>
        <Keyword>Wrox</Keyword>
        <Keyword>Book</Keyword>
        <Keyword>Sample</Keyword>
      </Keywords>
      <Shortcut>WroxSnippet</Shortcut>
      <Title>Wrox Sample Code Snippet</Title>
    </Header>
    <Snippet>
      <Code Language="CSharp">
        <![CDATA[
        private $type$ Add($type$ $parameterName1$, $type$ $parameterName2$)
        {
            return $result$;
        }
        ]]>
      </Code>
      <Declarations>
        <Literal>
          <ID>type</ID>
          <ToolTip>Type for parameters and result.</ToolTip>
          <Default>int</Default>
        </Literal>
        <Literal>
          <ID>parameterName1</ID>
          <ToolTip>Name of first parameter.</ToolTip>
          <Default>number1</Default>
        </Literal>
        <Literal>
          <ID>parameterName2</ID>
          <ToolTip>Name of second parameter.</ToolTip>
          <Default>number2</Default>
        </Literal>
        <Literal>
          <ID>result</ID>
          <ToolTip>Result value.</ToolTip>
          <Default>0</Default>
        </Literal>
      </Declarations>
    </Snippet>
  </CodeSnippet>
```

(continued)

Listing 19-10 *(continued)*

```xml
<!-- Second Code Snippet -->
<CodeSnippet Format="1.0.0">
  <Header>
    <Title>Sample Code Snippet</Title>
    <Shortcut>scsk</Shortcut>
    <Author>Keyvan Nayyeri</Author>
  </Header>
  <Snippet>
    <Code Language="CSharp">
      <![CDATA[
      // This is a simple code comment
      ]]>
    </Code>
  </Snippet>
</CodeSnippet>
</CodeSnippets>
```

The order of code snippets in a single file doesn't matter; the important point is the readability of your code-snippet codes. Of course, you should always try to write readable codes, so it's usually better and less confusing to avoid putting multiple code snippets in a single file.

Sample Code Snippet

For training purposes, here's another sample code snippet.

This example writes a code snippet to insert a class definition code template for an asynchronous-result class. This is a common class for asynchronous pattern implementation and can be constant between projects. Developers prefer to derive from such a class to implement their own logic for an asynchronous result. This class implements two interfaces: IAsyncResult and IDisposable.

Listing 19-11 shows the code for an asynchronous-result snippet.

Listing 19-11: Asynchronous-Result Code Snippet

```xml
<?xml version="1.0" encoding="utf-8"?>
<CodeSnippets xmlns="http://schemas.microsoft.com/VisualStudio/2005/CodeSnippet">
  <CodeSnippet Format="1.0">
    <Header>
      <Author>Keyvan Nayyeri (http://nayyeri.net)</Author>
      <Description>
        Sample code snippet to implement an asynchronous result class
      </Description>
      <HelpUrl>http://www.wrox.com</HelpUrl>
      <Keywords>
        <Keyword>Wrox</Keyword>
        <Keyword>Book</Keyword>
        <Keyword>Sample</Keyword>
      </Keywords>
      <Shortcut>AsyncResult</Shortcut>
      <Title>Code Snippet For Async Result Definition</Title>
```

```
    </Header>
    <Snippet>
      <Code Language="CSharp">
        <![CDATA[
using System;
using System.Collections.Generic;
using System.Linq;
using System.Text;
using System.Threading;

namespace $namespace$
{
    public class $className$ : IAsyncResult, IDisposable
    {
        AsyncCallback $callback$;
        object $state$;
        ManualResetEvent $manualResentEvent$;

        public $className$(AsyncCallback $callbackParam$, object $stateParam$)
        {
            this.$callback$ = $callbackParam$;
            this.$state$ = $stateParam$;
            this.$manualResentEvent$ = new ManualResetEvent(false);
        }

        object IAsyncResult.AsyncState
        {
            get { return $state$; }
        }

        public ManualResetEvent AsyncWait
        {
            get
            {
                return $manualResentEvent$;
            }
        }

        WaitHandle IAsyncResult.AsyncWaitHandle
        {
            get { return this.AsyncWait; }
        }

        bool IAsyncResult.CompletedSynchronously
        {
            get { return false; }
        }

        bool IAsyncResult.IsCompleted
        {
            get { return $manualResentEvent$.WaitOne(0, false); }
        }
```

(continued)

Listing 19-11 *(continued)*

```
        public void Complete()
        {
            $manualResentEvent$.Set();
            if ($callback$ != null)
                $callback$(this);
        }

        public void Dispose()
        {
            $manualResentEvent$.Close();
            $manualResentEvent$ = null;
            $state$ = null;
            $callback$ = null;
        }
    }
}

        ]]>
    </Code>
    <Declarations>
      <Literal>
        <ID>namespace</ID>
        <ToolTip>Namespace.</ToolTip>
        <Default>Wrox</Default>
      </Literal>
      <Literal>
        <ID>className</ID>
        <ToolTip>Class type name.</ToolTip>
        <Function>ClassName()</Function>
      </Literal>
      <Literal>
        <ID>callback</ID>
        <ToolTip>Callback variable name.</ToolTip>
        <Default>callback</Default>
      </Literal>
      <Literal>
        <ID>state</ID>
        <ToolTip>State variable name.</ToolTip>
        <Default>state</Default>
      </Literal>
      <Literal>
        <ID>manualResentEvent</ID>
        <ToolTip>ManualResentEvent name.</ToolTip>
        <Default>manualResentEvent</Default>
      </Literal>
      <Literal>
        <ID>callbackParam</ID>
        <ToolTip>Callback parameter name.</ToolTip>
        <Default>callbackParam</Default>
      </Literal>
      <Literal>
        <ID>stateParam</ID>
        <ToolTip>State parameter name.</ToolTip>
        <Default>stateParam</Default>
      </Literal>
```

```
        </Declarations>
      </Snippet>
    </CodeSnippet>
  </CodeSnippets>
```

This code has definitions for the code template of a class and produces literals for some fields and parameters as well as class names and namespaces. It sets the class name for the constructor automatically with the ClassName snippet function.

We won't get into details about this class and its implementation here, but these are familiar to readers who know the asynchronous design pattern in .NET. This class can be used to derive other classes for special purposes.

We can test this code snippet and see its result in action. Figure 19-9 and Listing 19-12 show an example.

Figure 19-9: Using an asynchronous-result code snippet

Listing 19-12: Using an Asynchronous-Result Code Snippet

```
using System;
using System.Collections.Generic;
using System.Linq;
using System.Text;
using System.Threading;

namespace Wrox
```

(continued)

Listing 19-12 *(continued)*

```csharp
{
    public class Keyvan : IAsyncResult, IDisposable
    {
        AsyncCallback callback;
        object state;
        ManualResetEvent manualResentEvent;

        public Keyvan(AsyncCallback callbackParam, object stateParam)
        {
            this.callback = callbackParam;
            this.state = stateParam;
            this.manualResentEvent = new ManualResetEvent(false);
        }

        object IAsyncResult.AsyncState
        {
            get { return state; }
        }

        public ManualResetEvent AsyncWait
        {
            get
            {
                return manualResentEvent;
            }
        }

        WaitHandle IAsyncResult.AsyncWaitHandle
        {
            get { return this.AsyncWait; }
        }

        bool IAsyncResult.CompletedSynchronously
        {
            get { return false; }
        }

        bool IAsyncResult.IsCompleted
        {
            get { return manualResentEvent.WaitOne(0, false); }
        }

        public void Complete()
        {
            manualResentEvent.Set();
            if (callback != null)
                callback(this);
        }

        public void Dispose()
        {
            manualResentEvent.Close();
```

```
            manualResentEvent = null;
            state = null;
            callback = null;
        }
    }
}
```

Managing Code Snippets

You have now learned how to build a code snippet. Next you need to learn how to manage code snippets in Visual Studio and import your code snippets to it.

For that, you can use the Code Snippets Manager tool available in Visual Studio, accessible via Tools ⇨ Code Snippets Manager or by pressing Ctrl+K and Ctrl+B, respectively. Figure 19-10 shows this dialog.

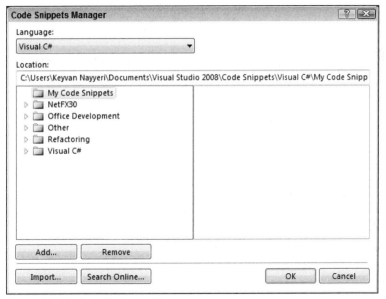

Figure 19-10: Code Snippets Manager

At the top of this window, you can choose the language from a drop-down list. This enables you to filter all available code snippets based on the language. Beneath this drop-down list is a label to show the path of items. The main part of the window is divided into two panes. The left pane is the list of categories and code-snippet names; the right pane provides some information about a code snippet. This information is taken from what you entered in the <Header> element of the code snippet.

Figure 19-11 shows one of the sample code snippets used in this chapter selected in the window.

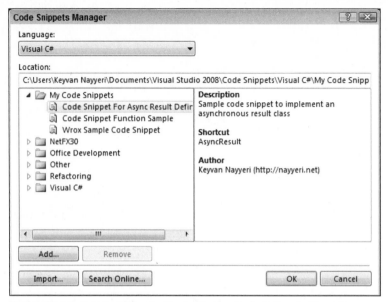

Figure 19-11: A code snippet selected in the Code Snippets Manager

The left pane of snippet categories includes a category for My Code Snippets, which is where your own code snippets will be added.

At the bottom left corner of the window are four buttons to add or remove a snippet folder and to import an existing .snippet file to Visual Studio or search online for other code snippets.

The most important item in this dialog is the Import button, which you can use to import snippets from existing .snippet files on your system. After choosing a .snippet file, you can specify the location to which the snippets should be imported to Visual Studio. These code snippets will be added to the My Code Snippets category and copied to a folder with the same name in the Code Snippets folder of your Visual Studio storage path (in Documents for Windows Vista or My Documents in Windows XP and 2003). After importing a code snippet to Visual Studio, it's available in appropriate projects for your development languages.

You can also write your own code snippets and share them with others in the .NET world via your blog or various .NET communities. Nowadays, having a blog seems mandatory for a professional developer! Some well-known .NET communities are listed in Appendix B.

Summary

In this chapter, you learned all about code snippets. After learning the concept of the code snippet and its applications, you looked closely at its anatomy. After that, you learned how to build a code snippet with XML codes, and explored all elements and attributes of a code-snippet document. Finally, you learned how to import code snippets and manage them in Visual Studio.

20

Templates

One of the aspects of visual development languages (like other development languages) is the way they keep application code in files that have templates. There are different templates for files and projects in a development language. For example, a console application has its own template while an ASP.NET web application has another template.

These templates are helpful because they save you from continually writing codes for each project or file every time you begin creating an instance of it. These project templates have been a part of Visual Studio from early versions, and new templates have been added on an ongoing basis by Microsoft, third-party vendors, and community members. Now, in Visual Studio 2008, you can use various project templates for different programming languages, technologies, and purposes.

The other benefit of these templates is that they provide consistency between all projects of the same type around the world. In addition, project development is possible for developers with different skills and knowledge.

There are several reasons why you need to be able to create custom projects and item templates and build your own templates:

❑ You may face a new technology and want to share some project templates for it. For example, one of my friends in the Community Server community wanted to build something as a starting point for developers to create Community Server modules and tasks. He ended up with a starter kit project (a kind of project template). As another example, Microsoft itself shipped a set of plug-ins for Visual Studio 2005 with different project templates to create Windows Presentation Foundation (WPF), Windows Communication Foundation (WCF), and Windows Workflow Foundation (WF or WWF) projects. These templates helped many developers begin developing applications for these technologies more quickly and easily.

❑ Sometimes when building a specific kind of project, there's a task that you do frequently that eats up your time. A simple solution is to create a template for this task and reuse it as needed.

❑ Developers create specific types of files, such as different derivations of XML or specific types of a C# class. You can simplify your code by creating item templates, rather than copying and pasting a piece of code to new files every time you want to create them. For example, a friend created an item template for an XML Integrated Query that he had named Xinq (it was a simple form of XLinq technology in the .NET Framework 3.5 for the .NET Framework 2.0). His implementation made it easy to create new items to query XML data.

Now that you have an idea of how helpful a project or item template can be, here's a list of related topics covered in this chapter:

❑ An introduction to project templates

❑ An introduction to item templates

❑ Differences between project and item templates

❑ The anatomy of project and item templates

❑ The structure of a template manifest file

❑ How to create a template manually

❑ How to create a template with the Export Template Wizard

❑ How to customize a template

❑ How to create custom template wizards

❑ Starter kits

After reading this chapter, you should know everything you need to begin creating project and item templates.

Visual Studio templates can be grouped into two categories: project templates and item templates. This chapter covers both types, including their similarities and differences.

Project Templates

Project templates cover an entire project, including all its references and files. A project template consists of all the files you need to create a type of project. Visual Studio has many built-in project templates, such as Windows Forms Application, Class Library, WPF Application, and ASP.NET Web Application.

All these project templates are grouped in categories based on their development languages, and you can choose them from the list in the New Project dialog box and assign names to them. Figure 20-1 shows this dialog box, with a Console Application template selected.

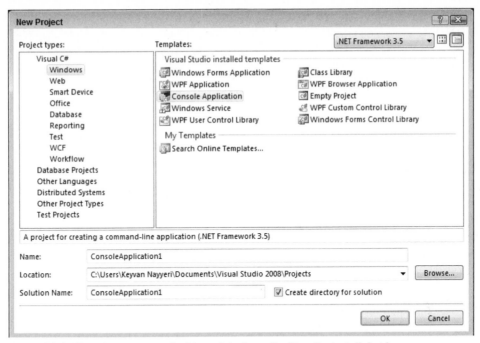

Figure 20-1: Choosing a new project template from the New Project dialog box

Using a project template, you can create a new project from a starting point that has already been created for you, one that has all the code templates that you need to add in order to create projects of specific types. This will save you a lot of time. For example, creating a console application from the dialog box shown in Figure 20-1 creates the files and references you need to write your code. Figure 20-2 shows the Solution Explorer expanded for a clean Console Application so you can see what's created there.

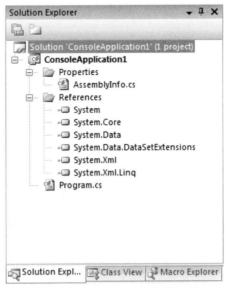

Figure 20-2: A clean Console Application project

Some references are added to the project, as well as an AssemblyInfo.cs file for assembly information, and a Program.cs file in which you can implement your code. This Program.cs file has a code template ready to go. All you need to do is add your logic to the `Main` method.

Item Template

An item template is another type of Visual Studio template. Unlike project templates that create entire projects (including files and references), item templates create files only.

As with project templates, Visual Studio has many item templates, such as Class, Application Configuration File, LINQ to SQL Classes, and WCF Service. Based on your project type, you may have access to different item templates in the Add New Item dialog. Figure 20-3 shows the Add New Item dialog for a Console Application to create an XML file.

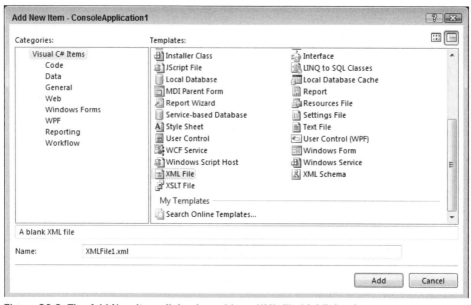

Figure 20-3: The Add New Item dialog box with an XML file highlighted

This creates an XML file with only an XML header element, enabling you to add your own XML codes there.

Like project templates, item templates are extremely handy and help you create new items and codes. For example, recall Chapter 17, "Extending the Debugger." You learned in that chapter that there's an item template for Debugger Visualizer that helps you create visualizers quickly by adding many of the necessary code templates for that.

There are some similarities and differences between project templates and item templates. Both of them create something in place for you and both of them add files with code templates, but project templates can contain more than this, whereas item templates just keep files.

From a technical point of view, there are also some similarities and differences. Both templates have a manifest definition and a set of files and icons (you'll see these technical details in a moment), but these manifest files have a different structure.

In the following sections you'll learn more technical details about Visual Studio templates and how to create them.

The Anatomy of Visual Studio Templates

The first technical aspect of Visual Studio templates you should learn about is their anatomy.

In fact, a Visual Studio template is nothing more than a ZIP archive file with a special structure. This ZIP file structure varies a little between project templates and item templates, but both templates have a *template manifest*, which is actually an XML file, along with some other files and an optional icon file for the template.

Project templates have an extra item, the project file, or project configuration file.

The template manifest, the main part of the template, is covered in the next section. The structure of this manifest XML file also varies a bit between project templates and item templates. Other elements of the template file are covered in the following sections as well.

Template Manifest

The manifest file of the template is the main part of the template and functions as its "heart." Without this manifest, the template is just a ZIP archive with some files included in it.

The manifest file is an XML file with a special structure. It has a .vstemplate extension, which makes it known to Visual Studio as a manifest.

When you create an XML file in Visual Studio and give it initial code, such as the code shown in Listing 20-1, Visual Studio automatically provides IntelliSense for you, so you can work easily with template manifest XML elements and attributes (see Figure 20-4).

Listing 20-1: Initial Code for a Template Manifest

```xml
<?xml version="1.0" encoding="utf-8"?>
<VSTemplate xmlns="http://schemas.microsoft.com/developer/vstemplate/2005">

</VSTemplate>
```

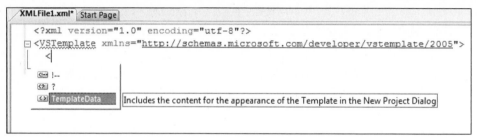

Figure 20-4: Visual Studio provides IntelliSense for template manifest files.

Applying that <VSTemplate> element with an XML namespace set to http://schemas.microsoft
.com/developer/vstemplate/2005 establishes that Visual Studio considers this XML document a
Visual Studio template and will provide IntelliSense, debugging features, and help options for it.

*At this point, you get three XML warnings because after validating your document against the Visual
Studio template schema, VS expects you to put some attributes and elements in this document. You'll
see these attributes and elements in a moment.*

Visual Studio template manifest files are validated against an XML schema that is a part of the
default Visual Studio installation located at [Visual Studio Installation Path]\Xml\
Schemas\1033\vstemplate.xsd. Visual Studio automatically validates your XML file against this
schema when you apply the aforementioned XML namespace.

A Visual Studio manifest XML document contains a <VSTemplate> element at the root. This element has
two attributes:

❑ Type: Specifies the type of template (item template or project template) and can generate
Project, ProjectGroup, and Item as its values.

❑ Version: Specifies in string form the version number of the .NET Framework to use for
the template.

Listing 20-2 is an update to the sample manifest.

Listing 20-2: Manifest after Adding Type and Version Attributes to the VSTemplate Element

```
<?xml version="1.0" encoding="utf-8"?>
<VSTemplate Type="Project" Version="1.0"
xmlns="http://schemas.microsoft.com/developer/vstemplate/2005">

</VSTemplate>
```

The <VSTemplate> element has four sub-elements that can be nested inside this root element:

❑ <TemplateData>: Keeps some general information about the template, such as its category and
icon, and sets the display properties of the template in the New Project or Add New Item dialog.
This is a required element.

❑ <TemplateContent>: Specifies the list of files included in the template. This is also a
required element.

❑   `<WizardData>`: This optional element keeps some XML data to pass to the custom wizard.

❑   `<WizardExtension>`: This optional element contains some information for a custom template wizard.

The order of the first two elements is important: `<TemplateData>` must appear before `<TemplateContent>`. In the following subsections you will take a closer look at these two elements.

<TemplateData>

`<TemplateData>` is responsible for providing general information about the template, such as its name, a description, an icon, and display properties. Table 20-1 lists all sub-elements of `<TemplateData>`, with a description of each.

Table 20-1: `<TemplateData>` Sub-elements

Element	Description
BuildOnLoad	Forces the solution to perform a build action right after creation
CreateInPlace	Creates project files at the target location, and nowhere else
CreateNewFolder	Can be used to create a new folder for project files. The default value is false
DefaultName	This is the default name that appears in the New Project or Add New Item dialog.
Description	Specifies a string value of text that appears as a description for the project or item in the New Project or Add New Item dialog.It has two optional attributes: ID and Package. ID is a Visual Studio resource identifier, and Package is a GUID that refers to a Visual Studio package ID. Both attributes can be used for advanced user scenarios.
EnableEditOfLocationField	Specifies that users can change the location field of the project or item
EnableLocationBrowseButton	Specifies that users can browse and choose other folders for storing the project
Hidden	Specifies that the template shouldn't appear in the New Project or Add New Item dialog. In this case, you don't need to set other sub-elements of `<TemplateData>`.

(continued)

Element	Description
Icon	The icon file name that should appear for a project or item in the New Project or Add New Item dialog. It has two optional attributes: ID and Package. ID is a Visual Studio resource identifier, and Package is a GUID that refers to a Visual Studio package ID. Both attributes can be used for advanced user scenarios.
LocationField	Specifies that the location field should be enabled, disabled, or hidden
LocationFieldMRUPrefix	Specifies the most recently used paths in the New Project or Add New Item dialogs
Name	The string value of the template name that appears in either the New Project or Add New Item dialog. It has two optional attributes: ID and Package. ID is a Visual Studio resource identifier, and Package is a GUID that refers to a Visual Studio package ID. Both attributes can be used for advanced user scenarios.
NumberOfParentCategoriesToRollUp	Can be used to display the template in parent categories. This is an integer value.
ProjectSubType	This string value specifies the project subtype of the template. Possible values are SmartDevice-NETCFv1 for .NET Compact Framework 1.0 and SmartDevice-NETCFv2 for .NET Compact Framework 2.0. Possible values for a project type of Web are CSharp, VisualBasic, and JSharp.
ProjectType	Specifies the project type category to display in the new Project or Add New Item dialog. This is a required sub-element of TemplateData and has four possible values: CSharp, VisualBasic, JSharp, and Web.
PromptForSaveOnCreation	Specifies whether the project should be saved on creation. This applies only to some specific project types that support it.
ProvideDefaultName	Specifies whether a default name should be provided for the template
RequiredFrameworkVersion	The enumeration value of the minimum .NET Framework version to use for the template. Possible values are 2.0, 3.0, and 3.5.
ShowByDefault	If set to false, the template will be displayed only in the specified <TemplateGroupdID>. The default value is true.

Element	Description
SortOrder	The sort order of the template in the New Project dialog
SupportsCodeSeparation	Specifies whether the template should support separate codes. This is an option for web projects, which you're likely familiar with from code-behind files in ASP.NET.
SupportsLanguageDropDown	Specifies whether a Language drop-down should be displayed. This is for projects that target multiple languages and is a Web project option.
SupportsMasterPage	Specifies whether the project supports master pages. This is also a Web project option.
TemplateGroupID	String value of an optional template group identifier for the template
TemplateID	The unique identifier of the template, given as a string. If you don't set it, then the name of the template is used instead.

Listing 20-3 updates the sample manifest with the addition of some sub-elements of the `<TemplateData>` element.

Listing 20-3: Manifest after Adding Sub-elements of the `VSTemplate` Element

```xml
<?xml version="1.0" encoding="utf-8"?>
<VSTemplate Type="Project" Version="1.0" xmlns="http://schemas.microsoft.com/
developer/vstemplate/2005">
  <TemplateData>

    <CreateNewFolder>true</CreateNewFolder>
    <DefaultName>MyProject</DefaultName>
    <Description>This is a sample project template for Wrox Pro Add-ins and
Extensions book</Description>
    <EnableEditOfLocationField>true</EnableEditOfLocationField>
    <Icon>Icon.ico</Icon>
    <Name>Sample Project Template</Name>
    <ProjectType>CSharp</ProjectType>
    <RequiredFrameworkVersion>3.0</RequiredFrameworkVersion>
    <TemplateID>{4C02F239-1F0E-4709-94A1-801A6488956C}</TemplateID>

  </TemplateData>
</VSTemplate>
```

\<TemplateContent\>

\<TemplateContent\> is the second required child element in \<VSTemplate\>. It defines the structure of template files and their names.

This element can contain one of the following child elements, but not more than one:

- ❑ \<Project\>: Contains definitions for files and folders to be added to the project
- ❑ \<ProjectCollection\>: Contains definitions for files and folders to be added to the project for multi-project templates
- ❑ \<ProjectItem\>: Contains definitions for the file that should be added with the item
- ❑ \<References\>: Specifies the list of assemblies to be added when an item or project is added

This element also can contain an optional \<CustomParameters\> element to define custom parameters, which are described later in the chapter.

The following subsections take a closer look at each of these elements.

\<Project\>

This element can keep a list of files and folders to be added to the project.

It has three attributes:

- ❑ File: This is a required attribute to specify the name of the project file in the template package.
- ❑ ReplaceParameters: Specifies whether there are some parameter values that should be replaced when the project is being created
- ❑ TargetFileName: Specifies the name of the project file. This is for cases when the project is created from a template. This is helpful when you want to change the name based on parameters.

This element also has some optional child elements:

- ❑ \<Folder\>: Defines a folder to be added to the project
- ❑ \<ProjectItem\>: Defines a file to be added to the project

You can use these child elements as many times as you like in a hierarchical manner in order to define the structure of a project.

Note that \<Folder\> and \<ProjectItem\> elements have some attributes and child elements of their own. \<Folder\> has two attributes:

- ❑ Name: This required attribute indicates the name of the project folder.
- ❑ TargetFolderName: This is the name of the folder used when it's being created from a template. This can be helpful when you want to change the name of a folder based on parameters.

The `<Folder>` element can contain other `<Folder>` and `<ProjectItem>` elements recursively to define a hierarchical structure.

`<ProjectItem>` doesn't have any child elements. It keeps the string value of a filename that should be added to the project. It has the following attributes:

- ❑ `OpenInEditor`: Specifies whether the item should be opened in the editor. The default is false.

- ❑ `OpenInHelpBrowser`: Specifies whether the item should be opened in the Help viewer. This is applicable only to local text and HTML files. The default is false.

- ❑ `OpenInWebBrowser`: Specifies whether the item should be opened in a web browser. This is applicable only to local text and HTML files. The default is false.

- ❑ `OpenOrder`: An integer value that represents the order of items to be opened. It must be a multiple of 10.

- ❑ `ReplaceParameters`: Specifies whether parameter values must be replaced when the project is being created from a template. The default is false.

- ❑ `TargetFileName`: Specifies the name of the project file. This is used when the project is created from a template. It is helpful when you want to change the name based on parameters.

Knowing these concepts, you can update the sample manifest as shown in Listing 20-4.

Listing 20-4: Sample manifest after Addition of the `Project` Element

```xml
<?xml version="1.0" encoding="utf-8"?>
<VSTemplate Type="Project" Version="1.0"
xmlns="http://schemas.microsoft.com/developer/vstemplate/2005">
  <TemplateData>
    <CreateNewFolder>true</CreateNewFolder>
    <DefaultName>MyProject</DefaultName>
    <Description>This is a sample project template for Wrox Pro Add-ins and
Extensions book</Description>
    <EnableEditOfLocationField>true</EnableEditOfLocationField>
    <Icon>Icon.ico</Icon>
    <Name>Sample Project Template</Name>
    <ProjectType>CSharp</ProjectType>
    <RequiredFrameworkVersion>3.0</RequiredFrameworkVersion>
    <TemplateID>{4C02F239-1F0E-4709-94A1-801A6488956C}</TemplateID>
  </TemplateData>
```

```xml
  <TemplateContent>
    <Project File="MyProject.csproj">
      <Folder Name="SampleFolder">
        <ProjectItem OpenInEditor="true">SampleText.txt</ProjectItem>
      </Folder>
      <ProjectItem>SampleCode.cs</ProjectItem>
    </Project>
  </TemplateContent>
```

```xml
</VSTemplate>
```

<ProjectCollection>

<ProjectCollection> is another element that can be nested within a <TemplateContent> element. This element for multi-project templates defines the organization of their items.

It doesn't have any attributes, but it has two optional elements:

- ❑ <ProjectTemplateLink>: Refers to a project in a multi-project template. It includes a ProjectName attribute. The value of this element refers to another template path to use for the project.

- ❑ <SolutionFolder>: Refers to a solution folder in a multi-project template for group projects. It has a Name attribute for its name. <SolutionFolder> can keep other <ProjectTemplateLink> and <SolutionFolder> elements in a hierarchical manner.

Listing 20-5 is the updated version of a sample manifest using <ProjectCollection>. Notice the modification of the <VSTemplate> element to change the Type attribute to ProjectGroup in order for it to act as a multi-project template.

Listing 20-5: Sample Manifest after Adding the ProjectCollection Element

```xml
<?xml version="1.0" encoding="utf-8"?>

<VSTemplate Type="ProjectGroup" Version="1.0"
xmlns="http://schemas.microsoft.com/developer/vstemplate/2005">
  <TemplateData>
    <CreateNewFolder>true</CreateNewFolder>
    <DefaultName>MyProject</DefaultName>
    <Description>This is a sample project template for Wrox Pro Add-ins and
Extensions book</Description>
    <EnableEditOfLocationField>true</EnableEditOfLocationField>
    <Icon>Icon.ico</Icon>
    <Name>Sample Project Template</Name>
    <ProjectType>CSharp</ProjectType>
    <RequiredFrameworkVersion>3.0</RequiredFrameworkVersion>
    <TemplateID>{4C02F239-1F0E-4709-94A1-801A6488956C}</TemplateID>
  </TemplateData>

  <TemplateContent>
    <ProjectCollection>
      <ProjectTemplateLink ProjectName="First Project">
        WindowsApps\Template1.vstemplate
      </ProjectTemplateLink>
      <ProjectTemplateLink ProjectName="Second Project">
        WindowsApps\Template2.vstemplate
      </ProjectTemplateLink>
      <SolutionFolder Name="">
        <ProjectTemplateLink ProjectName="Third Project">
          ClassLibraries\Template3.vstemplate
        </ProjectTemplateLink>
      </SolutionFolder>
    </ProjectCollection>
  </TemplateContent>

</VSTemplate>
```

Note that you have to create all templates that you link in the `<ProjectTemplateLink>` element, such as Template1, Template2, and Template3. All these templates must be provided with a template package at appropriate points.

<ProjectItem>

`<ProjectItem>` can be considered part of the item template, to add files to the project.

It has three optional attributes and doesn't have any child elements:

- ❑ `SubType`: Specifies the subtype of the item. This is helpful for choosing the suitable Visual Studio editor for the item.

- ❑ `ReplaceParameters`: Specifies whether the item has parameter values that should be replaced when the item is being added to the project. The default is false.

- ❑ `TargetFileName`: Specifies the name of the file. This is used when an item is created from a template. It is helpful when you want to change the name based on parameters.

Listing 20-6 is the updated version of a sample manifest with the addition of `<ProjectItem>`.

Listing 20-6: Sample Manifest after Adding the `ProjectItem` Element

```xml
<?xml version="1.0" encoding="utf-8"?>
<VSTemplate Type="Item" Version="1.0"
xmlns="http://schemas.microsoft.com/developer/vstemplate/2005">
  <TemplateData>
    <CreateNewFolder>true</CreateNewFolder>
    <DefaultName>MyProject</DefaultName>
    <Description>This is a sample project template for Wrox Pro Add-ins and
Extensions book</Description>
    <EnableEditOfLocationField>true</EnableEditOfLocationField>
    <Icon>Icon.ico</Icon>
    <Name>Sample Project Template</Name>
    <ProjectType>CSharp</ProjectType>
    <RequiredFrameworkVersion>3.0</RequiredFrameworkVersion>
    <TemplateID>{4C02F239-1F0E-4709-94A1-801A6488956C}</TemplateID>
  </TemplateData>


  <TemplateContent>
    <ProjectItem>class.cs</ProjectItem>
  </TemplateContent>

</VSTemplate>
```

<References>

This element specifies a list of assembly references that should be added to the project so that the code files work properly.

The `<References>` element doesn't have any attributes but it has a single child element: `<Reference>`. `<Reference>` is a required child element for `<References>`. It keeps information for an assembly. The `<Reference>` element itself is a container for another element: `<Assembly>`. `<Assembly>` keeps the name of the assembly when added to the project as a reference.

`<References>` and `<Reference>` elements can be added to templates that have an item as their `Type` attribute.

Listing 20-7 updates the sample manifest code again by adding the `<References>` element.

Listing 20-7: Sample Manifest after Adding the `References` Element

```xml
<?xml version="1.0" encoding="utf-8"?>
<VSTemplate Type="Item" Version="1.0"
xmlns="http://schemas.microsoft.com/developer/vstemplate/2005">
  <TemplateData>
    <CreateNewFolder>true</CreateNewFolder>
    <DefaultName>MyProject</DefaultName>
    <Description>This is a sample project template for Wrox Pro Add-ins and
Extensions book</Description>
    <EnableEditOfLocationField>true</EnableEditOfLocationField>
    <Icon>Icon.ico</Icon>
    <Name>Sample Project Template</Name>
    <ProjectType>CSharp</ProjectType>
    <RequiredFrameworkVersion>3.0</RequiredFrameworkVersion>
    <TemplateID>{4C02F239-1F0E-4709-94A1-801A6488956C}</TemplateID>
  </TemplateData>


    <TemplateContent>
      <References>
        <Reference>
          <Assembly>
            System, Version=2.0.0.0, Culture=neutral, PublicKeyToken=b77a5c561934e089
          </Assembly>
        </Reference>
      </References>
    </TemplateContent>

  </VSTemplate>
```

<WizardData>

This element just keeps some XML data to pass to the custom template wizard. It can be used for configuration of the wizard. Listing 20-8 shows this element in action.

Listing 20-8: Sample Manifest after Adding the `WizardData` Element

```xml
<?xml version="1.0" encoding="utf-8"?>
<VSTemplate Type="Project" Version="1.0"
xmlns="http://schemas.microsoft.com/developer/vstemplate/2005">
  <TemplateData>
    <CreateNewFolder>true</CreateNewFolder>
    <DefaultName>MyProject</DefaultName>
    <Description>This is a sample project template for Wrox Pro Add-ins and
Extensions book</Description>
    <EnableEditOfLocationField>true</EnableEditOfLocationField>
    <Icon>Icon.ico</Icon>
    <Name>Sample Project Template</Name>
    <ProjectType>CSharp</ProjectType>
    <RequiredFrameworkVersion>3.0</RequiredFrameworkVersion>
    <TemplateID>{4C02F239-1F0E-4709-94A1-801A6488956C}</TemplateID>
  </TemplateData>

  <TemplateContent>
    <Project File="MyProject.csproj">
      <Folder Name="SampleFolder">
        <ProjectItem OpenInEditor="true">SampleText.txt</ProjectItem>
      </Folder>
      <ProjectItem>SampleCode.cs</ProjectItem>
    </Project>
  </TemplateContent>


  <WizardData>
    <add key="item1" value="value1" />
  </WizardData>

</VSTemplate>
```

Later in this chapter, you'll learn more about creating custom template wizards.

<WizardExtension>

This element is responsible for defining the assembly and class names of a custom template wizard to use with the template. It has no attributes, but it has two required elements:

❑   `<Assembly>`: Refers to the assembly where the code logic for the wizard is implemented

❑   `<FullClassName>`: Refers to the full class name of the class where the code logic for the wizard is implemented. This class is a part of the assembly specified in the `<Assembly>` element.

You'll learn more about writing a wizard later in this chapter. For now, consider the example of this element shown in Listing 20-9.

Listing 20-9: Sample Manifest after Adding the `WizardExtension` Element

```xml
<?xml version="1.0" encoding="utf-8"?>
<VSTemplate Type="Project" Version="1.0"
xmlns="http://schemas.microsoft.com/developer/vstemplate/2005">
  <TemplateData>
    <CreateNewFolder>true</CreateNewFolder>
    <DefaultName>MyProject</DefaultName>
    <Description>This is a sample project template for Wrox Pro Add-ins and
Extensions book</Description>
    <EnableEditOfLocationField>true</EnableEditOfLocationField>
    <Icon>Icon.ico</Icon>
    <Name>Sample Project Template</Name>
    <ProjectType>CSharp</ProjectType>
    <RequiredFrameworkVersion>3.0</RequiredFrameworkVersion>
    <TemplateID>{4C02F239-1F0E-4709-94A1-801A6488956C}</TemplateID>
  </TemplateData>

  <TemplateContent>
    <Project File="MyProject.csproj">
      <Folder Name="SampleFolder">
        <ProjectItem OpenInEditor="true">SampleText.txt</ProjectItem>
      </Folder>
      <ProjectItem>SampleCode.cs</ProjectItem>
    </Project>
  </TemplateContent>


  <WizardExtension>
    <Assembly>
      WizardAssembly, Version=1.0.0.0, Culture=neutral,
PublicKeyToken=588519aa8589d06f, Custom=null
    </Assembly>
    <FullClassName>
      Keyvan.TemplateWizard
    </FullClassName>
  </WizardExtension>

</VSTemplate>
```

Creating a Template

Now that you have a good understanding of the template manifest and its elements, it's time to explore how to create a Visual Studio template. This process relies heavily on the manifest configuration, so the manifest had to be introduced first.

Creating a project template or item template can differ. For each there are two ways to create a template: automatic and manual. In the automatic option, you use a wizard to create the template, whereas in the manual process you do this with some codes, especially the manifest codes that were described in the previous section.

Using the Export Template Wizard to automatically create a template is easier, but the manual process gives you more power and flexibility. I'll begin with the manual process.

Creating a Template Manually

After reading a full description of a template manifest in the previous section, learning the manual process is pretty easy!

You need to follow certain steps, though, to create a project or item template manually:

1. Create your project or item file and write your codes there.

2. Create an XML manifest file with a .vstemplate extension and configure it to work with your project or item template.

3. Follow the instructions in the next subsections to deploy the template to Visual Studio.

Here's an example in which I create a project template for a Class Library project that contains a single code file named `SampleClass.cs` and references to appropriate assemblies. I first create a new Class Library project and add these items to it, and then test my application. After this, I create an XML file for my template manifest, a process you can see in Listing 20-10.

Listing 20-10: Template Manifest for a Manually Created Project Template

```xml
<VSTemplate Version="2.0.0"
xmlns="http://schemas.microsoft.com/developer/vstemplate/2005" Type="Project">
  <TemplateData>
    <Name>Sample Class Library Template</Name>
    <Description>A class library project template</Description>
    <ProjectType>CSharp</ProjectType>
    <ProjectSubType>
    </ProjectSubType>
    <SortOrder>1000</SortOrder>
    <CreateNewFolder>true</CreateNewFolder>
    <DefaultName>MyClass</DefaultName>
    <ProvideDefaultName>true</ProvideDefaultName>
    <LocationField>Enabled</LocationField>
    <EnableLocationBrowseButton>true</EnableLocationBrowseButton>
    <Icon>__TemplateIcon.ico</Icon>
  </TemplateData>
  <TemplateContent>
    <Project TargetFileName="MyProject.csproj" File="MyProject.csproj"
ReplaceParameters="true">
      <ProjectItem ReplaceParameters="true"
TargetFileName="SampleClass.cs">SampleClass.cs</ProjectItem>
      <Folder Name="Properties" TargetFolderName="Properties">
        <ProjectItem ReplaceParameters="true"
```

(continued)

Listing 20-10 *(continued)*

```
TargetFileName="AssemblyInfo.cs">AssemblyInfo.cs</ProjectItem>
        </Folder>
      </Project>
    </TemplateContent>
  </VSTemplate>
```

In a moment you'll learn how to install this project template.

Deploying a Template

After creating a template (including its manifest, icon, and project files), you need to put all the files in the same place, and then select them all and archive them as a ZIP file. You can see the list of files for my template here:

```
Properties
    AssemblyInfo.cs
__TemplateIcon.ico
ClassLibTemplate.vstemplate
MyProject.csproject
SampleClass.cs
```

Note that you shouldn't simply send the parent folder to a ZIP archive, because your template won't work in this case.

After creating the ZIP archive, you can install it in Visual Studio simply by copying the file to one of following paths:

❑   For project templates, you can copy the file to *[Document Path]*\Visual Studio 2008\ Templates\ProjectTemplates.

❑   For item templates, you can copy the file to *[Document Path]*\Visual Studio 2008\ Templates\ItemTemplates.

Although it's not a big concern for you as a developer of Visual Studio templates, you may be interested to know where built-in Visual Studio templates are located. The path that contains project templates is [Visual Studio Installation Path]\Common7\IDE\ProjectTemplates, and the path that contains item templates is [Visual Studio Installation Path]\Common7\IDE\ItemTemplates. At these paths you can find project and item templates grouped into languages.

For my project template, I copy it to the first path. Then I launch my Visual Studio IDE and open the New Project dialog. Notice the addition of my project template to the My Templates section of the Templates list in Figure 20-5.

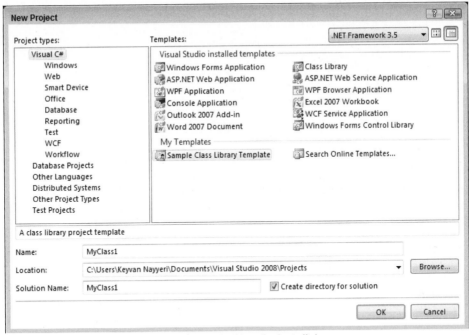

Figure 20-5: Project template is added to the New Project dialog

Now I can create a new project from this template. The final project has the same structure, as you would expect (see Figure 20-6).

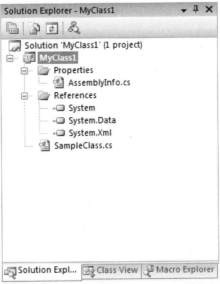

Figure 20-6: A new project is created from the project template.

As an alternative and easier option for deployment of Visual Studio templates, you can use the Visual Studio Content Installer, described in Chapter 13.

Export Template Wizard

The second and easier way to create a Visual Studio template is with the Export Template wizard. This wizard helps you create project templates and item templates without any knowledge of template structure.

The Export Template Wizard is accessible via the File ⇨ Export Template menu item. When you open this wizard, it first asks you to choose whether you want to create a project template or an item template and then to choose a project name from a drop-down list in order to create a template based on it (see Figure 20-7). To use this wizard you need to have a project opened. Since I created a project template in the previous section, here I create an item template.

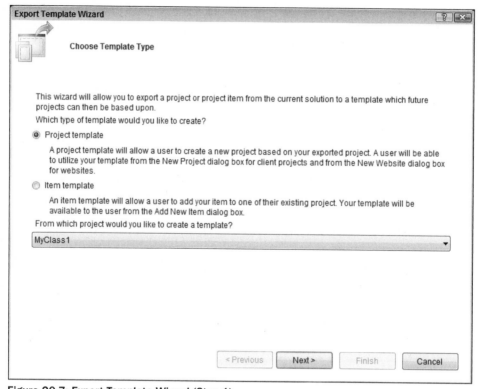

Figure 20-7: Export Template Wizard (Step 1)

In the next step, you need to choose which files you wish to include in the template (see Figure 20-8).

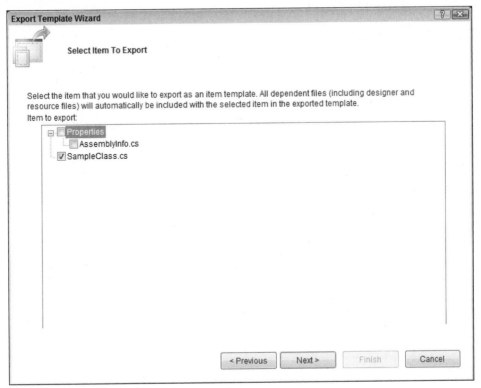

Figure 20-8: Export Template Wizard (Step 2)

In the third step, you choose which references you want to add to your template. Visual Studio lists all available references in your project (see Figure 20-9).

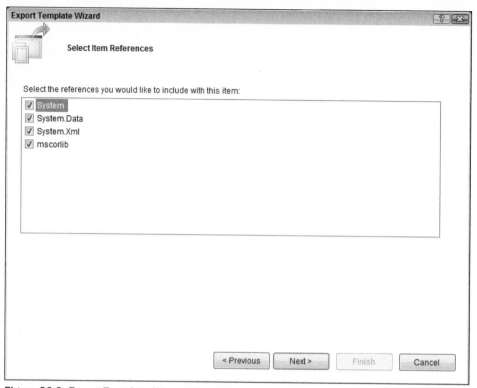

Figure 20-9: Export Template Wizard (Step 3)

Finally, in the last step, you can choose an icon for your template, as well as a template name and description. In addition, you can specify whether you want to import this template automatically to Visual Studio and display an Explorer window on the output files folder (see Figure 20-10).

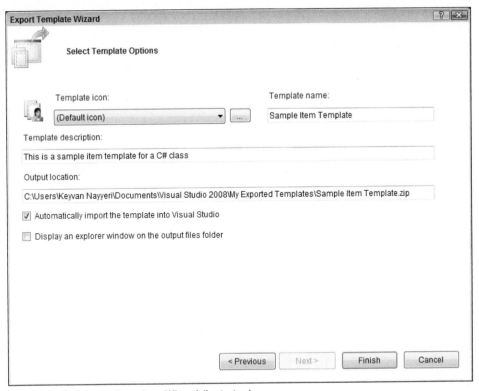

Figure 20-10: Export Template Wizard (last step)

After clicking Finish, Visual Studio creates the template for you and imports it to the IDE. Now you can see this item template in the Add New Item dialog box (see Figure 20-11).

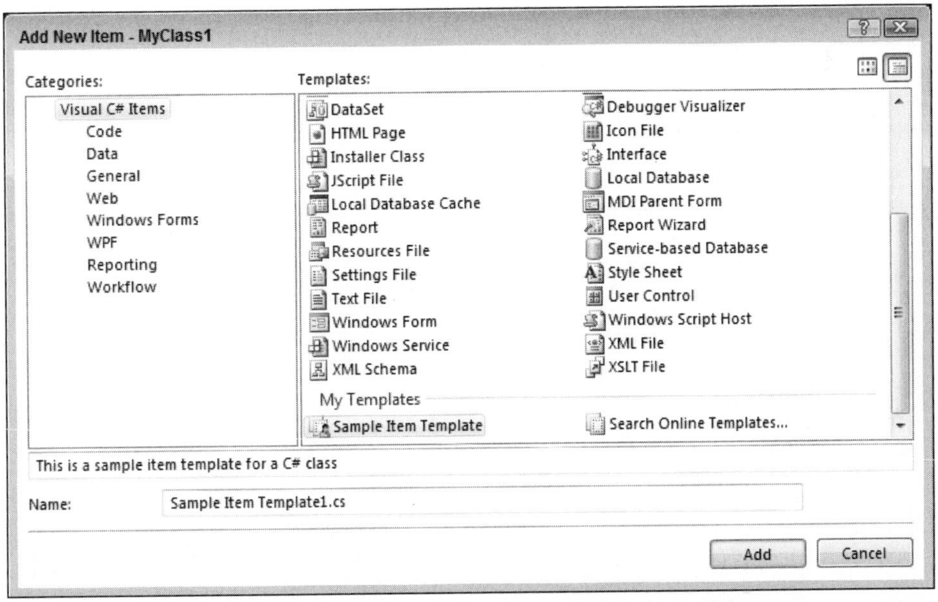

Figure 20-11: The New Item template is added to the Add New Item dialog box.

Customizing a Template

The previous implementation of the project template was its simplest form. For real-world scenarios you may need to pass some parameters and replace those parameters with appropriate values to achieve the template you need.

First of all, you need to insert parameter placeholders in your code files. These placeholders nest the parameter names inside two dollar signs ($). Listing 20-11 is an updated version of the `SampleClass` file with a few parameters.

Listing 20-11: Contents of `SampleClass.cs` Using Template Parameters

```
using System;
using System.Collections.Generic;
using System.Text;

namespace MyProject
{
    public class SampleClass
    {

        private int $firstField$ = $value1$;
        private int $secondField$ = $value2$;


    }
}
```

After inserting placeholders in the code, you can modify the template manifest to define these parameters and their values. To do this, add a `<CustomParameters>` element within the `<TemplateContent>` element. This element can contain one or more `<CustomParameter>` elements. Each `<CustomParameter>` element has `Name` and `Value` attributes. Using these two attributes, you can define the names and values of your parameters.

Listing 20-12 is the updated version of the template manifest to include parameters.

Listing 20-12 Adding Parameters to the Template Manifest

```
<VSTemplate Version="2.0.0"
xmlns="http://schemas.microsoft.com/developer/vstemplate/2005" Type="Project">
  <TemplateData>
    <Name>Sample Class Library Template</Name>
    <Description>A class library project template</Description>
    <ProjectType>CSharp</ProjectType>
    <ProjectSubType>
    </ProjectSubType>
    <SortOrder>1000</SortOrder>
    <CreateNewFolder>true</CreateNewFolder>
    <DefaultName>MyClass</DefaultName>
    <ProvideDefaultName>true</ProvideDefaultName>
    <LocationField>Enabled</LocationField>
    <EnableLocationBrowseButton>true</EnableLocationBrowseButton>
    <Icon>__TemplateIcon.ico</Icon>
  </TemplateData>
```

```
<TemplateContent>
  <Project TargetFileName="MyProject.csproj" File="MyProject.csproj"
ReplaceParameters="true">
    <ProjectItem ReplaceParameters="true"
TargetFileName="SampleClass.cs">SampleClass.cs</ProjectItem>
    <Folder Name="Properties" TargetFolderName="Properties">
      <ProjectItem ReplaceParameters="true"
TargetFileName="AssemblyInfo.cs">AssemblyInfo.cs</ProjectItem>
    </Folder>
  </Project>

  <CustomParameters>
    <CustomParameter Name="$firstField$" Value="number1"/>
    <CustomParameter Name="$value1$" Value="0"/>
    <CustomParameter Name="$secondField$" Value="number2"/>
    <CustomParameter Name="$value2$" Value="1"/>
  </CustomParameters>

</TemplateContent>
</VSTemplate>
```

Now if I create a new project from this template and open its `SampleClass` file, it contains the code shown in Listing 20-13.

Listing 20-13: Custom Parameters Are Replaced in the Code

```
using System;
using System.Collections.Generic;
using System.Text;

namespace MyProject
{
    public class SampleClass
    {
        private int number1 = 0;
        private int number2 = 1;
    }
}
```

Note that without setting the `ReplaceParameters` attribute to true for the project items, Visual Studio doesn't replace custom parameters with corresponding values.

Custom Template Wizards

One of the enhanced features of Visual Studio templates is their capability to add a custom wizard to the item to run right after the user creates the project or item from the template. An example of this scenario is described in Chapter 18 for VSPackages. You can create a new VSPackage project and configure it with the Visual Studio Package Wizard.

There are some benefits to having such a wizard:

- ❏ You can collect user inputs and use them in your project.
- ❏ You can add parameter values to the project for the template.
- ❏ You can add other files to the project.

When using a template wizard, you have access to DTE classes (described in detail elsewhere in this book) in order to manipulate your projects easily.

Creating a custom template wizard is as easy as implementing an interface.

Following are the general steps for writing a custom template wizard:

1. Build an assembly that implements the IWizard interface.
2. Install the assembly in the GAC (Global Assembly Cache).
3. Update your template manifest to use this assembly.

As an example of these steps, I'll update the sample project template created earlier in this chapter, when I described using its template manifest to create a Class Library project. I create a wizard to get parameter values from the user interface, rather than put them in the manifest.

The first steps are to create a Class Library project, add a public class to it, and implement the IWizard interface in it. The IWizard interface is located in the Microsoft.VisualStudio.TemplateWizard assembly. This interface has six methods to implement. These methods will execute on specific times in the life cycle of a project template. Some of them are restricted to item templates. The six methods are described in Table 20-2.

Table 20-2: IWizard Interface Methods

Method	Description
BeforeOpeningFile	Runs before opening a new item in the template
ProjectFinishedGenerating	Runs when the project has finished generating from the template
ProjectItemFinishedGenerating	Runs when the project item has finished generating from the template
RunFinished	Runs when the wizard has finished its tasks
RunStarted	Runs at the beginning of the template wizard
ShouldAddProjectItem	Specifies whether a project item should be added to the project

Here, for my sample, I'll just work with the RunStarted method in order to replace parameter values from what I get from the user in the user interface.

This method has four parameters:

- An object to be converted to a DTE object. It enables customization of the project
- A Dictionary of strings of parameter names and values
- A WizardRunKind enumerator value that specifies the kind of template being used
- An object array of a set of parameters that are passed to the wizard by Visual Studio

Here I rely on the `Dictionary` parameter to add my parameter values.

Before adding code details for implementing the IWizard interface, I create a Windows Form with two TextBoxes to get user inputs for my custom parameters, and an OK button so that I can use them in the template. The code for this form is shown in Listing 20-14.

Listing 20-14: InputForm Code

```csharp
using System;
using System.Collections.Generic;
using System.ComponentModel;
using System.Data;
using System.Drawing;
using System.Text;
using System.Windows.Forms;

namespace CustomTemplateWizard
{
    public partial class InputForm : Form
    {
        private string value1;
        private string value2;

        public InputForm()
        {
            InitializeComponent();
        }

        private void btnOk_Click(object sender, EventArgs e)
        {
            this.value1 = txtValue1.Text;
            this.value2 = txtValue2.Text;
        }

        public string GetValue1()
        {
            return this.value1;
        }

        public string GetValue2()
        {
            return this.value2;
        }
    }
}
```

GetValue1 and GetValue2 are two public methods that return two values for parameters.

Now I implement the IWizard interface in the WizardImplementation class (see Listing 20-15).

Listing 20-15: Implementing the IWizard Interface

```csharp
using System;
using System.Collections.Generic;
using System.Text;
using Microsoft.VisualStudio.TemplateWizard;

namespace CustomTemplateWizard
{
    public class WizardImplementation : IWizard
    {
        private InputForm inputForm;
        private string value1;
        private string value2;

        #region IWizard Members

        public void BeforeOpeningFile(EnvDTE.ProjectItem projectItem)
        {
        }

        public void ProjectFinishedGenerating(EnvDTE.Project project)
        {
        }

        public void ProjectItemFinishedGenerating(EnvDTE.ProjectItem projectItem)
        {
        }

        public void RunFinished()
        {
        }

        public void RunStarted(object automationObject, Dictionary<string, string>
replacementsDictionary,
            WizardRunKind runKind, object[] customParams)
        {
            inputForm = new InputForm();
            inputForm.ShowDialog();

            this.value1 = inputForm.GetValue1();
            this.value2 = inputForm.GetValue2();

            inputForm.Close();

            replacementsDictionary.Add("$firstField$", "number1");
            replacementsDictionary.Add("$value1$", this.value1);
            replacementsDictionary.Add("$secondField$", "number2");
```

```
                    replacementsDictionary.Add("$value2$", this.value2);
            }

            public bool ShouldAddProjectItem(string filePath)
            {
                return true;
            }

            #endregion
        }
    }
```

As you see, the `RunStarted` method is where you insert the main logic. In this method, I create an instance of `InputForm` and use it to display the form and store two parameter values in local private variables and add them, along with the other two parameters, to the Dictionary of parameters for appropriate parameter keys.

After this, I build my Class Library project and sign my assembly with a strong name, and then register this assembly in the GAC (Global Assembly Cache).

Listing 20-16 modifies my template manifest to include this assembly and remove previous parameters.

Listing 20-16: Modified Template Manifest to Use a Custom Wizard

```
<VSTemplate Version="2.0.0"
xmlns="http://schemas.microsoft.com/developer/vstemplate/2005" Type="Project">
  <TemplateData>
    <Name>Sample Class Library Template</Name>
    <Description>A class library project template</Description>
    <ProjectType>CSharp</ProjectType>
    <ProjectSubType>
    </ProjectSubType>
    <SortOrder>1000</SortOrder>
    <CreateNewFolder>true</CreateNewFolder>
    <DefaultName>MyClass</DefaultName>
    <ProvideDefaultName>true</ProvideDefaultName>
    <LocationField>Enabled</LocationField>
    <EnableLocationBrowseButton>true</EnableLocationBrowseButton>
    <Icon>__TemplateIcon.ico</Icon>
  </TemplateData>
  <TemplateContent>
    <Project TargetFileName="MyProject.csproj" File="MyProject.csproj"
ReplaceParameters="true">
      <ProjectItem ReplaceParameters="true"
TargetFileName="SampleClass.cs">SampleClass.cs</ProjectItem>
      <Folder Name="Properties" TargetFolderName="Properties">
        <ProjectItem ReplaceParameters="true"
TargetFileName="AssemblyInfo.cs">AssemblyInfo.cs</ProjectItem>
```

(continued)

Listing 20-16 *(continued)*

```
        </Folder>
      </Project>
    </TemplateContent>

  <WizardExtension>
    <Assembly>
      CustomTemplateWizard, Version=1.0.0.0, Culture=neutral,
  PublicKeyToken=e745066e7fcbe813, Custom=null
    </Assembly>
    <FullClassName>CustomTemplateWizard.WizardImplementation</FullClassName>
  </WizardExtension>

</VSTemplate>
```

You need a public key token that matches the one assigned to the assembly in the GAC, so be careful about this.

After packing my template and installing it in Visual Studio, it shows the Windows Form asking for user inputs every time I try to create a project from this template (see Figure 20-12), and it replaces these values in the generated class code (see Listing 20-17).

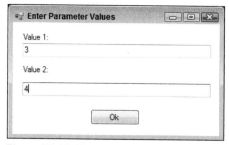

Figure 20-12: The custom template wizard appears after creating a project.

Listing 20-17: Custom Wizard Replaces Parameter Values in Code

```
using System;
using System.Collections.Generic;
using System.Text;

namespace MyProject
{
    public class SampleClass
    {
        private int number1 = 3;
        private int number2 = 4;
    }
}
```

Starter Kits

Starter Kits are a special kind of project template for sharing sample codes and documentation resources for special projects with other developers. Starter Kits can be considered an enhanced version of project templates. They not only have a set of project, configuration, code, and resource files, but also may have a set of documentation files to describe how to work with a specific technology.

Project templates and Starter Kits are similar concepts, but there are a few minor differences between them. Project templates are created to function as a starting point for projects, whereas Starter Kits are created to teach something and provide sample codes for a technology. A Starter Kit contains all the items in a project template, but it may also have some extra files for documentation.

The process of building a Starter Kit is similar to that for a project template, but based on the kind of Starter Kit that you're going to create and your needs for it, you may need to add some extra files for documentation.

Summary

Understanding Visual Studio templates was the main goal of this chapter. Project templates and item templates and their differences were the first topics. After that you read a complete discussion about the anatomy of Visual Studio templates and the structure of template manifest files.

The next topic was creating new templates, both manually and with the Export Template Wizard. Finally, you learned how to create custom template wizards and read a short discussion about Starter Kits as a special type of project template.

21

MSBuild

Like debugging, build and compilation is another main stage in the software development process. You learned all about extending the debugger in Visual Studio in Chapter 17; now it's time to look at the build and compilation process, and all the extensibility points that are provided by Visual Studio for this stage.

I don't need to describe the concept of build and compilation of software here, but how is this stage implemented in .NET? Some readers may have a background in this, but others may not. Microsoft has tried to provide an automatic way to simplify the process of building, compilation, deployment, and logging. Yes, deployment! You may say that deployment is another stage in software development and you're 100 percent right, but Microsoft has provided some means to tie these two stages and automate them.

In the first sections of this chapter you'll learn more about MSBuild and its applications, but first I'll provide a short introduction to this important topic, as MSBuild is a platform that enables you to write automated builds, thereby simplifying this stage of your projects.

In this chapter you'll learn about the following topics:

- ❏ The concept of MSBuild and its applications
- ❏ The anatomy of MSBuild files
- ❏ The structure of MSBuild files and common elements of MSBuild
- ❏ How to write MSBuild files
- ❏ How to write a custom MSBuild task
- ❏ How to use MSBuild files

As with Chapters 19 and 20, this chapter relies heavily on XML and related concepts because MSBuild files are XML documents. Unlike Chapters 19 and 20, which described all possible elements and attributes for an XML schema, I won't go into detail here about some uncommon elements and attributes; the vast number of these elements and attributes is beyond the scope of a chapter. However, you can get more information by reading online documentation and articles (such as MSDN documents).

This chapter is independent from .NET development languages to some extent, and you'll see a few sample projects showing how to build and deploy with MSBuild.

What Is MSBuild?

In Visual Studio 2005, Microsoft introduced a new technology called *MSBuild*. MSBuild stands for Microsoft Build Engine. MSBuild is a build platform for the .NET Framework and Visual Studio. This platform is completely built based on XML and has similar syntax to Apache Ant or NAnt. Apache Ant is a build platform for Java, while NAnt is another build platform for .NET written by the community.

In MSBuild you define what you have and what you want to get; then the platform does the job for you, taking your inputs and creating your results.

MSBuild is a part of the .NET Framework, which means that you don't need to have Visual Studio installed in order to get the benefits of this platform, even though there is a high correlation between Visual Studio and MSBuild.

MSBuild is completely supported by Microsoft development tools and is integrated with them, so you can use it without worrying about its interoperability with other technologies.

You can use MSBuild to write automated builds and deployments. You can write an MSBuild file to include your source-code files and compile them, using some references with a specific version of the .NET Framework, and then store the result in a package or even deploy it somewhere.

MSBuild is useful for writing custom builds and deploying the software automatically, but it's even more helpful than this when it comes to teamwork scenarios, where it becomes a main part of the work! Software teams use MSBuild to perform automated builds after each check-in to source control and to test the result and keep their projects up to date.

Continuous Integration

If you're not already familiar with it, *continuous integration* is a name for a practice in extreme programming (XP) whereby you commit any change that you make into the software immediately. Extreme programming is one of the Agile software development methodologies. It doesn't matter if your change is small or large; committing the changes enables other developers in your team to get the latest changes and keep themselves updated. For large projects, you need *automated continuous integration* — a process on the server that monitors the server of your code repository or source control for any changes and performs automated builds. MSBuild comes into the play at this point to help you write these automated builds.

Many continuous integration tools such as Cruise Control are completely integrated with MSBuild in order to perform builds on code from a source control repository, returning the result of successful or failed builds to team members as e-mail or RSS feeds, and to show them on internal team web pages.

Using MSBuild, you can also create ZIP packages of your software for release automatically and choose to include which items are in it. You can even use MSBuild for web deployment of ASP.NET projects.

MSBuild is also integrated completely with Microsoft Visual Studio Team Foundation Server (TFS), which is an enterprise source-control system for .NET development, and developers can use it to perform automated builds on their projects. All Visual Studio project files are MSBuild files and can be used with MSBuild easily.

The Anatomy of MSBuild Files

As mentioned, MSBuild files are XML documents with a specific schema (like the code snippets and Visual Studio templates described in Chapters 19 and 20). I'll describe this schema briefly in this chapter.

In general, MSBuild files have a .target extension, but they can also use other extensions. Some common examples of this are project files in Visual Studio such as .csproj and .vbproj.

Let's take a look at an example. Listing 21-1 shows the source code of a .csproj file for a C# Class Library project in the .NET Framework 3.5. It's the default code and I haven't added any new items or code to it.

Listing 21-1: MSBuild File for a C# Class Library

```
<?xml version="1.0" encoding="utf-8"?>
<Project ToolsVersion="3.5" DefaultTargets="Build"
xmlns="http://schemas.microsoft.com/developer/msbuild/2003">
  <PropertyGroup>
    <Configuration Condition=" '$(Configuration)' == '' ">Debug</Configuration>
    <Platform Condition=" '$(Platform)' == '' ">AnyCPU</Platform>
    <ProductVersion>9.0.21022</ProductVersion>
    <SchemaVersion>2.0</SchemaVersion>
    <ProjectGuid>{1E4CE5B4-8BA1-483F-813D-CAAD4DB62704}</ProjectGuid>
    <OutputType>Library</OutputType>
    <AppDesignerFolder>Properties</AppDesignerFolder>
    <RootNamespace>ClassLibrary1</RootNamespace>
    <AssemblyName>ClassLibrary1</AssemblyName>
    <TargetFrameworkVersion>v3.5</TargetFrameworkVersion>
    <FileAlignment>512</FileAlignment>
  </PropertyGroup>
  <PropertyGroup Condition=" '$(Configuration)|$(Platform)' == 'Debug|AnyCPU' ">
    <DebugSymbols>true</DebugSymbols>
    <DebugType>full</DebugType>
    <Optimize>false</Optimize>
    <OutputPath>bin\Debug\</OutputPath>
    <DefineConstants>DEBUG;TRACE</DefineConstants>
    <ErrorReport>prompt</ErrorReport>
    <WarningLevel>4</WarningLevel>
  </PropertyGroup>
  <PropertyGroup Condition=" '$(Configuration)|$(Platform)' == 'Release|AnyCPU' ">
    <DebugType>pdbonly</DebugType>
    <Optimize>true</Optimize>
    <OutputPath>bin\Release\</OutputPath>
    <DefineConstants>TRACE</DefineConstants>
```

(continued)

Listing 21-1 *(continued)*

```xml
      <ErrorReport>prompt</ErrorReport>
      <WarningLevel>4</WarningLevel>
  </PropertyGroup>
  <ItemGroup>
    <Reference Include="System" />
    <Reference Include="System.Core">
      <RequiredTargetFramework>3.5</RequiredTargetFramework>
    </Reference>
    <Reference Include="System.Xml.Linq">
      <RequiredTargetFramework>3.5</RequiredTargetFramework>
    </Reference>
    <Reference Include="System.Data.DataSetExtensions">
      <RequiredTargetFramework>3.5</RequiredTargetFramework>
    </Reference>
    <Reference Include="System.Data" />
    <Reference Include="System.Xml" />
  </ItemGroup>
  <ItemGroup>
    <Compile Include="Class1.cs" />
    <Compile Include="Properties\AssemblyInfo.cs" />
  </ItemGroup>
  <Import Project="$(MSBuildToolsPath)\Microsoft.CSharp.targets" />
  <!-- To modify your build process, add your task inside one of the targets below
and uncomment it.
        Other similar extension points exist, see Microsoft.Common.targets.
  <Target Name="BeforeBuild">
  </Target>
  <Target Name="AfterBuild">
  </Target>
  -->
</Project>
```

This XML document begins with a root `<Project>` element that has an XML namespace set to `http://schemas.microsoft.com/developer/msbuild/2003`. As you know from reading Chapters 19 and 20, after setting this namespace, Visual Studio loads the corresponding schema file for your XML document, and you can use IntelliSense to more easily write your code (see Figure 21-1).

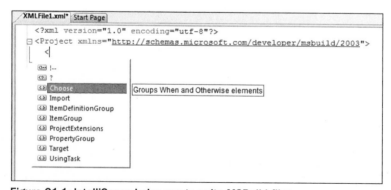

Figure 21-1: IntelliSense helps you to write MSBuild files.

Within this <Project> root element are some groups of elements that are described in the rest of this chapter. Using these elements, you define different pieces of code and resources that you want to include in your build, as well as appropriate references for it, the .NET Framework version to use for building, and the type of build action to perform. You can also declare options for your build to deploy your result.

MSBuild Structure

Let's take a look at technical details.

An MSBuild file consists of a collection of element groups. The following groups are the main parts of an MSBuild file:

- ❑ **Items:** These declare inputs to the MSBuild file and can be used to perform build actions and tasks.

- ❑ **Properties:** Properties can be used for configuration of MSBuild files and are key-value pairs.

- ❑ **Targets:** With targets, you can group a collection of tasks and perform them together. For example, a target may compile items and put the result in a particular folder.

- ❑ **Tasks:** Tasks are units of actions that should be performed when a build process is occurring. Tasks can help to group these actions logically.

The following subsections describe these main parts and demonstrate how to use them. However, before talking about these groups of elements, let me say a few things about the root <Project> element here.

This element has three optional attributes:

- ❑ DefaultTargets: A list of targets that you want to be built if a particular target is not specified. You can separate items with a semicolon.

- ❑ InitialTargets: A list of targets that you want to be built before other targets. You can separate items with a semicolon.

- ❑ ToolsVersion: This string attribute specifies the toolset version with which this project should always be built.

This root <Project> element also has eight child elements:

- ❑ <Choose>: This groups two other elements: <Otherwise> and <When>. It helps to evaluate child elements to keep a set of <ItemGroup> or <PropertyGroup> elements.

- ❑ <Import>: Using this element, you can import the content of other project files to the current file.

- ❑ <ItemDefinitionGroup>: This keeps a group of item metadata definitions.

- ❑ <ItemGroup>: Keeps a collection of item elements. You need to declare all items that you want to include in the build in this element.

❑   <ProjectExtensions>: With the help of this element, you can pass some custom information to your build. The XML content of this child element is ignored by MSBuild itself, but you can use it for custom configurations and settings.

❑   <PropertyGroup>: Keeps a group of property elements. You need to declare all property elements for your MSBuild files here.

❑   <Target>: This element groups a set of tasks in the build process into a single unit.

❑   <UsingTask>: This acts as a map between an assembly where you implement the logic of a task and the <Task> element corresponding to it.

Listing 21-2 represents the initial code that you can use to get started with writing an MSBuild file.

Listing 21-2: Initial Code for an MSBuild File

```xml
<?xml version="1.0" encoding="utf-8"?>
<Project xmlns="http://schemas.microsoft.com/developer/msbuild/2003">

</Project>
```

Of course, this simple code yields an XML warning in Visual Studio because according to the MSBuild schema, it expects some child elements for the root <Project> element.

Let's look at the main parts of an MSBuild file.

Items

Items are inputs to the MSBuild file. The goal is to get these inputs and perform a task on them and finally return an output. Items consist of a collection of item groups. Later you can use these items in your tasks to perform some actions on them.

In MSBuild you can declare items within the <ItemGroup> element. Here you insert your items in elements with different names and put the name of the item in the Include attribute. An example of this scenario is shown in Listing 21-3.

Listing 21-3: Declaring Items

```xml
<ItemGroup>
  <Compile Include="Program.cs" />
  <Compile Include="MyClass.cs" />
</ItemGroup>
```

You can either insert multiple files in different elements or insert them all in one single element and use a semicolon to separate them in the Include attribute. Keep this in mind as a general technique in the rest of this chapter. For example, Listing 21-4 updates Listing 21-3 to use a single element.

Listing 21-4: Inserting Multiple Items in a Single Attribute in a Semicolon-Separated List.

```xml
<ItemGroup>
  <Compile Include="Program.cs;MyClass.cs" />
</ItemGroup>
```

You have access to several item types inside the `<ItemGroup>` elements listed here:

- `<BaseApplicationManifest>`
- `<BootstraperFile>`
- `<CodeAnalysisDictionary>`
- `<CodeAnalysisImport>`
- `<COMFileReference>`
- `<Compile>`
- `<COMReference>`
- `<Content>`
- `<EmbeddedResource>`
- `<Folder>`
- `<Import>`
- `<NativeReference>`
- `<None>`
- `<ProjectReference>`
- `<PublishFile>`
- `<Reference>`
- `<Service>`
- `<WebReferences>`
- `<WebReferenceUrl>`

The application of many of these elements is obvious from their names, and you can find the application of others from online documentation. Some of these elements are frequently used, while others are used only occasionally. Moreover, you can declare your own item element types if necessary.

You can refer to these item collections with the @(ItemCollectionName) format in your MSBuild files, such as @(Compile) or @(Reference).

Wildcards

When adding your items, sometimes it's appropriate to add a set of files with the same extension. For example, it's common to add all C# files with the .cs extension to the project. In such cases, you can use wildcards to simplify your work, as Listing 21-5 shows.

Listing 21-5: Using Wildcards to Include Several Items

```
<ItemGroup>
  <Compile Include="*.cs" />
</ItemGroup>
```

Exclude Items

You can also exclude specific items from the group with the `Exclude` attribute of your items collection element. This is useful when you use wildcards to choose several items but don't want particular items from the list (see Listing 21-6).

Listing 21-6: Using the `Exclude` Attribute to Exclude Items

```
<ItemGroup>
  <Compile Include="*.cs" />
  <Compile Exclude="MyClass.cs" />
</ItemGroup>
```

Item Metadata

Passing some metadata about items to project files is a common scenario when authoring MSBuild files. There is some metadata information about the items in a project that's a part of MSBuild by default, such as `<FullPath>`, `<RootDir>`, `<Filename>`, and `<Extension>`. You can refer to this well-known default metadata with a %(MetadataName) pattern such as %(CreatedTime).

You can also pass your own metadata with items as well. For example, Listing 21-7 passes the encoding of the item (UTF8) by adding an `<Encoding>` child element to the item collection element.

Listing 21-7: Adding Metadata Information to Items

```
<ItemGroup>
  <Compile Include="*.cs">
    <Encoding>UTF8</Encoding>
  </Compile>
</ItemGroup>
```

An `<ItemGroup>` element can also have some other attributes, such as `Condition`, to include or exclude items under some conditions. Later you'll see how conditions work in MSBuild.

Properties

Properties are a set of key-value pairs for configuring your MSBuild project files. You can use properties to send custom parameters to your tasks in a project file.

There is a huge list of property names in MSBuild, well beyond the scope of this chapter. You can access them with IntelliSense or view the list with online documentation.

Reserved built-in properties (as well as your custom properties), along with environment variables, have similar syntax when you want to cite them in your project files. This syntax is $(PropertyName) — for example, $(ApplicationIcon) or $(DebugType).

Property names aren't case sensitive, so you can refer to them in different ways: $(DebugType), $(debugType), $(Debugtype), $(debugtype), ($DEBUGTYPE), and many other combinations are all correct.

Environment variables are properties that belong to the environment in which you're running an MSBuild file, such as the output and path. All these environment variables are represented in MSBuild as properties and can be used like properties. For example, Path is a variable that refers to the path of the project files.

Properties can be passed to an MSBuild file via command-line arguments as well. This is covered later in the chapter.

Listing 21-8 shows an example of using properties in MSBuild.

Listing 21-8: Using Properties in MSBuild

```
<PropertyGroup>
  <WarningLevel>2</WarningLevel>
  <CreateOnFly>true</CreateOnFly>
</PropertyGroup>
```

The preceding code uses a reserved property (WarningLevel) as well as a custom property (CreateOnFly).

Targets

Targets are another main part of the MSBuild structure. Targets group some tasks in a single unit to run together in a particular order.

You can use targets to perform different tasks on the project based on the user's choices. For example, you can compile and build a ZIP package for the project when the user chooses that option, or build and deploy it to the Web when that option is chosen.

A target has a name with which the user can call it. Each target has one or more MSBuild or user-defined tasks (you'll read about them in a moment).

Listing 21-9 shows a simple example of declaring a single <Target> element.

Listing 21-9: Using the Target Element

```
<Target Name="Compilation">
  <Csc Sources="@Compile" />
</Target>
```

This code uses the C# compiler task in order to compile the items that are defined in the <Compile> item element(s). As mentioned before, you can use @(ItemCollectionName) syntax in order to refer to item collection elements in MSBuild files.

Tasks

A task is a unit of executable code. During the build process on a project, .NET needs to apply some specific actions to the project. You can define these actions via tasks in MSBuild.

A task is a kind of code logic and it can't run inside an XML file like MSBuild, so you need to implement this logic somewhere outside the MSBuild file and then refer to it in the MSBuild file.

MSBuild supports several common tasks out of the box, and Microsoft has tried to include all common scenarios in the built-in tasks. However, sometimes you will need to implement the logic for your own tasks. MSBuild is extensible enough to let you do this. In the next section you learn how to write a custom task.

To declare a task in MSBuild, you must use a `<Target>` element (as you saw in the previous section). You can embed as many task elements as you like inside a `<Target>` element.

Listing 21-10 demonstrates an example of this.

Listing 21-10: Declaring Tasks

```
<Target Name="Compilation">
  <Csc Sources="@(Compile)" />
  <Copy SourceFiles="@(FilesToCopy)" DestinationFolder="c:\Destination" />
</Target>
```

This target has two tasks. The first task compiles all files declared in the `<Compile>` element(s) and the second task simply copies some declared files in the `<FilesToCopy>` element(s) to a destination path.

How to Write a Custom Task

The process of writing a custom task for MSBuild is relatively easy. You need to implement the ITask interface located in the Microsoft.Build.Framework assembly.

Therefore, the first step is to create a Class Library project and add a reference to the Microsoft.Build. Framework assembly. Then you create a class that implements the ITask interface. Listing 21-11 shows an example.

Listing 21-11: Implementing the ITask Interface to Create a Custom Task

```
using System;
using System.Collections.Generic;
using System.Linq;
using System.Text;
using Microsoft.Build.Framework;

namespace CustomTask
{
    public class SimpleLoggerTask : ITask
    {
        #region ITask Members

        public IBuildEngine BuildEngine
        {
            get
            {
                throw new NotImplementedException();
            }
```

```
            set
            {
                throw new NotImplementedException();
            }
        }

        public bool Execute()
        {
            throw new NotImplementedException();
        }

        public ITaskHost HostObject
        {
            get
            {
                throw new NotImplementedException();
            }
            set
            {
                throw new NotImplementedException();
            }
        }

        #endregion
    }
}
```

The ITask interface has one method and two properties to override. BuildEngine and HostObject are two properties to designate the build engine and host object associated with the task. The Execute method is the main place where you can implement your logic for the task. This method is called by MSBuild to perform the task. The function returns true if the task is done successfully; otherwise, it returns false.

The implementation of a task can be easier than this, however, because Microsoft has created a default implementation for the BuildEngine and HostObject properties and has provided an abstract base class from which you can derive and override the Execute method.

You can use the Task class located in the Microsoft.Build.Utilities assembly to do this. Implementation of this abstract base class doesn't require anything more than overriding the Execute method. This saves you from some extra work.

This is the approach I use in the next example, which implements simple logic for my task and just logs a message in a logger to see how it works. Listing 21-12 is my initial implementation of this task.

Listing 21-12: Initial Implementation of SimpleLoggerTask

```
using System;
using System.Collections.Generic;
using System.Linq;
using System.Text;
using Microsoft.Build.Utilities;

namespace CustomTask
{
    public class SimpleLoggerTask : Task
    {
        public override bool Execute()
        {
            Log.LogMessage("Inside the task!");
            return true;
        }
    }
}
```

Adding your own attributes to the task is straightforward. Just add a property to your class and this will be considered an attribute for your task in MSBuild. Moreover, you can mark a property with the Required attribute to identify it as a required attribute in MSBuild.

Listing 21-13 updates SimpleLoggerTask to have two attributes.

Listing 21-13: Adding Attributes to the Custom Task

```
using System;
using System.Collections.Generic;
using System.Linq;
using System.Text;
using Microsoft.Build.Framework;
using Microsoft.Build.Utilities;

namespace CustomTask
{
    public class SimpleLoggerTask : Task
    {
        private string optionalAttribute;

        public string OptionalAttribute
        {
            get
            {
                return this.optionalAttribute;
            }
            set
            {
                this.optionalAttribute = value;
            }
        }
```

```
        private string requiredAttribute;

        [Required]
        public string RequiredAttribute
        {
            get
            {
                return this.requiredAttribute;
            }
            set
            {
                this.requiredAttribute = value;
            }
        }

        public override bool Execute()
        {
            Log.LogMessage(string.Format("Inside the task! OptionalAttribute = {0}
    - RequiredAttribute = {1}"),
                this.optionalAttribute, this.requiredAttribute);
            return true;
        }
    }
}
```

This code adds two properties for both an optional and a required attribute and then updates the Execute method to log these two attributes as well.

Now I can compile this code into an assembly and proceed to the next step.

Registering a Custom Task in MSBuild

Now that I've implemented my custom task in an assembly successfully, I can add a new task element to my MSBuild file and register this file there.

To do this, I need to add a <UsingTask> element to the root <Project> element. This element gets a TaskName attribute, which specifies the name of the task, and an AssemblyFile attribute, which can be set to either the assembly name or the address of the assembly.

I create a new MSBuild project file like the one shown in Listing 21-14.

Listing 21-14: Registering a Custom Task in MSBuild

```xml
<?xml version="1.0" encoding="utf-8"?>
<Project xmlns="http://schemas.microsoft.com/developer/msbuild/2003">
  <UsingTask TaskName="SimpleLoggerTask"
            AssemblyFile="C:\CustomTask\CustomTask.dll" />
  <Target Name="SimpleLogger">
    <SimpleLoggerTask optionalAttribute="Keyvan" requiredAttribute="Nayyeri" />
  </Target>
</Project>
```

After registering my custom task, I was able to use it inside a <Target> element and set its attributes.

Running this MSBuild file, I get the following result in the command prompt:

```
Microsoft (R) Build Engine Version 3.5.21022.8
[Microsoft .NET Framework, Version 2.0.50727.1433]
Copyright (C) Microsoft Corporation 2007. All rights reserved.

Build started 12/2/2007 7:59:44 AM.
Project "C:\Chapter 21\customtask.target" on node 0 (default targets).

  Inside the task! OptionalAttribute = Keyvan - RequiredAttribute = Nayyeri

Done Building Project "C:\Chapter 21\customtask.target" (default targets).


Build succeeded.
    0 Warning(s)
    0 Error(s)

Time Elapsed 00:00:00.05
```

In the next sections you'll learn how to run an MSBuild file.

Conditions

Conditional elements and attributes are a common part of MSBuild elements. They help you to perform actions or select items when a condition is true.

The `Condition` attribute of an MSBuild element is the most common example of using conditions in MSBuild. This attribute accepts a set of conditions. If the condition evaluates to true, then that specific task, action, or operation will be applied. These conditions are very similar to logical operands in the C# language. For example, Listing 21-15 is an example of the `Condition` attribute.

Listing 21-15: Using the `Condition` Attribute

```
<Target Name="Compilation" Condition="Exists('@(Compile)')">
  <Csc Sources="@(Compile)" />
</Target>
```

This procedure checks whether items in the `<Compile>` element exist, and then performs a C# compilation task on them if so. Otherwise, it ignores this task.

The other type of conditional statements in MSBuild are the combinations of `<Choose>`, `<When>`, and/or `<Otherwise>` elements. Using these elements, you can perform tasks under some conditions and manage the logic of your project file. These elements provide a structure similar to `If` and `Else` statements in C#.

The `<Choose>` element is just a container for `<When>` and `<Otherwise>` elements. It can contain one or more `<When>` elements and one and only one `<Otherwise>` element. When an element has a `<Condition>` attribute and the condition evaluates to true, the content inside the `<When>` element is parsed. You can insert several `<When>` elements inside a `<Choose>` element for different conditions. `<Otherwise>` is the element that plays the role of `<Else>` in C#. When other conditions aren't true, the content of this element is parsed.

Note that only <Choose>, <ItemGroup>, and <PropertyGroup> elements can be inserted inside <When> and <Otherwise> elements.

Consider the example shown in Listing 21-16.

Listing 21-16: The Choose, When, and Otherwise Elements

```
<Choose>
  <When Condition="'$(CompileType)' == 'CSharp'">
    <ItemGroup>
      <Compile Include="*.cs" />
    </ItemGroup>
  </When>
  <When Condition="'$(CompileType)' == 'VB'">
    <ItemGroup>
      <Compile Include="*.vb" />
    </ItemGroup>
  </When>
  <Otherwise>
    <ItemGroup>
      <Compile Include="*.*" />
    </ItemGroup>
  </Otherwise>
</Choose>
```

This example checks for the CompileType property. If it's set to CSharp, then C# files will be included in the compilation. If it's set to VB, then Visual Basic files will be included. Otherwise, all files will be included.

How to Use MSBuild Files

Now that you have a good background in MSBuild and can write MSBuild files, it's time to learn how to use those files.

Some MSBuild files are the auto-generated project files for different project types in Visual Studio, and they run with default targets when you perform a Build, Rebuild, or Clean action on your projects and solutions. When you write MSBuild files manually, however, you need to run them yourself.

To do this, you need to get the help of the command line and a command that comes with the .NET Framework. This command is nothing more than the MSBuild command.

This command has some switches. You can view the complete list of these switches, with their description, by running one of the following commands from the command line:

msbuild /?

or

msbuild /help

Let's take a look at some common switches and the use of this command. Obviously, one of the arguments to pass to this command is the path of the MSBuild project file. Other arguments vary based on your needs and choices.

One simple option is to run the MSBuild file just by passing its address. For example, I can write the following command to run the MSBuild file that I wrote as a sample to show you how to write a custom task:

```
msbuild "C:\Chapter 21\customtask.target"
```

This simply runs the MSBuild file with all its targets and returns the following output, which provides a simple report of the build process as well as what I specified in my custom task to be written:

```
Microsoft (R) Build Engine Version 3.5.21022.8
[Microsoft .NET Framework, Version 2.0.50727.1433]
Copyright (C) Microsoft Corporation 2007. All rights reserved.

Build started 12/2/2007 7:59:44 AM.
Project "C:\Chapter 21\customtask.target" on node 0 (default targets).
  Inside the task! OptionalAttribute = Keyvan - RequiredAttribute = Nayyeri
Done Building Project "C:\Chapter 21\customtask.target" (default targets).


Build succeeded.
    0 Warning(s)
    0 Error(s)

Time Elapsed 00:00:00.05
```

If I want to run an MSBuild file with a specific target, I can simply pass the target name with /t or /target switches. It's also possible to specify multiple target names by using a semicolon-separated list of targets for these switches. Here I specify the SimpleLogger target, for example:

msbuild "C:\Chapter 21\customtask.target" /target:simplelogger

Here you can see the output:

```
Microsoft (R) Build Engine Version 3.5.21022.8
[Microsoft .NET Framework, Version 2.0.50727.1433]
Copyright (C) Microsoft Corporation 2007. All rights reserved.

Build started 12/2/2007 8:02:21 AM.
Project "C:\Chapter 21\customtask.target" on node 0 (simplelogger target(s)).
  Inside the task! OptionalAttribute = Keyvan - RequiredAttribute = Nayyeri

Done Building Project "C:\Chapter 21\customtask.target" (simplelogger target(s)).


Build succeeded.
    0 Warning(s)
    0 Error(s)

Time Elapsed 00:00:00.04
```

The last point I'd like to mention here is about passing your parameters to MSBuild via command-line arguments.

To do this, you can pass your properties via the /property or /p switches. These switches get the combination of property key-value pairs with /property:<n>=<v> syntax, where <n> is the name of the property and <v> is the value of it. Here you can pass multiple property key-values via a semicolon-separated list.

For example, the following command passes two properties named author and publisher, with values 2 and Wrox, to my command, respectively.

```
msbuild "C:\Chapter 21\customtask.target" /property:author=Nayyeri;publisher=Wrox
```

Sample MSBuild File

I'll finish this chapter by providing a real-world example of MSBuild. First, I'll write a simple Windows Presentation Foundation (WPF) application with XAML to create a single .xaml file, and then I'll write an MSBuild file to compile this application.

Before talking about the MSBuild side, consider the following simple WPF application, which consists of a single XAML file. This XAML file doesn't have anything except a button (see Listing 21-17). Even if you don't know WPF very well, this WPF application is easy to understand. It will give you the general idea so you won't need to worry about XAML codes.

Listing 21-17: Sample WPF Application

```xml
<Window xmlns="http://schemas.microsoft.com/winfx/2006/xaml/presentation"
    xmlns:x="http://schemas.microsoft.com/winfx/2006/xaml"
    Title="WPF Application" Height="200" Width="250">
  <StackPanel Margin="60">
    <Button Background="LightBlue">
      Click Me!
    </Button>
  </StackPanel>
</Window>
```

I need to write an application definition XAML file as well. This global App.xaml file doesn't contain anything special. It sets the preceding window as the startup object for the application (see Listing 21-18).

Listing 21-18: App.xaml

```xml
<Application xmlns="http://schemas.microsoft.com/winfx/2006/xaml/presentation"
    xmlns:x="http://schemas.microsoft.com/winfx/2006/xaml"
    StartupUri="Window1.xaml">
  <Application.Resources>

  </Application.Resources>
</Application>
```

Now I begin writing my MSBuild file. In the first step, I create the `<PropertyGroup>` element, which holds properties representing information about my application, such as its assembly name, its output type, and its output path (see Listing 21-19).

Listing 21-19: Adding the `PropertyGroup` Element

```xml
<?xml version="1.0" encoding="utf-8"?>
<Project xmlns="http://schemas.microsoft.com/developer/msbuild/2003">
  <PropertyGroup>
    <AssemblyName>WPFApplication</AssemblyName>
    <OutputType>winexe</OutputType>
    <OutputPath>.\</OutputPath>
  </PropertyGroup>
</Project>
```

After this, I add an `<ItemGroup>` element to my file with the references necessary for compilation of my application (see Listing 21-20).

Listing 21-20: Adding References

```xml
<?xml version="1.0" encoding="utf-8"?>
<Project xmlns="http://schemas.microsoft.com/developer/msbuild/2003">
  <PropertyGroup>
    <AssemblyName>WPFApplication</AssemblyName>
    <OutputType>winexe</OutputType>
    <OutputPath>.\</OutputPath>
  </PropertyGroup>

  <ItemGroup>
    <Reference Include="System" />
    <Reference Include="System.Xml" />
    <Reference Include="WindowsBase" />
    <Reference Include="PresentationCore" />
    <Reference Include="PresentationFramework" />
    <Reference Include="UIAutomationProvider" />
    <Reference Include="UIAutomationTypes" />
    <Reference Include="ReachFramework" />
    <Reference Include="System.Printing" />
    <Reference Include="System.Runtime.Serialization" />
    <Reference Include="System.IdentityModel" />
  </ItemGroup>

</Project>
```

The next step is to add another `<ItemGroup>` element for my file items. This `<ItemGroup>` element has an `<ApplicationDefinition>` element for my App.xaml file and a `<Page>` element for my window file (see Listing 21-21).

458

Listing 21-21: Adding File Items

```xml
<?xml version="1.0" encoding="utf-8"?>
<Project xmlns="http://schemas.microsoft.com/developer/msbuild/2003">
  <PropertyGroup>
    <AssemblyName>WPFApplication</AssemblyName>
    <OutputType>winexe</OutputType>
    <OutputPath>.\</OutputPath>
  </PropertyGroup>
  <ItemGroup>
    <Reference Include="System" />
    <Reference Include="System.Xml" />
    <Reference Include="WindowsBase" />
    <Reference Include="PresentationCore" />
    <Reference Include="PresentationFramework" />
    <Reference Include="UIAutomationProvider" />
    <Reference Include="UIAutomationTypes" />
    <Reference Include="ReachFramework" />
    <Reference Include="System.Printing" />
    <Reference Include="System.Runtime.Serialization" />
    <Reference Include="System.IdentityModel" />
  </ItemGroup>

  <ItemGroup>
    <ApplicationDefinition Include="App.xaml" />
    <Page Include="Window1.xaml" />
  </ItemGroup>

</Project>
```

Finally, I add to my file two built-in target files for C# and the .NET Framework 3.0 compilation, with Import elements (see Listing 21-22).

Listing 21-22: Importing Built-in Targets

```xml
<?xml version="1.0" encoding="utf-8"?>
<Project xmlns="http://schemas.microsoft.com/developer/msbuild/2003">
  <PropertyGroup>
    <AssemblyName>WPFApplication</AssemblyName>
    <OutputType>winexe</OutputType>
    <OutputPath>.\</OutputPath>
  </PropertyGroup>
  <ItemGroup>
    <Reference Include="System" />
    <Reference Include="System.Xml" />
    <Reference Include="WindowsBase" />
    <Reference Include="PresentationCore" />
    <Reference Include="PresentationFramework" />
    <Reference Include="UIAutomationProvider" />
    <Reference Include="UIAutomationTypes" />
    <Reference Include="ReachFramework" />
    <Reference Include="System.Printing" />
    <Reference Include="System.Runtime.Serialization" />
```

(continued)

Listing 21-22 *(continued)*

```
    <Reference Include="System.IdentityModel" />
  </ItemGroup>
  <ItemGroup>
    <ApplicationDefinition Include="App.xaml" />
    <Page Include="Window1.xaml" />
  </ItemGroup>

  <Import Project="$(MSBuildBinPath)\Microsoft.CSharp.targets" />
  <Import Project="$(MSBuildBinPath)\Microsoft.WinFX.targets" />

</Project>
```

I save this MSBuild file and name it SampleWPF.target, and then run it with the following command from the command line:

msbuild "C:\Chapter 21\samplewpf.target"

This results in the following output:

```
Microsoft (R) Build Engine Version 3.5.21022.8
[Microsoft .NET Framework, Version 2.0.50727.1433]
Copyright (C) Microsoft Corporation 2007. All rights reserved.

Build started 12/2/2007 8:10:50 AM.
Project "C:\Chapter 21\samplewpf.target" on node 0 (default targets).
  Could not locate the .NET Framework SDK. The task is looking for the path to
  the .NET Framework SDK at the location specified in the SDKInstallRootv2.0 v
  alue of the registry key HKEY_LOCAL_MACHINE\SOFTWARE\Microsoft\.NETFramework.
    You may be able to solve the problem by doing one of the following:  1.) In
  stall the .NET Framework SDK.  2.) Manually set the above registry key to the
  correct location.
PrepareForBuild:
  Creating directory "obj\Debug\".
CopyFilesToOutputDirectory:
  Copying file from "obj\Debug\WPFApplication.exe" to ".\WPFApplication.exe".
  samplewpf -> C:\Chapter 21\WPFApplication.exe
  Copying file from "obj\Debug\WPFApplication.pdb" to ".\WPFApplication.pdb".
Done Building Project "C:\Chapter 21\samplewpf.target" (default targets).


Build succeeded.
    0 Warning(s)
    0 Error(s)

Time Elapsed 00:00:01.66
```

After running this command and getting this result, MSBuild creates a few files and folders for me. One of these files is WPFApplication.exe. Running this executable file, I get the result shown in Figure 21-2.

Figure 21-2: Sample WPF application

As you can see, there is no `<Target>` element in this MSBuild file, but it uses the built-in Build target to create the output.

Summary

This chapter was about MSBuild and custom builds in .NET and Visual Studio. First you read an introduction to MSBuild and its applications, and then explored its anatomy. In the main part of the chapter you learned about different groups of elements in MSBuild. At the end of the chapter, you learned how to use MSBuild files in order to build and package an application.

Of course, MSBuild is a broader topic than what we can cover in one chapter, so it wasn't possible to discuss all of its details here. I tried to provide a general overview of important and common topics, but you can follow this thread with online documentation such as MSDN for further reading.

22

Macros

In Chapter 3, "Quick Tour," you had a short introduction to macros, including a very simple example to get an initial feel for them. As you learned there, macros can be written only with Visual Basic; and as this book focuses on C# as the primary development language, I moved the content for macros to this part of the book. Macros remain a major aspect of Visual Studio extensibility and therefore must be discussed.

As you learned earlier, a macro is the answer to the need for a time-saving solution for repetitive tasks in daily work with computer software. Many Microsoft products support macros, especially those products built based on an IDE with an editor. For example, products such as Office Word, Office Excel, and Visual Studio have excellent built-in support for macros.

The purpose of this chapter is to show you everything you need to know in order to use macros and write your own macros for Microsoft Visual Studio. The chapter covers the following topics:

- ❑ An introduction to macros
- ❑ Anatomy of macros
- ❑ Macros IDE
- ❑ Macro Explorer
- ❑ Different ways to build a macro
- ❑ How to record a macro
- ❑ How to write a macro
- ❑ How to debug a macro
- ❑ How to deploy a macro
- ❑ Simplifying the process of running a macro

After covering these topics, you will have a basic understanding of macros and how to work with Visual Studio macros. This chapter teaches by way of example — walking through the source code of the examples will clearly demonstrate the details of macro development. A good background in Visual Basic syntax is required for understanding this chapter.

Introduction to Macros

Repetitive tasks are a part of our daily life. Life itself can be considered a set of repetitive tasks, set among other tasks that happen occasionally or just once. The same is true for using an application. You know that when you use a program frequently, you have to do some repetitive tasks, often daily. It's unavoidable; we don't use an application unless we need it and it can meet those needs. That involves executing some specific steps, which done every day or every week quickly become repetitive — and tedious.

A professional application is one that's able to automate these repetitive tasks and simplify them to save the user's time. Accomplishing this has been one of the main goals of the software industry from its inception, and that goal hasn't changed.

Repetitive tasks occur in any application we use regularly, but there are more of them when the application is built on an IDE with a text editor that we frequently use. Microsoft has great support for macros as a way to automate these tasks in its products. Even the earliest versions of Microsoft Office products and Microsoft Visual Studio supported macros out of the box; the same is true for current versions and this is likely to continue for newer versions.

One of Microsoft's main goals in creating macros is providing extensibility options for its products. Another goal is to make it possible for ordinary users (i.e., nondevelopers) to simplify their work with these products, without any knowledge of programming. Therefore, you can record a macro and generate the programming code from it to accomplish this goal. However, being able to add more details and build a macro for specific tasks requires programming knowledge. Whether you record a macro or write it yourself, it's still a programming code package that must run on Visual Studio.

Before the .NET technology became available, macros could be written with the Visual Basic for Applications (VBA) programming language, and Microsoft Office products and Microsoft Visual Studio IDE were using this language for their macros. After the .NET Framework came into play, however, Microsoft replaced this language with a .NET version of Visual Basic and shipped a special version of Visual Studio named Visual Studio Tools for Office (VSTO) to support development for Microsoft Office products. However, there isn't much difference between Visual Studio macros and Office macros. Here, we'll just focus on Visual Studio macros.

In Visual Studio, macros have their own IDE, named Macros IDE, which you can use to write your macros. You can also interact with macros from Visual Studio IDE with Macro Explorer without opening the Macros IDE, but your options are limited in comparison with what you have in Macros IDE. Macros IDE and Macro Explorer are covered later in this chapter.

Macros are a part of projects, but these projects are different from other programming projects that you use for .NET development in Visual Studio. Unlike programming projects, macro projects aren't a part of a solution — they are independent of programming projects and solutions. This means that a macro can be run for several programming projects and doesn't depend on a specific project or solution. This enables you to write a macro and run it for multiple projects without any problem.

Macro projects are also independent of the particular type of programming project and can be run for different types. Generally, macro projects should be considered a completely new thing, totally separate from programming projects.

In the next section, you'll learn about the anatomy of a macro from a programming point of view.

The Anatomy of a Macro

This section provides a brief introduction to the anatomy of macros, as this is a key part of our discussion in this chapter. Macros live in macro projects. As mentioned in the previous section, macro projects are different from normal programming projects in Visual Studio. On an upper level, macro projects are a part of a *macro system*. This system can be considered as a container for all macro projects in Visual Studio. Some people consider this macro system to be the single solution for macro projects, and they're right — indeed, this system is very similar to a solution.

Macro projects are independent of each other. A macro project is saved in a single .vsmacros file. This enables the macro to be deployed easily just by moving a single file.

A macro project can have one or more modules. Each module can contain one or more macros, along with other helper variables and methods for your macros. Therefore, a macro project can contain more than one macro, and the same is true for a module file. However, all these modules and macros are stored in a single .vsmacros file for the macro project. A good example of this is the Samples macro project that is part of the default Visual Studio installation; this includes some modules, and each of these modules contains more than one macro.

Listing 22-1 shows the initial code for a module when you add it to a macro project.

Listing 22-1: Initial Code of a Module in a Macro Project

```
Imports System
Imports EnvDTE
Imports EnvDTE80
Imports EnvDTE90
Imports System.Diagnostics

Public Module Module1


End Module
```

The first part of a module is its *references*. Like a normal .NET class, you must add references to anything that you need to use in your code.

The rest of the code for a module is its *body*. Here you can put your variables and methods.

A macro is a Visual Basic subroutine that lives in a module, without any parameters and with public scope. A macro system in Visual Studio looks for all available public subroutines without parameters in a macro project and adds them to its macros list.

Listing 22-2 shows such a macro (named SampleMacro) without any code implementation.

Listing 22-2: Sample Macro Code

```
Imports System
Imports EnvDTE
Imports EnvDTE80
Imports EnvDTE90
Imports System.Diagnostics

Public Module Module1
    Sub SampleMacro()

    End Sub
End Module
```

All variables and methods in a module are available globally in a macro project, unless you change their scope to private. Therefore, you can call a method from another module without using its fully qualified reference. You can have two methods with the same name in two different modules, but when referring to them you must use their fully qualified reference.

Along with modules, you can add classes and codes to a macro project and store them with the project. Like modules, however, these classes will be stored in a .vsmacros file for the macro project. You can use classes and codes as helpers for your modules.

Unlike programming codes, macros aren't compiled to be distributed. They must be deployed with source code, so you need to move the source code of a macro in order to deploy and distribute it. The storage structure of a macro (which uses a single .vsmacros file for everything) comes in handy and makes life easier. Later in this chapter, you'll read more about deploying macros.

Macros IDE

The Macros IDE (shown in Figure 22-1) is the main place for developing macros. This IDE is accessible via Tools ⇨ Macros ⇨ Macros IDE or by pressing Alt+F11.

Figure 22-1: Macros IDE

Macros IDE has same look and feel as Visual Studio IDE, with a similar structure and elements. However, Macros IDE is different from Visual Studio IDE in that it's just for developing macros. Although it differs in this way from Visual Studio IDE, it's a part of Visual Studio and can't be loaded as a stand-alone program. When you try to create a new macro from Visual Studio IDE (via Macro Explorer) or choose a macro to edit, Macros IDE appears to enable you to work on your macro's code.

The Structure of Macros IDE

The structure of Macros IDE is very similar to Visual Studio IDE. In addition to some windows that can be docked to one of the corners, a main editor at the center of the IDE is the main part of Macros IDE, and it is here that you write and edit codes for your macros.

As you saw previously, it's possible to write add-ins for Macros IDE just as you do for Visual Studio IDE. These add-ins can help automate some tasks and simplify coding. In general, Macros IDE should be considered a similar IDE to Visual Studio IDE, with a few differences, but these are still two separate IDEs.

Main Elements of Macros IDE

The default look of Macros IDE is very simple, and some windows aren't enabled. It just has the Project Explorer and Class View windows opened and docked to the left. However, you can enable some other important windows, such as Error List or Task List.

The following sections describe the main elements of Macros IDE so you can become familiar with them.

Project Explorer

As stated previously, Macros IDE doesn't have a Solution Explorer. Instead, it has a Project Explorer, which is very similar to the Solution Explorer (see Figure 22-2).

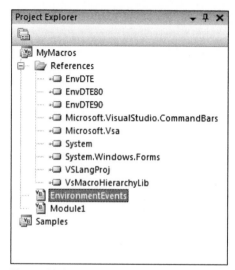

Figure 22-2: The Macros IDE Project Explorer

Project Explorer can hold macro projects and files, and you can use it to manipulate your macros. This Project Explorer in Macros IDE plays the role of Macro Explorer in Visual Studio IDE, and both windows are synchronized. In other words, if you make any change in Project Explorer, that change will take effect in Macro Explorer, and vice versa.

Class View

Class View in the Macros IDE, shown in Figure 22-3, has the same role as Class View in the Visual Studio IDE. This means that you can use this window to view the hierarchy of classes, including their properties and methods, and to view all classes and references available in your macro project.

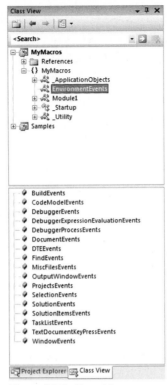

Figure 22-3: Class View window

Error List

The Error List window, shown in Figure 22-4, displays a list of errors for your macro project. Its function is similar to that of the Error List window in the Visual Studio main IDE.

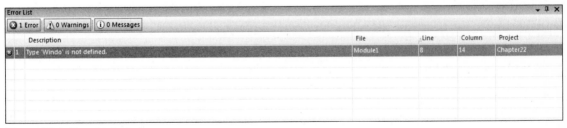

		Description	File	Line	Column	Project
	1	Type 'Windo' is not defined.	Module1	8	14	Chapter22

Figure 22-4: Error List window

This window is helpful because it shows a list of errors, warnings, and messages for your macro project, including all syntax errors made during the writing of the code. This enables you to catch any errors while you're coding.

Macro Explorer

Although Macro Explorer is a Visual Studio window, it's appropriate to cover it in this chapter because of its close relation to macros.

Macro Explorer shows all macro projects and their contents (such as modules and files) in a hierarchy. It's very similar to Project Explorer in Macros IDE, and, as mentioned previously, they're synchronized.

You can right-click on different items in this window to gain access to some common options and tasks for that item. These options are different for each item based on its type. For example, right-clicking on the root Macros item gives you access to three options: loading a macro project, creating a new macro project, and opening Macros IDE (see Figure 22-5).

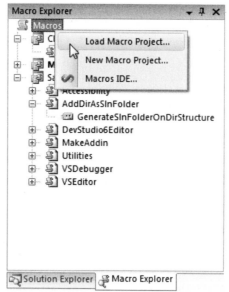

Figure 22-5: Right-click menu for the Macros item in Macro Explorer

Using the Macro Explorer window, you can rename a macro project (see Figure 22-6), add a new module to it, and more. Note that you could add other types of items to a macro project via Project Explorer in Macros IDE, but here you're limited to modules only.

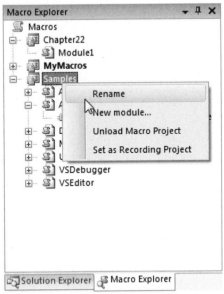

Figure 22-6: Right-click menu for a macro
project in Macro Explorer

In the macros system of Visual Studio, you're not able to remove a macro project. Instead, you can unload it from the system. Doing this excludes the macro project and all its macros from the system but keeps the physical .vsmacros file of the project on disk storage. You can unload a macro project by clicking the Unload Macro Project item in the right-click menu of a macro project. Later, you can load this project by right-clicking on the root Macros item in Macro Explorer and choosing the Load Macro Project item.

The last option for a macro project is to mark it as a recoding project. This is described in the next section. You can also edit, rename, or delete a module, or add new macros to it, in the window shown in Figure 22-7. Double-clicking on a module or choosing an item that needs an editor (such as Edit or New Macro) opens the Macros IDE, where you can edit the module.

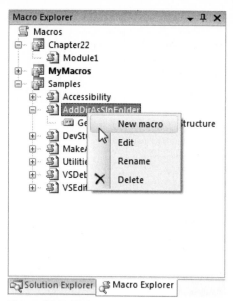

Figure 22-7: Right-click menu for a module in Macro Explorer

If you open a module to see its content and it contains at least one macro, then you can see all the macros for a module as its children items, indicated with a cassette icon. Macro items provide the same options as modules. Double-clicking on a macro runs it. This can also be accomplished by right-clicking on the macro and choosing the Run item (see Figure 22-8).

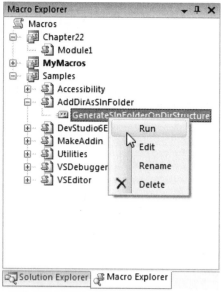

Figure 22-8: Right-click menu for a macro in Macro Explorer

Running and Stopping a Macro

After building a macro (described in the next section), you'll obviously want to run it. There are various options to do this. Two options were described in the last section. Here, I'll now add some others to give you more options based on your situation:

❑   Double-click on the name of the macro in Macro Explorer.

❑   Right-click on the name of the macro in Macro Explorer and choose Run.

❑   Choose Tools ➪ Macros ➪ Run Macro when the macro item is selected in Macro Explorer.

❑   Open the source code of the macro module in Macros IDE and move the cursor to the name of the definition of the macro. Then click the Play button in the toolbar or press F5 to start the macro, or do same via the Debug ➪ Start item in the Macros IDE menu.

❑   Run the macro from the command prompt.

❑   Assign Toolbar items, menus, or shortcut keys to macros and use them to run the macro.

The rest of the discussion in this section requires a long-running macro in order to show some items in the user interface. Therefore, I've written a simple macro, shown in Listing 22-3, and named it LongRunningMacro.

Listing 22-3: A Long-running Macro

```
Imports System
Imports EnvDTE
Imports EnvDTE80
Imports EnvDTE90
Imports System.Diagnostics

Public Module LongRunningModule
    Sub LongRunningMacro()
        System.Threading.Thread.Sleep(5000)
    End Sub
End Module
```

This code simply calls the `System.Threading.Thread.Sleep(5000)` class to keep the thread running for five seconds. This enables us to monitor it for this period.

When run, a macro performs all the repetitive tasks that are defined for it step by step if there is no error in the macro project containing the macro. While the macro is running, two icons will appear in the Visual Studio IDE and Windows taskbar, and both are the same (a rotating cassette icon). The icon that appears in Visual Studio IDE is shown in Figure 22-9, and the icon that appears in the Windows taskbar is shown in Figure 22-10. To see these icons, run the macro in Listing 22-3.

Figure 22-9: Macro icon in Visual Studio IDE

Figure 22-10: Macro icon in the Windows taskbar

Both icons specify that a macro is running in Visual Studio IDE. They disappear whenever the macro stops running.

In order to stop a macro from running (for which there may be several reasons, such as its having an infinite runtime), you can right-click on the macro icon in the Windows taskbar and choose the only item there: Stop Visual Studio macros. You can see this in Figure 22-11.

Figure 22-11: Stopping a macro

Note that if you have multiple macros running in Visual Studio, this stops all of them.

Building a Macro

Now that you've learned some basics about the Visual Studio macro system, it's time to jump into the main topic of this chapter and talk about building macros — which should be the main goal of everyone reading this.

There are two general ways to build a macro:

❑　Record a macro with the Visual Studio macro recorder tool

❑　Write a macro with programming codes

The first option is easier to use and is a quick way to build a macro. Even better, it doesn't require any programming knowledge. You start recording and do all the repetitive steps in the IDE; the macro recorder converts what you do with the mouse and keyboard into programming code.

In fact, the result of this first option is similar to the second one, which is simply writing programming code with Visual Basic language to build a macro. This isn't as easy and quick as the first option, but with this method you have access to many more tools to build more enhanced macros.

The following sections provide a detailed discussion about both options for building a macro.

Recording a Macro

The idea of recording a macro is very simple. Recall that the main goal of creating a macro is to automate a repetitive task. Therefore, a macro can be built just by recording these tasks and playing them again.

This is in theory, but in fact you have to create a mechanism to record these tasks. Fortunately, this is done for you by Microsoft, and you can easily use a macro recorder for your task. This recorder is easy to use — you simply start recording a macro, follow all the steps to accomplish your repetitive task, and then stop the recorder. Between the start and stop actions, you can choose different menus, click on items, and enter keyboard inputs. The macro recorder converts whatever you do to Visual Basic codes to build a macro. After this, you can save the macro with your desired name and run it as many times as you like.

As nice as this sounds, and even though the macro recorder is a great tool and can record many common and simple macros, it can't build enhanced macros that need to interact with specific APIs of the system. For that, writing a professional macro needs development with programming codes.

To summarize, these are some benefits of the macro recorder:

❑   You can build a macro quickly.

❑   Non-developer users can build macros without having knowledge in .NET and programming (although almost all Visual Studio users are developers).

❑   You can use the macro recorder as a starting point for writing your macros. In other words, you can use the recorder to record some parts of your macros automatically and generate the codes. This saves you the time and effort involved in writing all the codes manually.

In the next subsection, you'll learn how to use the macro recorder to build your own macros.

Selecting the Recording Project

The macro recorder needs to recognize a macro project as the recording project in order to store all generated codes for the macro in a module for the project. This is a single project among all the macro projects available in the Visual Studio macro system. By right-clicking on a macro project in Macro Explorer and selecting Set as Recording Project, you can make this choice.

By default, the macro recorder stores all codes for a macro in a module named RecordingModule in the recording project. The name of the recorded macro will be TemporaryMacro.

The default recording macro project in Visual Studio is MyMacros project, which is created by Visual Studio for you.

Recording the Macro

The macro recorder begins recording a macro as soon as you start it. You can do this either by choosing the Tools ⇨ Macros ⇨ Record TemporaryMacro item or pressing Ctrl+Shift+R.

After starting the macro, a new toolbar appears in Visual Studio IDE, as shown in Figure 22-12. This toolbar isn't a part of the default Visual Studio toolbars and only appears when you are recording a macro. You can use it just as you use normal toolbars, but note that these changes won't be saved as a part of the recording macro.

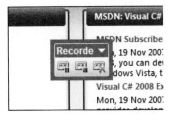

Figure 22-12: Recorder toolbar

The recorder toolbar has three buttons:

- **Pause Recording/Resume Recording:** This button pauses the recording process and resumes it afterward.

- **Stop Recording:** This button stops the recording process and saves all the necessary data in the TemporaryMacro code.

- **Cancel Recording:** This button cancels the recording process and doesn't store any data for your macro.

The macro recorder saves everything you do in Visual Studio IDE. This "everything" includes such tasks and operations as the following:

- Clicking on toolbar items

- Clicking on menu items

- Pressing keyboard keys

- Choosing the OK option for any dialog box that may appear when you open a menu or toolbar item

Visual Studio generates appropriate codes for any operation that you perform and stores these codes in the TemporaryMacro macro.

Let's look at an example and record a macro to see how it works.

First, I create a new macro project and name it MacroRecorderSample. Next, I set this project as the recording project and start the macro recorder.

In this macro I perform the following actions and then stop my macro to store it. Here I want to automate a task I always do with my code — that is, formatting my source code and saving everything after that. This time, I simplify this task for add-in class files:

1. Open a Visual Studio add-in project.

2. Open the Connect.cs file.

3. Choose the Edit ⇨ Advanced ⇨ Format Document item from the menu.

4. Click the Save All button on the toolbar.

If I open the TemporaryMacro code to see what is added there, it should resemble what is shown in Listing 22-4.

Listing 22-4: Generated Code for TemporaryMacro After Recording

```
Option Strict Off
Option Explicit Off
Imports System
Imports EnvDTE
Imports EnvDTE80
Imports EnvDTE90
```

```
Imports System.Diagnostics

Public Module RecordingModule
    Sub TemporaryMacro()
        DTE.Windows.Item("Connect.cs").Activate()
        DTE.ExecuteCommand("Edit.FormatDocument")
        DTE.ExecuteCommand("File.SaveAll")
    End Sub
End Module
```

As you see, this code contains the steps corresponding to the actions I performed while recording the macro. Note that this isn't a rule, and you shouldn't expect Visual Studio to always generate one line of code for each step, but generally it does generate a line of code for each operation you perform.

In the first line of code it loads the Connect.cs file. In the second line it runs the Format Document command. At the end, it saves everything.

You can see the results in Figure 22-13 (before running the macro) and Figure 22-14 (after running the macro).

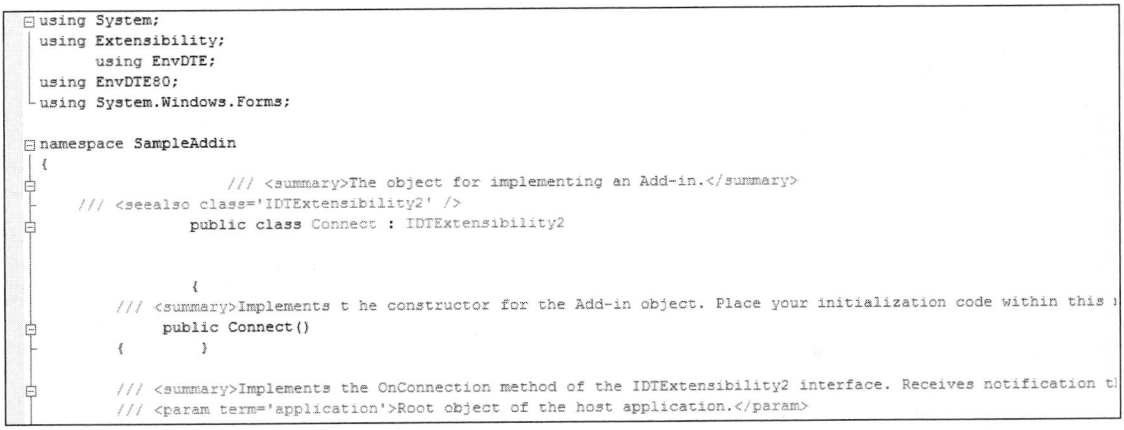

Figure 22-13: Connect.cs before running the macro

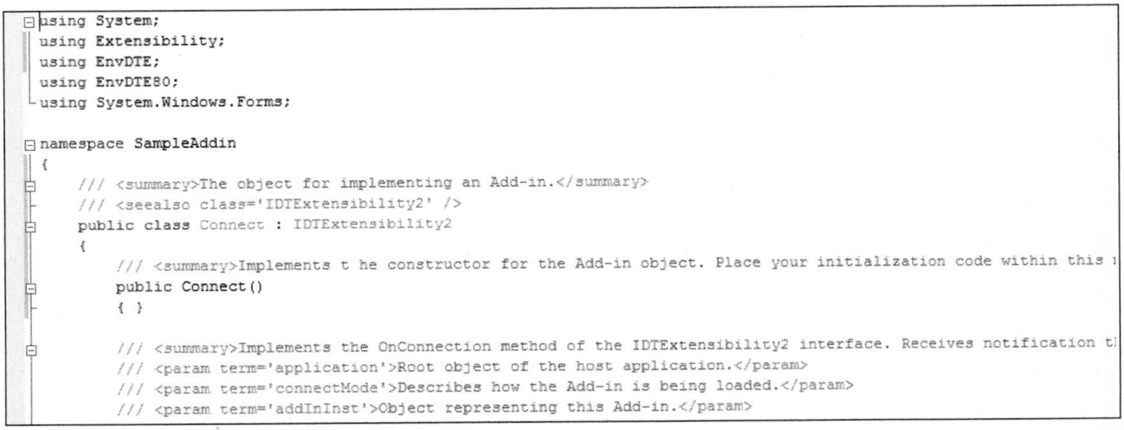

Figure 22-14: Connect.cs after running the macro

After Recording

After recording your macros, you have auto-generated code for them. As mentioned before, usually you want to extend this auto-generated code for your needs. After recording, you can modify existing code according to those needs.

For example, suppose that you want to modify the preceding macro to format the latest open document, rather than have the Connect.cs file with a more general macro. In addition, suppose that you want to build the whole solution at the end (after saving all changes). You will end up with the code that's presented in Listing 22-5.

Listing 22-5: Modified Version of the Recorded Macro

```
Option Strict Off
Option Explicit Off
Imports System
Imports EnvDTE
Imports EnvDTE80
Imports EnvDTE90
Imports System.Diagnostics

Public Module RecordingModule
    Sub TemporaryMacro()
        DTE.ExecuteCommand("Edit.FormatDocument")
        DTE.ExecuteCommand("File.SaveAll")
        DTE.ExecuteCommand("Build.BuildSolution")
    End Sub
End Module
```

This modified code removed the first step in Listing 22-4 to avoid activating a specific Connect.cs file, and then added a new line of code at the end to perform a build action on the solution regardless of the name of the solution.

Now if I run this macro, it formats the source code of the latest opened document, saves all changes, and performs a build action on the solution.

This is a common scenario and demonstrates a good technique for saving time and resources in coding macros from the base. In general, you can record macros for specific file, project, or solution names and items, and then remove any lines that call these specific names in order to have a generic macro.

The other common task after recording a macro and probably modifying the source code is renaming the macro and moving it to a new location. You want to have your macros under a meaningful project, module, and macro name. You can choose one of the macro projects as the recording project to store your macro, but Visual Studio chooses the module name (RecordingModule) and macro name (TemporaryMacro) for you. You can rename your macro to something else by right-clicking on the name of the macro and choosing the Rename option. It's also possible to rename a module in the same way. In both cases Visual Studio renames the module and macro name and all the names in the source code automatically.

For this example, I renamed the macro to SampleMacro, and the module to MacroRecorderModule. Always try to choose meaningful and related names for your macros and modules, because after moving a module to other machines and releasing it for other users, they need to know what each macro does, and these names can help indicate that.

Developing a Macro

The main topic of this chapter is macro development, or writing a macro with programming codes, and there is only one programming language that you can use for this: Microsoft Visual Basic. Macro development is the most common way to build macros because you get the benefit of everything provided for macro development, including rich APIs and the referencing of other components.

The following sections describe what you need to know about macro development and some related topics.

Getting Started

Earlier in this chapter, you saw the default code for a module that Visual Studio generates for you. For easy reference, it's presented here again in Listing 22-6.

Listing 22-6: Default Code for a Module

```
Imports System
Imports EnvDTE
Imports EnvDTE80
Imports EnvDTE90
Imports System.Diagnostics

Public Module Module1


End Module
```

This is the starting place from which you can develop a macro. First, let's take a quick look at this generated code. This code consists of two parts: *header references* and the *module body*. The module body is where you add your codes, but references are familiar to every .NET developer. Default references are to the System namespace as well as to Document Tools Extensibility (DTE) APIs for different versions of Visual Studio. DTE is described in more detail in Chapter 4. The final reference is to the System. Diagnostics namespace for checking the diagnostics of your macros and some other purposes.

As is obvious from these namespaces, you have access to default .NET types and classes along with DTE classes in your code. Usually these classes make up the main part of your code, but sometimes you need to add references to other namespaces and components. In such cases, all you need to do is add appropriate references to these namespaces or components in your modules, and probably in your macro projects. After that, you can use these references in your code. I don't go into the details of doing this here, because knowing these principles is a prerequisite for reading this book.

As described previously, writing a module is as simple as adding a new public subroutine, with no parameters, to a module. In this subroutine you can implement your logic and perform different tasks with DTE APIs. However, in order to have structured code and develop your macros, you normally have to use other methods and your own classes to split the code implementation into logical parts. This is a topic beyond the scope of this book, but all developers know these software development principles. When you put calls to other methods in your code and create new object instances of classes to use them, the process of running your macro moves to new locations and runs your code from other places.

When coding a macro, you can get the benefits of Visual Studio IntelliSense for your macros in Visual Studio Macros IDE and its editor (see Figure 22-15). Over the years, I (and many developers like me) have found this helpful for coding.

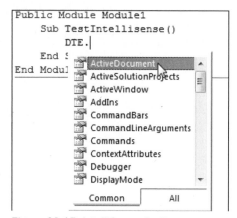

Figure 22-15: IntelliSense for the macro editor

Here's a sample macro to demonstrate how a macro is developed. This macro is built to save the current open document if its changes aren't saved already.

First, take a look at the code implementation of this macro in Listing 22-7.

Listing 22-7: Code Implementation of the SaveDocument Macro

```
Imports System
Imports EnvDTE
Imports EnvDTE80
Imports EnvDTE90
Imports System.Diagnostics

Public Module GettingStarted
    Sub SaveDocument()
        If (Not DTE.ActiveDocument.Saved) Then
            SaveAndCheck()
```

```
            End If
        End Sub

        Private Sub SaveAndCheck()
            If (DTE.ActiveDocument.Save() = vsSaveStatus.vsSaveCancelled) Then
                System.Windows.Forms.MessageBox.Show("Couldn't save the document")
            End If
        End Sub
    End Module
```

As you can see, the SaveDocument macro checks whether the current active document is saved or not. If it's not saved, then the macro calls the private SaveAndCheck method, where it saves changes and shows a MessageBox if the save has failed.

If you run this macro (it's provided in the code downloads for this chapter) when a document such as a text file is open and has unsaved changes, then it saves the changes for you. This is shown in Figures 22-16 and 22-17. Even though you can't see the full effect because the screen shots are black and white, notice the difference in contrast of the vertical line at the left of the text on each screen.

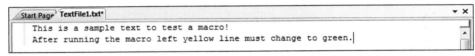

Figure 22-16: Text document before running the macro

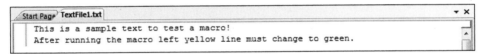

Figure 22-17: Text document after running the macro

Dealing with the User Interface

The preceding material about macros didn't use any user interface elements, but it's possible to display user interface elements such as Windows forms or input boxes to end users via a macro.

In windows forms, you can use a designer and Toolbox items to design your user interface, but for macros you need to build everything on-the-fly, using programming codes. Here are some examples to give you the idea.

The first common case occurs when you need to get input values from the user when running a macro. An InputBox is a good choice to do this. Listing 22-8 shows an example of displaying an InputBox to get user inputs, and a MessageBox to display errors and notifications.

Listing 22-8: Using an InputBox to Get User Inputs

```
Sub InputBoxSample()
    Dim input As String = InputBox("Enter something here:", "InputBox Sample")
    System.Windows.Forms.MessageBox.Show(String.Format("You entered: '{0}'",
input), _
                                        "Result",
System.Windows.Forms.MessageBoxButtons.OK, _
System.Windows.Forms.MessageBoxIcon.Information)
End Sub
```

Figures 22-18 and 22-19 show the result of running this macro.

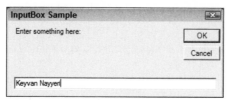

Figure 22-18: InputBox to get input from users

Figure 22-19: MessageBox to display errors and notifications to users

The other common case is when you want to show a WinForm to a user. For that you need to build your form and change its appearance on-the-fly, and then show it to the user. An example of this is shown in Listing 22-9, and you can see its output in Figures 22-20 and 22-21.

Listing 22-9: Displaying a Windows Form to Users

```
Sub WinFormSample()
    Dim form As New System.Windows.Forms.Form
    form.Width = 300
    form.Height = 200
    form.Text = "WinForm Sample"
    form.Name = "frmMain"

    Dim button As New System.Windows.Forms.Button
```

```
        button.Name = "btnSample"
        button.Width = 100
        button.Height = 25
        button.Left = 90
        button.Top = 70
        button.Text = "Click Me!"
        AddHandler button.Click, AddressOf button_Clicked

        form.Controls.Add(button)
        form.ShowDialog()
End Sub

Sub button_Clicked(ByVal sender As Object, ByVal e As EventArgs)
        System.Windows.Forms.MessageBox.Show("You clicked on a button!")
End Sub
```

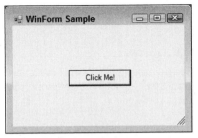

**Figure 22-20: Showing a Windows
Form to users**

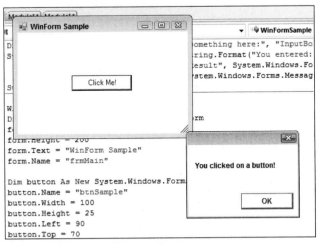

Figure 22-21: Result MessageBox

The preceding code first creates a form and a button and sets their appearance properties. It then adds an event handler for button-click events, and finally adds this button to the form and displays it.

In the same way, you can also show dialog boxes to end users by writing programming codes and showing them on-the-fly.

System Events

All the macros you've seen until this point were ones that you can run manually. Sometimes, however, you'll be interested in running a macro automatically when an event occurs in the IDE. For example, suppose that you want to notify the user when the build progress of a project is complete.

For cases such as these, you can write macros to respond to system events. Some built-in events are defined in the Visual Studio macros system, and you can write your own events as well.

Built-in system events are grouped into 23 categories, as described in Table 22-1.

Table 22-1: System Events Categories

Category	Description
BuildEvents	Events for solution builds
CodeModelEvents	Events for the code model
CommandBarEvents	Events when the CommandBarControl is clicked
CommandEvents	Events for a specified command
DebuggerEvents	Events for the debugger
DebuggerExpressionEvaluationEvents	Events for when the debugger starts or stops the evaluation of expressions
DebuggerProcessEvents	Events for when a debugger process starts or stops
DocumentEvents	Events for the document
DTEEvents	Events for the DTE
FindEvents	Events for the find operation
MiscFilesEvents	Gets a ProjectItemsEvents object for the solution
OutputWindowEvents	Events for the output window
ProjectItemsEvents	Events for all project items in a solution
ProjectsEvents	Gets an event object for all projects in the solution
PublishEvents	Events for publishing
SelectionEvents	Events for selection operations
SolutionEvents	Events for the solution

Category	Description
SolutionItemsEvents	Gets a ProjectItemsEvents object for the solution
TaskListEvents	Events for the task list
TextDocumentKeyPressEvents	Gets an object for key-press events in the text editor
TextEditorEvents	Events for the text editor
WindowEvents	Events for the window
WindowVisibilityEvents	Events for when a tool window is showing or hiding

To implement a macro for a specific event, you need to open the macro project in Macros IDE and open the EnvironmentEvents module for the project. This module contains some auto-generated codes that you often don't need to worry about, but you can add system events to this module and implement your code logic for them.

If you open this module in Macros IDE, you can see two combo boxes at the top of the code editor. The left one contains a list of system-event categories. When you choose an event category, the right combo box shows all the available events for that event category. If you choose an event, then VS adds a code template for that event to the module, along with some appropriate parameters for that event type, and you can implement your code there. For example, I chose BuildEvents from the left list and OnBuildDone from the right list to show a MessageBox when the build is done (see Figure 22-22).

Figure 22-22: Choosing event category and event type.

After choosing this event type, VS generates code like what is shown in Listing 22-10.

Listing 22-10: Auto-generated Code for the Event

```
Private Sub BuildEvents_OnBuildDone(ByVal Scope As EnvDTE.vsBuildScope, ByVal
Action As EnvDTE.vsBuildAction) _
Handles BuildEvents.OnBuildDone

End Sub
```

Now I add a single line of code to this event handler to implement my logic (see Listing 22-11).

Listing 22-11: Adding Code Implementation to the Event Handler

```
Private Sub BuildEvents_OnBuildDone(ByVal Scope As EnvDTE.vsBuildScope, ByVal
Action As EnvDTE.vsBuildAction) _
Handles BuildEvents.OnBuildDone

    System.Windows.Forms.MessageBox.Show("Build Done!", "Build", _
                            System.Windows.Forms.MessageBoxButtons.OK,_

System.Windows.Forms.MessageBoxIcon.Information)

End Sub
```

After this, I get a MessageBox that notifies me whenever I build my projects or solutions in Visual Studio (see Figure 22-23).

Figure 22-23: Notification
after the build is done

Using a Macro Code in Other Macro Projects

Obviously, you sometimes need to use a code you have written for a macro in other macro projects. For example, you may need to use a subroutine or function in other macro projects. In this case, writing anything from the base doesn't seem like a good idea, so you look for an approach to import your code from the original macro project.

Generally, there are two ways to export and import the source code of a module:

❑ Export the module to a file, and then import this file to the other project.

❑ Copy the module to a Visual Basic class library project (or any other project type) in the main IDE and compile it into an assembly, and then reference this assembly in other macro projects.

Here I describe the first approach; the second is easy to do if you have a good knowledge of .NET.

To export a module:

1. Right-click on the name of the module in Project Explorer in Macros IDE.

2.   Choose the export option for your module. It's the name of your module following "Export" text.

3.   In the dialog, specify a path for your module and save it.

To import a module:

1.   Right-click on the name of the project in Project Explorer in Macros IDE.

2.   Choose the Add ⇨ Add Existing Item option.

3.   Find your module and add it to the project.

Debugging a Macro

Debugging is a constant of software development. It's also a very broad topic, and discussing it in depth is beyond the scope of this book. However, this section describes some common techniques for debugging macro codes in Visual Studio.

There are two ways to start a macro in Macros IDE when you're developing it. The first way was mentioned earlier: choose Debug ⇨ Start from the menu or press F5 on the keyboard. This will run a macro in debug mode, but there is an alternative for this that doesn't use the debugging mode to start the macro. While this isn't helpful for debugging, you can do it by choosing Debug ⇨ Start Without Debugging from the menu or pressing Ctrl+F5 on the keyboard. For debugging purposes, you should avoid the latter option and start a macro with debugging (see Figure 22-24).

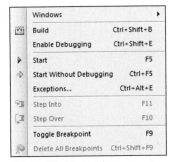

Figure 22-24: Debug menu in Macros IDE

Macros IDE provides the same debugging tools as the main Visual Studio IDE, such as the Breakpoint window and the Immediate window. The debugging techniques are similar, and I simply point to them.

You can enable debugging by choosing Debug ⇨ Enable Debugging or pressing Ctrl+Shift+E, or disable it by choosing Debug ⇨ Disable Debugging or pressing Ctrl+Shift+D. This shows or hides the Watch window at the bottom of Macros IDE, which enables you to monitor the values of variables. It also runs the macro with the debugger.

Note that running a macro in debugging mode doesn't allow you to stop it by right-clicking on the macro icon in the Windows taskbar. If you do so, nothing happens and the macro keeps running.

You can put breakpoints in your code in the same way that you put them in other code. For those readers who may not know them, here are three ways to add a breakpoint for a line of code:

❑ Press F9 when the cursor is moved to a specific line of code.

❑ Right-click everywhere on the line and choose Breakpoint ⇨ Insert Breakpoint.

❑ Click on the left column of the editor for each line.

After putting in a breakpoint for a line, a red bullet appears in the left column of the code editor. You can remove the breakpoint by following the preceding instructions.

When the macro runs and reaches the breakpoint, it pauses there; and you can use visualizers and the Watch window to monitor the values of variables and test the progress of your code.

In addition to these debugging options, you also have access to the other debugging options that were available in the main Visual Studio IDE when you reach a breakpoint such as stepping into a method, stepping over a method, or stepping out of a method.

While writing macros, you usually deal with some common objects and classes such as DTE. As some of these objects are COM components, you can't monitor them with visualizers or watch a window. If you do so (for example, by pressing Shift+F9 after selecting DTE to watch it), nothing will be displayed for you.

As an example, I've written the macro in Listing 22-12 in order to debug it. In this example, I resize the main Visual Studio IDE to half its current size if its width and height are larger than 800; otherwise, a MessageBox appears.

Listing 22-12: Sample Macro for Debugging

```
Imports System
Imports EnvDTE
Imports EnvDTE80
Imports EnvDTE90
Imports System.Diagnostics

Public Module DebuggingModule
    Sub TestDebugging()
        Dim mainWidth As Integer = DTE.MainWindow.Width
        Dim mainHeight As Integer = DTE.MainWindow.Height

        Try
            Resize(mainWidth, mainHeight)
        Catch ex As Exception
            System.Windows.Forms.MessageBox.Show("Width and height must be larger
than 800.")
```

```
          End Try

      End Sub

      Private Sub Resize(ByVal width As Integer, ByVal height As Integer)
          If (width < 800) Or (height < 800) Then
              Throw New ArgumentException("Width and height must be larger than
800.")
          End If

          DTE.MainWindow.Width = width / 2
          DTE.MainWindow.Height = height / 2
      End Sub
  End Module
```

In this code, I check for width and height in a subroutine and throw an `ArgumentException` under some conditions, handling it with a `Try..Catch` block in the macro routine. In the `Catch` block, I call a method. Suppose that I want to test whether my code moves to the `Catch` block to show the MessageBox. In other words, I want to test whether an exception occurs in this code.

To do this, I put a breakpoint in the `Catch` section of my `Try..Catch` block (see Figure 22-25), and then run my macro in debugging mode when the main IDE is resized to something smaller than 800 × 800.

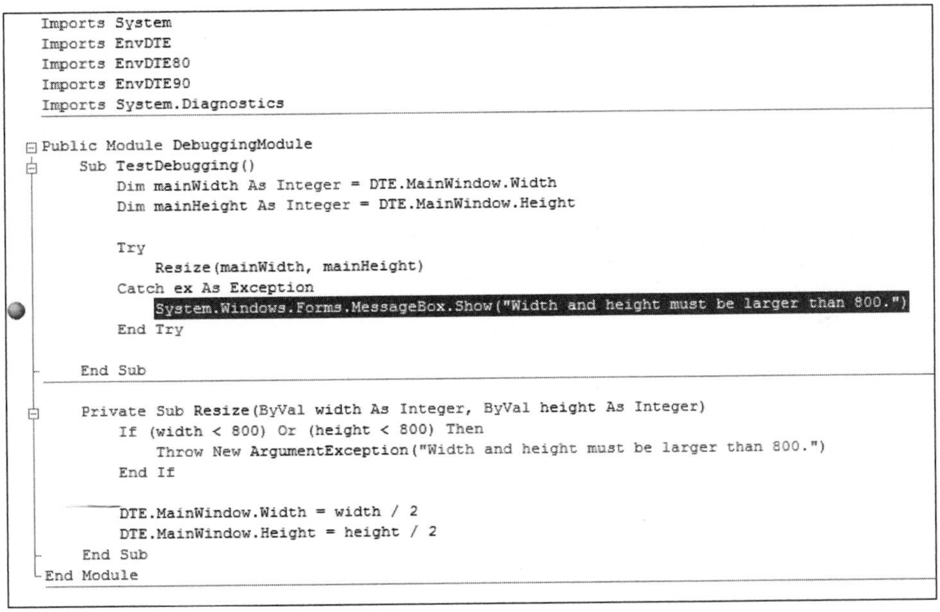

```
Imports System
Imports EnvDTE
Imports EnvDTE80
Imports EnvDTE90
Imports System.Diagnostics

Public Module DebuggingModule
    Sub TestDebugging()
        Dim mainWidth As Integer = DTE.MainWindow.Width
        Dim mainHeight As Integer = DTE.MainWindow.Height

        Try
            Resize(mainWidth, mainHeight)
        Catch ex As Exception
            System.Windows.Forms.MessageBox.Show("Width and height must be larger than 800.")
        End Try

    End Sub

    Private Sub Resize(ByVal width As Integer, ByVal height As Integer)
        If (width < 800) Or (height < 800) Then
            Throw New ArgumentException("Width and height must be larger than 800.")
        End If

        DTE.MainWindow.Width = width / 2
        DTE.MainWindow.Height = height / 2
    End Sub
End Module
```

Figure 22-25: Putting a breakpoint in macro code

After running this code in debug mode and reaching the breakpoint, the code stops. At this point I can see that the code in my `Catch` block is running and can make sure that an exception has occurred in my code. If I move my mouse over the name of the `mainWidth` variable to determine its value, as shown in Figure 22-26, I can see that it has the 219 value that causes this exception.

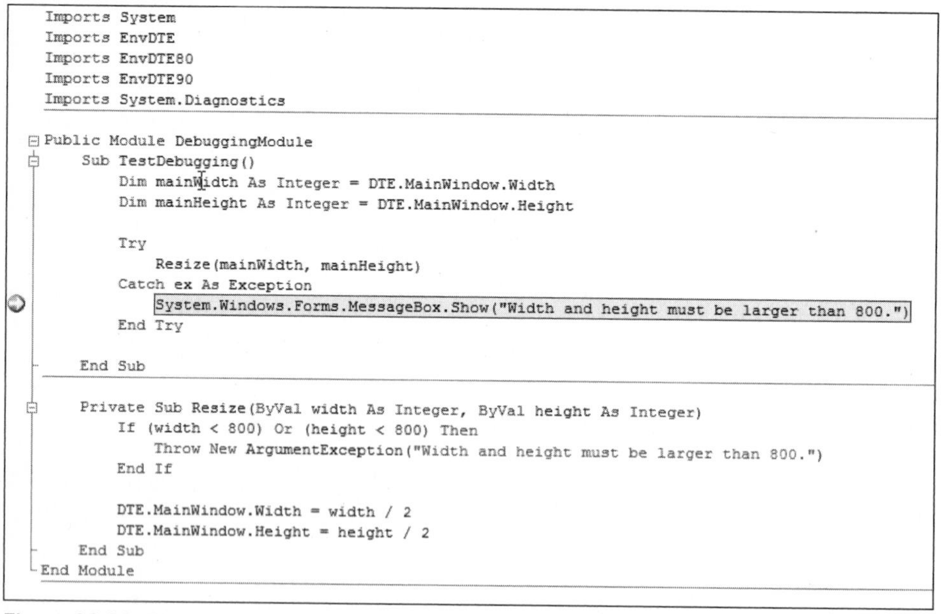

```
Imports System
Imports EnvDTE
Imports EnvDTE80
Imports EnvDTE90
Imports System.Diagnostics

Public Module DebuggingModule
    Sub TestDebugging()
        Dim mainWidth As Integer = DTE.MainWindow.Width
        Dim mainHeight As Integer = DTE.MainWindow.Height

        Try
            Resize(mainWidth, mainHeight)
        Catch ex As Exception
            System.Windows.Forms.MessageBox.Show("Width and height must be larger than 800.")
        End Try

    End Sub

    Private Sub Resize(ByVal width As Integer, ByVal height As Integer)
        If (width < 800) Or (height < 800) Then
            Throw New ArgumentException("Width and height must be larger than 800.")
        End If

        DTE.MainWindow.Width = width / 2
        DTE.MainWindow.Height = height / 2
    End Sub
End Module
```

Figure 22-26: Diagnosing the macro in debugging mode with a breakpoint and a visualizer

Deploying a Macro

Suppose that you have written an excellent macro that runs without any errors or exceptions. This macro is only helpful to you unless you can deploy and release it to let others use your work.

Unlike other types of applications that you can build with Visual Studio and build installers (and then compile into DLL files), macros are code packages that you can move. This is a negative point for macros because it doesn't enable you to build normal installers and deploy them like other software. However, thanks to the structure of macro-files storage, deployment gets easier.

As you read earlier, everything for a macro project is stored in a single .vsmacros file. You can move this single file to other machines in order to deploy a macro. By default, Visual Studio uses a specific path to store all macros. You can go there to find your macro file and copy it to other machines.

To find or change this path, choose Tools ⇨ Options, and then Projects and Solutions ⇨ General from the opened window. Now you can see or change the path of the "Visual Studio projects location" (see Figure 22-27). All macros are stored in different folders in a folder named VSMacros80 in this path.

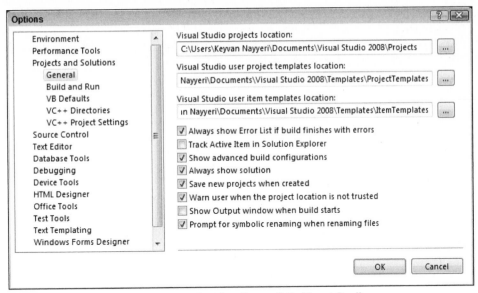

Figure 22-27: You can change the project location path in Visual Studio.

In the opposite direction, if you want to load a macro project from a .vsmacros file to the Visual Studio macros system, right-click on the Macros item in the root of Macro Explorer in VS IDE and choose the Load Macro Project item. Then select the file to load its macro project.

You have to follow the same steps in order to use source code downloads for this chapter.

As an alternative option for easier deployment of your macros, you can use the Visual Studio Content Installer, which automatically deploys your macros to appropriate paths. The Visual Studio Content Installer is covered in Chapter 13, "Deploying Add-Ins," in detail. For now, just be aware that you need to be careful about the values of the `<FileContentType>` and `<FileName>` elements in your VSContent file, making sure they're set to appropriate values for macro deployment and your macro's filename.

Some Points About Macros

The following points about macros and the macro recorder are worth knowing for everyone:

❑   If a macro project can't build without errors, then a macro inside that project can't run even if it doesn't have any errors. You might think that a macro code would be independent of its project and run anyway. For example, in ASP.NET web applications, you can run and view a page that has no errors even if other pages do. Here, however, a macro project and everything inside it must be error-free in order to run.

❑   When working from Macro Explorer, Visual Studio considers the latest opened window as the window that was active before running the macro. This prevents it from considering the Macro Explorer itself as the latest active window. Keep this in mind when writing and running macros.

Run Macros Easier

In the previous section, you learned some ways to run macros, but you would probably agree that not all these ways are desirable, especially when it comes to deploying and moving macros from one machine to another. All of these methods were dependent on Macro Explorer or Macros IDE, and this limits users, as these must be opened to run a macro and this is time-consuming.

This section describes how you can provide some tools to simplify the running process for macros by adding new menu items and toolbar buttons or by assigning shortcut keys to macros.

Adding Toolbar Buttons and Menu Items

The first options are adding new menus or menu items and adding new toolbars or toolbar items for your macros. This can help you run some common macros quickly and easily. For example, you can add a new menu and name it Macros, and then add your macros as items to this menu and run them whenever you like. Or you can create a new toolbar and add your macros as its items.

In both cases, you first need to choose Tools ⇨ Customize from the main Visual Studio IDE menu, which brings up the window shown in Figure 22-28.

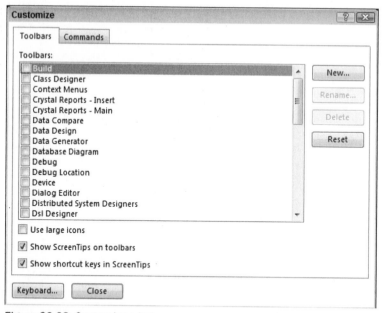

Figure 22-28: Customize window

This window has two tabs: Toolbars and Commands. Using some options provided in these two tabs, you can add new toolbars to VS IDE as well as new menu items based on different categories.

The Toolbars tab is where you can add, rename, or delete toolbars. You can add new toolbars by clicking the New button and entering the name of the toolbar. This adds a new toolbar to the center of the IDE with the name you select and without any button. This is a floating toolbar by default, but you can dock it to corners or fix it. In Figure 22-29, I've added a new toolbar and named it Macros for my example. To add buttons to a toolbar, you need to use the Commands tab, which is described next.

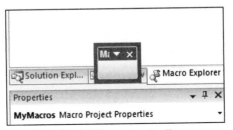

Figure 22-29: Adding a new toolbar

The second tab in the Customize window is Commands, as shown in Figure 22-30. You can use this tab to add new commands to Visual Studio IDE as menus, menu items, or toolbar items.

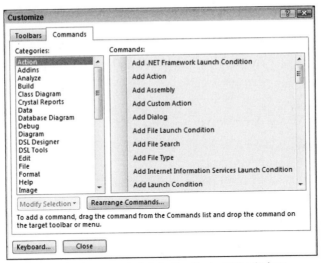

Figure 22-30: Commands tab in the Customize window

This tab is divided into two panes: Categories and Commands. Commands are grouped into categories, and you can choose the appropriate categories in the left pane to see their commands in the right pane.

You can drag and drop items from the Commands pane into VS menus to add them as new menu items, or to toolbars to add them as new toolbar items. A Macros category is available in the Categories pane.

When you choose this category, all macros available in the Visual Studio macros system will be shown in the Commands pane. You can drag and drop macros from here to anywhere you like. In Figure 22-31, I've dragged and dropped two macros that I wrote for this chapter to my newly created Macros toolbar.

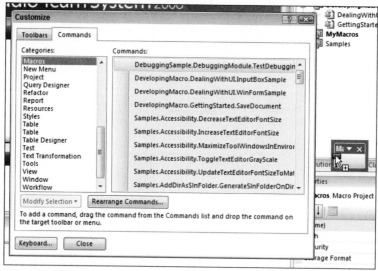

Figure 22-31: Adding macros to a toolbar

Note that you can also drag and drop items to menus, rather than toolbars, to use them as new menus or menu items.

After moving items to a toolbar or menu, you can right-click on them to perform various tasks, such as reset, delete, rename, and choose button image (see Figure 22-32).

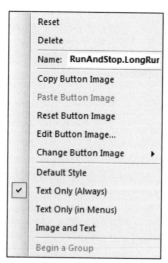

Figure 22-32: After moving an item

Finally, I rename my buttons in the toolbar to meaningful names and then move the toolbar somewhere suitable. (The toolbar is shown in Figure 22-33).

Long Running Test Debugging

Figure 22-33: Macros toolbar

Assigning Shortcut Keys

The other way to simplify the process of running a macro is to assign a shortcut to that macro in order to run it easily by pressing a key.

To assign a shortcut key to a macro, first choose Tools ⇨ Options from the main IDE menu. In the left tree, choose Environment, and then Keyboard from the list of options (see Figure 22-34).

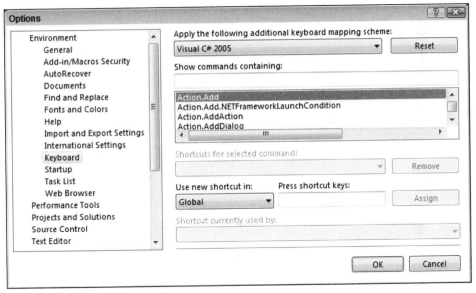

Figure 22-34: Keyboard options

In the right pane is a list of available commands for assigning a shortcut. You can either choose the name of your macro or type the "macros" text in the textbox above it to quickly access the available macros in Visual Studio (do not press Enter after typing the text and just wait until it lists all the macros).

After choosing your macro, you can click on the textbox under the Press Shortcut Keys label and then press your shortcut keys to see them in the textbox. After you have confirmed that this is the correct shortcut for your macro, click the Assign button to assign the shortcut to the macro (see Figure 22-35). Note that Visual Studio shows all commands that are already using your selected shortcut so you can avoid removing currently used shortcuts.

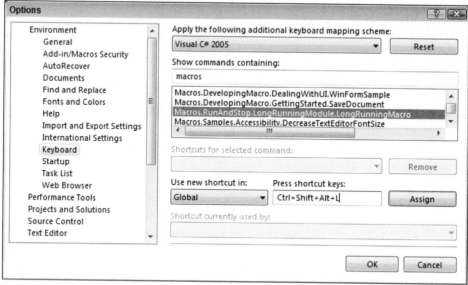

Figure 22-35: Assigning a shortcut key to a macro

Sample Macro

At the end of this chapter you can see a sample macro in action, with a full description. This way, you can get a clearer idea about macro development. This example is a default sample macro in Visual Studio named GenerateSlnFolderOnDirStructure, and it is available in the AddDirAsSlnFolder module in the Samples project.

This macro gets a folder path and adds all of its content to a solution folder in Visual Studio if a solution is open.

The source code of this module is shown in Listing 22-13.

Listing 22-13: AddDirAsSlnFolder Module Source Code

```
Imports EnvDTE
Imports EnvDTE80
Imports System.Diagnostics

Public Module AddDirAsSlnFolder

    ' A list of folder names, file names, and extensions that we do not want to add
    '  to the solution.
```

```vb
    Dim excludedExtensions As New System.Collections.Specialized.StringCollection
    Dim outputWindowPaneTitle As String = "Add directory as solution folder report"

    ' Function to filter out folder names, file names, and extensions that we do
not
    ' want to add to the solution.
    Function IsFileExcluded(ByVal filePath As String) As Boolean
        Dim extension As String
        Dim fileName As String

        extension = System.IO.Path.GetExtension(filePath)
        extension = extension.ToLower()

        fileName = System.IO.Path.GetFileName(filePath)
        fileName = fileName.ToLower()

        If (excludedExtensions.Contains(extension)) Then
            Return True
        Else
            If (excludedExtensions.Contains(fileName)) Then
                Return True
            Else
                Return False
            End If
        End If
    End Function

    ' Recursively walk all the files and folders within a specified path,
    ' and add them to the specified solution folder.
    Sub GenerateSlnFolderOnDirStructure2(ByVal currentPath As String, ByVal
currentSlnFolder As EnvDTE80.SolutionFolder)
        Dim folders As String()
        Dim files As String()
        Dim file As String
        Dim folder As String

        folders = System.IO.Directory.GetDirectories(currentPath)
        files = System.IO.Directory.GetFiles(currentPath)

        ' Examine all the files within the folder.
        For Each file In files
            If (Not IsFileExcluded(file)) Then
                Dim projItem As ProjectItem
                Try
                    projItem =
currentSlnFolder.Parent.ProjectItems.AddFromFile(file)

                    If (Not (projItem Is Nothing)) Then
                        If (Not (projItem.Document Is Nothing)) Then
                            projItem.Document.Close(vsSaveChanges.vsSaveChangesNo)
                        End If
                    End If
```

(continued)

Listing 22-13 *(continued)*

```
                Catch
                    Dim outputWindowPane As EnvDTE.OutputWindowPane
                    outputWindowPane = GetOutputWindowPane(outputWindowPaneTitle,
True)
                    outputWindowPane.OutputString("The item """ + file + """may
have not been added to the solution." + vbLf)
                End Try
            End If
        Next

        ' Examine all the subfolders.
        For Each folder In folders
            Dim folderName As String
            Dim newSlnFolder As SolutionFolder
            Dim proj As Project

            If (Not IsFileExcluded(folder)) Then
                folderName = System.IO.Path.GetFileName(folder)
                proj = currentSlnFolder.AddSolutionFolder(folderName)
                newSlnFolder = proj.Object
                GenerateSlnFolderOnDirStructure2(folder, newSlnFolder)
            End If
        Next
    End Sub


' Macro to import a folder on disk into a solution folder structure.
' Before running this macro, you must:
' 1) Change the path pointed to by startFolder to a path on your computer.
'    You could also call this macro through the command window, supplying
'    a start path argument.
' 2) Ensure that a solution file is open and saved to disk.
Sub GenerateSlnFolderOnDirStructure(Optional ByVal startFolder As String = "")
    Dim currentSlnFolder As EnvDTE80.SolutionFolder
    Dim proj As Project
    Dim sln2 As EnvDTE80.Solution2
    Dim folderName As String

    If (String.IsNullOrEmpty(startFolder)) Then
        startFolder = InputBox("Enter the folder path to import")
        If (String.IsNullOrEmpty(startFolder)) Then
            Return
        End If
    End If

    If (System.IO.Directory.Exists(startFolder) = False) Then
        MsgBox("The specified folder could not be found")
        Return
    End If

    GetOutputWindowPane(outputWindowPaneTitle, True).Clear()

    If System.IO.Directory.Exists(startFolder) = False Then
```

```
            Dim outputWindowPane As EnvDTE.OutputWindowPane
            outputWindowPane = GetOutputWindowPane(outputWindowPaneTitle, True)
            outputWindowPane.OutputString("The path entered could not be found" +
vbLf)

            Exit Sub
        End If

        excludedExtensions = New System.Collections.Specialized.StringCollection
        ' If you do not want a file with a particular extension or name
        '  to be added, then add that extension or name to this list:
        excludedExtensions.Add(".obj")
        excludedExtensions.Add(".ilk")
        excludedExtensions.Add(".pch")
        excludedExtensions.Add(".pdb")
        excludedExtensions.Add(".exe")
        excludedExtensions.Add(".dll")
        excludedExtensions.Add(".sbr")
        excludedExtensions.Add(".lib")
        excludedExtensions.Add(".exp")
        excludedExtensions.Add(".bsc")
        excludedExtensions.Add(".tlb")
        excludedExtensions.Add(".ncb")
        excludedExtensions.Add(".sln")
        excludedExtensions.Add(".suo")
        excludedExtensions.Add(".vcproj")
        excludedExtensions.Add(".vbproj")
        excludedExtensions.Add(".csproj")
        excludedExtensions.Add(".vjsproj")
        excludedExtensions.Add(".msi")

        sln2 = DTE.Solution
        folderName = System.IO.Path.GetFileName(startFolder)
        proj = sln2.AddSolutionFolder(folderName)
        currentSlnFolder = proj.Object
        GenerateSlnFolderOnDirStructure2(startFolder, currentSlnFolder)
    End Sub

End Module
```

This example uses the GetOutputWindowPane method from the Utilities module in the Samples directory, so if you want to run this code in a different project, then you need to copy the Utilities module into your project as well.

This module contains three methods:

❑   IsFileExcluded: Checks a folder or file to see whether it must be excluded. It's a helper method for other methods.

❑   GenerateSlnFolderOnDirStructure2: This is a helper method for the GenerateSlnFolderOnDirStructure macro method. It uses a recursive algorithm to iterate through all available folders and files and adds them to the solution folder that is passed to it as a parameter.

499

❑ GenerateSlnFolderOnDirStructure: This is the macro method. It gets an optional folder name to add its content to a solution folder. This method uses previous helper methods to do its job.

Along with these methods, this module has two members:

❑ excludedExtensions: This is a StringCollection that holds a collection of extensions that must be excluded and cannot be added to the solution folder.

❑ outputWindowPaneTitle: This is a String value that keeps the title of the output window pane.

The following sections provide a complete description of the three methods that play a role in this module.

IsFileExcluded

Shown in Listing 22-14, the IsFileExcluded function returns a Boolean result specifying whether a file or folder must be excluded or not.

Listing 22-14: IsFileExcluded Function

```
Function IsFileExcluded(ByVal filePath As String) As Boolean
    Dim extension As String
    Dim fileName As String

    extension = System.IO.Path.GetExtension(filePath)
    extension = extension.ToLower()

    fileName = System.IO.Path.GetFileName(filePath)
    fileName = fileName.ToLower()

    If (excludedExtensions.Contains(extension)) Then
        Return True
    Else
        If (excludedExtensions.Contains(fileName)) Then
            Return True
        Else
            Return False
        End If
    End If
End Function
```

In this function, the extension and fileName variables keep the extension and name of the file that is passed to the function. Then, in a simple nested If Then Else statement, it checks both extension and fileName to make sure they're included in excludedExtensions. If they're included (or if at least one of them is included), then it returns true. Otherwise, it returns false.

GenerateSlnFolderOnDirStructure2

GenerateSlnFoldronDirStructure2 (see Listing 22-15) is a method that gets two parameters: currentPath, which is the string value of a path, and currentSlnFolder, which is a

SolutionFolder. This method calls itself recursively to add all folders and files beginning from a specified path, one by one, to the solution folder.

Listing 22-15: GenerateSlnFolderOnDirStructure2 Method

```
Sub GenerateSlnFolderOnDirStructure2(ByVal currentPath As String, _
                                     ByVal currentSlnFolder As
EnvDTE80.SolutionFolder)
    Dim folders As String()
    Dim files As String()
    Dim file As String
    Dim folder As String

    folders = System.IO.Directory.GetDirectories(currentPath)
    files = System.IO.Directory.GetFiles(currentPath)

    ' Examine all the files within the folder.
    For Each file In files
        If (Not IsFileExcluded(file)) Then
            Dim projItem As ProjectItem
            Try
                projItem = currentSlnFolder.Parent.ProjectItems.AddFromFile(file)

                If (Not (projItem Is Nothing)) Then
                    If (Not (projItem.Document Is Nothing)) Then
                        projItem.Document.Close(vsSaveChanges.vsSaveChangesNo)
                    End If
                End If
            Catch
                Dim outputWindowPane As EnvDTE.OutputWindowPane
                outputWindowPane = GetOutputWindowPane(outputWindowPaneTitle, True)
                outputWindowPane.OutputString("The item """ + file + _
                                        """may have not been added to the
solution." + vbLf)
            End Try
        End If
    Next

    ' Examine all the subfolders.
    For Each folder In folders
        Dim folderName As String
        Dim newSlnFolder As SolutionFolder
        Dim proj As Project

        If (Not IsFileExcluded(folder)) Then
            folderName = System.IO.Path.GetFileName(folder)
            proj = currentSlnFolder.AddSolutionFolder(folderName)
            newSlnFolder = proj.Object
            GenerateSlnFolderOnDirStructure2(folder, newSlnFolder)
        End If
    Next
End Sub
```

This method has two variables: Files and Folders. Files is an array of strings for the names of all files available in the current folder and Folders is an array of strings for the names of all subfolders within the current folder.

The main body of this method consists of two loops. The first loop iterates through all available files in the current folder and adds them to the solution folder. The second loop iterates through all subfolders in the current folder and calls itself recursively for each of them. The result is that all subfolders are added to the solution folder. In both loops, the program calls the IsFileExcluded helper function to exclude the file or folder.

In the first loop, it adds the file to the currentSlnFolder and then creates a ProjectItem for it. At the end, it closes this item without saving changes.

In the second loop, it gets the folderName from the folder path and then adds a new solution folder to the currentSlnFolder for this folder with the same name. It then calls itself recursively by passing the folder and newSlnFolder as parameters.

GenerateSlnFolderOnDirStructure

Listing 22-16 shows the macro method in which the main implementation of the macro is located. It gets an optional startFolder parameter of type String, which is the path of the folder to begin adding to the solution folder.

Listing 22-16: GenerateSlnFolderOnDirStructure Method

```
Sub GenerateSlnFolderOnDirStructure(Optional ByVal startFolder As String = "")
    Dim currentSlnFolder As EnvDTE80.SolutionFolder
    Dim proj As Project
    Dim sln2 As EnvDTE80.Solution2
    Dim folderName As String

    If (String.IsNullOrEmpty(startFolder)) Then
        startFolder = InputBox("Enter the folder path to import")
        If (String.IsNullOrEmpty(startFolder)) Then
            Return
        End If
    End If

    If (System.IO.Directory.Exists(startFolder) = False) Then
        MsgBox("The specified folder could not be found")
        Return
    End If

    GetOutputWindowPane(outputWindowPaneTitle, True).Clear()

    If System.IO.Directory.Exists(startFolder) = False Then
        Dim outputWindowPane As EnvDTE.OutputWindowPane
        outputWindowPane = GetOutputWindowPane(outputWindowPaneTitle, True)
        outputWindowPane.OutputString("The path entered could not be found" + vbLf)
        Exit Sub
```

```
            End If

            excludedExtensions = New System.Collections.Specialized.StringCollection
            ' If you do not want a file with a particular extension or name
            ' to be added, then add that extension or name to this list:
            excludedExtensions.Add(".obj")
            excludedExtensions.Add(".ilk")
            excludedExtensions.Add(".pch")
            excludedExtensions.Add(".pdb")
            excludedExtensions.Add(".exe")
            excludedExtensions.Add(".dll")
            excludedExtensions.Add(".sbr")
            excludedExtensions.Add(".lib")
            excludedExtensions.Add(".exp")
            excludedExtensions.Add(".bsc")
            excludedExtensions.Add(".tlb")
            excludedExtensions.Add(".ncb")
            excludedExtensions.Add(".sln")
            excludedExtensions.Add(".suo")
            excludedExtensions.Add(".vcproj")
            excludedExtensions.Add(".vbproj")
            excludedExtensions.Add(".csproj")
            excludedExtensions.Add(".vjsproj")
            excludedExtensions.Add(".msi")

            sln2 = DTE.Solution
            folderName = System.IO.Path.GetFileName(startFolder)
            proj = sln2.AddSolutionFolder(folderName)
            currentSlnFolder = proj.Object
            GenerateSlnFolderOnDirStructure2(startFolder, currentSlnFolder)
        End Sub
```

In this method, the program first determines whether `startFolder` is passed to it; otherwise, it will ask for this value via an InputBox. After this, it checks for the availability of such a folder and displays a MessageBox if it doesn't exist. Then it exits from the method.

The next step is to prepare the output window with an appropriate title and to show an error message in this window if `startFolder` doesn't exist.

Excluding some extensions from the addition is the next step in this method. `sln2` refers to the current solution, and `sln2.AddSolutionFolder(folderName)` adds the start folder to a solution folder. The last step is to pass `startFolder` and `currentSlnFolder` to `GenerateSlnFolderOnDirStructure2`, which recursively adds all files and subfolders to the solution folder.

Running the Macro

Running this macro is similar to other macros, so you can simply double-click on it to run it. However, an alternative option is to run this macro via a command prompt by passing a parameter to specify the `startFolder` parameter. If you choose not to do this via a command prompt, it's possible to enter the path via an InputBox after running the macro.

First, I create a console application to test my macro for it. When this project (and hence its solution) is open, I run the macro, which first opens up an InputBox to ask for the `startFolder`. Now I give it a folder path in order to copy its files and subfolders to the same solution folder in my solution (see Figure 22-36).

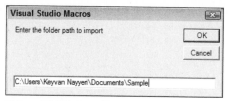

Figure 22-36: InputBox to enter the path

After pressing Enter or clicking the OK button, this macro copies all files and subfolders from this path to my solution as a solution folder with the same name (see Figure 22-37).

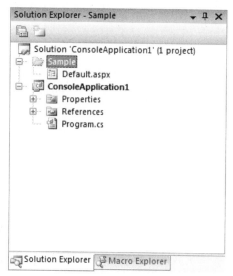

Figure 22-37: Result of running the macro

Summary

In this last chapter you learned about one of most common extensibility options in Visual Studio, the macro. First you were introduced to macros and their anatomy and got familiar with the Macros IDE and different elements of Visual Studio for working with macros, such as Macro Explorer. After that you learned how to run and stop macros, and then looked at the ways to build a macro using Macro Recorder and development code.

You also read a full discussion about options for recording your macros with Macro Recorder and customizing the generated code. In addition, you now know how to use programming codes to develop a macro. The next sections described debugging and deploying macros as two main steps in macro development. You also learned how to simplify running macros in the IDE via various techniques. Finally, you worked through a sample macro that enabled you to see a real macro in action and understand how everything works together.

Third-Party Add-Ins and Extensions

Here is a list of third-party add-ins and extensions written by companies, open-source projects, and community members. Some of these add-ins and extensions are completely free, some of them have a free and a commercial version, and others are completely commercial. Note that many more third-party add-ins and extensions could be listed here, but I chose some of the more well-known and helpful ones, to let you discover some real-world examples of what you saw in theory in this book.

❑ **Regionerate** (http://rauchy.net/regionerate) This is a free open-source tool that enables developers to apply layout rules to C# code.

❑ **ReSharper** (www.jetbrains.com/resharper) A commercial add-in with support for C#, Visual Basic, ASP.NET, XML, and XAML. One of the most famous Visual Studio add-ins, it enables functionality for developers such as code analysis, code refactoring, code generation, code templates, and unit testing.

❑ **Regex Kit Visualizers** (http://tools.osherove.com/Default.aspx?tabid=187) Regex Kit is a set of visualizers to debug four types in Visual Studio: *String*, *Regex*, *Match*, and *MatchCollection*. These visualizers were written by Roy Osherove and are completely free. Using them you can debug regular expressions and strings and find their matches in an input string. It has a very simple user interface that enables you to see everything necessary about your regular expressions and to debug your code.

❑ **CopySourceAsHTML** (http://jtleigh.com/CopySourceAsHtml) CopySourceAsHtml (CSAH) is a free open-source add-in for Microsoft Visual Studio that enables you to copy source code, syntax highlighting, and line numbers as HTML code. With smart codes, CSAH uses VS code highlighting settings from APIs. This add-in is helpful for anyone who wants to copy and paste a source code to his or her blog or site.

❑ **Cache Visualizer** (http://blog.bretts.net/?p=11) Cache visualizer is a free Visual Studio visualizer to monitor an ASP.NET 2.0 cache. It's free and open source and can be helpful for ASP.NET developers who frequently work with caches.

❏ **NCover** (http://ncover.org/site) This is a code coverage tool for .NET. Code coverage is a concept in test-driven development (TDD) and unit testing. In a nutshell, it specifies the percentage of source codes that are covered by unit testing.

❏ **TestDriven.NET** (http://testdriven.net) TestDriven.NET is a Visual Studio add-in that integrates with several Visual Studio unit testing tools such as NCover, NUnit, MbUnit, and Team System. It enables you to unit test your code with a single click in the VS environment.

❏ **GhostDoc** (http://roland-weigelt.de/ghostdoc) GhostDoc is an add-in for Visual Studio that generates XML comments for C# and Visual Basic from the XML comments in base classes or interfaces or by auto-generation from names and types. XML comments are helpful for documentation of code in C# and Visual Basic.

❏ **NDepend** (http://ndepend.com) This is a static code analysis tool that helps you to analyze your codes and assemblies for their dependencies. It also provides Code Query Language (CQL) to query for different elements of code in your projects. It includes an add-in that integrates with Visual Studio, and has a free and a commercial edition.

❏ **AnkhSVN** (http://ankhsvn.tigris.org) AnkhSVN is a Visual Studio add-in that integrates Subversion source control with Visual Studio. Subversion (abbreviated as SVN) is a free open-source project for source and version controlling.

❏ **T4 Editor** (http://t4editor.net) The Text Templating Transformation Toolkit (known as T4) is a technology developed by Microsoft and used for code generation in some products such as DSL tools. This is a part of the Visual Studio SDK but it lacks a good design-time feature. A third-party T4 editor written by Clarius Consulting offers better features, including enhanced design-time support.

❏ **XML Debugger Visualizer** (http://projectdistributor.net/Releases/Release.aspx?releaseId=278) XML visualizer is a free open-source visualizer for Visual Studio to monitor XML files and types and debug them in a visual manner.

Resources

Communities

- **Visual Studio Homepage** — http://microsoft.com/visualstudio
- **Visual Studio Extensibility Developer Center** — http://msdn.com/vsx
- **Visual Studio Extensibility on MSDN** — http://msdn2.microsoft.com/en-us/library/bb187341(vs.80).aspx
- **Visual Studio Shell Homepage** — http://msdn.com/vstudio/shell
- **Visual Studio Forums** — http://forums.microsoft.com/MSDN/default.aspx?ForumGroupID=6&SiteID=1
- **Visual Studio Extensibility Forums** — http://forums.microsoft.com/MSDN/ShowForum.aspx?ForumID=57&SiteID=1
- **ASP Alliance** — http://aspalliance.com
- **CodePlex** — http://codeplex.com
- **DotNetSlackers** — http://dotnetslackers.com
- **Code Project** — http://codeproject.com
- **DevX** — http://devx.com

Blogs

- **Visual Studio Extensibility Team** — http://blogs.msdn.com/vsxteam
- **Aaron Marten** — http://blogs.msdn.com/aaronmar

- ❏ **Keyvan Nayyeri** — `http://nayyeri.net`
- ❏ **Scott Hanselman** — `http://hanselman.com`
- ❏ **Roy Osherove** — `http://weblogs.asp.net/rosherove`
- ❏ **Phil Haack** — `http://haacked.com`
- ❏ **James Lau** — `http://blogs.msdn.com/jameslau`
- ❏ **Scott Guthrie** — `http://weblogs.asp.net/scottgu`
- ❏ **Allen Denver** — `http://blogs.msdn.com/allend`
- ❏ **Don Demsak** — `http://donxml.com`
- ❏ **Gareth Jones** — `http://blogs.msdn.com/garethj`
- ❏ **Steven Smith** — `http://aspadvice.com/blogs/ssmith`
- ❏ **Ken Levy** — `http://blogs.msdn.com/klevy`
- ❏ **Carlos Quintero** — `http://msmvps.com/blogs/carlosq`
- ❏ **Deepankar Dubey** — `http://blogs.msdn.com/ddubey`

Books

- ❏ Professional Visual Studio 2008 (ISBN: 9780470229880)
- ❏ Professional Visual Studio 2005 (ISBN: 9780764598463)
- ❏ Professional VB 2008 (ISBN: 9780470191361)
- ❏ Professional C# 2008 (ISBN: 9780470191378)
- ❏ Professional ASP.NET 3.5: in C# and VB (ISBN: 9780470187579)
- ❏ Professional ADO.NET 3.5 with LINQ and the Entity Framework (ISBN: 9780470182611)
- ❏ Professional XML (ISBN: 9780471777779)
- ❏ Professional WPF Programming: .NET Development with the Windows Presentation Foundation (ISBN: 9780470041802)
- ❏ Professional WCF Programming: .NET Development with the Windows Communication Foundation (ISBN: 9780470089842)
- ❏ Professional Windows Workflow Foundation (ISBN: 9780470053867)
- ❏ Professional Visual Studio 2005 Team System (ISBN: 9780764584367)
- ❏ Professional Team Foundation Server (ISBN: 9780471919308)
- ❏ Professional Silverlight 1.1 (ISBN: 9780470193938)

Index

A

X

Get more from Wrox.